Contents

Explore the Trails and Tales of the Hoosier State's Best Outdoor Resource

DON GULBRANDSEN

RiverRock
PUBLICATIONS

RiverRock Publications LLC
Indianapolis, Indiana
Email: riverrockpublications@gmail.com

ISBN: 979-8-9953461-0-4

All photos by Don Gulbrandsen

Design and editorial production by Patricia Frey
Cover design by Jason Hinman/Mojo Media
Maps by Don Gulbrandsen and Jason Hinman/Mojo Media

Front Cover Photographs (clockwise from top left): Indiana
Dunes; Turkey Run; Shades; Whitewater Memorial; Chain
O'Lakes

Back Cover Photographs (from left): Shakamak;
McCormick's Creek; O'Bannon Woods

Printed in the United States of America

Preface

Indiana's 24 state parks are immensely popular: in 2023–2024, more than *12 million people* visited the properties. What do people do when they visit? Most of them hike, cited as the most popular activity by 70 percent of visitors in surveys conducted by the Indiana Department of Natural Resources.

That means millions of people are tromping around Indiana state parks each year, and a lot of them have questions about the properties and which trails they should be hiking. I love hiking guidebooks, but I've never found one that gives me all the information I need before visiting an Indiana state park. Apps and online guides fill in some of the gaps but not all of them. "Someone needs to write a really good book about hiking in Indiana state parks," I thought to myself. "And maybe that person is me."

That thought first occurred to me in 2018, and I did some initial research and writing. It was enjoyable work; not only are these parks fun to hike, but they also have great origin stories. Unfortunately, my schedule didn't match my aspirations. I hadn't even visited and hiked all the parks yet and with a full-time career consulting in the nonprofit sector, I knew it would be a few years before I could focus on the project.

Fast forward to 2025: the opening I was looking for finally presented itself. I launched a project to revisit every park (I had logged No. 24 in 2021), hike the trails I'd missed (plus re-hike many others I enjoyed), and comprehensively photograph every property (I captured more than 4,000 images). I researched and wrote as I went, so that by October 2025, I'd revisited every park at least once and written a comprehensive guide to each.

The result is the book you're currently reading. My goal was to create a curated, personalized guide to enjoying the trails—and other features—of Indiana's 24 state parks. In an era where people now wonder whether a machine wrote the words they're reading, I'm proud to say that *none* of the writing in this book came from AI—only from hours spent on the trails, learning firsthand about all the great things our parks have to offer.

In many ways, this book is a love letter—both to Indiana state parks and to hiking or running trails. I started hiking as a child. I was born in Illinois, but when I was six my family moved to Colorado. My parents had never been outdoorspeople but with a great view of the Rocky Mountains from our suburban Denver home, they caught the bug. Over the next several years we camped and hiked all over Colorado, exploring many of the state's gorgeous national parks and forests.

When we moved backed to the Midwest, my parents drifted away from the outdoor life, but I was hooked. In addition to camping and hiking, fishing and canoeing were my passions, and I was often joined by my patient wife, Tari (who had never camped before marrying me), and son, Kendal. In my late 30s, I added trail running to my favorite activities. Eventually, I sold the canoe and fished less, but today I spend more time than ever on the trails, either hiking or running.

I first moved to the Hoosier State nearly two decades ago, and I've explored every corner and all 92 counties. Compared to its neighbors, Indiana gets low marks for environmental protection and a lack of outdoor resources, but the state parks offer an exception to this perception. In reading this book, I hope you enjoy learning about the parks and get inspired to spend more time in them. After that, it's a small step from hiking to joining a Friends group, donating time or money to help your favorite property, or urging elected officials to protect and fund the state parks. And when you do that, you'll feel the satisfaction of knowing that you've done your part to ensure that your grandchildren—and their grandchildren—will be able to experience the joy of hiking a trail in an Indiana state park.

Acknowledgments

An ambitious project like this one requires a quality team, and I was fortunate to have the support of several exceptional people.

I've worked with Joe Funk and Jason Hinman of Mojo Media for many years and always enjoy collaborating with them. You can see Jason's handiwork in this book's cover and maps. Thanks to both of you for your help!

Tracy Schubert and I are former colleagues, and I knew that her outdoor experiences and background in reference books made her the right editor to help clean up the text. Thanks, Tracy, for your fine and timely efforts!

I started working with Patti Frey nearly 20 years ago; asking her to design the pages of my own book was a no-brainer. Thanks, Patti, for doing an amazing job (as usual)!

My parents, Don and Maureene Gulbrandsen, were instrumental in nurturing my love of hiking and the outdoors thanks to our many mountain trips during my Colorado childhood. I'm thankful to them for sharing a gift that continues to enrich me.

Katie Birge is my son's partner, a native Hoosier, and fiercely proud of her state. Thanks, Katie, for helping me appreciate Indiana's history and natural wonders!

Kendal Gulbrandsen is our only child, but my wife and I insist that when it came to kids we focused on quality over quantity. He moved to Indiana first, took us to our first Indiana state park (McCormick's Creek), and played an important role in many of my favorite state park experiences. Thank you, Kendal, for being both a wonderful son and hiking/running partner!

Most of my gratitude in life flows to Tari Gulbrandsen, my amazing wife and the person who made this book possible. She is my No. 1 hiking buddy and accompanied me on many of the walks described in this book. Even more importantly, she has provided love and support beyond what I could have ever imagined receiving when I first met her in a small Iowa town many years ago. Thank you, Tari; I love you and look forward to many more hikes together.

Introduction

History of the Indiana State Park System

Indiana's state parks exist primarily because of the efforts of one man: Indianapolis businessman Richard Lieber. Born in Dusseldorf, Germany, in 1869, Lieber made his way to the Hoosier State in 1891, worked as a reporter, and later started successful chemical and bottling companies. Lieber believed that an active life was essential for a healthy life. Inspired by a trip to Yosemite National Park in 1900 and later trips to the Rocky Mountains, Lieber soon embraced conservation and the restorative power of nature—views that meshed well with those of President Theodore Roosevelt, whom Lieber met in 1908 while serving as a delegate for a White House–hosted conservation congress.

Lieber actively promoted conservation in Indiana and served as chairman of the Fourth National Conservation Congress, held in Indianapolis in October 1912. At the event, Lieber met with future president Woodrow Wilson, and the pair forged an effective partnership working on conservation issues.

Indiana's 1916 Centennial presented Lieber just the opportunity he was seeking: to use the celebration to launch a state park system. He convinced Governor Samuel Ralston to establish a State Parks Committee with Lieber as chairman. By the end of 1916, the 20-person committee, without the benefit of any state funding, had accomplished its goal: McCormick's Creek and Turkey Run State Parks had been acquired, dedicated, and were welcoming visitors. That was just the beginning. By the early 2000s, 24 parks were operating, providing millions of visitors the high-quality outdoor experiences that Lieber had dreamed of being able to offer his fellow Hoosiers.

Hiking Indiana State Parks

Hiking in an Indiana state park is best classified as a "low adventure" activity—fun, nature-focused, and good exercise but there is minimal challenge or risk involved. You can't stray too far from civilization because there are no wilderness areas in the

A rocky stairway lifts hikers out of Box Canyon on Turkey Run's Trail 2.

state parks. If you're a backpacker, you might be disappointed; Shades is the only property with a backpacking campground and the trail serving it extends just two and a half miles.

But if you're a dedicated day hiker looking for a quality natural experience on well-maintained trails supported by ample parking, restrooms, and running water, Indiana state parks are hard to beat. The properties are spread all over the state and sample a variety of memorable habitats—from the Lake Michigan dunes in the north to western Indiana's sandstone ravines to the cave-and-sinkhole karst terrain in the south. Twenty-two of the parks offer a well-maintained campground for overnight stays. Seven properties (soon to be eight) have an inn for those seeking a little more comfort. All the parks have a nature center and/or interpretive naturalist programs to educate visitors about flora, fauna, and history. And in addition to hiking, the properties offer a wide array of outdoor activities, including mountain biking, horseback riding, fishing, kayaking, fossil hunting, and much more.

Hiking Basics

The dangers may be limited in Indiana state parks, but they are still there and you need to prepare accordingly. Here are some tips for what to wear and what to carry when you hike.

Clothing

Even in the heat of summer, I prefer wearing long pants to protect my legs from ticks, spiders, poison ivy, and other annoyances that I encounter. I have multiple pairs of lightweight hiking pants with zip-off legs, which allow me to convert to shorts when the conditions are favorable.

For the top half of my body, I use moisture-wicking fabrics and layers. Your base layer (touching your skin) should be a fabric that moves moisture off your body. In cold weather, use merino or alpaca wool. In warmer temps, polyester works well. Avoid cotton, which retains moisture and can make you miserable on a long hike. In cold weather, wear or pack an insulating layer, such as a light down puffer or a fleece. In all conditions, a top waterproof layer (Gor-Tex or equivalent) is a must-have. Pack it even if it's dry and/or warm when you start.

Footwear

I get a kick out of looking at what people wear on their feet while hiking the state park trails—everything from cheap flipflops to high-tech mountaineering boots. The ideal is somewhere in between.

Indiana's hiking trails are tame compared to what you find in the mountains to the east and west of us, but some of the state's top trails follow stream beds that can be wet, slippery, and lined with ankle-twisting stones. You'll appreciate the traction and support provided by a pair of quality mid-height hiking boots or low hiking shoes. I prefer waterproof models, but some hikers avoid Gore-Tex and other waterproofing fabrics in shoes because they tend to trap moisture and can make your feet feel hot and sweaty.

Many hikers eschew boots in favor of trail running shoes, which are a hybrid between regular running shoes and hiking boots. This might be the perfect choice for Indiana state park trails. The best trail runners are light but built with abrasion-resistant materials and rugged, grippy outsoles. Most dispense with waterproofing, choosing instead to be quick-draining and engineered for "mud evacuation"—in other words, wet feet are just part of the fun.

What to Carry

While hiking the state parks, I encounter plenty of people who look like they parked at the trailhead, hopped out, and started walking, carrying nothing but a smartphone and the clothes on their backs. For many trails on many days, this might be fine, but I prefer being prepared to spend several hours outside, in varying weather conditions, no matter how short my intended hike.

Every hiker who intends to spend any amount of time on the trail should invest in a daypack with a volume in the 15–25-liter range—big enough to carry everything for you and a partner on typical state park outing. Go to a quality outdoor store and try on daypacks to find one that fits. Key features include ample padding on the shoulder straps and back; outside storage pockets for quick access to oft-used items; and adjustable/locking straps at the chest and stomach to keep the pack from bouncing.

The first thing you need to carry in your pack is water. Either plan on carrying water bottles or buy a "reservoir compatible" model and a separate water reservoir—or else a pack that comes with a removeable water reservoir. Select a 3L reservoir, which should be adequate for most Indiana outings. The rule of thumb is to carry at least one liter of water per person for every five miles you plan to hike—more if the weather is going to be hot.

In addition to extra layers of clothing, what else should you carry in your daypack?
- ✓ First-aid kit (including items for blister prevention/management)
- ✓ Pocket knife/multitool
- ✓ Flashlight and/or headlamp
- ✓ Emergency rain poncho
- ✓ Buff/neck gaiter
- ✓ Bandanna
- ✓ Spare socks

- ✓ Sunglasses/spare glasses
- ✓ Small towel
- ✓ Insect repellent
- ✓ Spare hat and gloves (cold weather)
- ✓ Food

Concerning the last item, I always throw a few granola bars or some trail mix in the bottom of my pack and snack as I go to keep my energy levels up. Sometimes I pack a full sack lunch. Keep it simple but always have some food with you to avoid a calorie crash on the trail.

Some backcountry hikers might wonder why I left off basics like fire starters and toilet-management tools. It was intentional. In Indiana state parks, never start a fire outside a picnic or camping area and confine your toilet activities to the ample facilities available in every park. Those are the rules.

What about trekking poles? I own some but rarely use them in the state parks. Hikers with limited mobility may find trekking poles a wonderful tool for increasing their confidence, easing wear-and-tear on their legs, and extending their range. Plus, there are a handful of truly rugged trails—including at Turkey Run, Shades, and Clifty Falls—where hikers of every ability might benefit from an assist provide by trekking poles.

Hiking Through the Seasons

Many people equate hiking with the summer months, but Indiana is a year-round hiking destination. I'm on the trails 12 months a year and can report that some of my favorite state park hikes have occurred in the dead of winter. The properties tend to be quiet and devoid of people. Views are better because the leaf cover is gone. Ice is your biggest risk, especially in the properties with creek-bed trails, including Turkey Run, Shades, and Clifty Falls. Serious winter hikers should invest in and carry a set of microspikes.

Summer is my least favorite hiking season in Indiana. I love the greenery and extended sunlight, but heat, humidity, dense forest undergrowth, and active insects can make a long summer day on the trails challenging. And the crowds, especially on good-weather weekends, can be overwhelming at the more popular parks.

Spring and autumn are Indiana's top hiking seasons, highlighted by cool temps, sparse crowds, and the splendor of nature in transition. It's a tossup as to which is my favorite. Spring is special because of the explosion of ephemeral wildflowers on the forest floor and the treetop bounty of northward migrating birds. Fall is highlighted by the colorful palette of changing leaves. The yellows, oranges, and reds flow from north to south from late September through early November, offering several weeks of prime hiking at the different properties.

Flora and Fauna
Plants and Their Habitats
True to Indiana's natural heritage, all the parks feature significant acreage of hardwood forest. Most of this land has been clearcut, and the forests are of the replanted second-growth (or even third-growth) variety. The state has just a handful of stands of untouched old-growth forest, including at Spring Mill and Turkey Run.

In spring forests, you'll encounter one of nature's best shows—the wildflower bloom. From March through May, before the trees leaf out, green shoots emerge from the forest litter followed by the yellows, purples, and pinks of their wildflowers. Many state parks offer guided hikes to view and identify wildflowers.

Other habitats take center stage in the state parks, including prairie. Originally, about 15 percent of Indiana (primarily in the northwest and western parts of the state) was prairie but most of that was plowed under for row crops. Several parks boast restored grasslands and one, Prophetstown, has made prairie its primary habitat. Hike Indiana's grassland trails in summer to experience their gorgeous wildflower blooms.

Wetland habitats once covered a quarter of the state but now account for less than 4 percent of Indiana's land area. Many state parks protect various types of wetlands, which are critical habitat for both plant and animal life. The northern parks, in the glacial lakes region, boast significant wetland acreage but properties all over the map protect and provide access to beautiful marshlands.

Problem Plants
Not all the vegetation in state parks is viewed positively. Case in point: Indiana provides ideal habitat for poison ivy. You will encounter it—often in abundance—at every state park property. Learn to identify poison ivy and keep your eyes open for it. To protect yourself, stay on the trails and wear long pants, which provide a barrier if you accidentally brush against it.

A bigger plant risk to our parks is the spread of invasive species, including Japanese honeysuckle, multiflora rose, autumn olive, garlic mustard, and many others. Invasives swallow up space and resources without contributing much positive in return. They crowd out desirable native plants that are used as food and habitat by native animals. Removing invasives is an ongoing project at most properties, with volunteer groups doing much of the work.

Mammals
Top-tier predators, including mountain lions and black bears, were extirpated from Indiana in the late 1800s, and today are only very rare visitors to the state. Large mammals that you might see include bobcats (whose populations are growing), coyotes, and white-tailed deer, which you are likely to encounter in every state park.

Trail 10 takes a two-mile trek down the Lake Michigan beach at Indiana Dunes.

Red and gray fox, river otters, beaver, raccoons, mink, and opossum are among the common medium-sized mammals in the parks. Various squirrels, bats, moles, voles, mice, chipmunks, and rabbits round out the common small mammals.

Snakes

Many would-be hikers ask, "Are there snakes?" For Indiana state parks, the answer is "yes, but not that many." This is especially true of the venomous kind that concern people the most. Four venomous species are native to Indiana, but they are rare. The cottonmouth hasn't been seen for years and may have been extirpated. The massasauga and timber rattlesnakes are both endangered. Very limited numbers of the small massasauga live in wetland habitats in the northeast corner of Indiana. The large but reclusive timber rattler is present in Brown County State Park and occasionally observed there. The eastern copperhead, native to the southern third of Indiana, is more common but secretive and its cryptic coloring makes it difficult to spot. Snakes that you are likely to encounter on or along state park trails include garter snakes, water snakes, and rat snakes—all important predators in their ecosystems.

Birds

Because of its mix of habitats and location along major migratory routes, Indiana is a premiere destination for bird watchers, boasting more than 400 species identified. The state parks represent some of the best places to watch birds, and many of the properties are included as stops on the Indiana Audubon Society's highly regarded Indiana Birding Trail.

Every hiker with even a tiny interest in birds is encouraged to download and use Cornell's Merlin app for your smartphone. It's the easiest way to identify birds by call or photo and works without an internet connection. It's the perfect companion for a walk in the woods, and you'll be surprised at just how many species inhabit our parks.

Insects, Ticks, and Spiders

If you use AllTrails, you know that many reviews focus on two subjects: 1. How muddy are the trails? and 2. How bad are the bugs? It was my goal in this book not to obsess about those topics, because I think they are minor and manageable issues for Indiana hikers. But I admit there are some little critters to consider when planning a hiking trip.

Ticks are the most worrisome, because they are common and can carry life-altering diseases. Protect yourself by wearing long pants and generously applying insect repellent on your bare legs, pant legs, shoes, and socks. Some people take things a step further by tucking their pant legs into their socks.

Few hikers talk about spiders, but I've had to seek medical help twice to treat infected spider bites I picked up on the trails. Both bites were on my calves and received while I was wearing shorts…meaning I probably could have prevented the bites with long pants.

Mosquitos, biting flies, and gnats inhabit the general category of flying annoyances. Protect yourself with clothing and a generous application of insect repellent at the start of each hike. The repellent won't do much to deter gnats and deer flies, so buy yourself an inexpensive head net and throw it in the bottom of your daypack—it just might save a hike someday.

Indiana State Park Basics

Entry Fee

All properties but Falls of the Ohio charge a fee to enter the park. (Falls of the Ohio charges a fee for its museum-quality Interpretive Center.) Starting in 2026, most parks charged $7 per resident vehicle and $15 per non-resident vehicle, though some properties were higher. Because of ongoing tight budgets, it is possible that these rates will increase in the future.

Instead of trying to avoid fees or feeling guilty when there is no one at the gatehouse and you get in for free, every Indiana state park hiker should buy an annual pass. In 2026 passes, good for a given calendar year, cost $50 for residents and $120 for nonresidents. Disabled citizens and those over 65 can buy reduced-price passes for $25. It's a good deal if you make multiple park visits each year plus it's a great way to invest in a tremendous natural resource.

Hiking with Dogs

Dogs are welcome on all the trails in every Indiana state park but must be closely attended and kept on a leash, no longer than six feet, at all times.

Hiking with Horses and Bikes

Not everyone agrees with me, but I urge hikers in the Indiana state parks to stick to hiking-only trails as much as possible—even in parks where it is legal for hikers to use mountain biking and bridle trails. My motivations are safety and quality of experience—for hikers, cyclists, and horseback riders. I enjoy horseback trail riding and mountain biking and have hiked many multiple-user trails, especially in the western U.S., where the practice is much more ingrained. Unfortunately, I've had some negative experiences. It's hard to relax and immerse yourself in nature when you're constantly on the lookout for cyclists or horses and the potential for a collision or conflict is always there.

The shared mileage of officially designated horseback-and-hiking trails is limited. Pokagon and O'Bannon Woods have short, manageable stretches where hiking and bridle trails overlap, but Tippecanoe River is the only property with several miles of horseback-and-hiking trails. I've explored a couple of these routes and don't think they provide a quality hiking experience. As a result, I've excluded them from the Tippecanoe River chapter.

Mountain bike trails are more complicated to consider. In many parks, especially in southern Indiana (Harmonie, O'Bannon Woods, and Versailles), local mountain biking groups have built and maintain extensive trail networks, designated as biking-and-hiking routes.

But mountain bike trails are a different beast than hiking trails, engineered for flow rather than getting efficiently or scenically from Point A to Point B. I like running on mountain bike trails, but I find some biking routes tedious to hike. Plus, you must be on the constant lookout for riders and ready to step off the trail. Posted rules dictate that bikes must yield to pedestrians, but that rarely happens. Cyclists tend to be friendly and attentive, but rarely slow down, let alone stop, when encountering hikers.

With these realities in mind, I have excluded most of the state park mountain biking trails from this book. I've made a couple of exceptions for parks where it's nearly impossible to hike without using a bike trail (O'Bannon Woods) or where pedestrian traffic is heavy (Fort Harrison) and the user culture supports shared pathways.

Overnighting in the Parks

Indiana offers myriad options for staying overnight within the state parks. As noted earlier, all but two properties (urban parks Falls of the Ohio and Fort Harrison) feature a campground, many have cabins, and several have modern hotel-style inns.

Long Lake is the perfect spot to pause while hiking Trail 6 at Chain O'Lakes.

The campgrounds are uniformly excellent across the state park system, well maintained and appointed with all the infrastructure needed for a great experience. As someone who learned to camp by sleeping in a tent on the ground (still my preference), I have one gripe: most of the campgrounds are designed to serve recreational vehicles and camper/trailers. The campgrounds can feel a little crowded, highly social, and very civilized. For these reasons, tent campers might want to look for nonelectric or primitive sites, which are available at several campgrounds.

Technology and Communications

Cell service is spotty at most parks, and nonexistent in many places, especially on the trails. Don't count on using your smartphone for communications or accessing the Internet.

This low-tech reality doesn't bother me, though I still carry my smartphone. I simply download all the files I might need at home, including maps, brochures, and campground reservations. In addition, my phone serves as my backup camera, mileage tracker, bird identifier, and book reader.

All these possible uses remind us of one more item for your daypack: a power bank for recharging. Without a power bank, you'll likely join the legion of people leaving their phones to recharge in restrooms, picnic shelters, and other electrically supplied park buildings.

Navigating the Parks and Trails

One of my reasons for writing this book is to provide a quality navigational tool for Indiana state park users. But that doesn't mean there are zero resources currently available. In fact, there are a couple that you should utilize in addition to this book.

The most important existing resource is the official state park property maps—printed, folded guides that show every road, trail, and highlight. They offer an overview of park history and amenities and include very brief trail descriptions. You can purchase these maps for $1 at gatehouses, park offices, and visitor centers. Alternatively, visit each park's website and download the pdf version of the map for free. Do this before you visit; in many parks you may not find a cell signal strong enough to access the map on the fly.

As much as I enjoy and use the property maps, I also understand their shortcomings. They are often inaccurate and detail-light with regards to hiking trails. Plus, they are infrequently updated; it can take years to record changes.

Online resources have proliferated in recent years and the best for Indiana state park hikers is AllTrails, which offers both a web version and smartphone app. The free version is robust, but I recommend subscribing, which allows you to download maps to your phone. Much of the info on AllTrails is crowdsourced and further organized and embellished by AI, with mixed results. The reviews aren't always helpful, but the maps are valuable—to a point. Trail placement, topographic details, elevation profiles are excellent, but not all trails are included.

Supporting Indiana State Parks

Indiana's state parks are owned by its citizens but unfortunately, we live in an era where many public resources are underappreciated and underfunded. Among my goals for this book is to encourage more people to visit their state parks and take steps to support and protect them.

First and foremost, spend time in the parks and have fun. Hiking is a great activity but there are many other things to do, and they can be enjoyed by people of all ages and abilities. When you find something you really enjoy, share the experience by inviting a friend or family member to join you on your next outing.

Next, support the parks financially. Buying your annual park pass provides important operating funds for the properties, but you can go a step further by using charitable gifts to support the parks. The Indiana Natural Resources Foundation is the official nonprofit fundraising arm of the Indiana DNR. Money raised is used for projects throughout Indiana, including at the state parks. The Indiana Parks Alliance is an independent nonprofit that provides advocacy and funding for the state parks and state nature preserves. One of its current initiatives is the Trails for Tomorrow campaign, focused on raising funds for repairing and improving hiking routes in Indiana state parks and recreation areas.

Advocacy is one of the most important activities that state parks users can engage in to support their favorite properties. Elected leaders at the county and state level need to hear from people who use the parks. Tell them why the parks are important, what work needs to be done, and encourage them to increase funding.

Finally, consider becoming a Friend of one or more state parks. The officially sanctioned Friends groups have emerged as an essential resource for the parks, providing volunteer hours, event management, and financial support. In recent years, they have taken on multiple responsibilities previously held by staff. Currently, 19 properties are supported by 18 active Friends groups (Turkey Run and Shades have a combined group). Check the DNR website to see if your favorite park has a group and get a link to their online profile.

How to Use this Book

Each chapter in this book follows a standard format. First, I introduce each each park (presented alphabetically) through an actual hiking or running experience on the trails. Next, I explore each park's unique history. After reviewing the highlights of the modern-day properties, we get to the heart of the book: hiking and running guides for every trail in every state park in Indiana. I rate each route, describe its layout and difficulty, and offer a brief guided tour with essential information for your best hiking or running experience. Simple maps are provided to aid navigation.

The ratings run from one to five stars and are mine alone. Five-star trails are the best—worth a long drive to hike each as a standalone route. You'll find 22 five-star trails sprinkled throughout the book, representing memorable hikes at 14 different properties.

Most of the trail distances reported represent the state's official measurement, as published in the property maps. In a few instances, when my own experience or a reputable source disagreed with the official measurement, I reported a different distance. Unless otherwise noted, the distances represent the one-way length of the trail profiled; actual hikes might be much longer for out-and-back routes or trails accessed by a connector route.

INDIANA STATE PARKS

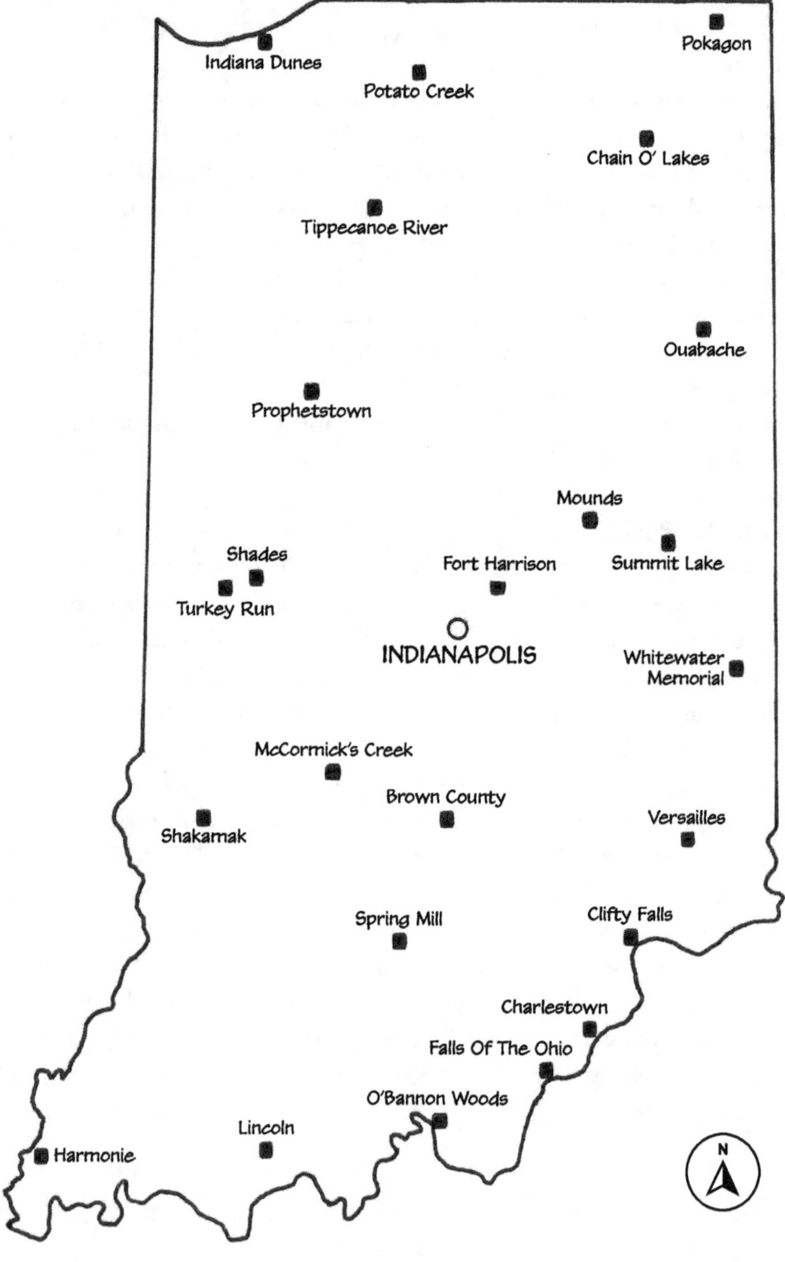

1
Brown County State Park

Brown County looms large in the Indiana state park system—both literally and figuratively. At 15,815 acres it is the largest state park in land area and one of the busiest, hosting 1.5 million visitors annually. Brown County also gets generous media attention and has a national reputation, frequently appearing on "best state park" lists. Its hilly topography, expansive vistas, and spectacular fall colors all bolster its reputation.

Yet ask a serious Hoosier hiker about Brown County and you might get a lukewarm response. There are some excellent trails, but Brown County gets overshadowed by the hiking available in other Indiana state parks as well as in nearby state forests and Hoosier National Forest, which butts up to the park's southern boundary.

Brown County, in fact, has a vast trail system, the largest in any Indiana state park, but most of the trail mileage is geared toward users other than hikers. More than 30 miles of mountain bike trails are concentrated in the northwest part of the park, while the southern third of Brown County is etched with more than 70 miles of bridle trails.

During a recent late fall, midweek trip I was reminded that Brown County deserves kudos for its hiking, too. Because traffic and crowds aren't my thing, I had purposely delayed my visit until the trees were past peak color. I've heard stories about the chaos on the roads during peak color, but I've never visited at that time.

Fortunately, cars were few and far between on this weekday, and there were still a few pockets of gold remaining in the trees. I ventured down Ogle Lake Road and parked at the lot below the dam. This is the epicenter for hiking in the park, offering access to Trails, 4, 5, 7, 8, 9, and 11—about 13 miles total. My goal was to hike all those routes except Trails 9 and 11.

Starting on Trail 7, I hiked across the dam and along the south shore of Ogle Lake. From the trail's elevated viewpoint, it's possible to look down on the lake and see fish, turtles, and other life in and near the water. Along the way I passed junctions with Trail 11 and Trail 4, the latter joining Trail 7 to cross the upper end of the lake on a boardwalk. On the far side, I turned right and followed Trail 4 up a wooded valley, a rare flat section of Brown County hiking trail.

Hesitation Point is the perfect spot for a break while hiking Trail 8.

The path soon intersected with Trail 5 through Ogle Hollow Nature Preserve. This 41-acre preserve was designated by the state in 1970 to protect the rare yellowwood trees found here. I explored the small lollipop path in the heart of the preserve, stopping to relish the quiet and take a few pictures, before returning to the main trail and climbing 200 feet out of the hollow. Trail 5 ended at a parking lot near the entrance to Buffalo Ridge Campground; a nearby bench offered a good spot to rest.

Trail 4 started on the opposite side of the parking lot. I passed through a beautiful section of forest with lingering gold leaves, then descended to Ogle Lake. Back at Trail 7, I retraced my steps across the boardwalk at the upper end of the lake but turned left at the next junction. The last section of Trail 7 was a level but twisting path along the north shore of the lake, good for fishing access and bird watching.

Back at my parking spot near the dam, I turned my attention to Trail 8, also known as the HHC Trail in tribute to the Hoosier Hikers Council, which rebuilt the route in 2002–2007. Since 1995, the Council has been responsible for building and maintaining some of the best hiking trails in Indiana. At Brown County, in addition to Trail 8, the Council laid out the beautiful Trail 11 connection to Trail 9 that departs south from Ogle Lake.

I left the parking lot westbound on Trail 8, took the right fork, and started a gentle climb up a quiet, wooded ravine. Leaving the ravine required a left turn and a long climb, initially with the help of a huge staircase. At the end of the climb was the trail's high spot, Hesitation Point (elevation of 1,002 feet), a popular viewpoint and great place for lunch. As I ate, two mountain bikers zipped by on the trail running near my picnic table.

Back on Trail 8, I headed west. For the next 1.5 miles the path roughly followed the park road on its way to West Lookout Tower. The attractive, two-story structure was built by the Civilian Conservation Corps in 1936. With the forest regrown around the tower, only a narrow vista to north remained, but it was gorgeous.

I retraced my steps on Trail 8, then turned right at the first intersection to hike the last mile to the car. It had to be all downhill, right? The first stretch obliged, twisting here and there through the woods for a 150-foot descent into a ravine—only to surprise me with a fresh climb. Such is the nature of southern Indiana hiking. Back at the car, I had the usual post-hike emotions: happy to be done but with a little twinge of not wanting to leave the woods. It had been a great day on the Brown County trails.

Brown County History

Brown County followed a circuitous and unlikely path to becoming a state park. Initially, there wasn't much interest in establishing a park in this location. Richard Lieber, first director of the Indiana Department of Conservation and acknowledged "father" of the state park system, owned property in the area, but Brown County was not among his priority properties.

Why? The area today looks nothing like it did in the early 20th century. And, in fact, the area has changed dramatically throughout its long geologic history.

Today's wooded hills were, 250 million years ago, lying at the bottom of a shallow inland sea. The area was part of a large silty and sandy delta formed by the outflow of a huge river. Over time, the deposits hardened into a variety of sedimentary rocks: limestone, shale, and sandstone.

Modern-day Brown County is a story written by water, which eroded away the limestone and shale, leaving the tougher sandstone—exposed in places in today's park as colorful, layered rock—protecting the tops of the taller hills and ridges. Forests took hold in this landscape and became the predominant feature.

Fast forward to the 19th century. Land-hungry settlers cleared trees and started growing crops. But trees and row crops thrive in very different types of soil. After logging a plot, early farmers would plant wheat and get just a few years of harvest before the topsoil was gone. To survive, they cleared more land and planted again, a process that went on for decades. Meanwhile, railroads helped build a market for lumber cut from the seemingly endless forests. By 1920 the Brown County hills were bare, the once-vast forests mostly gone. The remaining farmers were poor and barely eking out a living from the played-out soil.

At this time, Nashville, Indiana, real estate broker and insurance agent Lee Bright was convinced that Brown County needed a state park to provide an economic boost.

Bright reached out multiple times to Richard Lieber but gained no traction for his efforts. When game warden Fred Ahlers suggested to Bright that there was money available to purchase land for state fish and game reserves, Bright changed tactics.

Division of Fish and Game superintendent, George Mannfeld was interested, and he helped convince Lieber to acquire state property in Brown County using the fish and game reserve funds. Bright was appointed as a land acquisition agent by the state in 1924. He got to work immediately, amassing 7,600 acres of land for the state. Much of the land had been abandoned or purchased on the cheap at tax sales, but he also bought 18 owner-occupied properties.

Land acquired, the Brown County Game Reserve opened and a game farm raising pheasants and quail was established. One of the reserve's earliest priorities was reforestation, a visionary decision that transformed the landscape and, a century later, makes it difficult to imagine bare hills and farmland. White-tailed deer and other game animals were reintroduced (deer had been extirpated in 1877). In 1929, seven-acre Strahl Lake was built and stocked with gamefish. And meanwhile, land acquisitions continued, with the reserve growing to 10,000 acres by 1927.

Discussions about establishing a state park adjacent to the game reserve started in 1928. A year later, Brown County commissioners acquired and transferred to the state 1,1,29 acres that bordered the game reserve; a small Brown County State Park opened on the land in 1929.

Change came quickly to the new park, which proved very popular. Providing lodging for visitors was an early priority for Richard Lieber, who arranged construction of several cabins and a small lodge as a gathering place. Lieber used the lodging complex to honor Indiana's popular political satirist Kin Hubbard, who had passed away in 1930. Hubbard's characters were country folk from Brown County, Indiana, most notably the wisecracking Abe Martin. To mark its opening in 1932, the small lodge was dedicated as Abe Martin Lodge; the cabins were each named after other Hubbard comic characters.

In 1934, the first Civilian Conservation Corps crews arrived and set to work improving the park; they stayed until the program ended in 1942 and are responsible for much of the existing infrastructure. During their years in residence, the young men planted countless trees and built the dam creating Ogle Lake. They also constructed roads, trails, bridges, lookout towers, picnic shelters, the saddle barn, and an amphitheater.

In 1940 the game reserve was folded into the state park with the combined property surpassing 13,000 acres. Over time, additional land was added bringing Brown County State Park to its current size. Today, Brown County State Park protects the core of what is now the largest contiguous forest in the state—proof of the amazing healing power of nature and what the efforts of committed conservationists can achieve.

Brown County Today

The north gate of Brown County State Park is located on Highway 46 about 59 miles from Indianapolis city center. The large park has two other entrances. The West Gatehouse is the required entry point for RVs and vehicles towing trailers. The remote entrance off Highway 135 in the southeast corner of the park is for the Horseman's Campground only.

Brown County's large size and good segregation of amenities help offset the negative impacts of its many visitors, who can find many fun activities in the park. The main parking lot for mountain bikers is just inside the North Gate near the swimming pool. Horseback riders can visit the historic Saddle Barn for guided rides or trailer their own horses to the Highway 135 entrance. Fishing is popular at the two lakes. Ogle Lake, the larger of the two reservoirs, allows launching small motorless rowboats, canoes and kayaks.

Brown County is a popular spot for birdwatching, especially for forest species during the spring migration, but also for waterbirds in and near the two lakes. Wildlife watchers can look for a variety of species, including gray and red fox, coyote, raccoons, mink, and occasional bobcats. The park is also home to an interesting mix of amphibians and reptiles, including relatively rare and secretive timber rattlesnakes and copperheads.

Lodging options abound inside Brown County State Park. Abe Martin Lodge is open year-round and has 84 rooms in addition to a restaurant, gift shop, and ample space to lounge. Surrounding the lodge are 56 rustic cabins, some of which date back to the earliest days of the state park. A more recent addition is 20 two-story family cabins that can sleep up to eight people.

Brown County has the most expansive camping options of any Indiana state park. There are three traditional campgrounds, clustered together near the center of the park. Together they offer 429 sites, all but 28 featuring electrical hookups. On top of this, there is a rally campground for groups (60 sites), the Horseman's Campground (204 sites, including 118 with electricity), and a youth tent area.

If you don't camp and can't get into Abe Martin Lodge, don't worry; tourism-focused Brown County is loaded with lodging options, including hotels, cabins, resorts, home rentals, and just about anything you can imagine. Nashville, just two miles west of the North Gatehouse has high-quality restaurants, breweries, and distilleries, as well as artisan outlets featuring the work of many talented people.

Hiking Brown County

Brown County is a great destination for walkers—just stick to the hiking trails. The bridle trails are closed to hiking, and while you are allowed to hike on the mountain bike trails, they get busy and attract riders who are serious and fast.

Trail 6 circles the shores of Strahl Lake, offering exceptional water views.

Hiking in the park is concentrated in two areas. The first is near Abe Martin Lodge. Hiking from the lodge, its large parking lot, or nearby cabins provides access to Trails 1, 2, and 3—more than four miles of easily connecting path. Despite the proximity to the busiest area of the park, these trails are beautiful and offer a quiet, nature-filled experience.

Ogle Lake, in the west central part of Brown County, is the other center of hiking. From the parking lot near the small reservoir's dam, you can hike to hike to six different interconnected trails and cover nearly 13 miles of path without having to return to your car.

Two other trails are near well-known park landmarks. Trail 10 starts near the park office and fire tower, and Trail 6 starts behind the Nature Center.

Hiking in southern Indiana's hill country is more challenging than in other parts of the state. While some trails are easier than others, there are no *easy* trails at Brown County State Park, and all have at least one climb that will test you. Keep that in mind before you head out on a trail with kids or adults who have mobility or stamina issues.

Trail Running

The forested hills that make Brown County popular with hikers make it a compelling—but challenging—destination for trail runners. Maybe the biggest challenge, in addition to steep climbs, is the disconnected nature of the trails. In theory, you could connect trails with road sections, but the park roads are twisting, narrow, heavily traveled, and not safe for runners.

Instead, be cautious and stick to the trails. If you are staying in or near Abe Martin Lodge and content with a shorter route, run trails 1, 2, and 3, which link together for four-plus miles. The best option for runners, though, is to use the Ogle Lake Trailhead as a base. From that central point, you can access Trails 4, 5, 7, 8, 9, and 11 for 13 miles of running. An additional half-mile run beyond Trails 4/5 through the campground to the nature center gives you safe access to Trail 6. All these routes are scenic but hard; be prepared for steep climbs and descents.

A final option is to run on the mountain bike trails, which is allowed. For example, runners wanting to incorporate isolated Trail 10 into a route can strategically use mountain bike trails to connect with hiking Trails 4, 5, and 8.

TRAIL GUIDES

Trail 1—Lodge Trail

Rating: ★ ★ ★ **Configuration:** Lollipop
Distance: 0.9 miles **Difficulty:** Moderate

Tour: This trail starts near the northwest corner of Abe Martin Lodge and offers a quick and satisfying escape into nature punctuated by climbs that will get your heart pumping. Park in the lodge lot and start hiking along the access road on the west side of the complex. Trails 1 and 2 start together down a staircase near one of the rustic cabins. (Don't park in this area; the spaces are for cabin guests.) At the bottom of the stairs, Trail 1 departs left and heads up a beautiful ravine. The forested slopes and bird calls make you feel like you're in a wild place—even though you're surrounded by roads. The first quarter mile is a gentle downhill to the start of the loop; stay to the right and begin an up-and-down 100-foot ascent. Enjoy views highlighted by a varied mix of maturing trees and a small stream trickling through the ravine to your right. The trail tops out near the main park road, turns left, and starts a gentler descent back to the start of the loop.

Trail 2—CCC Trail

Rating: ★ ★ ★ **Configuration:** Loop
Distance: 2.0 miles **Difficulty:** Moderate

Tour: This trail was laid out in the 1930s by Civilian Conservation Corps workers and the bridges and other structures are a tribute to their hard work. Follow the parking directions for Trail 1, but keep walking along the cabin access road to the official start of Trail 2 and the recommended clockwise trip around the loop. The trail initially follows the hillside below Abe Martin Lodge, which looms above, then swings into a valley occupied by both a pretty stream and a bridle path, which parallel below you to the left. Civilization intrudes as the first of several large family cabins appears on the top of the hillside to your right. After three-quarters of a mile, the last of the cabins disappear, and the trail swings to the right out of the main valley and starts climbing. After crossing the lodge access road and paralleling the main park road for a while, the climb's destination becomes apparent: North Lookout Tower, a reconstruction of the original CCC structure. Take a few minutes to visit this attractive building which offers an expansive northward vista. Behind the tower, Trail 2 starts a steady 200-foot descent through the forest to one of the park's other impressive CCC landmarks: Lower Shelter. This sprawling rock structure has a large parking lot, an access alternative to avoid the busy lodge area. Crossing the small stream and scaling the CCC-era stone steps takes you to the wooden stairway shared by Trails 1 and 2, the route back to Abe Martin Lodge.

Trail 3—Saddle Barn Loop

Rating: ★ ★ ★ ★　　　　**Configuration:** Loop
Distance: 1.25 miles　　　　**Difficulty:** Moderate

Tour: Trail 3 offers both variety and unexpected natural beauty in a relatively short distance. Follow the parking and access instructions for Trail 1, continuing along the cabin road to the start of Trail 3. The first highlight comes quickly: the CCC-constructed stone amphitheater, which today can be rented for a wedding in the woods. The trail drops down a staircase; look to the right. Horses from the saddle barn might be visible through the trees. The trail emerges into a large open area and passes the barn, which dates from the park's earliest days. Guided trail rides are still popular; keep your eyes open for riders as you hike. After the saddle barn area, Trail 3 returns to the woods and starts climbing, paralleling a park road. Turning southwest, the trail follows a steep stairway into a narrow ravine, crosses a tiny creek, and starts downstream on the other side. This stretch is one of the prettiest in the park, feels remarkably isolated, and is rich with bird life. After rock-hopping over a larger creek and crossing the bridle path, Trail 3 climbs back toward the lodge and meets Trail 2. Turn right to return to your starting point.

BROWN COUNTY
STATE PARK

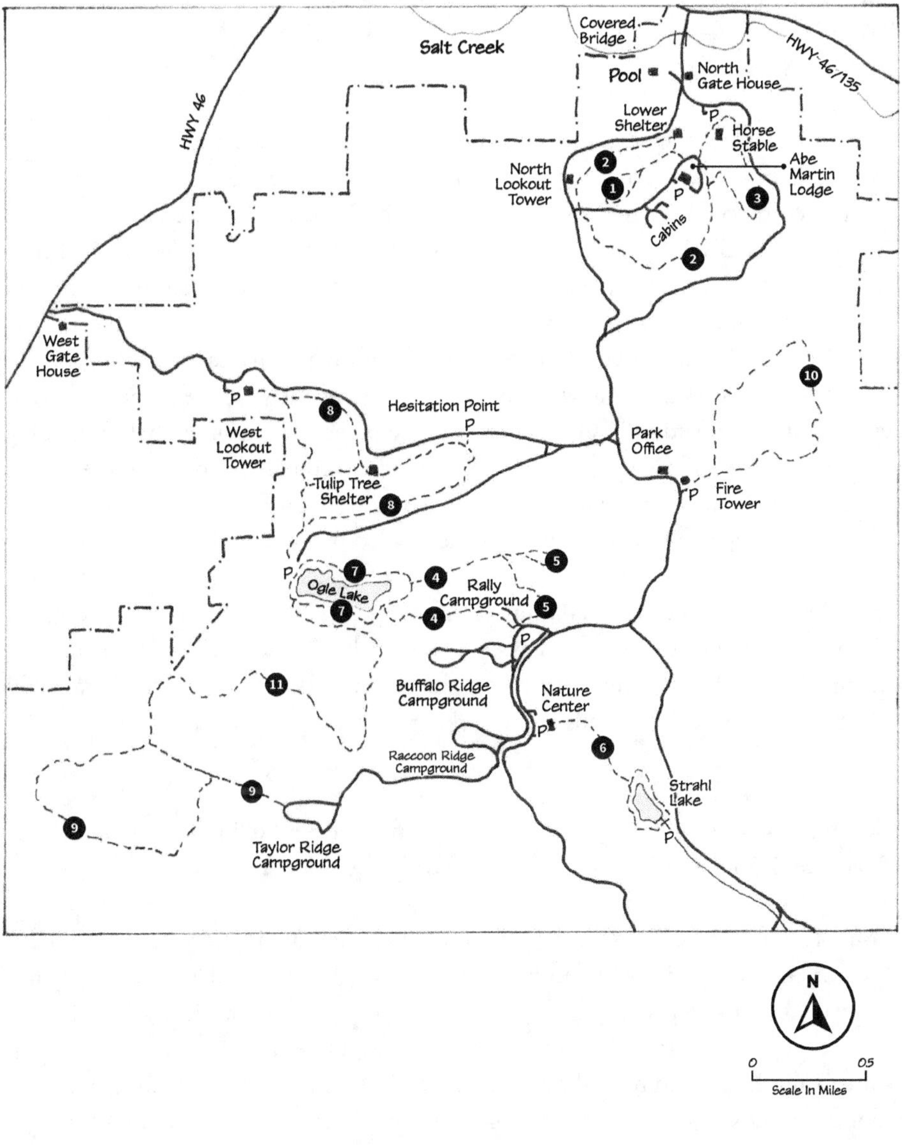

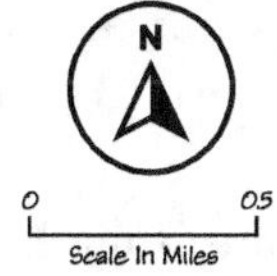

Trail 4—Rally Campground Trail
Trail 5—Ogle Hollow Nature Preserve Trail

Rating: ★ ★ ★ ★   **Configuration:** Loop and Lollipop
Distance: Trail 4—1.25 miles;   **Difficulty:** Moderate
Trail 5—0.75 miles

Tour: Trails 4 and 5 share a trailhead and function as a single large loop with a small extension into Ogle Hollow Nature Preserve. Follow the main park road to the campground entrance. Take the first right, before the Buffalo Ridge entrance and park in the first lot. Trail 4 departs to the west and descends gently for the first half mile through an attractive upland forest. The downhill gets progressively steeper as the trail switchbacks into a deep ravine before reaching the shores of Ogle Lake and joining with Trail 7. Turning left takes you to a parking lot that is an alternate access for this hike. Instead, turn right, following the path to the upper end of the 17-acre lake and crossing it on a boardwalk. On the far side, the paths split again, with Trail 4 going to the right. An informational sign and map offer a rough idea of the route ahead, which is nearly level for the next half mile as you walk up a quiet tributary valley. A steep slope topped by the ridge you just descended parallels to the right. Soon, Trail 4 ends and Trail 5 begins; turn left to explore the nature preserve on a short lollipop trail. Returning to the main trail, turn left and start the climb back to the parking lot. Keep your eyes open for rare yellowwood trees, which have smooth bark similar to beech but branch into multiple trunks. After gaining 300 vertical feet on a beautiful north-facing slope, Trail 5 ends at the parking lot where you started.

Trail 6—Strahl Lake Trail

Rating: ★ ★ ★ ★   **Configuration:** Lollipop
Distance: 1.5 miles   **Difficulty:** Moderate

Tour: Farmer Jimmie Strahl sold his property to the state in 1924 so that it could become part of the Brown County Game Reserve. A few years later he was memorialized when a small lake was built on the site. Trail 6 circumnavigates the lake and connects it to the Nature Center, which is the best place to start this hike. The path starts behind the building and goes downward immediately, the beginning of a 300-foot drop to the lakeshore. The trail passes through a gently sloped valley featuring a small stream and a relatively young forest. The trail takes a final staircase down to the edge of Strahl Lake and the start of the loop section; pause to look for herons, ducks, and other waterfowl. Turn right to follow a shoreline path that in places is just inches above the water. Cross the small dam and take the short side trip to get a good look at the unique spillway, which turns 90 degrees and sends water cascading across a natural rock face of sedimentary layers. Below the dam, you'll see the small parking lot and picnic area that offer alternative access for Trail 6. Returning to the east lake shore, note the large pine plantation that was planted in the park's early years. Continue circumnavigating the lake, crossing tributaries on boardwalks, to reach the beginning of the half-mile climb back to your starting point.

Trail 7—Ogle Lake Trail

Rating: ★ ★ ★ **Configuration:** Loop
Distance: 1.5 miles **Difficulty:** Moderate

Tour: The Ogle Lake parking lot is the focal point for the best hiking in this park. The lake was built in the 1930s as a water source but, ironically, lacks a potable water source in the 21st century. Hike Trail 7 counterclockwise by climbing the stairs to the top of the dam and turning right. At the dam's end, turn left, pass the Trail 11 junction, and follow the south shore. The trail rollercoasters up and down but mostly sits above the lake, providing views of fish, turtles, ducks, and other water life. It's also eroded, so watch your step as you navigate roots and stairs that need repairs. Trail 4 joins in the southeast corner of the lake and the two paths cross a boardwalk together at the head of the reservoir. Turn left where the paths fork and follow the north shore. The path here is also eroded but more level. It also follows closer to the water, offering good fishing access. After a final climb to a picnic area, Trail 7 drops back below the dam to the parking lot and your starting point.

Trail 8—HHC Trail

Rating: ★ ★ ★ ★ ★ **Configuration:** Double Loop with Extensions
Distance: 3.5 miles **Difficulty:** Moderate

Tour: Many hikers consider Trail 8 the top hiking destination in Brown County State Park. It offers length, a nicely engineered layout, surprising solitude, and good payoffs with Ogle Lake, Hesitation Point, and the West Lookout Tower anchoring the points of the rough triangle it follows. Follow the directions for Trail 7 but start your hike at the west side of the Ogle Lake lot, away from the dam. You reach a fork after a quarter mile; go right to navigate the loop counterclockwise. For the next mile and a quarter, wend your way up a quiet ravine that feels far from civilization—even though roads follow the tall ridgetops on both sides. The trail makes an abrupt left turn and scales a steep hillside with the help of a huge staircase. The trail reaches its highest elevation at Hesitation Point; take a few minutes to cross the road and enjoy the vista. Trail 8 roughly follows the West Gate Entrance Road to West Lookout Tower for the next mile and a half. At a fork near Tulip Tree Shelter, go right. (Turning left offers a shortcut back to Ogle Lake

Trail 2 takes hikers to the viewpoint at the North Lookout Tower.

that avoids the lookout.) Stay right at a second fork to take an out-and-back trip to the lookout, which soon appears above you. Returning on the lookout stub, turn right at the first Trail 8 fork to descend into and climb out of a pretty, isolated ravine. At the top of the next hill, you encounter the opposite end of the shortcut you passed earlier; from here it's an easy downhill cruise back to the parking lot.

Trail 9—Taylor Ridge Trail
Trail 11—Vollmer Trail

Rating: ★ ★ ★ ★   **Configuration:** Lollipop with Extension
Distance: Trail 9—3.0 miles;   **Difficulty:** Challenging
Trail 11—2.75 miles

Tour: Trails 9 and 11 provide the only hiking route in 10 O'Clock Line Nature Preserve, the largest in the state. This is also one of the most remote and little-traveled areas of the park. Taylor Ridge Trail, a simple lollipop into the preserve, is the oldest of the two paths and accessible only from the campground of the same name (near site 324). It has no parking. Hoosier Hikers Council provided better access by building a beautiful connector from Ogle Lake, now dubbed Trail 11. Follow the parking and start-of-hike instructions for Trail 7; depart on Trail 11 from the south end of the dam. Immediately scaling a steep slope sets the tone for the hike, which has several challenging climbs. After reaching the first summit, the trail drops back into a ravine then climbs a shoulder to another ridge—marking 400 vertical feet in just the first mile—then repeats this pattern one more time en route to Trail 9. Turn left at the junction with the older trail, which has a different personality: muddier, more overgrown. After a quarter mile, the campground access departs to the left; the round trip adds an extra mile to the hike. Past the campground turnoff, Trail 9's loop descends southward into a densely vegetated valley with a small creek, then turns west and follows the waterway downstream for three quarters of a mile. Nearing the park boundary, the trail turns north and begins a steep climb out of the ravine and back to the connection with Trail 11.

Trail 10—Fire Tower Trail

Rating: ★ ★ ★   **Configuration:** Loop
Distance: 2.2 miles   **Difficulty:** Moderate

Tour: This trail starts next to the park's fire tower, a popular attraction that is worth climbing if there's no line (there is a limit of six people at a time on the rickety structure). Turn right on the Trail 10 loop, following a gently descending, wide path. When leaves are off the trees, views of distant hills begin to appear. Soon, the CCC-era Peachtree Shelter emerges from the forest ahead of you. Though trees now obscure the vista to the southeast, the recently renovated structure is a nice spot to stop. The trail swings north from the shelter and continues descending, following a small waterway to the trail's low point and a rock-hop across a larger stream. The path in this area illustrates the good and the bad of Trail 10. The good: the quiet, in one of the loneliest corners of the park, makes the area feel like wilderness. The bad: a heavily eroded, sometimes muddy walkway and lots of invasive vegetation. Trail conditions improve somewhat throughout the climb to regain the 300 feet of elevation, taking you back up to the tower. The path narrows and firms up as you move upward, twisting through the trees and hopping over roots. A small pond in the woods, filled with frogs, eggs, and tadpoles in the spring, is a special treat. After one final steep push, you reach the end of the loop and turn right to return to the trailhead.

2
Chain O'Lakes State Park

A few years ago, I dreamed up and executed a grand adventure plan for Chain O'Lakes State Park. The property has two distinctly different trail systems: one on land and one on water. The land-based system covers 29 miles, the longest hiking/running trail network in an Indiana state park. The water-based system extends five miles and connects nine of the park's 13 glacial lakes, offering hours of flatwater paddling. My plan involved sampling a generous helping of both trail systems in a single day. Doable? Absolutely! Would I be exhausted afterwards? Undoubtedly!

I arrived at Chain O'Lakes on a late-October Friday in perfect weather that was forecast to stay that way. I set up my tent in the park's huge campground, enjoyed a nice dinner, and was in my sleeping bag early. I woke up at sunrise, dressed, and ate a light breakfast in the chill air. Soon I was running slowly down Trail 6, easing my body into what would be a long day.

Chain O'Lakes has a stellar reputation among trail runners. The network of rolling, scenic trails feels like it was designed with running in mind. My plan was to cover roughly 11-12 miles and visit eight lakes.

Despite the early hour, I was buoyed by the scenery—autumn was in full swing. The world was a pleasing mix of green, orange, red, and gold. The lakes, mirrorlike in the calm air, reflected the color palette from the surrounding forests. I wanted to keep running just to discover more beautiful scenes.

After running along Sucker, Long, Dock, and both Finster lakes, an old schoolhouse caught my attention. I left it for now, focused first on running Trail 9. After completing the challenging loop around Krieger Lake—a marshy kettle with abundant birds—I returned to Stanley School. It was time for a break, and a docent had just opened the historic building for visitors. I was a muddy, sweaty mess but curious, so sheepishly entered the front door. The volunteer encouraged me to come to the front of the one-room schoolhouse, but I declined, citing my filth. She kindly offered an historic overview from a safe distance, and then it was time for me to depart.

A fall hike through the upland forest on Chain O'Lakes Trail 12.

My route continued west and took me around Bowen Lake, after which I joined Trail 7, which roller-coastered over low hills and followed the creek linking Weber and Sand Lakes. A couple of kayaks were making their way upstream toward Weber Lake; I would explore this waterway myself later in the day.

I followed Trail 5 around beautiful Sand Lake, the largest and deepest in the park. After passing the beach, I found Trail 3, followed it to Trail 10, and made my way back to the campground and the end of my run. I felt great but tired and hungry. I fired up the stove, made brunch, and settled in for a rest—but not for too long. By early afternoon I was hiking on Trail 3 back to Sand Lake.

At the livery, I rented a kayak for two hours, donned my life jacket, and started paddling northwest. The view from the water was amazing. Paddling was hard on my upper body but let me rest my fatigued legs. I reached the stream outlet, passed under the footbridge I had crossed earlier that morning, and started my journey to Weber Lake.

This was the fun part of the trip. Flow in the connecting stream was negligible, but it was narrow and twisting, requiring deft paddle work to steer around the trees in the water. Complicating matters was the steady flow of traffic in both directions. Some people were struggling, but with patience and good humor everything worked out.

Weber Lake is not large, so I paddled quickly through it, hoping to reach Mud Lake within my one-hour turnaround target. Traffic dwindled and the next stream was wider and easier to navigate. Eventually I floated into Mud Lake and saw a couple of fishing boats that likely launched at Miller Lake farther downstream.

I had reached my goal in my allotted time, but my arms and chest were screaming. Despite wanting to rest a little longer, I turned around and started my return trip. Back on the stream to Sand Lake, traffic was even heavier, and the going slower than before, but I finally passed the last kayak and escaped to open water. With my arms raising the white flag, I paddled at a modest pace and pulled into the livery with a couple minutes to spare. On the walk back to the campsite, I reflected on what had been an amazing day—Chain O'Lakes had lived up to its reputation as the perfect place for a multi-trail adventure.

Chain O'Lakes History

Between 20,000 and 16,000 years ago, what today is Chain O'Lakes was covered by an ice sheet up to a mile thick. The glacier flowed from the north, carrying and depositing rocks, gravel, and sand eroded from Canadian bedrock. And though ice eventually covered two thirds of Indiana, the glacial lobes advanced and retreated periodically, depending on the temperatures.

It was during the final retreat north that the glaciers sculpted the park's current landscape. Giant blocks of ice broke off the glacier face and were partially buried by sand, gravel, and other deposits. Eventually, these huge ice blocks melted, leaving kettle lakes and drainage streams. Today, we see 13 such lakes in the park, along with the creeks connecting nine of the lakes and former lakes that have filled in and today are marshes, bogs, or just low spots among the hills.

Post-glaciers, the land in and around the future state park developed fertile soils and was covered with forests, wetlands, and small pockets of grasslands. It was a resource-rich landscape in which humans thrived. A variety of native cultures lived in the area for thousands of years but by the early 1800s, only scattered bands of Miami and Potawatomi could be found; historical records indicate there was a settlement on the north shore of Indian Lake, now called Bowen Lake.

William Bowen was the first white person to settle in the modern-day park. In 1840 he built a house near the north shore of the lake that now bears his name—in the same area that native tribes had been living just a few years before. Bowen was one of many farmers drawn to the area because of rich soils and forests that were considered less dense and easier to clear than in the southern part of the state. Today, Noble County is still a thriving agricultural area.

But the glacial features that make Chain O'Lakes appealing for recreation—lakes, wetlands, and sandy/gravelly hills—discouraged farming in enough places that the future parkland retained some of its wild charms well into the 20th century.

Interest in turning the area into a park can be traced back to 1937. In 1946, a state land planner surveyed 23 sites around Indiana in search of a site for a "natural lake state park." His recommend choice: the property that became Chain O'Lakes. The following year the legislature allocated $37,500 for initial land acquisition and three counties (Noble, Whitley, and Allen) raised $250,000 for the park from tax levies.

Unfortunately, local opposition to the park emerged (mostly because of the tax increase), lawsuits were filed, and the funds were frozen in escrow until 1956. When the suits were finally thrown out, the first 50 acres were purchased in December of that year. In 1959 Governor Harold Handley pushed the legislature to allocate another $300,000 to the park, and land acquisition began in earnest.

On June 12, 1960, with the title to more than 1,300 acres in hand, Chain O'Lakes State Park was formally dedicated. Since that time, the park has more than doubled in size and undergone an exciting transformation. To this day, Chain O'Lakes continues to add new amenities, build trails, and improve the experience for the 420,00-plus people who visit every year.

Chain O'Lakes Today

Chain O'Lakes is 145 miles from downtown Indianapolis. The park is much closer to Fort Wayne—28 miles from the city center—and many Allen County residents consider it their home park.

Today, the state park covers 2,718 acres. Of this, 212 acres is water, but it feels like much more than that. Chain O'Lakes gets more out of its property than just about any other state park in Indiana. There are more trails, water-based sports, scenic vistas, places to camp, and activities to participate in than you would expect to find in a park twice this size.

What really sets Chain O'Lakes apart is its paddling trail. Yes, other properties have designated water trails but at no other Indiana state park can you find an inter-connected chain of small lakes and calm streams that seem to have been designed with casual paddling in mind. The park does a wonderful job of promoting this resource, thanks to the popular five-mile Nine Lake Paddle Challenge, five launch points around the park, and a well-run rental center on Sand Lake offering canoes and kayaks.

Not surprisingly, fishing is popular at the park; largemouth bass, crappie, and bluegill are the top game species. In addition to paddling and fishing, Sand Lake also offers swimming. The beach is located on the southeast shore and is open Memorial Day weekend to Labor Day.

Chain O'Lakes offers visitors multiple opportunities to see and learn about the area's flora and fauna, and it is an especially diverse property. In addition to the lakes and wetlands, the park has dense riparian and upland forests as well as 200 acres of restored prairie. More than 731 acres of the park have been protected as Glacier Esker Nature Preserve. The park is a stop on the Indiana Birding Trail and has a wonderful mix of species year-round.

History shines at the park's preserved Stanley School, open from late April through October. The one-room schoolhouse was used 1915-1954 and offered a K-8 education for up to 30 children at a time. The current building was the fourth incarnation of the school; the three predecessors were all destroyed in fires.

There are multiple options for overnighting at Chain O'Lakes. The huge main campground has 413 sites: 331 electric, 49 nonelectric, and 33 primitive (tents only and pit toilets). Trails 1, 3, 6, and 10 lead to the campground and it is easy to hike or run from there to Sand Lake and all its amenities. In addition to the main camp-ground, Chain O'Lakes offers a rally camp for adult groups, a youth group tent area, and a paddle-in canoe campground on the east shore of Rivir Lake with four primitive sites.

For a more civilized stay inside the park, Chain O'Lakes offers 18 cabins, which occupy a beautiful, wooded hillside above Long Lake.

Outside the park, chain hotels can be found in Columbia City, 20 minutes south and in Kendallville 25 minutes northeast of the park. Both towns have grocery stores, restaurants, and other outlets for buying supplies.

Trail 6 leads to a beautiful dockside view on Long Lake.

Hiking Chain O'Lakes

With 29 miles of pathway and mountain bikes and horses prohibited, Chain O'Lakes has the largest hiking- or running-only trail network among Indiana state parks. It is an exceptional resource, fully interconnecting and well maintained. Because the park has been embraced by the trail running community, the paths tend to be wide and not overly technical. Steep hills are rare. Signage is comprehensive and most intersections include route-finding maps. And the scenery? If you enjoy walking through an ever-changing palette of forests, natural lakes, wetlands, and prairies—complete with a rich diversity of birds and wildlife—you'll be pleased. The big question is, with so many trails, what do you hike if your time is limited?

Trails 2 and 8 are gorgeous and give the best introduction to the park. Start near Stanley School to add some history to the mix. If you have more time and energy, add Trail 7 to create one of the best five-mile hikes in Indiana. Trail 5 loops around Sand Lake for an easy and pleasant one-plus-mile stroll—a good follow-up to renting a kayak, canoe, or boat and having enjoyed some time on the water. Campers should take advantage of Trail 6, a beautiful loop that cuts through the east side of the campground.

Trail Running

Though Chain O'Lakes leans hard into its identity as the state's premiere paddling destination, it's arguably Indiana's best place to run trails. Chain O'Lakes has been embraced by its local running community, which has built a large and growing trail network designed and maintained to meet the needs of runners. On top of that, Chain O'Lakes hosts three major trail running events throughout the year.

Every trail at the park is run-friendly, so it's hard to pick a wrong one. The big question is how far you want to go. Visit the ignitetrailseries.com to find maps for two established long-run options: the 13.1-mile loop used by the half and full marathon every December; and the 25-mile loop used in October by the group's signature 50/75/100-mile races. The latter route is noted by permanent marker posts through Chain O'Lakes—unique for an Indiana state park. In a fun twist, the markers include a small sign celebrating past race winners.

For runners looking for a shorter distance, Trail 4 is a good place to start. The route consists of four conjoined loops; extend your desired distance by adding more loops. Grow the run even more by adding parts of Trails 11, 7, 5, and/or 12, all of which intersect with Trail 4. There are a few places to access Trail 4 but the parking area between the Norman and Miller Lake boat ramps is the only trailhead with a pit toilet.

TRAIL GUIDES

Trail 1

Rating: ★★★   **Configuration:** Loop
Distance: 1.5 miles   **Difficulty:** Moderate

Tour: This is a convenient, scenic, and short hike from the campground, connecting via Trail 6 from Site 379 to Glacier Ridge Shelter. If you aren't camping, park at the Dock Lake boat ramp, walk west down the access road and turn right to follow Trail 1, which climbs past the park headquarters on the lake's west side. Turn right at the junction with Trail 2, cross the bridge over the stream connecting Bowen and Dock Lakes; Trail 1 follows the north shore of the latter. Thick vegetation limits water views but enjoy the beautiful riparian forest. Turn right at the next intersection and cross the waterway connecting Dock and Long Lakes. A junction with Trail 6 sits beyond the bridge; turn left and follow the combined trails, starting one of the few long uphills in the park. Trail 1 breaks to the right on its own and continues climbing to Glacier Ridge, your endpoint if you started from the campgrounds. Non-campers,

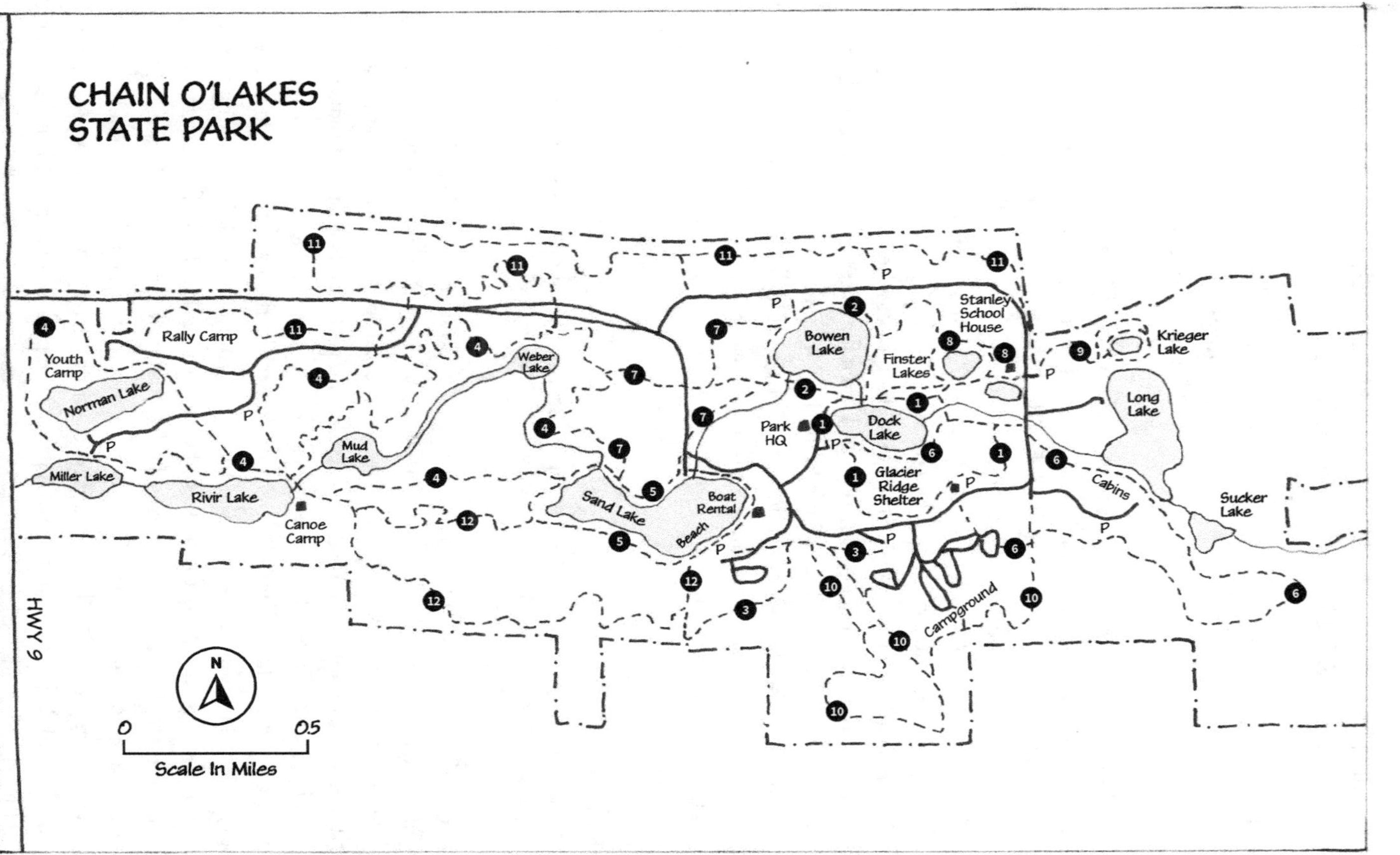

CHAIN O'LAKES
STATE PARK
Youth Camp
Rally Camp
Norman Lake
Miller Lake
Mud Lake
Rivir Lake
Canoe Camp
Weber Lake
Sand Lake
Beach
Boat Rental
Bowen Lake
Park HQ
Dock Lake
Finster Lakes
Glacier Ridge Shelter
Stanley School House
Krieger Lake
Long Lake
Cabins
Sucker Lake
Campground
HWY 9
N
0
0.5
Scale In Miles
P

keep going, passing the fish cleaning station before starting a quarter-mile descent through a second-growth forest to your starting point.

Trail 2

Rating: ★ ★ ★ ★   **Configuration:** Lollipop
Distance: 1.0 miles   **Difficulty:** Moderate

Tour: Bowen Lake may be the prettiest of the park's 13 named bodies of water and Trail 2 follows its circular shoreline for most of its route, offering one sublime view after another. The trailhead is on the right side of the park road, about a half mile after making the turn toward Stanley School. Despite what the official property map shows, this is a lollipop route starting on the lake's northwest side. Follow the downhill path from the parking lot to a three-way junction with Trail 7; turn left and follow the eroded track toward the water to navigate the Trail 2 loop clockwise. You can access the water's edge frequently as you hike—stop, look, and listen for waterfowl and wading birds. Pass the connector to Trail 8 and continue to the T with Trails 1 and 6; turn right and cross the bridge over the short channel between Dock and Bowen Lakes. Trail 2 follows the latter's south and west shores, in the process crossing the channel to Sand Lake. The trail takes a more inland track for its final stretch and a climb to the junction with the trailhead connector.

Trail 3

Rating: ★ ★ ★   **Configuration:** Lollipop (close loop with Trail 12)
Distance: 1.3 miles   **Difficulty:** Easy

Tour: Trail 3 uses a pleasant, forested route to convey campers from the campground to Sand Lake and two junctions with Trail 12, which you can use to create a loop and an interesting return hike. Trail 3 starts next to campground Site 10 and passes the visitor lot, where non-campers should park. The path heads west and makes a steady downhill toward the beach, in the process passing two junctions with Trail 10, before reaching a Trail 3 fork. Take the right option to do the loop counterclockwise. You soon pop out of the woods, and the trail peters out at a road. Walk along the pavement or through the grass to the large beach parking lot. Look for the start of Trails 5 and 12 at the lot's northeast corner, follow the trail for a short distance west along Sand Lake (enjoying the great views), and turn left with Trail 12 at the next junction. The wide, straight path, likely an old road, climbs gently through the trees and soon becomes Trail 3. Follow it almost to a gate at the park boundary and turn left. From here the path descends through an attractive second-growth forest to a creek crossing next to an intersection. Turn right; the left turn is an alternative route back to the beach. After following the stream for a short distance, Trail 3 climbs gently through the woods back to junction with the campground connector.

Trail 4

Rating: ★ ★ ★

Distance: 5.7 miles

Configuration: Multiple Loops

Difficulty: Moderate

Tour: Trail 4 has grown in recent years thanks to the efforts of a local running group. It is now a series of four conjoined loops that provide access to Chain O'Lakes' less-visited west side. Runners will enjoy the routes, but hikers may find the wide, winding trails—like mountain bike routes but less engineered and lacking structures—a little monotonous. Trail 4's most popular hike is the large eastern loop. Park at the Weber Lake access, on the right side of the main road a quarter mile past the gatehouse. To hike the loop clockwise, go left/east from the trailhead, following the mowed path through the woods. The path descends to a wetland area, crosses a bridge, and joins Trail 7 with a right turn at the intersection. The next section is exceptional, following the crest of a glacial esker and then the narrow channel between Sand and Weber Lakes; on summer weekends you'll likely see kayakers. The route takes a right turn and joins Trail 5, soon crossing the channel you've been following and offering wonderful views of Sand Lake. Trail 4 departs up a steep hill to the right and heads into a little-traveled region of the park. Unofficial side trails provide access to small Mud Lake, prettier than its name suggests. Soon Trail 4 reaches one of Chain O'Lakes' unique assets, the canoe campground. The scenic shoreline setting on Rivir Lake is a good place for a break; there is even a pit toilet. Trail 4 splits beyond the bridge over the channel. Left leads to the loop around Norman Lake; turn right to stay on the main loop. Turn right again almost immediately at an unmarked junction to follow your return route. This is a new run-focused trail section, and it is somewhat forgettable, winding up and down every side valley for two miles before a short, scenic visit to the shore of Weber Lake. A brief, steep climb delivers you to your vehicle. To hike the western loops of Trail 4, park between the boat ramps for Miller and Norman Lakes. Trail 4 circles the latter, passing the youth and rally camps. Extend your hike or run by adding loops north of Rivir and Mud Lakes.

Trail 5

Rating: ★ ★ ★ ★

Distance: 1.3 miles

Configuration: Loop

Difficulty: Easy

Tour: The official trailhead for Trail 5 is one shared with Trail 7 on the north shore of Sand Lake. It's a good starting point, allowing hikers to avoid busier options near the beach and boat rental. Hike west from the start, following the lake's north shore and leaving the busiest section for last. Sand Lake is the park's biggest, deepest, and most visited but it's a gem nonetheless; you'll find yourself stopping frequently to take in the views. Trail 4 joins for a time and the combined paths cross the channel leading to Weber Lake, a fun spot to watch kayakers. Continue walking around Sand Lake's western shore, passing junctions with Trails 4 and 12; the latter joins Trail 5 for the pretty south shore trek to the beach. This is where everything changes, especially if you're visiting on a summer weekend. Pick your way through the people and past the nature center/concession stand, boat livery (where you rent kayaks and other craft), and boat ramp. A short jaunt over the channel to Bowen Lake delivers you back to your vehicle.

Trail 6

Rating: ★ ★ ★ ★   **Configuration:** Loop

Distance: 3 miles   **Difficulty:** Moderate

Tour: Trail 6 is a wonderful hike for people staying in the cabins or campgrounds, but day-trippers should enjoy it, too. Glacier Ridge Shelter is a good starting point. Head south across the road into the campground; turn left then left again to reach the "primitive" area. Trail 6 restarts next to Site 407 and heads into a scrub forest on a mowed path to a poorly marked intersection with Trail 10. Make a left/right jog to stay on Trail 6, which continues through a pretty, more mature forest. After descending a large staircase, the trail loops through the woods past small Sucker Lake, visible through the trees. Soon, you get a full-on water view thanks to a dock reaching out into gorgeous Long Lake. Back on the trail, note the stairs climbing to the hilltop cabins. At the road, turn right on the pavement, walk 100 yards, and look for the trail restart on the left. Trail 1 joins the route for a short distance, then Trail 6 breaks off on its own to follow the south shore of Dock Lake. The vegetation is dense, and water views are limited, but take note of the beautiful forest, which contains some of the largest trees in the park. Turn left/south on combined Trail 1 and 6 near the boat ramp (an alternate starting point) and make the final climb through the woods past the fish cleaning station to Glacier Ridge.

Trail 7

Rating: ★ ★ ★ ★ ★   **Configuration:** Loop

Distance: 2 miles   **Difficulty:** Moderate

Tour: Trail 7 connects with, and is a fine add-on, for hikes on Trails 2, 4, and 5 but it's a wonderful walk on its own, offering a tour of Chain O'Lakes' glacial landscape. The trailhead in on the north shore of Sand Lake; depart to the west on a path shared with Trail 5, enjoying water views as you walk. Trail 7 (joined by Trail 4) departs to the right and starts following the channel—created by glacial meltwater—between Sand and Weber Lakes. Don't be surprised by kayakers on warm-weather weekends. Trail 7 leaves the channel, climbs, and follows a curving ridge of glacial deposits, an esker. After crossing the park road, a fork offers two options for following Trail 7. The right is shorter, while the left is longer and uses part of Trail 2 near the east shore of Bowen Lake to complete the loop. Both options converge next to the scenic channel connecting Bowen and Sand Lake, with Trail 7 following this waterway back to the starting point.

Trail 8

Rating: ★ ★ ★ ★   **Configuration:** Loop (with four connectors)
Distance: 1.5 miles   **Difficulty:** Moderate

Tour: At its heart, Trail 8 is a self-guided nature walk (look for the brochure online or at the trailhead) around the two Finster Lakes. But four connector paths radiating off the loop as well as junctions with Trails 1 and 2 create options for longer walks. Park at the Stanley School lot. To follow the nature trail stations in numerical order, depart on the trail north of the school. Tiny Turtle Pond is the first landmark, on your right. Soon, the largest of the paired Finster Lakes appears through the trees, but without access; the trail sits on a ridge above the lake. A path to the right connects with Trail 2, offering a looped side trip to Bowen Lake. After descending from the ridge, you encounter a second connector to Trail 2 followed by a junction with Trail 1. This area offers exceptional views from the south shore of Finster Lakes. Trail 8 continues east along the water. At a fork, turn left to complete the loop and return the way you came or turn right to follow an optional route near the smaller of the Finster Lakes back to the school.

Trail 9

Rating: ★ ★ ★   **Configuration:** Lollipop
Distance: 1.3 miles   **Difficulty:** Moderate

Tour: Trail 9 passes through an interesting mix of habitats and is great for birdwatchers but the experience is marred by a huge utility line. Nonetheless, this is a quality hike and starts in the lot near Stanley School. The first segment passes through a gorgeous, restored prairie, passes under the power line, then climbs a glacial ridge above Krieger Lake. The main trail makes a sharp U-turn, though an unmarked path going straight also accesses the lake. After cresting the ridge, the trail makes a gradual descent to a boardwalk on the east side of the small lake—which is the last open

Bowen Lake, from the Trail 2 bridge over the inlet from Sand Lake.

water in a large kettle-hole marsh. The birdlife is rich and varied, so take some time to listen and look. Continue off the long boardwalk to follow Krieger Lake's west shore. Either walk back to your outbound route or look for the steeper, unmarked shortcut departing from the lake's northwest corner.

Trail 10

Rating: ★★   **Configuration:** Lollipop
Distance: 2.5 miles   **Difficulty:** Moderate

Tour: Trail 10 offers a convenient hike for campers and is useful to runners circumnavigating the park, but it's Chain O'Lakes' least-interesting path. It's mostly a mowed track cut through scrubby former farmland, dotted with young trees and burdened by too many invasive plants. You can access Trail 10 from the campground and Trails 3 or 6, but a good starting point is the parking lot south of the turnoff to the cabins. The first section is a long and straight (probably an old road) and includes an intersection with Trail 6. After swinging west along the southern edge of the campground, you reach a T that marks the start of the loop. Turning right follows the west side of the campground to a junction with Trail 3. Turn left, then left again, to stay on Trail 10. A connector to the left offers a shortcut option or stay on the main trail—twice crossing a channelized ditch, a reminder of the area's farming history—to return to the start of the loop and the return trail to your vehicle.

Trail 11

Rating: ★ ★

Distance: 4.4 miles

Configuration: Point to Point

Difficulty: Easy

Tour: Trail 11 is popular with runners (and in the winter, cross-country skiers) and traversed by two of the park's popular trail races. The path connects Stanley School with the Rally Camp, roughly following Chain O'Lakes' northern boundary. Much of the route is a wide, flat, and mowed path gently winding through the woods—nondescript but pleasant. Park at Stanley School and head north on the mowed path to a service road, continuing to a gate. Turn left, pass under the power line, then wind your way through a relatively young forest for nearly three miles. The trail turns south and passes near the gatehouse. A side trail to the left is a new run-focused route that winds back to the west to the Weber Lake trailhead. Back on the main route, Trail 11 crosses to the south side of the park road and continues west for another mile to its end at the Rally Camp. Return the way you came or use Trails 4, 7, 2, 1, and 8 as a similar-length-but-more-scenic alternate route.

Trail 12

Rating: ★ ★ ★

Distance: 3.5 miles

Configuration: Loop

Difficulty: Moderate

Tour: Trail 12 has the distinction of being the host loop for the springtime Glacial Esker 6-12-24 Hour endurance trail race. The rest of the year it's just a nice hike, often overlooked by people seeking more lake-focused routes. Park at the beach; the trail leaves from the northwest corner of the lot. The first section, joined by Trail 5, follows the scenic south shore of Sand Lake. Trail 12 then departs to the left and says goodbye to the water. This stretch, through a maturing forest, is beautiful and wild feeling. A bench next to a stream through a small valley offers a nice resting spot. The path Ts and turns left on an old service road; the canoe camp is a short walk to the right from this intersection. The trail swings east then south and follows a ridge above the creek crossed earlier. After recrossing the stream, Trail 12 begins a stretch hugging the park's southern boundary—cornfields lie just a few yards away and there is even a section through a restored prairie. After returning to the woods, Trail 12 eventually intersects with Trail 3 and turns north on a former road that takes hikers back to the beach parking lot.

3
Charlestown State Park

This is a story about a time that Charlestown State Park surprised me.

It was a hot summer day, and I had business in the Louisville area that took all morning to complete. When I finished, I couldn't help but notice the ominous skies. Heavy thunderstorms were forecast, and they were starting to boil up in the steamy atmosphere. I shrugged off the weather, jumped in the car, and put my plan into action: I was going to hike at Charlestown State Park before the skies opened.

After passing the gatehouse, I turned left and followed the road to its dead end at a small parking lot—the start of Trail 1.

My reasons for choosing Trail 1 were simple: I had never hiked it before, it was about the length I wanted to walk (2.4 miles), and it was the closest trail to the park entrance. Beyond those simple facts, I didn't know much about the route. I quickly changed into hiking clothes and boots but was frozen by the boom of a nearby thunderclap. Rain started falling and I jumped back in the car to plot my next steps.

Not ready to give up, I took advantage of a strong cell signal to scan the weather radar. It turned out I was just catching the northern edge of a large storm. After it passed me, I'd have at least 90 minutes of clear weather.

Fifteen minutes later, the rain had stopped, and I was on the trail. The first section was nondescript—straight, wide, and graveled, probably a former road. The woods were young and scrubby; invasive honeysuckle appeared on both sides of the path. Meanwhile, the thunder echoed almost nonstop. Louisville, just a few miles south, was getting pounded. Feeling unsettled by the weather, I moved quickly down the trail.

Then everything abruptly changed. A narrow footpath broke away from the former road and started winding downhill and into a maturing forest. After navigating in and out of a shallow ravine, the trail descended even more and entered what felt like a completely different world.

Trail 2 descends into dense forest to a beautiful limestone-lined creek.

I had reached Fourteenmile Creek valley, the defining feature of Charlestown's eastern side. In places the muddy stream was visible through the dense forest. Four of the park's trails—1, 3, 4, and 5—traipse into the valley. I had hiked Trail 3 in the past. It was nice but didn't prepare me for what I found on Trail 1.

This part of the Fourteenmile Creek valley felt more like The Shire than southern Indiana. Massive moss-covered trees, ferns, and mushrooms were all around me. Wood thrushes, more than I had ever heard in one place, called happily from the forest canopy. The thunder still rumbled in the distance, but I forgot about being in a hurry. Every direction held an interesting detail to be examined, a scene to be photographed. My pace slowed to a crawl, and the outside world dissolved away.

As I walked, the scene became even more enchanting. Giant chunks of limestone littered the forest flow, sending the trail to and fro as it navigated the obstacle course. The massive rocks looked ancient; coated with moss and sprouting all kinds of plant life, they could have been lying there undisturbed for centuries. Above on the hillside, rocky outcrops revealed the source of the giant stones. In some places, cave-like depressions looked like the home of little forest folk who I imagined must be all around me. The thunder stopped, and the sun emerged briefly from behind the clouds, its light filtering through the trees.

Then, as I climbed out of the forested valley, I was jolted by what could have been a scene from a postapocalyptic movie. To my right, a massive concrete pier appeared ghostlike in the densely wooded valley. Up the hill ahead of me was another concrete structure, crumbling and covered with moss and lichen. The trail continued beyond it, climbing arrow-straight up a gentle grade.

As I examined the mysterious human artifacts, I realized this was an abandoned railroad right-of-way, complete with the remnants of a huge bridge that once crossed the valley. The scene reminded me that, not many years ago, this property was part of the Indiana Army Ammunition Plant. Remnants of the industrial facility—which manufactured gun powder—are more prominent on the west side of the park. This eastern area was largely left to nature, serving as a wild buffer zone around the potentially explosive factory.

I hiked on, with modern America intruding in the form of vehicle noise from nearby Highway 62. The trail turned left off the old railroad line and plunged back into quiet woods for its last half mile. Suddenly, thunder started again; another storm was brewing, and this one would hit the park. I got to my car, jumped in, and started the long drive home—and none too soon. The skies opened just a few miles down the road. Over the next few hours, nearly four inches of rain fell on the park.

Despite my close call with bad weather, Charlestown had delivered a surprising hiking experience. As I drove home, I was already plotting my next visit.

Charlestown History

Charlestown once lay at the bottom of ancient tropical seas and over time layers of silt and sand built up and were compressed into the sedimentary rocks now exposed in the park. Some of the deposits are Devonian limestone from about 390 million years ago. These fossil-bearing rocks are from the same formation visible at nearby Falls of the Ohio State Park. Other parts of Charlestown are underlain by Silurian limestone, which dates back even further, 419-443 million years ago.

Charlestown resides in a karst landscape, meaning that water has dissolved away parts of the limestone bedrock, leaving sinkholes on the surfaces and drainage channels underground. Charlestown lacks the caves found at other state parks in the karst region, but you pass sinkholes and springs along the trails as you hike through the park.

Glaciers shaped significant features of the park that we see today. The Ohio River and Fourteenmile Creek were not covered by ice and were scoured out by meltwater from glaciers that stopped just north of the park about 20,000 years ago.

With its water, woodland resources, and rugged, protective topography, the Charlestown area has been attractive to humans for thousands of years. Artifacts from indigenous people who lived here about 4,000 years ago were unearthed in 2006 during construction of the Ohio River boat ramp. A formation called Devils Backbone may have been the site of a fortified Mississippian period structure, built about 1,000 years ago—but that's a complicated story.

State geologist E.T. Cox surveyed the site in 1873 and noted the presence of a prehistoric rock structure and burial site, which he described as an "Indian cemetery." Racist attitudes of the day couldn't imagine a native source and attributed the structure to legendary Welsh Prince Madoc; folk tales claim he was the first European to visit America. He was said to have been at Devil's Backbone around 1170. This fanciful tale can be dismissed but we'll never learn much about the native people responsible for the site: after Cox's survey the area was quarried, and evidence of human habitation removed.

The property below Devil's Backbone soon gained fame as a popular getaway for residents of nearby Louisville. In 1886, the Louisville and Jefferson Ferry Company purchased 118 acres on the peninsula between Fourteenmile Creek and the Ohio River as part of a scheme to generate more traffic. The property had been a church camp called Fern Grove, and the company built a hotel and dancehall to entice visitors. It became a popular getaway for both picnics and overnight trips. For a time the ferry company was happy with its investment.

Eventually, business waned but in 1923 Louisville publishing magnate David Rose saw a money-making opportunity. He purchased Fern Grove, renamed it Rose Island, and began transforming it into an "amusement park." Not quite the thrill-ride

Trail 1 squeezes its way through massive, moss-covered boulders.

collection that we expect today, this amusement park had a swimming pool, merry-go-round, small roller-coaster, zoo (complete with a black bear), miniature golf course, and shooting gallery. Trails scaled Devil's Backbone, Shetland ponies provided rides for little kids, and cabins offered additional overnight accommodations. Visitors could now drive to the park and walk across a suspension bridge over Fourteenmile Creek to reach the fun, but most people still arrived by steamboat.

After booming for several years—attracting as many 135,000 visitors each year—the park fell on hard times during the Depression. David Rose battled to keep his dream alive, but it all fell apart in 1937. That year, the Ohio experienced its greatest flood in modern history, leaving Rose Island under 10 feet of water. The property was damaged beyond repair, and David Rose simply abandoned his amusement park.

Three years later, Rose Island and the rest of the modern-day park land took a sharp turn in its history when it was acquired for the new Indiana Army Ammunition Plant (INAAP). This massive industrial facility included three separate ordnance plants that manufactured smokeless gun powder for artillery shells during World War II, the Korean War, and the Vietnam War. The full facility covered 18,000 acres and contained 1,700 buildings, 190 miles of roads, and 92 miles of railroad tracks. At its peak, the plant employed more than 27,000 people, two thirds of whom were women.

Despite production surges during wartime, INAAP's importance declined over the years and portions of the facility were retired and parcels of land donated for other purposes. In January 1990, the Department of Defense included INAAP on a list of facilities targeted for closure; production ceased in October 1992, and the future of the land was placed in the hands of a local reuse authority.

Not surprisingly, Clark County eyed the property for future economic growth. The westernmost acres eventually became the River Ridge Commerce Center, which today hosts warehouses, office buildings, and small manufacturing facilities. The future of the east side was less clear. One proposal included using it for a large cardboard manufacturing plant, but a strong local contingent eyed the land for a park, the idea that ultimately carried the day.

In 1993, the first 859 acres were transferred to the state, followed by another 1,125 acres in 1994. Construction of recreational infrastructure started in 1995, and the property was officially dedicated as Charlestown State Park in 1996. It was the first—and still only—Indiana state park named for a town. Over the years, land donations and purchases, plus a final transfer of 2,600 acres of former INAAP property expanded Charlestown to its current 5,100 acres.

Prior to the creation of INAAP, much of the property had been covered with crops and pastures; most of the forest had been cut down. The Army's 50 years of management ended up being a positive for most of the land, especially in the vicinity of Fourteenmile Creek. The Army directed tree-planting efforts, and the dense forests reestablished themselves in many areas, providing an outstanding palette for developing a new recreational area.

Charlestown Today

Charlestown State Park is 105 miles from downtown Indianapolis, about an hour and 45-minute drive via Interstate 65 and state highways 160 and 62. The park is in the Louisville metro area and only about a half-hour drive from the Kentucky city's downtown.

Charlestown is a young park and still a work in progress. Staff readily admit this but have big plans for Charlestown—while cautioning that it will take years to build out the infrastructure. More trails are in the park's future, including a paved, multiuse trail. Additionally, the park has 1,500 acres that are "restricted" and in need of intense rehabilitation because of military plant remnants. Another challenge is invasive plants, which thrive in the disturbed habitats and need constant attention.

Despite its in-progress status, Charlestown already offers plenty to entice visitors, including Rose Island. When the park opened, there wasn't much left of the amusement park thanks to flooding and looting, and there was no way to cross Fourteenmile Creek. The access issue was solved with the 2011 opening of the historic Portersville Bridge. The beautiful iron truss structure, built in 1912, originally spanned the East Fork of the White River between Dubois and Daviess counties. It was dismantled, moved, and reassembled at the site of the former suspension bridge to Rose Island.

On the "island"—actually a peninsula—the park has done a great job of telling the story of the moribund amusement park. Following nearly a mile-long path, visitors can examine the park's remains while learning more thanks to a series of interpretive signs and hand-cranked audio players.

Despite its recent human history, nature abounds at Charlestown. The spring wildflower bloom draws raves; it's possible to see as many as 20 different species during the peak season from mid-March to May 1. The park is a stop on the Indiana Birding Trail and known for large numbers of migrating spring warblers. Mammals that you might encounter include white-tailed deer, coyotes, raccoons, and river otters.

Fishing for bass, catfish, and bluegill is available in Fourteenmile Creek, and the Charlestown Landing area has a boat ramp for launching into the Ohio River.

For overnighting in the park, Charlestown has a modern campground with 192 sites available for year-round use. Because the park lacks an inn or cabins, you'll have to venture outside for less-rustic accommodations. Charlestown has a modern hotel just a mile from the park entrance or you can drive to nearby interstate interchanges for more options. The area is suburban and has an ample supply of restaurants and retail outlets.

Hiking Charlestown

Charlestown is a great hiking destination, especially if you enjoy mixing history into your walks. The park features eight numbered/named routes covering more than 16 miles. Most of the trails are scenic, rugged, and wild feeling but many also feature interpretive signage explaining park history.

Yet there are some shortcomings that you need to account for when visiting Charlestown. It's a big park, and most of the trails don't connect with each other. That means hiking one trail, then getting in your vehicle and driving to the next trailhead. Trails 3, 4, and 7 are the only ones that connect enough to provide a single, long(ish) hike, about six miles.

Another problem—and this speaks to why Charlestown feels "unfinished"—is the lack of supporting infrastructure, especially restrooms and drinking water. Trail 2 and the 5K Course are the only routes with a full-featured trailhead. Trail 6 has a vault toilet near its two endpoints. For other trails, plan accordingly. The small parking area and lack of toilet and water are especially surprising for the popular Trail 3, 4, and 7 trailhead.

Trail Running

Charlestown is a running-centric state park, the only property with a dedicated and maintained 5K course (located near the Clark Shelter/Oak Shelter picnic area). The course is used by local cross-country teams for practice and meets and is open to all runners.

All seven of the numbered trails are runnable, especially if you don't mind some technical challenge (i.e. roots and rocks). Because there are many steep sections and lots of limestone on the trail—or eroding dirt paths—footing can be slick in wet weather.

The biggest challenge is assembling routes from the mostly disconnected pieces. One strategy is to use the park roads (which see light vehicle traffic) to link sections together, especially in the central area of the park. Trails 2 and 5 are my favorite for running. Traversing both, linked by a round trip on the roads, results in a seven-mile outing. Tack on the 5K course and you'll have a nice 10-miler. Running Trails 3, 4, and 7 is a challenging (hilly) six-mile outing. Add a two-mile round-trip road run to the campground, plus a circuit on Trail 5 for a nine-plus-mile run.

Trail 7 visits the ruins of the once-popular Rose Island Amusement Park.

TRAIL GUIDES

Trail 1

Rating: ★ ★ ★ ★ ★　　　　**Configuration:** Loop
Distance: 2.4 miles　　　　**Difficulty:** Moderate

Tour: This outstanding hike starts just a couple of minutes off Indiana Highway 62. Turn left at the T-intersection just beyond the gatehouse and follow the road to the parking lot at its end. The trailhead is at the south end of the lot. To hike the loop counterclockwise, stay straight on the trail, which starts off wide and graveled—probably a former road. After a third of a mile, follow the unmarked narrow trail that departs to the right (the main path turns and ends just past this point). The hike changes markedly from here, descending, winding, and entering a more mature woodland. After climbing in and out of a small ravine, the trail turns and drops even further into a gorgeous bottomland forest with massive trees and lush undergrowth. Fourteenmile Creek appears in sporadic glimpses through the woods to the right though always stays a distance away. To the left, limestone outcroppings begin to appear, and soon massive, moss-covered rocks litter the forest floor, forcing the trail to detour around and sometimes through the obstacles. Keep your eyes open for highlights in every direction: mushrooms, cave-like depressions in the rock wall, a rich variety of bird life. After winding through the valley for three quarters of a mile, the trail turns and starts climbing upward; soon the concrete footing of an abandoned railroad bridge, covered in moss and lichen, appears alongside the trail. One of the bridge's huge pilings can just be seen through the trees deeper in the valley. Beyond the bridge, the trail follows the former rail line uphill for a quarter mile before turning left into the woods for the final leg of the loop.

Trail 2

Rating: ★ ★ ★ ★　　　　**Configuration:** Loop
Distance: 1.4 miles　　　　**Difficulty:** Moderate

Tour: Just a short drive beyond the gatehouse, this trail offers an easy escape into a forest that feels wild and remote and in the spring is a wonderful place to see wildflowers. Park at Clark Shelter (toilets and water nearby) and look for the Trail 2 sign at the west end of the lot. Hike across the wide, mowed 5K Course Trail straight into the woods. The first section is a gentle descent into a forest that matures as you walk; large trees become more common, and a deepening valley appears to your right. The trail gets more rugged, hopping over roots, descending stairs, and crossing side valleys on small bridges until rendezvousing with the stream, which may be dry in the summer.

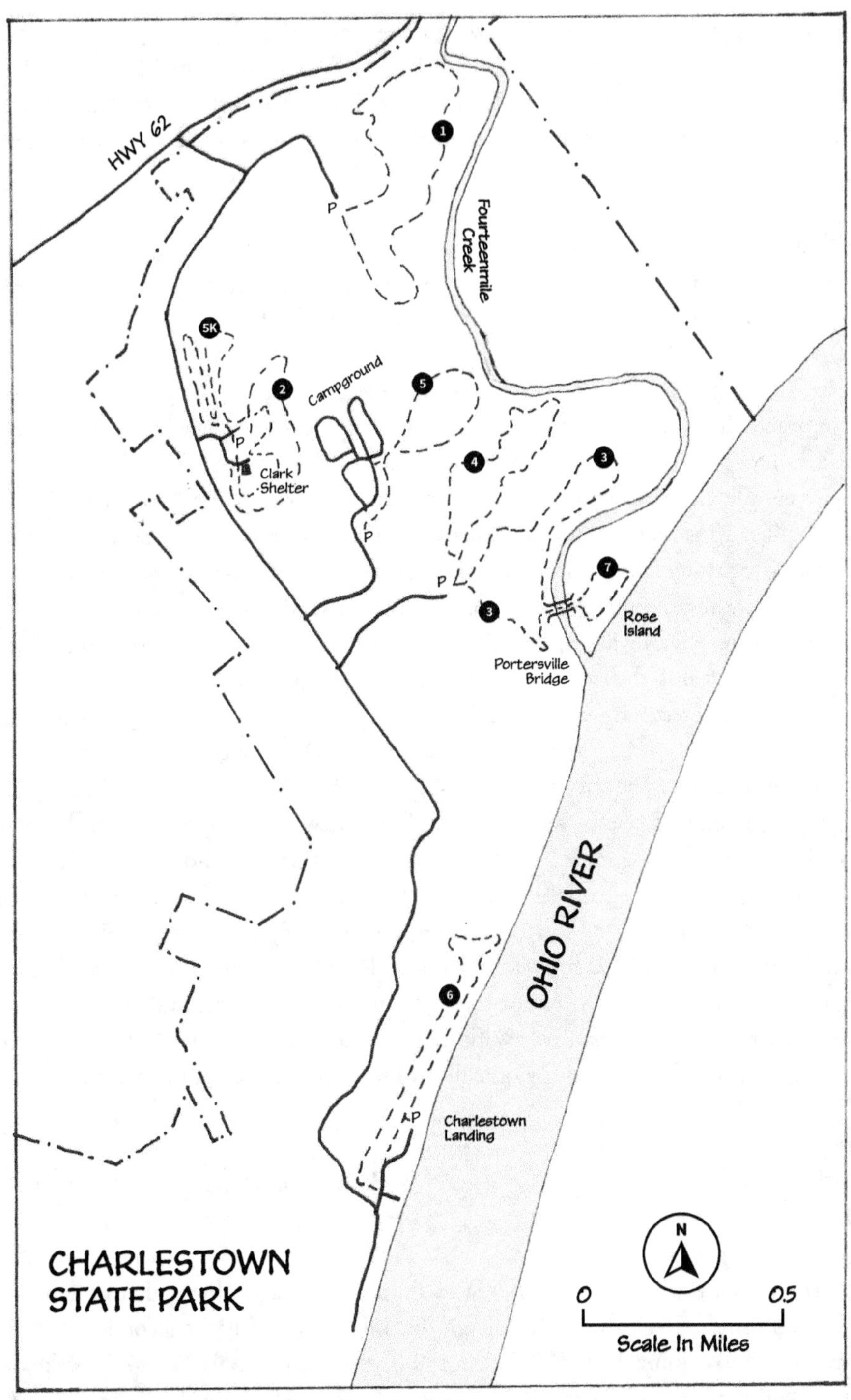

HWY 62
Fourteenmile Creek
1
5K
2
Campground
5
Clark Shelter
4
3
P
P
P
P
7
Rose Island
3
Portersville Bridge
OHIO RIVER
6
Charlestown Landing
P
N
CHARLESTOWN STATE PARK
0
0.5
Scale In Miles

When water is flowing, it dances down a limestone bed, spilling over low falls. It's a magical scene, complete with a viewing platform. The return trip makes a steep climb alongside a small tributary. When flowing, the stream offers a pretty, cascading water feature to distract from the uphill trudge. At the top, you pop out of the trees at the picnic area; your vehicle will be visible to your left, a short walk away.

Trail 3

Rating: ★ ★ ★ ★   **Configuration:** Loop
Distance: 2.1 miles   **Difficulty:** Challenging

Tour: Trail 3 has three distinct segments that together make a satisfying hike that few people actually complete: most use only the paved portion to get to and from Rose Island. That's a mistake because the remainder of the trail offers the best views of Fourteenmile Creek, the waterway that dominates the prettiest part of Charlestown. The trailhead for Trails 3, 4, and 7 sits next to the park's service area; there are no restrooms or water here. Begin your hike on the road-like paved trail, which soon starts descending steeply. It's easy walking and shaded, so not unpleasant. At the bottom, Portersville Bridge appears. Crossing it takes you to Trail 7/Rose Island but instead turn left into the trees on a narrow path. This attractive section winds through a bottomland forest with Fourteenmile Creek to your right. The murky water has negligible current—it is an arm of the dammed-up Ohio here—and turtles and fish are sometimes seen. The stream eventually goes its own way, while the trail continues through a quiet, wild-feeling section of forest before swinging to the left and climbing a ravine for the final segment. The trail in this area is straight and eroded, with rock dumped here and there to stabilize things. A trailside highlight is the stone remains of an old homestead, marked with an interpretive panel installed in 2025. The Hay Family Farm dates to 1797 and is infamous in local history because in 1887 Samuel Hay was murdered by his neighbor Jacob Robinson after the two men had a dispute over ownership of an access road. With that morbid history to ponder, the final nondescript section of trail speeds by quickly and soon you're back at the parking lot.

Trail 4

Rating: ★ ★ ★   **Configuration:** Lollipop
Distance: 2.9 miles   **Difficulty:** Challenging

Tour: Trail 4 is the park's longest but lacks the standout scenic highlights available on the other routes. That noted, it's an enjoyable hike—especially the second half if you travel the loop counterclockwise. Park at the same lot as for Trails 3 and 7 but take the branch off the paved trail to the left. The "stick" on the "lollipop" has been upgraded with crushed rock and large limestone chunks—signs that this trail has issues with standing water and mud. At the T intersection, turn right to do the loop counterclockwise. Be patient; the first half mile is scrubby and surrounded by invasives. That is followed by an eroded downhill section that can get muddy and slick. The trail improves markedly when it enters a beautiful older forest and winds its way into the heart of the valley. Soon, Fourteenmile Creek comes into view through the trees, some of which are huge in this forgotten bottomlands hamlet. After passing close to the creek, the trail is blocked by a tributary and turns left up its valley to climb back to the blufftop. This side of the loop is pretty and does a nice job of switchbacking and following the hillside to minimize both the grade and erosion. After closely following the shrinking limestone-bottomed stream (which is dry much of the year) to near its source, Trail 4 turns left to rejoin its crushed-stone connector and return to the parking lot.

Trail 5

Rating: ★ ★ ★   **Configuration:** Lollipop (Loop from campground)
Distance: 1.2 miles   **Difficulty:** Moderate

Tour: This trail into Fourteenmile valley pops a lot of bang into a short distance. Campers can hike this route from a trailhead near Site 17 but everyone else should park at the lot adjacent to the Campground Control Station. The first section is a straight, flat "tunnel" through the trees. Pass the turnoff to the campground (where you can find a convenient vault toilet) then turn right on the main loop. The trail begins a gentle descent into mature forest; a ravine is visible through the trees to your right. (You can't see it, but Trail 4 is skirting the opposite side of the same ravine.) The trail swings left and bottoms out at an overgrown viewing platform; Fourteenmile Creek is somewhere out there beyond the dense trees. The trail turns inland and immediately starts climbing. It's a pretty stretch, passing multiple moss-covered limestone outcrops; bird songs ring from the treetops. An interesting highlight soon pops up mid-trail: an Army Corps survey marker, reminding you that this used to be a military installation. The pleasant loop ends all too soon, with a return to the straight-line connector.

Trail 6

Rating: ★ ★ ★   **Configuration:** Loop
Distance: 2.3 miles   **Difficulty:** Challenging

Tour: This is a classic payoff hike. You have to endure two boring utility rights of way to enjoy a half mile of fantastic hiking—and other sections that aren't too bad. Park on the far west side of Charlestown Landing within sight of the boat ramp. Take the short connector trail through the trees and turn right on the paved road. There is no sign, but this is Trail 6 and, yes, it's also a service road. After passing a fenced-in water utility, Trail 6 dwindles to a wide dirt path. The tall trees and driftwood remind that you are in the bottomland of a big river, and you can catch glimpses of the Ohio to your right. To your left, the forested bluffs rise abruptly, topped by large limestone outcrops. As the trail curves inland, you hear running water and soon cross a bridge over a scenic tributary cascading over rocks as it seeks the Ohio. Continuing, another surprise: a large stone ruin, the remains of a 19th century lime kiln. In a fascinating twist, this kiln was likely owned by Jacob Robinson, the man responsible for the 1887 murder mentioned on a Trail 3 interpretive panel. The trail turns and switchbacks upward, offering nice views of the kiln from above. The sound of running water returns and two waterfalls, lying below a footbridge, appear. It's as pretty a scene as you'll find in Indiana. After climbing the opposite side of the valley, the trail reaches the blufftop and its worst section, below a power line. Soldier on and the line eventually ends, leaving you on an attractive, forested path near the bluff's edge. Looking left, you can see the trail you previously walked far below. As the trail turns and descends through rocky sections, the park road appears on your right. When you pop out of the trees with the Ohio in front of you, turn left and walk the pavement's edge to the service road you started on.

Trail 7

Rating: ★ ★ ★ ★   **Configuration:** Loop (with many side paths)
Distance: 0.9 miles   **Difficulty:** Easy (access is Moderate/Challenging)
(2.1 miles round trip via Trail 3)

Tour: This is more of a historical walking tour than a hike, but whatever you call it, Rose Island is one of the most interesting destinations in Indiana. Unfortunately, it's not an outing for everyone: the return climb has a long stretch of 10-20 percent grades that might be too much for people with physical limitations. Follow the instructions for Trail 3 and proceed to Trail 7 by crossing the historic Portersville Bridge, enjoying exceptional views of Fourteenmile Creek. On the far side, you'll find an introduction to Rose Island, which has fantastic interpretive resources. Take your time to read the many panels and listen to the hand-powered recordings. Though described as a loop on the property map, Trail 7 is really a main trail with multiple side paths. The best strategy is to walk down the main path (covered in crushed limestone) taking side trips to view different sites. At the end, explore the hotel and river landing area. If the water is low, it's worth crawling through the brush to get a scenic view of the river. (Some maps show a trail following the water but it's largely impassable.) From the hotel area, follow a trail heading

The top tier of the beautiful waterfall beneath a bridge on Trail 6.

inland to complete the loop. The hill rising to your right is the Devil's Backbone, which is only open for guided hikes during the winter. After passing the zoo area and the pool, the trail emerges from the woods back at the bridge.

5K Course Trail

Rating: ★   **Configuration:** Loop
Distance: 3.1 miles   **Difficulty:** Easy

Tour: This trail is not much of a hike but offers a great resource for runners, local cross-country teams, or even walkers looking for a laid-back, off-road experience. The 5K course is laid out in the vicinity of Oak and Clark shelters as well as Trail 2. It loops in and out of the surrounding woods, so is both nicely shaded and spectator friendly. There is plenty of parking as well as toilets and water. The starting line, marked with a sign, is in the open field north of the playground. Other than mileage markers, the course has no signage and can be confusing in places. Walk/run west from the start, turn left before the parking area, and cross the road. You'll see a wide opening in the trees that marks the 5K route. The path stays wide throughout and is either mowed grass or dirt. If you come to a cross path, stay straight. And when you return from the woods to the picnic area, always follow the long grass edge to your right until you come to the next opening—until you complete the fourth/last loop. At that point, turn left, circle around the road to Oak Shelter, then turn right to finish where you started.

4
Clifty Falls State Park

My wife, Tari, and I still look back fondly on a four-day, three-park tour of southern Indiana that we took several years ago. After the trip—which was great from start to finish—we agreed that the highlight was an overnight stay and hike at Clifty Falls.

We started with a too-short visit to Spring Mill and a tour of the Pioneer Village before driving to Jasper to meet friends for dinner. The next morning, we drove east to Madison for lunch and a walk through the historic community along the Ohio River. From there, it was a mere two-mile jaunt to our lodging at Clifty Inn. Pulling up in front of the inn, we both agreed it looked like a college dorm. Fortunately, the vibe inside was much different. The inn offered nice rooms, good service, and an outstanding dinner, all punctuated by blufftop views of the river valley.

The inn is also a perfect starting point for hikers, and we were up early the next morning to get on the trails. We followed Trail 1 past the nature center and descended into the deep, narrow Clifty Creek valley. At a three-way junction, we turned left on Trail 2 and switchbacked down to the bed of Clifty Creek. Turning right, we followed Trail 2 upstream.

September is the park's dry season, and the falls tend to disappear. The lack of water meant that Clifty Creek was barely flowing—good because Trail 2 was passable without wading. Calling this route a "trail" was a stretch; it was really a rocky passage on a stream bed at the bottom of a narrow canyon. Wet feet are likely when the stream runs higher. Hiking here after heavy rains is sometimes impossible.

The other advantage of fall hiking on Trail 2 is amazing scenery. Autumn had arrived in the park, and the trees were responding with yellows, golds, and oranges. Bathed in sunlight, we found ourselves enjoying one of the most beautiful hikes we had ever experienced in Indiana. Because we had departed early, fellow hikers were few and far between. We delighted when the first creature we encountered was a whitetail doe.

Despite the natural beauty and good conditions, this was not an easy hike. The creek bed's limestone rocks can be ankle-turners, and we had to slow down and step

Trail 2 is a scenic and adventurous hike up the rocky bed of Clifty Creek.

gingerly. On the other hand, the fossil-rich rocks were a source of endless entertainment. As we looked down to confirm our next step, it was common to find brachiopods, corals, and other ancient sea creatures preserved in the limestone.

Soon, a junction with Trail 5 appeared on the right (east) bank and we had a decision to make. As much as we would enjoy hiking to trail's end below Big Clifty Falls, we knew they were dry and there wouldn't be much to see. Instead, we started climbing the switchbacks up and out of the canyon. Near the top, we reached a T-intersection. The trail to the left led to also-dry Tunnel Falls. We turned right and followed Trail 5 south along the edge of the canyon.

We soon reached the south end of the "tunnel" that named the falls. Brough's Tunnel is 600 feet long and was built to carry the Madison & Indianapolis Railroad out of the Ohio valley, but the company's 1854 bankruptcy ended the project. The cave-like bore, home in winter to hibernating bats, used to be open for exploration, but has been closed because of a rockfall. We rested for a few minutes at the entrance, littered with fallen boulders, then pressed on.

The hike beyond the tunnel was beautiful but not for the faint of heart. Trail 5 followed a narrow shelf carved into a steep rock wall on the canyon's east side. Impressive formations, showing hundreds of distinct limestone layers, towered overhead. Stone stairs eased the way in places but in other spots the trail had to navigate around huge fallen rocks. We took our steps with care, trying to ignore the drop-off to the right. At the bottom of a huge staircase (the access from the Lilly Memorial), Trail 5 turned into Trail 4 and the route began offering glimpses into the past, including stonework dating back to the doomed attempt at railroad building.

Arriving at an intersection, we pondered a left turn and a steep climb to visit dry Hoffman Falls or a right turn back down into the canyon. We turned right, thankful for the downhill but soon realizing that eventually we would have to pay for our decision. Arriving at the dry bed of Hoffman Creek near where it joins Clifty Creek, we crossed the stones and looked payback straight in the face—Trail 4 climbed right back up an even steeper hill than we had just descended. Tari offered her oft-repeated quip: "When you hike with Don, there's always going to be another uphill." I couldn't argue.

Trail 4 ended at Trail 3. We turned left, climbed stone steps through and around rock formations, and crested the canyon near the Poplar Grove Picnic Area. From there it was a short walk on trails and roads back to the inn. We had just enough time to shower before check-out and the next leg of our trip, a drive to Brown County State Park, a night at Abe Martin Lodge, and a trek on that park's Trail 8. That, too, was a great hike but while sharing our thoughts about the trip on the drive home, we both agreed: We should have stayed a second night at Clifty Inn.

Clifty Falls History

The rock layers in the Clifty Falls canyon tells an amazing geologic story—one that begins during the Ordovician Period, more than 400 million years ago, when the state park lay at the bottom of a shallow sea. Over time, layers of mud, dead plants, and animals accumulated and were compressed into alternating layers of limestone and shale, which we now call the Dillsboro Formation. This thick layer of rock today makes up the bottom of Clifty Canyon. It is rich with fossils—preserved sea life in the form of brachiopods, corals, trilobites, crinoids, and bryozoans.

Immediately on top of the Dillsboro is a different type of rock, also from the Ordovician Period and known as the Saluda Member. This thinner layer (35-40 feet) of limestone is stronger than the Dillsboro and harder to erode. It forms the crest of the park's four major waterfalls. Above the Saluda Member are layers of younger rock, dating back to the Silurian Period, which form the uppermost cliffs along the top of Clifty Canyon.

The formation of the canyon and waterfalls is a more modern story, lasting from 2.6 million to only 12,000 years ago, with glaciers as the central character. Before the last Ice Age, the Clifty Falls area looked very different; there were no canyons, and the Ohio was a very small stream. The final glacier stopped north of the park and its meltwaters eroded away the soft Dillsboro Formation and scoured a deep canyon for Clifty Creek. The stronger Saluda Member resisted, forming the park's waterfalls. Though the glaciers are long gone, water is still working its magic. With every flood,

Clifty Creek and its tributaries grind away more rock, deepening the canyon and pushing the cascades farther upstream.

Clifty Falls has always had a close relationship with Madison, Indiana; in fact, part of the park falls within its city limits. Madison was laid out in 1810 and grew quickly; it was an important river port and entry point for the young state of Indiana, which entered the union in 1816. It was also where the state's first railroad, the Madison & Indianapolis (M&I) was built, starting in 1836. The railroad was a state-owned venture but transferred to private ownership in 1847.

Though initially successful, the railroad was hampered by the Madison Incline, a grueling 7,000-foot climb out of the river valley on the steepest standard-gauge grade in the U.S.—nearly 6 percent. Enter Ohio businessman John Brough. In 1852, he agreed to buy the M&I on the condition he build a new route out of the valley. His preferred option was to climb up Clifty Creek and Dean's Branch before rejoining the existing trackage. Seven hundred workers started cutting the new route up the rocky canyon, including boring a 600-foot tunnel. Since dynamite hadn't been invented, it was backbreaking work, largely done by hand.

By 1854, Brough was out of money, and no track had been laid. The M&I declared bankruptcy and Brough returned to Ohio, where he later was elected governor. But his reputation was tarnished in Indiana, where his failed railroad project was called Brough's Folly.

Fast forward six decades. Madison civic leaders wanted to establish a new state park in the beautiful canyon just west of town. The never-used railroad excavations were a viewed as a positive because they would make it easier to build out the park.

Conservation Commission Chairman Richard Lieber supported the Madison efforts and convinced the state to match $15,000 raised locally for the park. In late 1920, the money was used to purchase the first 617 acres, the land was donated to the state, and the park was established. A year later, construction on infrastructure started. In 1922, Lieber had a stone farmhouse converted into a six-bedroom guest house—the first incarnation of Clifty Inn.

For more than 40 years, Clifty Falls remained the same size, but its amenities went through many changes. The years 1933–1940 were especially important, because two Civilian Conservation Corps camps were active in the park. The young men built the gatehouses, south entrance road, nature center (originally a saddle barn), trails, shelters, and lookout tower. In 1965, a donation of land from the State Mental Hospital, lying just to the east, more than doubled the size of the park. Additional land acquisitions over the years expanded Clifty Falls to its current 1,519 acres.

Clifty Inn has undergone tremendous changes during its century in business. Many of the upgrades were done to expand capacity or simply keep up with the times, but in 1974 nature forced a major rebuilding project. On April 3 of that year,

One of the many mutilayered limestone formations along the route of Trail 5.

a massive tornado—part of a historically large tornado outbreak—plowed through the park, leveling trees and destroying half of the inn. The lodge reopened a year later and over the next 50 years saw the addition of a conference center, new amenities, and major renovations. Today, with 71 rooms, indoor pool, restaurant, and lots of lounging space inside and out, Clifty Inn is a star of the Indiana state park system.

Clifty Falls Today

Clifty Falls is close enough to Indianapolis for a day trip—it's only a 100-mile drive via Interstate 65 and Indiana Highways 256 and 56. The park is closer to Louisville, Kentucky (about an hour's drive), and Cincinnati, Ohio (about 90 minutes away), than Indiana's largest city.

Clifty Falls is a small park (only five properties are smaller) but packs a lot of activities within its borders. Viewing the falls is likely the most popular thing to do, and all six can be viewed by driving and short walks. Did I say *six*? In addition to the four best-known cascades (Big Clifty, Little Clifty, Tunnel, and Hoffman), the property map now notes Dogwood and Redbud Falls, which are visible from the high bridge over Little Crooked Creek, just inside the south gatehouse. Remember that the falls are seasonal. They usually flow in the spring and after heavy rains but can go completely dry at other times.

Despite its proximity to Madison, Clifty Falls is an important sanctuary for all things wild. The park is a stop on the Indiana Birding Trail and noted for being a great year-round birding destination. Mammals are also common, especially white-tailed deer, but you might also encounter bobcats, raccoons, weasels, and red foxes. Visit the Nature Center, near Clifty Inn, to learn more about the park's natural treasures and its extensive summertime slate of interpretive naturalist–led programs.

For overnighting at the park, it's hard to beat Clifty Inn, which offers comfortable rooms, a restaurant, lounge areas, and an indoor pool year-round. (The park also has an outdoor pool, open during the summer months, located a half mile north of the inn.) For a little more adventure, consider camping at Clifty Falls. The centrally located campground has 106 electric and 63 nonelectric sites. It connects to the park's path network via Trail 9, so is hiker friendly.

If you can't get a room in the park, don't worry; Madison has both national hotels and locally owned lodging options. The attractive river town has historic sites, shops, restaurants, breweries, and various entertainment venues and events.

Hiking Clifty Falls

Thanks to the rugged environs of Clifty Creek canyon, this park offers hiking distance, variety, scenery, and challenge far beyond what you would expect from such a small property. The park has 10 numbered trails totaling more than 14 miles of hiking. It also boasts some of the most challenging trails in Indiana—with steep climbs, sharp drop-offs, and sometimes dangerous footing—which may not be suitable for young children or folks with health or mobility issues.

Clifty's numbered trails are mostly short and/or point-to-point, so you must combine them to create longer loop routes. My favorite is nicknamed the Canyon Loop Trail. It starts at the north end of the park and mostly stays out of the canyon, except to cross Clifty Creek at the south end of the park. The route follows, in order, Trails 8, 2, 3, 4, 5, 6, and 7. It's about six miles long and highlighted by the canyon's four named falls, mature forests, amazing rock formations, and remnants of the failed 1850s railroad construction.

Trail 2 is a must-hike but must be combined with other routes to form a loop. I suggest starting on Trail 3 from Poplar Grove Picnic Area and hiking up Clifty Creek on Trail 2 from the south. Trail 5 is your exit point to the east but if the falls are flowing it's worth hiking an out-and-back on the north end of Trail 2. Use Trails 5, 4, and 3 to return to Poplar Grove.

There are parking lots and trail access points all along Canyon Road, so you can create a variety of short hikes on different trails without having to commit to a huge loop. The road is also useful for return hikes; a long stretch has a dedicated bike/hike lane.

Trail Running

As good as Clifty Falls is for hiking, it is not a great running destination. Most of the trails have stretches with challenging footing or are narrow with steep drop-offs. The trails near the falls are busy when the weather is good, so pass-bys on narrow paths are common.

But that's not to say you can't run at Clifty Falls. The northern two miles of Trail 8 are ideal for running but plan to turn around when the descent into Clifty Creek starts near the southern end. More promising is the southern end of the park around Poplar Grove Picnic Area and the swimming pool. In that area, Trails 1 and 3 are runnable in most places but challenging thanks to steep hills. Trail 9 and 10 are the most-running-friendly paths but offer limited scenic value. Using these trails in various combinations, a runner starting at the picnic area, Clifty Inn, or the campground could put together a nice five-mile route.

The park roads are another option for runners. A long stretch of road, from Tunnel Falls to the Nature Center, is one way with a dedicated bike/hike land and perfect for running.

TRAIL GUIDES

Trail 1

Rating: ★ ★ ★   **Configuration:** Point to Point
Distance: 1.3 miles   **Difficulty:** Challenging

Tour: This short but hilly trail is convenient for hikers staying at Clifty Inn. If you're not departing from the inn, park at the Nature Center, which is worth a short visit to learn more about the park and its natural resources. Trail 1 departs south out of the parking lot, gently descending to the Observation Tower. The tower is short—just a couple of flights of stairs—and doesn't offer much of a view thanks to trees, but it's worth the quick climb to explore. The trail turns sharply at the tower and starts a steep downgrade, one of the biggest hills in the park, taking you about halfway down the side of the canyon. At the bottom you enter a level stretch that was part of the planned railroad grade. Another tunnel was constructed in this area, but later dynamited and the rubble cleared. An intersection provides connections to Trail 2 (which goes down to Clifty Creek) and Trail 3 (which follows the mid-canyon grade); take the right fork to stay on Trail 1. You immediately start reclaiming the elevation you just lost, but this climb is much gentler than your earlier descent. After the climb to the blufftop, Trail 1 follows Canyon Road and eventually ends at Trail 3 near Poplar Grove Picnic Area.

Trail 2

Rating: ★ ★ ★ ★ ★   **Configuration:** Point to Point
Distance: 3.0 miles   **Difficulty:** Very Challenging

Tour: Based on online reviews, many people don't like this hike nearly as much as I do. Why? It's hard. The "trail" follows Clifty Creek nearly all the way to Clifty Falls and most of the time you're walking (slowly) on a jumble of broken limestone and trying to avoid turning your ankle. If you're lucky, the creek will be low and the walking easier. If the creek's up but still passable, you'll have to do some wading, and the limestone may be slick. The payoff is an amazing trek through a canyon that is beautiful, wild, and unique for Indiana. The official starting point is Poplar Grove Picnic Area; park at the southernmost lot. Hop on the trail across the road and turn left/south. Follow the sign that points you downhill to Trails 1, 2, and 3, then follow Trail 2 when the routes diverge midway down the canyon. Keep descending until you reach the bed of Clifty Creek. Turn right (north) and start walking, taking your time on the rocky surface. Keep scanning the right bank, because in some places a path running on shore will give you a break from the rocks. Speaking of rocks, keep your eyes on them: they contain fossils of ancient marine animals, lots of them. But also look up to see scenic rocky bluffs, mature forests, birds, and wildlife—this hike has it all. If you're struggling on the creek bed, don't worry; there are two more exit points to the right. The first, after a half mile, connects with Trail 4. The second, three quarters of a mile later, climbs to Trail 5. Beyond this point, Trail 2 continues almost another mile (expect to wade when the creek is running high) before dead-ending near Clifty Falls; unfortunately, views of the falls are limited. To finish the hike, turn around, walk back down the creek, and exit at one of the three connecting trails that scale the east side of the canyon.

Trail 3

Rating: ★ ★ ★ ★   **Configuration:** Point to Point
Distance: 0.8 miles   **Difficulty:** Challenging

Tour: There are multiple places to access Trail 3 but to get the full experience, park at the south end of Poplar Grove and follow the instructions for Trail 2. At the three-trail intersection, take a hard right to follow Trail 3. You quickly notice that something unnatural about this trace—the path is level and there seems to be a shelf following below. It turns out you're on the railroad grade excavated in the 1850s but never used. At a junction with Trail 4 (which heads down into the canyon), Trail 3 turns right and climbs back up the bluff, passing a rock outcrop and using limestone steps to rapidly gain elevation. At the top, turn left, passing a sign to Poplar Grove, but your hike isn't over yet. Continue down the hill to a bridge over the layered limestone bed of Hoffman Branch; the falls of the same name are directly to your left. Continue to the Trail 3's end, at a viewing platform and another meeting with Trail 4. Unfortunately, the falls are difficult to see—here or anywhere else on the trails—and often the first in the park to dry up. Retrace your route back to the Poplar Grove turnoff to finish your hike.

Trail 4

Rating: ★ ★ ★ ★   **Configuration:** Y-Shaped
Distance: 0.75 miles   **Difficulty:** Challenging

Tour: This short trail offers easy access to Hoffman Falls but its main purpose is providing two routes connecting Trails 3 and 5. Park at the Hoffman Falls lot and start hiking straight down to the falls' observation deck—which, unfortunately, doesn't offer much of a view. Trail 3 goes left from here and crosses the small creek above the falls, but follow Trail 4 down a steep, rocky, root-covered path to the right. Take your time; the footing can be tricky. The trail soon splits; the uphill path to the right enters

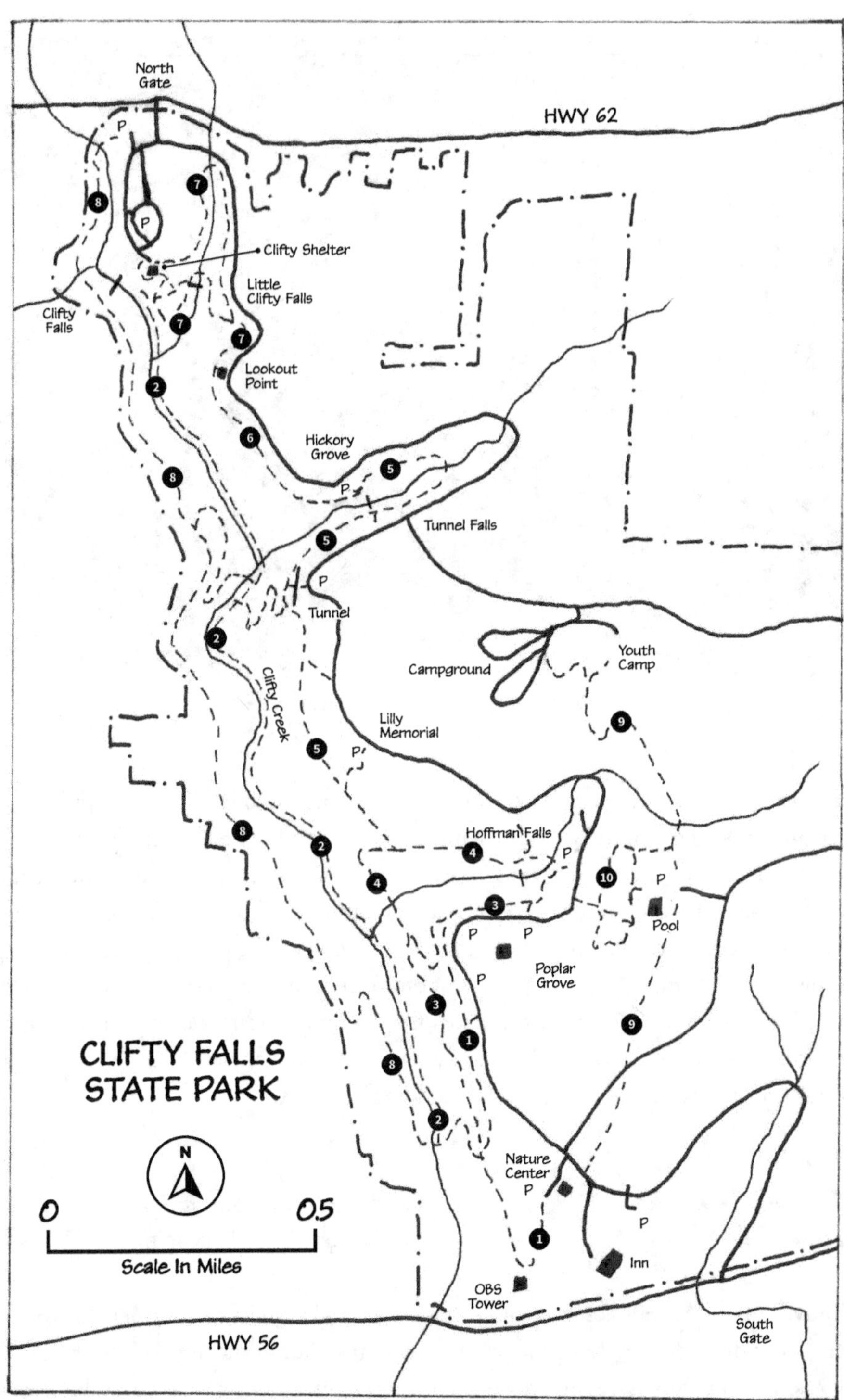
North Gate
HWY 62
P
8
7
P
Clifty Shelter
Little Clifty Falls
Clifty Falls
7
7
Lookout Point
2
6
Hickory Grove
5
8
Tunnel Falls
5
P
P
Tunnel
2
Campground
Youth Camp
Clifty Creek
Lilly Memorial
9
5
P
Hoffman Falls
8
2
4
P
10
P
4
Pool
3
P
P
P
Poplar Grove
P
9
3
1
CLIFTY FALLS
STATE PARK
N
8
2
Nature Center
P
0
0.5
Scale In Miles
1
Inn
P
OBS Tower
HWY 56
South Gate

Big Clifty Falls from Lookout Point, at the junction of Trails 6 and 7.

an area rich with remnants of the 1850s rail construction, including stone pilings for a planned trestle. Stop to consider that this work was all done by men nothing more than simple tools and horses. Trail 4 turns into Trail 5 at the base of the tall, vertical staircase leading to the Lilly Memorial, a lookout built by the CCC. Continue your Trail 4 hike by retracing your steps to the junction and following the downhill leg (now on your right). At the bottom, you can turn right and follow Hoffman Branch to connect with Trail 2 but instead cross the stream and start the climb back out of the canyon. Trail 4 ends at the junction with Trail 3. To complete a loop back to your car, turn left and follow Trail 3 to the Hoffman Falls overlook.

Trail 5

Rating: ★ ★ ★ ★ ★   **Configuration:** Point to Point
Distance: 1.2 miles   **Difficulty:** Very Challenging

Tour: This short trail is scenic but difficult; its rocks, stairways (stone and wood), and steep drop-offs might be too much for young children and anybody with mobility issues. But this is a must-do hike at Clifty, with some of the park's best rock formations along with a tunnel and other remnants of the doomed 1850s railroad project. Trail 5 has four different access points, but the Lilly Memorial overlook is a good place to park and start hiking. At the bottom of the steep staircase, turn right (Trail 4 goes to the left) and enjoy a wonderland of forest and rocks. The stacked, thin layers of Silurian limestone—some exposed by railroad excavations—rise to the right while huge trees tower overhead. Interesting mosses, ferns, flowers, and fungus cover rocks, roots, and other features on the ground. Elsewhere, you walk on huge blocks of limestone (moved by human and horsepower) laid to provide a stable foundation for tracks that never arrived. With highlights in every direction, it's easy to get distracted; don't. The footing can be slick and in places a fall off the downslope edge could have serious consequences. A huge rubble pile marks the southern entrance of the never-used tunnel—600 feet long but less than six feet high. A recent rock fall closed the bore to visitors. A 2025 inspection was not promising and a member of the park staff shared with me that it might be closed permanently. Just past the tunnel, a connector departs to the left for the canyon floor and connections with Trails 2 and 8. Going forward on Trail 5, you pass the much more visible north end of the tunnel and soon Tunnel Falls is visible through the trees to the left. The trail follows Dean's Branch upstream beyond the falls then descends to the creek's limestone bed on an odd stair/ladder structure. There is no bridge for crossing, so prepare for wet feet in all but the driest conditions. The final section of the trail ducks under a limestone overhang before becoming Trail 6 at the base of the stairway up to Hickory Grove parking area. For a return trip to Lilly Memorial, either retrace your steps on the trail or walk the park road, which has a dedicated bike/hike lane for part of the route.

Trail 6

Rating: ★ ★ ★   **Configuration:** Point to Point
Distance: 0.5 miles   **Difficulty:** Moderate

Tour: This short segment acts as a connection between Trail 5 and Trail 7. To hike Trail 6 on its own as a one-mile round trip, park at the Hickory Grove lot, walk down the stairs, and turn right. (Trail 5 goes to the left.) In places, Trail 6 is barely off the shoulder of the park road, but after a time it drops away and gets more interesting. Rock formations, small waterways, and flowers (in season) provide plenty to look at as you hike. And just like that—it's over. The trail ends at Lookout Point, which offers open cross-canyon views of Clifty Falls; there is even a viewing platform with a binocular device. Trail 7 continues north from here, and Little Clifty Falls is just a short walk away.

Trail 7

Rating: ★ ★ ★ ★　　　　　　　**Configuration:** Loop (with multiple side routes)
Distance: 1.25 miles　　　　　　**Difficulty:** Moderate

Tour: Trail 7 is probably best described as a network of trails—it can be a little disorienting when trying to navigate to its various waypoints. But it's a wonderful walk with many scenic highlights, including Big Clifty and Little Clifty Falls. Park in the large lot just inside the north gate and start walking on the trail departing from the southwest corner. The first stop comes quickly—the classic overlook of Big Clifty Falls, which is somewhat overgrown in the summer. (Spring is arguably the best time to hike this trail, with open views and robust falls.) Follow the Trail 7 marker and turn right at the next "Big Clifty Falls" sign and walk down the stone steps. This stub trail ends on a boardwalk under an overhang and offers a lower and closer-feeling view of the cascade. Return to the trail and follow the "Little Clifty" signs; turn right at the first junction. You soon arrive at a popular landmark, Cake Rock, a huge chunk of limestone that appears to be teetering on the cliff edge. Continue hiking, walk down a stair, and you find yourself on a bridge over Little Clifty Falls. There are decent views from the far side of the canyon. Turn right at the next junction; soon you cross a tributary with its own small waterfall. At the top of the next hill, Trail 7 becomes Trail 6: this is Lookout Point, which has nice across-the-canyon views of Big Clifty Falls. Retrace your steps to the last junction and take the right fork. This last section of trail climbs along Little Clifty Creek above the main falls. It's a pretty valley with smaller cascades (at least when the water is flowing). The trail crosses a bridge near the canyon's head, then returns downstream, climbing gently on its final leg back to the parking lot.

Trail 8

Rating: ★ ★ ★ ★　　　　　　　**Configuration:** Point to Point
Distance: 4.5 miles　　　　　　**Difficulty:** Challenging

Tour: The park has just a narrow strip of land lying west of Clifty Creek but it's a beautiful upland forest that lies mostly in a state nature preserve. Fewer people visit this part of the park, making Trail 8 an exceptional hike for a quiet, remote-feeling experience. Turn right after entering the north gate and park at the first lot on the right, the trailhead. You're just yards from Highway 56/62 but don't let the road noise scare you off; it will disappear in a couple of minutes. Hike down the large stairway to the banks of Clifty Creek. In 2025, volunteers reinstalled the large limestone blocks that make crossing simple at most flow stages. For most of its first couple of miles, Trail 8 is wide and gently rolling. The mature forest is usually alive with songbirds,

Trail 7 crosses Little Clifty Creek just above the falls of the same name.

and Clifty Creek burbles and splashes to your left. Shortly, you can hear the falls, too, but don't look for a viewpoint; there isn't a safe/legal one from this side of the canyon. After about a mile, a side trail departs down into the canyon, where it intersects with Trail 2 and Trail 5—part of a possible loop back to your starting point. Instead, keep moving forward on Trail 8, which offers occasional views across the deep canyon. On your right, a couple of houses beyond the trees reveal how close civilization lies to this wild place. But enjoy the hike, with periodic tributaries providing both climbs and scenic water features. After a couple of miles, the trail starts descending for good and its character changes markedly. Narrower, rocky, and slippery, the challenging path demands both attention and a slower pace. Eventually you reach Clifty Creek again—the end of Trail 8 and the start of Trail 2. The creek is wide and rocky here, easily crossed or hiked most of the year, but challenging or even impassable when the water is high. Trail 2 provides a couple of different options for hikes back to where you parked, or you can play it safe and retrace your route on Trail 8.

Trail 9

Rating: ★★   **Configuration:** Point to Point
Distance: 1.0 miles   **Difficulty:** Moderate

Tour: This utilitarian pathway has distinctly different personalities north and south of the swimming pool parking lot. If you're not camping, park at the nature center and start your hike at the trailhead across the road from the center. The first half mile or so is an open, mowed path running straight through a scrubland that is currently undergoing restoration. The occasional manhole covers mean that this a probably a utility right of way. Hike through it as quickly as you can. When you reach the pool, walk straight across the parking lot and the restart of the trail will soon come into sight. It's dramatically different in this section. The trail winds through a beautiful upland forest on its way to the campground. After passing a junction with Trail 10, you'll cross the first of two streams. The second bridge is a good place to turn around (the forest ends near here) unless you want to see the campground. You can retrace your route on the return trip or create a more ambitious loop using Trail 10, a connector to Poplar Grove, Trail 3, and Trail 1.

Trail 10

Rating: ★   **Configuration:** Loop
Distance: 1.0 miles   **Difficulty:** Easy

Tour: This short loop offers convenient hiking for swimming pool visitors, but it traverses a woodland in the middle of habitat restoration. While it may provide a better experience in a few years, right now it barely merits attention in a park packed with highlight hikes. To explore Trail 10, park at the west end of the pool lot and walk the short connector to the main loop. Turn right to walk counterclockwise. Pass the right turn toward Trail 9 and follow the loop left deeper into the woods. The forest has mixed-age trees but lots of openings, which has made it possible for invasives to become established. You may see signs of brush removal work that hopefully will lead to a native-dominated ecosystem. After two-thirds of a mile, you cross a connector path; turning right goes to Poplar Grove, while turning left returns to the pool. Continue walking the main loop and soon the pool comes into sight. After passing the far end of the connector, take the next right back to your car.

5
Falls of the Ohio State Park

Looking back on 2020, I'm still not sure how most of us survived the pandemic. COVID-19 disrupted our lives as no previous crisis had before. We lost our jobs, our routines, and—worst of all—friends and family who succumbed to the disease.

For many, including me, time outdoors became an important coping strategy. In July my son, Kendal, and I took an enjoyable three-day tour of parks and trails in southern Indiana. One of our most memorable stops was Falls of the Ohio State Park, which is short on hiking but offers a wonderful mix of nature, history, and fossils.

Falls of the Ohio is an outlier in the Indiana state park system. It's the smallest and least-visited property and being located just across the Ohio River from Louisville has a decidedly urban character. We parked near the beautiful Interpretive Center and took in an exhilarating view of the city skyline, big river, and exposed fossils beds. But first, we needed to get the lay of the land.

The Interpretive Center, which charges an admission fee, is highly recommended. Highlights include a well-made film and exhibits explaining the rich history of the falls—both natural and human. After an hour of learning, we were ready to explore.

The river levels were low, exposing both the upper and lower fossil beds. We worked our way down the limestone layers, carefully stepping over broken rocks and driftwood from the spring flood. The beds were covered with silt, but near the water's edge we started to find the treasure we were seeking.

As a kid, I was obsessed with dinosaurs and convinced my parents to take a trip to Dinosaur National Monument, which straddles the Utah-Colorado state line. That park's Jurassic fossil beds are mind-blowing: a rock-bound tangle of huge reptile skeletons covering a full hillside.

But that's not what Falls of the Ohio looks like. Initially I was underwhelmed by the fossilized invertebrates I found under foot, but then the sheer number of small creatures preserved in stone got me thinking. The brachiopods, corals, and crinoids I was staring at had lived in the bottom of a tropical sea *390 million years ago*. And now I was walking on that ancient seabed within sight of a modern city—wow.

The Louisville skyline on the horizon beyond the Falls of the Ohio fossil beds.

We continued walking upstream, toward the prominent railroad bridge that delineates the park's eastern boundary, stopping frequently to examine interesting fossils. Eventually we circled back to the Interpretive Center and looked for the start of our next hike. We found the unmarked entrance to the Woodland Loop Trail at the southwest corner of the parking lot.

We followed the faint trail toward the water but turned as footprints followed the edge of the dense forest to our right. To the left was a rocky beach dotted with trees; the river lay beyond. Soon a movement in the forest caught our attention. A young button buck looked warily at us from the dense undergrowth. He paused then ran deeper into the forest. A young doe followed him.

We continued walking, following a line of driftwood until a broad creek blocked our path, forcing a turn inland. The going was slow as we hopped over a huge jumble of driftwood logs and walked into the trees. Beyond the forest's far edge, we could see the flood-control levee rising above us. A more established trail appeared, and we followed it through the trees in the general direction of the Interpretive Center.

The bottomland forest was wild and unkempt; logs and tree debris, both fallen in place or delivered by flood water, riddled the ground. Huge cottonwoods loomed overhead. A hiker coming the other direction asked whether we'd seen the pair of deer he'd encountered the previous day. We told him to keep his eyes open for his whitetail friends.

Back at the parking lot, we decided to climb the levee to the Ohio River Greenway and hike the paved trail on its crest to the George Rogers Clark homesite—an isolated chunk of the state park located a mile-and-a-half away. It was a long, hot walk, without many highlights or much of a payoff: the site is just that, an empty swath of grass. But after we were done, we could comfortably say we had enjoyed most of what Falls of the Ohio had to offer. And, for a few hours at least, we had left our pandemic-damaged world far behind.

Falls of the Ohio History

During the Devonian Period, roughly 390 million years ago, southern Indiana lay at the bottom of a warm, shallow sea. The Devonian is known as the Age of Fishes, but the ancient Indiana sea was populated with a rich variety of marine life, including corals, crinoids, brachiopods, sponges, and trilobites. Those common invertebrates died and were covered with deep layers of sediment, eventually to be preserved as the fossils in layers of limestone that we see today.

When visiting Falls of the Ohio, you will encounter references to two different fossil beds: the younger upper (which can be seen near the Interpretive Center) and older lower. Analyzing the beds more closely, researchers have isolated five distinct layers of fossils. Not surprisingly, each layer contains a different mix of bottom-dwelling sea creatures, and among the five strata more than 600 unique species have been identified. The bottommost layer—which is the largest at the park—is nicknamed The Coral Zone. It is difficult to walk on this layer without stepping on exposed coral fossils.

In "modern" times—the past two million years—glaciers shaped the landscape that we see today. The Ohio was once a small river but flowing glacial meltwater scoured out the basin and turned it into a huge river.

The glacier runoff exposed the Devonian limestone beds but couldn't erode them away, leaving a series of rapids that fall 26 feet over about two miles. The whitewater zone formed the only significant barrier on the Ohio's route to the Mississippi and became a magnet for human activity. The first people arrived between 10,000 and 18,000 years ago, likely nomadic hunters drawn to the area's rich animal resources. Fish congregated below the Falls, and birds thrived in the area thanks to food resources. The shallows created by the rapids were important crossing points for all kinds of mammals, including large herds of migrating bison.

During the Woodland Period, 1,000-3,000 years ago, humans adopted agriculture and became more settled in the Falls region. The Mississippian Period that followed over the next 500 years was the era of the mound builders, who laid out large villages that contained more than one thousand residents. When European explorers and settlers arrived at the Falls, the Shawnee controlled much of the Ohio valley; they lived in small villages and subsisted on hunting, fishing, and farming.

The Shawnee people were largely driven from the Ohio valley in the 1670s by their enemies from the Iroquois Confederation. About this same time, the French arrived and laid claim to the region; the British soon followed and took ownership in the wake of the French and Indian War. Settlers streamed west but the Shawnee, trying to reclaim their territory, attacked the newcomers. Wars, first with the British and later the Americans, broke out repeatedly over the next several years. After General "Mad Anthony" Wayne defeated the Shawnee and their allies at the Battle of Fallen Timbers in 1795, the native presence along the Ohio melted away.

Meanwhile, U.S. General George Rogers Clark, a hero of the American Revolution, had begun laying the foundation for settlement around the Falls, including the future city of Louisville. In 1778 Clark left a small group of settlers on what became known as Corn Island just upstream from the Falls. He continued west to fight the British and hoped the pioneers would create an outpost to support the war effort. The following year, the families moved to the mainland and established what became Kentucky's largest city.

Clark returned to the area after the war deeply in debt because he hadn't been reimbursed by the government for his war expenses. He bought seven acres of land and in 1803 built a cabin on what became known as Clark's Point—today it's the George Rogers Clark Homesite unit of the state park.

Clark's younger brother William joined him to help with struggling business interests. But the younger Clark was soon drafted by President Thomas Jefferson to take on a major project: leading the Corps of Discovery to explore the Louisiana Purchase. Co-leader Merriweather Lewis soon arrived at the Clark cabin. After recruiting several expedition members from the local population, America's most famous explorers started their journey west from the Falls on October 26, 1803. George Rogers Clark, his health failing, eventually moved away from his riverside cabin in 1809.

In the years that followed, Louisville grew as the Ohio became one of America's most important transportation corridors. The river around the Falls was transformed to accommodate the booming boat traffic. In 1830, a canal was built to bypass the Falls; at the time it was the world's largest. In 1881, the first dam to regulate the river's flow was completed. And in the 20th Century, a larger canal and two different dams were built. The second dam—the McAlpine, finished in 1961—improved navigation but ended up inundating three quarters of the fossil beds, which were an important attraction and research site.

Steps were taken to preserve the fossil beds that remained above water at least part of the time. The Falls of the Ohio was recognized at a National Natural Landmark in 1966 and in 1981 the area was designated the country's first National Wildlife Conservation Area. A state park was the next goal and in 1987 the Falls of the Ohio Foundation formed to raise money to build an Interpretive Center. In 1990, the state park was dedicated, and four years later the Interpretive Center opened.

Falls of the Ohio Today

Falls of the Ohio is in suburban Clarksville, just across the river from Louisville, Kentucky. The park is about an hour and 45-minute drive from downtown Indianapolis via Interstate 65 but using recreational trails you could safely *walk* from Kentucky's largest city in about an hour.

At just 165 acres, Falls of the Ohio is by far Indiana's smallest state park. It is also listed as the least-visited, hosting just 119,000 people in 2023–2024. But these figures may cover only people who paid admission to the Interpretive Center and not the

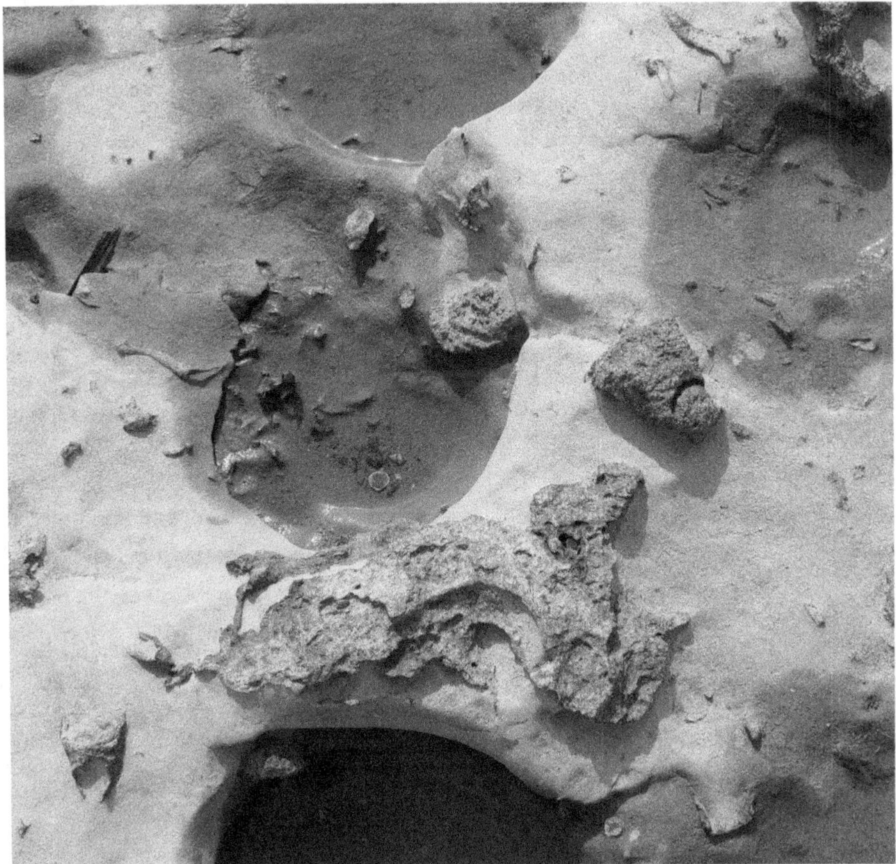

The fossil beds are covered with the remains of Devonian Era sea creatures.

many who casually visit to fish, wander the fossil beds, or walk the Woodland Loop. It is rare to see the park empty.

The Interpretive Center, a beautiful 16,000-square-foot building with commanding views of the fossil beds, is the logical place to start any visit to Falls of the Ohio. The admission price is a little steep—and not covered by your state parks pass—but the Center is a recommended stop, especially during your first visit.

The fossil beds are understandably the park's primary draw. Consider joining one of the regular hikes led by park staff to see and learn more about the rich variety of fossils.

Unlike most of Indiana's other parks, there can be a wrong time to visit Falls of the Ohio. When the river is high, all or part of the fossil beds may be under water. Extreme flooding while I was writing this book in spring 2025 filled the river basin to just feet below the Interpretive Center. August through October is considered the best time to explore the fossil beds. During most years, low water during this season makes even the island portions of the park accessible by foot. Otherwise, the fossil beds on the far side of the river channel can only be reached by boat.

Many people launch boats to take advantage of the high-quality fishing available in the park; fishing from shore is also allowed and a popular pastime for many visitors. The park's boat ramp is located at the isolated George Rogers Clark Homesite, about a mile and a half drive east of the main park using city streets. It is also permissible to park in the Interpretive Center lot and carry lightweight craft—canoes or kayaks—over the fossil beds to the water's edge.

The state park, while small, is part of the much larger Falls of the Ohio National Wildlife Conservation Area. The federal property covers 1,404 acres surrounding the state park. The area is especially known for its abundant bird life—something that drew famed naturalist and artist John James Audubon to the Falls in 1808–1810. Today, the state park is a noted stop on the Indiana Birding Trail. The area boasts an amazing mix of 275 species—shorebirds, waterfowl, and woodland birds.

The state park hosts special events throughout the year. A favorite is the Rock the Rocks concert held every fall, which serves as a fundraiser for Falls of the Ohio Foundation. National touring acts play live sets on the fossil beds starting just before sunset. The audience watches from camp chairs and blankets positioned on higher levels of limestone. The backdrop is jaw-dropping: The fossil beds, the river, and the Louisville skyline.

There are no overnight accommodations inside the park, but the region abounds with thousands of hotel rooms. Campers have limited options in and around Clarksville, but may want to stay at Charlestown State Park, about a half-hour away.

Hiking Falls of the Ohio

This small property—something of an urban oasis—offers the least traditional hiking experience of any state park. But the park lends itself to exploration on foot and visitors may walk several miles while exploring everything Falls of the Ohio has to offer. The short Woodland Loop is the only traditional hiking trail in the park, but you could spend hours walking the expansive fossil beds along the water's edge. The Ohio River Greenway is part of a much large network of regional recreational paths; at Falls of the Ohio, it connects the main part of the park with the George Rogers Clark Homesite unit.

Trail Running

Neither the Woodland Loop nor fossil beds lend themselves to running. The Ohio River Greenway offers the best running opportunities. The paved path is popular with walkers, runners, and cyclists and extends for several miles in both directions from the park.

TRAIL GUIDES

Woodland Loop Trail (Trail W)

Rating: ★ ★   **Configuration:** Loop
Distance: 0.75 miles   **Difficulty:** Moderate

Tour: This short walk follows the only traditional hiking path in the park. Note that there are no signs, the trail is faint in some areas, and you'll have to scramble over driftwood piles in a couple of spots. Access the park from Riverside Drive and park in the lot behind the Interpretive Center. Cost is $2; pay cash or online at one of two small stations. The trail starts at a gate by the west corner of the parking lot. It begins wide and easy to follow but then branches and fades. Keep the edge of the dense forest on your right and you'll be okay. The faded path dead ends at a deep stream bed, which is the park boundary; turn right and follow Cane Run upstream into the forest. You will likely have to clamber over a mass of driftwood. Just before you get to the far edge of the woods, a path materializes and swings to the right. With a clear trail underfoot, navigation back to the parking lot is much easier and you can focus on the huge cottonwood trees, interesting mushrooms, and abundant bird life that highlight the walk. The trail emerges from the woods by a picnic area on the east side of the parking lot.

Fossil Beds

Rating: ★ ★ ★   **Configuration:** No trails; walking on open bedrock
Distance: N/A   **Difficulty:** Moderate

Tour: While you won't find a trail, this is one of the most interesting and scenic walks in Indiana. It offers outstanding views of the Ohio River and the Louisville skyline while under foot you will encounter countless fossils of marine invertebrates that lived 390 million years ago. To access the fossil beds, follow the marked concrete path departing from the Interpretive Center parking lot. When it ends, work your way down the layers of rock toward the water. You are allowed to walk anywhere you want on the beds, which extend from Cane Run in the north to the railroad bridge in the south—about three quarters of a mile along the waterfront. Collecting the fossils is prohibited. Accessibility is affected by the river level. Spring is usually the worst season to visit. The Ohio is usually lowest, and hiking best, August-October. During this time of year, flood gates are closed on the weir that encloses the park. In most years, it is possible during these dry periods to walk to the fossil beds on the islands across from the main park. Expect to do some shallow wading but the hike is safe and rewarding.

Ohio River Greenway

Rating: ★ ★   **Configuration:** Point to Point
Distance: 1.5 miles   **Difficulty:** Easy
(3 miles round trip)

Tour: Technically, this paved recreational trail is just outside the park (it marks the northern boundary of the main unit) but it conveniently links the property's two disconnected areas. The greenway is part of an extensive recreational trail system that follows the Ohio for several miles and even offers access from Jeffersonville to downtown Louisville via the spectacular Big Four Bridge. To walk to the George Rogers Clark homesite from the Interpretive Center parking lot, either scramble up the side of the levee to the trail or take the easy route to the greenway by walking back out the state park entrance drive. The elevated trail is wide open, allowing you clear, pleasant views down on the bottomland forest and into Clarksville neighborhoods. But the openness means no shade, so be ready for intense sun. The trail turns and closely follows Harrison Avenue for its last half mile, where the forest is replaced by private residences with back lawns running down to the river. The state park soon appears on the left. Unfortunately, the area doesn't have much to see because a replica of Clark's cabin burned in an arson fire in 2021. There's a boat ramp offering nice views of the river, some picnic areas, and a small replica slave shack, which lacks interpretive signage.

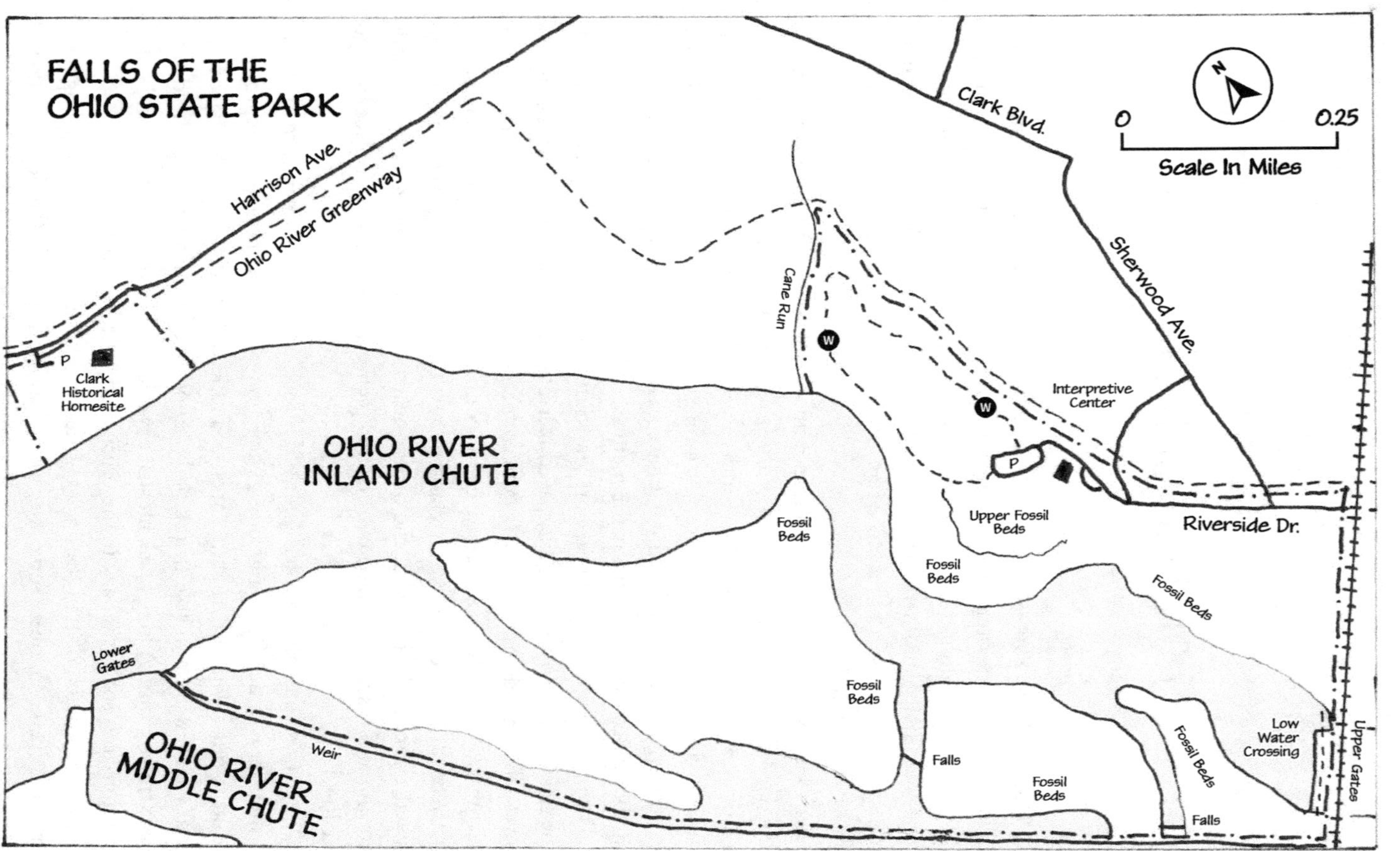
FALLS OF THE OHIO STATE PARK
Clark Blvd.
0
0.25
Scale In Miles
Harrison Ave.
Ohio River Greenway
Cane Run
Sherwood Ave.
W
W
P
Interpretive Center
P
Clark Historical Homesite
OHIO RIVER INLAND CHUTE
Upper Fossil Beds
Fossil Beds
Fossil Beds
Fossil Beds
Riverside Dr.
Fossil Beds
Lower Gates
Weir
Fossil Beds
OHIO RIVER MIDDLE CHUTE
Falls
Fossil Beds
Falls
Fossil Beds
Low Water Crossing
Upper Gates

6

Fort Harrison State Park

Fort Harrison State Park—or "Fort Ben" as it is known by many—is unique in the Indiana state park system. It's a relatively young park, dedicated in 1996, and an urban park, just minutes from downtown Indianapolis. It's also a historically significant U.S. military landmark, having once hosted a major Army base. Because of these features, Fort Harrison has a mix of amenities, and a personality, that is unlike any other state park in Indiana.

Fort Harrison serves me in a couple of important ways. First, it's an easy and satisfying day-hiking destination. Just a short drive from my Indianapolis home, I can be on a beautiful, forested trail—12 months a year—in a half hour. Planning for a Fort Harrison visit is unnecessary. There are ample toilets and water sources on site and if I'm hungry, before or after the hike, I have a choice of several great restaurants in the neighborhood just beyond the park's main gate.

For me, the other big draw at Fort Harrison is the myriad running opportunities. Whether I want to run dirt trails, paved recreational trails, or park roads—or all the above—this park delivers. The park even connects directly with the popular Fall Creek Greenway, which offers a safe route by foot or bicycle to downtown Indianapolis.

A recent weekend trip to Fort Harrison was typical of my experiences at the park. My wife, Tari, and I parked at the big lot near Delaware Lake, which has a modern restroom and is surrounded by tree-covered picnic tables, the perfect place for a post-hike lunch.

We started our hike on Fall Creek Trail, which was busy thanks to the beautiful summer weather. The path soon swung alongside its namesake, a beautiful, clear stream popular with fishermen, canoeists, and kayakers (though no formal access or rental facilities are available in the park). Soon, we heard squeals up ahead from a small family group. A long black rat snake was leisurely crossing the trail and creating a big uproar. It soon was back in the brush, and we continued forward.

The first stretch of trail featured a varied mix of hardwood trees highlighted by some massive sycamores. Soon we climbed away from Fall Creek and followed a

Spring offers hikers amazing wildflower displays on Lawrence Creek Trail.

low bluff above a bottomland forest. This section, located in Warbler Woods Nature Preserve, used to stay at stream level for longer. On the bottoms, it frequently flooded and was usually muddy; the new alignment is a big improvement.

The trail eventually returned to the stream and followed a series of stairs, boardwalks, and observation decks sitting well above the water. The views of the Fall Creek were outstanding. On the far banks, a disc golf course could be seen cutting through the trees.

After the observation deck, the trail started climbing uphill and away from the stream. Soon, we reached the paved Harrison Trace recreational trail. Turning either direction takes you on an easy stroll back to the parking lot, but we decided to cross and continue on the dirt trail. Shallow-and-weedy Duck Pond appeared in front of us; water lilies and pads covered the water's surface. We paused on the rock-covered dam to enjoy the flowers then took a right turn to follow the northern side of the Camp Creek Trail loop.

The pretty, shaded trail made a mostly downhill trek through an open forest with frequent views of small Camp Creek. We frequently heard voices around us: walkers, runners, and cyclists using one of three nearby trail sections running parallel to our route.

Camp Creek Trail eventually turned right and dumped onto Harrison Trace. We turned left then right at a fork in the Trace. Either way would have worked because the trail wraps around both sides of Delaware Lake en route to the parking lot.

As we passed, Delaware Lake, watching fishermen who always seem to be present in the warm months, we discussed lunch options: Mexican? Pizza? Thai? Hikers have those and more in the fun and flourishing Fort Ben neighborhood that has sprung up on remnants of the old Army base adjoining the park. In fact, Fort Harrison is one of the few Indiana state parks where it's realistic to reside within walking or biking distance of the main gate. For us, the park was just a short car ride away—a welcome natural resource for a couple of city dwellers.

Fort Harrison History

Some of the land that now constitutes Fort Harrison State Park was farmed in the 1800s. Elisha Reddick was the first settler in the area; he purchased 132 acres in 1823. It wasn't until 1901 that the property's purpose took a dramatic turn. That year, former president and Indiana resident Benjamin Harrison passed away and his son, Lieutenant Colonel Russell Harrison, started working to both maintain the U.S. Army's presence in Indianapolis and honor his father's legacy.

In the wake of the Spanish-American War, the U.S. was building its military capability, so the younger Harrison's efforts found supporters. His first project involved transforming the U.S. Arsenal in Indianapolis, on the city's near-east side, into a battalion military post. Local opposition derailed that project, so Harrison pivoted to selling the Arsenal and using the proceeds to finance an all-new base farther from downtown. In 1903, the Army sold the Arsenal and purchased 1,994 acres of land in Lawrence Township, nine miles northeast of Indianapolis. Three years later, another 423 acres were acquired, and construction began on the new Fort Benjamin Harrison.

Much of the property was hilly, cut by small streams, and forested—which suited the Army as it desired a property that would serve well for training troops. During its early years, the fort was a garrison for the 10th and 23rd U.S. Infantries and the Indiana State Militia. Nonetheless, the facility's long-term future was in doubt until the outbreak of World War I, when Fort Harrison became a key training center. At its peak in 1917, the fort hosted 12,000 men, three officer training camps, and a hospital.

Between the world wars, Fort Harrison retained its role as a busy military installation. It was home to the 11th Infantry, artillery and tank platoons, and the Army's Baker and Cooks school. Citizen Military Training Camps, designed to counteract anti-military sentiment and promote citizenship, started in 1925 at Fort Harrison and ran for 15 years. Because they provided a month of free food and lodging, the camps were popular during the Depression. During that same era, Fort Harrison hosted the Indiana headquarters of the Civilian Conservation Corps, which was responsible for construction and reforestation projects in state parks around Indiana.

The outbreak of World War II brought a new burst of activity to Fort Harrison. Deemed too small for training troops, it became an important induction and logistical support center. A large hospital was constructed, and Army Chaplain and Finance schools opened. In 1944 and 1945, the fort hosted a camp for German and Italian prisoners of war. Then the war ended, and almost every element of the fort was deactivated; it was targeted for closure. For a short time, Fort Harrison was transferred to the Air Force, but it returned to the Army in 1950.

In the late 1950s, Fort Harrison blossomed again, this time as the home of the Army's Finance Center. A huge new facility, providing office space for thousands of employees, was constructed. Located south of the state park on 56th Street, the building remains the home of what is now called the U.S. Army Financial Management Command.

Over the next few decades, various Army training centers, the Army bands, the Indiana National Guard, and other entities used what remained of the old fort but the end was in sight. In 1991, budget cuts put Fort Harrison on a list for closure and by the end of the year the facility was decommissioned. The next year, a local citizens group organized to protect the 1,100 forested acres of the fort—the largest contiguous tree-covered property in central Indiana. Governor Evan Bayh lent his support to turn the area into a state park and, in 1995, the efforts paid dividends: the Department of the Interior deeded 1,700 acres of the old fort to Indiana for recreational purposes. In 1996, the property was dedicated as Indiana's 22nd state park and opened to the public.

Fort Harrison Today

The main gate for Fort Harrison State Park is located at the intersection of 59th Street and Post Road in Indianapolis. (Technically, the park is in Lawrence, which is an independent municipality within the capital city.) The park is about a half-hour drive from the heart of downtown Indy via Interstates 70/465 and 56th Street. You could probably bike to the park on the Fall Creek Greenway in about 75 minutes.

As noted previously, much of the park's 1,700 acres is forested. As a result, the park is valued as much for its preservation role as for its recreation role. There are four state nature preserves within Fort Harrison's boundaries, together protecting more than a third of the park's land area. Two of the preserves, Bluffs of Fall Creek and Chinquapin, are isolated from the main area of the park and closed to the public.

Unlike most of the state park system, this is a day-use-only park; it opens at sunrise and closes at sunset. That means there is no camping in Fort Harrison. But there are plenty of other interesting things to do including picnicking, fishing, and horseback riding. In the winter, the park boasts one of Indianapolis' biggest and best sledding hills. The Fort Golf Course is rated as one of the best public links in the state. And, in a nod to its military history, the park is home to the Museum of 20th Century Warfare and periodic battle reenactments produced by a dedicated cadre of volunteers.

The park's natural beauty is among its drawing cards, and the bird watching is outstanding; Fort Harrison is a stop on the Indiana Birding Trail. Delaware Lake

Fall Creek Trail winds through Warbler Woods Nature Preserve.

and Fall Creek are great places to see waterfowl, the open areas are home to grassland birds, and the dense forests attract many species during the spring and fall migration.

There is no camping in the park, but you can overnight at the Fort Harrison State Park Inn, located just outside the main gate. Unfortunately, it takes a long walk or run on the shoulder of the entrance road to access the trail system. There is one hotel, about a mile from the park, in the Fort Ben neighborhood. If you're willing to expand your search and drive a little, there are more than 34,000 hotel rooms in the Indianapolis metro area, as well as some commercial campgrounds.

Hiking Fort Harrison

Fort Harrison State Park is popular with hikers and boasts a 13.45-mile trail system… but the reality of those trails needs a little explanation.

Fort Harrison has only three hiking-focused dirt or mowed trails: Fall Creek, Camp Creek, and Tree Line, which together cover about four miles. Much of the park's foot traffic follows the 2.75-mile Harrison Trace, a wide, paved recreation trail that cuts through the heart of the park from west to east. Fort Harrison also has two "single-track multi-use hike-and-bike" trails: Lawrence Creek and Schoen Creek, located in the southwest part of the park. Together, these constitute 6.6 miles of trail. While they were designed for mountain biking, these trails get heavy traffic from hikers and runners. This fact makes Fort Harrison an exception to my usual advice for hikers to stay off mountain bike trails. Both types of users are generally aware of the other and safely respectful of their presence.

Trail Running

Fort Harrison is popular with the Indianapolis running community. It's rare to visit the park without seeing at least a few people putting in miles on the roads and trails. The park also hosts organized races throughout the year, the most notable being the Indy Half at Fort Ben in the fall. While the race starts and ends just outside the park, most of the 13.1 miles are run through or along the edges of Fort Harrison State Park. It's a challenging, hilly route but fall colors and cool temperatures make it popular.

My favorite trail running routes are the two hike-and-bike trails, Schoen Creek and Lawrence Creek; the latter easily rates as one of the top trail runs in Indiana. The two paths flow wonderfully through beautiful forests in the southwest corner of the park. They climb up and down, but the grades are reasonable. They are close enough to each other that you can combine them for a nice seven-mile route.

The best access for both trails is the Lawrence Creek trailhead parking lot, along the road to the Visitors Center and Park Office. The beginning of Lawrence Creek is obvious (across the road) but Schoen Creek starts 100 yards south of the lot, across the bridge and to the left.

TRAIL GUIDES

Camp Creek Trail (CC)

Rating: ★★★★   **Configuration:** Partial Loop (complete using Harrison Trace)
Distance: 2.0 miles   **Difficulty:** Moderate

Tour: Camp Creek Trail is accessed on both ends using Harrison Trace and is fully contained within the latter route's paved loop on the east side of the park. Most of the trail is in Warbler Woods Nature Preserve and feels remarkably wild—with the large trees and many birds it's easy to forget you're hiking in a big city. To follow the Camp Creek loop counterclockwise, park at the Delaware Lake lot and follow the paved Harrison Trace around the north side of the lake. Take the first right and two quick lefts to reach the Camp Creek trailhead. The route winds pleasantly through an open, maturing, second-growth forest, moving up and down ravines and crossing small waterways. After a half mile, you encounter a pile of broken concrete, a reminder that this area once was an Army training ground. After passing a wide, unmarked path and a memorial bench, you find yourself on the bluff above Camp Creek and hiking one of the loveliest trail segments in Indiana. Huge trees and wonderful elevated views of the stream are highlights. At Duck Pond, turn left onto the rock-covered dam, pass the outlet, and look for Camp Creek Trail's left turn back into the woods. (Going straight at this junction takes you back to Fall Creek Trail, my preferred return route.) Though you're on the north bank of the same creek and your outbound route is visible in many places, this leg is less interesting: the forest is younger and the stream views inferior (though it's still a nice hike). The trail dead ends at Harrison Trace; turn left to return to Delaware Lake and the parking lot.

Fall Creek Trail (FC)

Rating: ★★★   **Configuration:** Point to Point (with extra loop)
Distance: 1.1 miles   **Difficulty:** Moderate

Tour: This pretty path follows its namesake stream through a maturing, varied forest with stretches that are more riparian and others that are more upland. Park at Delaware Lake; the trailhead is at the northeast corner of the lot. The trail makes a beeline for Fall Creek then turns right and follows upstream. Look for wildflowers in the spring and massive sycamore trees all year long. The trail soon enters Warbler Woods Nature Preserve, and the creek swings away to the left. The adjacent bottomlands are prone to springtime flooding, which is why the trail was relocated from that area to its current route on higher ground. The first of two unmarked side trails departs uphill to the

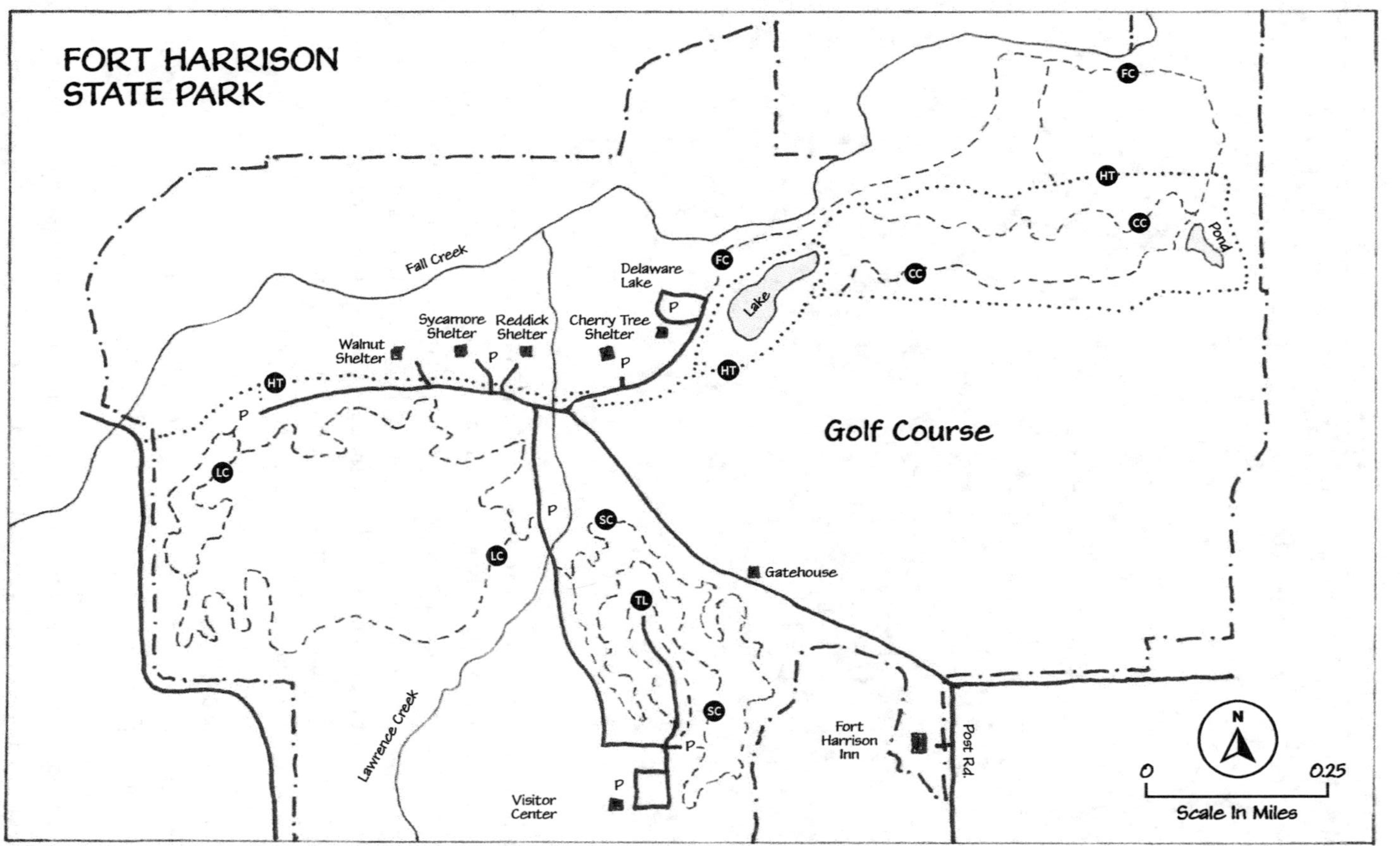

FORT HARRISON
STATE PARK
Fall Creek
Delaware Lake
Lake
Pond
FC
HT
CC
CC
FC
Sycamore Shelter
Reddick Shelter
Cherry Tree Shelter
Walnut Shelter
P
P
P
HT
HT
Golf Course
LC
LC
P
SC
Gatehouse
TL
SC
Fort Harrison Inn
Post Rd.
P
P
Visitor Center
Lawrence Creek
N
0
0.25
Scale In Miles

Camp Creek Trail begins its woodland jaunt along its namesake stream.

right; they form a loop and connect with Harrison Trace for people desiring a shorter route. Fall Creek returns just as the trail navigates a series of stairways and boardwalks that include observation decks with excellent elevated views of the stream. Fall Creek soon turns left, and the trail starts climbing before eventually swinging right and leveling out. At the top of the hill, the trail ends at Harrison Trace and offers multiple options for returning to the start: turn either direction on the paved path or continue straight to access either leg of the Camp Creek Trail loop.

Harrison Trace (HT)

Rating: ★ ★   **Configuration:** Lollipop (two loops)
Distance: 2.75 miles   **Difficulty:** Easy

Tour: Some purists think that pavement turns hiking into nothing more than a walk but that's short-sighted in an urban park like Fort Harrison. The Trace is a great entry-level introduction to the woods, offers easy access to people with mobility issues, and is friendly to both foot- and wheel-powered recreationalists. It's also an important connector for other trails. To get a full tour, park at the Walnut Trailhead at the west end of the park; the Trace connector departs to the north. Turning left takes you to the bike/hike/run entrance on Boy Scout Road and the Fall Creek Greenway. Instead, turn right and hike through pretty Walnut Grove, past three picnic shelters, and across Lawrence Creek and the Delaware Lake access road. Now in the woods, stay to the right and start climbing along the south bank of the lake. This section is notorious on the Indy Half Marathon: it's a late-race uphill slog to the eastern edge of the park. At the top, the Trace turns left and starts descending another steep section before returning to the lake. Stay to the right at the intersection, walk past the Delaware Lake parking area/restrooms, and continue to the junction with the main Trace. Turn right to return to your car.

Lawrence Creek Hike-and-Bike Trail (LC)

Rating: ★ ★ ★ ★ ★ **Configuration:** Loop
Distance: 3.6 miles **Difficulty:** Moderate

Tour: This trail was engineered as a mountain bike path and as such flows nicely (especially for trail running) but it feels a lot like a hiking trail. The route traverses a beautiful upland forest—Lawrence Creek Nature Preserve—that has a spring wildflower display as gorgeous as you can find in the state park system. Park at the Lawrence Creek Trailhead (which can fill up quickly) and cross the road to access the trail. Head to the left to reach the main loop. Hikers and runners can go either direction; cyclists must go counterclockwise (to the right), which is my preferred direction on foot. Keep your eyes open for all types of travelers—cyclists, runners, dogs, etc.—and be ready to step off the trail. The first half of the trail is especially beautiful, running up and down small valleys and snaking around many big trees; the builders fit a remarkable length of trail in a small area without overwhelming the environment. You'll get periodic glimpses of roads and grassy areas, but they don't detract from the overall experience. The route gets a little confusing near the Walnut Trailhead (an alternate access) where an unmarked branch breaks to the left. Straight is the official route, left is shorter, and both reach the same endpoint. You can treat this section as a side loop if you want additional distance. Continue around the main loop as it winds up and around multiple ravines. The trail in this area feels remote but occasional car noise from Boy Scout Road and the outlines of houses through the trees remind you suburbia is just beyond the edge of the forest. The last section of the loop is beautiful but nondescript and the end comes surprisingly fast, proving how engaging the route can be.

Schoen Creek Hike-and-Bike Trail (SC)

Rating: ★ ★ ★   **Configuration:** Loop
Distance: 3.0 miles   **Difficulty:** Moderate

Tour: Like nearby Lawrence Creek this route has been engineered for mountain bikes and flows nicely through an attractive woodland. But it gets less traffic, especially from hikers, probably because it's compressed in a small area, has open sections passing near buildings, and has more mud and roots than its sister trail. But Schoen Creek is still worth a run or hike, especially in the warm, green months when the route is prettiest. The official trailhead is at the top end near the Millenium Grove Picnic Area, but most people park at Lawrence Creek. From the latter access, walk south on the road's edge, cross the creek, and look for the trail start to the left. Turn left (the opposite direction of cyclists) on reaching the main loop. The first section climbs and follows a low ridge parallel to the main park road and a small stream. After descending to and crossing the stream, the trail passes a ruined building foundation on the right and the gatehouse on the left. After switchbacking to the top of the ridge, the path winds through a grove of massive, old trees before coming to the forest edge and passing a wetland. On entering the Camp Glenn area, the trail goes just behind some of the repurposed military buildings before reaching the official trail access and parking area. For the next mile, Schoen Creek Trail tracks closely to the Tree Line Trail as they circumnavigate Millenium Grove Picnic Area. Turning back into the forest, the pretty final stretch descends gently to the end of the loop and the left turn back to the parking area.

Tree Line Trail (TL)

Rating: ★   **Configuration:** Loop
Distance: 1.0 miles   **Difficulty:** Easy

Tour: This nondescript mowed path offers a family-friendly walk—maybe as part of lunch at the Millenium Grove Picnic Area that it circumnavigates—as well as a lesson in native Indiana trees. Seventeen species are identified with interpretive signs along the trail; pick up a companion brochure at the visitor's center if you want more information. If you're not picnicking, park at the lot for the Schoen Creek Trail and walk the short distance west to the Tree Line Trailhead.

7

Harmonie State Park

One of the best ways to immerse yourself in a state park is to spend a night or two inside the property's boundaries. Among other things, an overnight stay lets you enjoy those edge-of-darkness hours in the morning and evening, when people are fewer and animals are more active. Explore, look, and listen during these times and you'll often be amazed at what you encounter.

I've camped since I was a kid and still try to get out a few times each year. I'm one of those tenting-only purists—"if you're not sleeping on the ground, you're not really camping" is my motto. Unfortunately, at this point in my life, my aching back sometimes hates this attitude.

I recently found myself with a two-day summertime window for exploring Harmonie State Park. I'd visited a few times before but was always in a hurry, on my way to somewhere else. This time, I'd make the three-hour drive from Indianapolis and camp overnight, leaving myself plenty of time to relax and explore every corner of the park.

I arrived on a weekday to find the 200-site campground mostly empty. When I asked an employee if this was typical, she replied, "Who really enjoys Indiana camping in the summer? But wait until fall. This place will be packed." Frankly, the mostly empty facility was fine with me. Families walked or rode their bikes along the tree-covered lanes, and I had a couple of nice conversations with fellow campers, but mostly it was quiet.

With the temperature pushing 90 degrees, I dawdled at my campsite, which was pretty and shaded by a huge tulip tree, and ate a snack. The site was within steps of Trail 2, which was my primary reason for choosing it, and I decided I'd better get hiking. I loaded my backpack with plenty of water, sprayed my body with a thick layer of DEET, and started walking. My plan was to walk a double-loop combining Trails 2 and 4, total length about four miles.

Trail 2—straight, wide, and gravel covered—descended rapidly through a mature forest. At some point in its history—like many of the trail segments at

A wooden stairway eases the climb for hikers exploring Trail 5.

Harmonie—this had been a road. An abrupt left turn led to a bridge over a small stream and a T-intersection. Turning right would have led me to the Wabash River, about a half-mile hike. But that was an adventure for the next day, so I turned left and followed the stream to Trail 4. It looked like another former road, confirmed at a hefty bridge with wheel-width treads. I took the first left, onto a narrow path, entering the trail's main loop, my favorite hiking segment in the park.

For the next half mile, Trail 4 skirted the northern boundary of Harmonie Hills Nature Preserve. There is no old growth in the park but much of the forest was logged nearly two centuries ago and never clear cut again. As a result, there are many areas like this, with huge trees, a dense overhead canopy, and an open forest floor. Previous spring hikes on this trail revealed a wonderland of ephemeral flowers. On this hike, the blooms were long gone but the woods were beautiful, nonetheless.

After crossing the park road, the route joined Trail 1 for a time, sticking a little too close to the asphalt for my liking. Trail 1 split away to the south near Cherry Hill Shelter—a nice starting point for Trails 1, 4, and 6—but I continued west, sometimes within sight of the road.

Soon I started encountering intersections with mountain bike trails. The volunteer Harmonie State Park Trail Builders has been busy in recent years, carving roughly 20 miles of bike trails into the hilly southwest corner of the park.

Trail 4 made a sharp northward turn and entered a long tangent that clearly was a retired road. I remembered the hills on this stretch from previous hikes—down, up, down, up—tiring but made easier by the road builders' cuts and fills. Soon I was back on the connector trail and made a right turn onto a new section of Trail 2.

This part of the path was wide and easy, making a gentle uphill as it followed the stream up the valley. Some familiar-looking purple flowers on the path's edge caught my eye—hostas. I had similar blooms in my yard back home in Indianapolis. Like daffodils I'd seen here on springtime hikes, these introduced flowers were evidence of a long history of settlement before this property became a public park.

Trail 2 emerged from the trees near the campground entrance. I turned left on the asphalt and made the trek to my campsite at the far end of the facility. I was hot, sweaty, and still had a tent to set up and flying insects to battle. But I also had a cold beverage waiting in the cooler and trees loaded with a variety of birds to stare at. Summer camping can be a challenge, but I knew it was going to be a beautiful evening in the outdoors.

Harmonie History

The land that now makes up Harmonie State Park once lay at the bottom of a shallow, tropical sea. Over the course of millions of years, thick deposits of sand and silt accumulated and were compressed into layers of sedimentary rock—limestone, shale, and sandstone. Trapped within the rock were scattered deposits of organic matter that over time became coal and petroleum.

Today, this geologic region—roughly 400 miles by 200 miles in size—is known as the Illinois Basin, and it is an active coal and petroleum producing area. It lies under its namesake state as well as smaller parts of southwest Indiana and western Kentucky. Harmonie is near the region's southern boundary.

The soil was rich in southwest Indiana and the Wabash River an important transportation conduit, features that attracted white settlers looking to start a new life. A riverside plot of land just north of the modern-day park was a magnet for two successive utopian societies starting in 1814. The first was a group of breakaway German Lutherans led by George Rapp. After first settling in Pennsylvania, the Rappites bought 3,500 acres along the Wabash and moved west. There they carved a settlement out of the forest and called it Harmony—sometimes spelled as Harmonie—which grew and thrived for the next decade.

In the early 1820s, the Rappites found themselves too isolated from trade markets as their manufacturing expanded. Dedicated abolitionists, they were also in conflict with slave owners in nearby Kentucky. After deciding to relocate back to Pennsylvania, the Rappites sold Harmony to Scottish industrialist Robert Owen in 1825 and by May of that year had vacated the settlement.

The wealthy, reform-minded Owen had a different type of utopia in mind. After renaming the town New Harmony, he launched what was to become America's first socialist experiment. As a communal utopia, the experiment was a failure, and the socialistic society was dissolved in 1827. Yet the settlement succeeded in many other ways, in part, because it attracted an amazing mix of talented people. Over time, New Harmony became one of the country's leading centers for education, science, and the arts. The town had the country's first public library as well as a public school system open to both sexes. While Robert Owen returned to Great Britain in 1828, his sons stayed and become important Indiana leaders. Robert Dale Owen was a state legislator and U.S. congressman; David Dale Owen was a state and federal geologist; and Richard Owen was state geologist and the first president of Purdue University.

South of New Harmony, the forested hills along the river had been cleared and farmed by settlers going as far back as the era of the original Harmony settlement. The farms remained long after the utopian ideas had drifted away. The first winds of change emerged in 1889 when oil reserves were discovered thanks to a well drilled in the middle of Terre Haute. Development of the resource was slow, until 1938, when the large Griffin oil pool was tapped along the Wabash in Gibson County, just upstream from Harmonie.

The first oil well—the 2,382-foot-deep Joel Vail No. 1—was drilled in what would become the state park in 1945. Eventually, 50 wells would be established in the future park. Most have played out and been capped but several are still operating. You can see signs of the oil industry at various places in Harmonie, including a retired pump-jack on display near the site of the former swimming pool. Tank trucks visit the park regularly to collect the oil.

Plans to establish a new state park in southwest Indiana can be traced back to at least 1964 but it took the generosity of Elmer Elliot and his daughters to jumpstart the process. Elliot was a conservation-minded farmer who wanted to see his property used for recreation by the people of New Harmony. He died in 1965 at the age of 100. The next year his daughters donated 700 acres of Elliott land and Harmonie State Park was officially established.

At about the same time as the land donation, Indiana was awarded $1.1 million as one of the first federal Land and Water Conservation Fund grant recipients. The money was earmarked for land acquisition at Harmonie. The park was originally slated to comprise 4,200 acres.

The plans ran into roadblocks, including landowners reluctant to sell. The state was forced to acquire land using eminent domain, which created bad feelings in the area. Also, most of the selling owners retained mineral rights, which is why the park still has several independently owned and operated oil wells within its boundaries.

By 1972, the park had expanded to 3,000 acres but its infrastructure was limited. Finally, in 1974, the state legislature committed $2 million to complete the land acquisition and spur development of the park that so many love today.

Harmonie Today

Today, Harmonie State Park covers 3,450 acres and offers visitors a variety of recreational activities. The park is the most distant property from Indianapolis—189 miles away, requiring about three hours of driving using Interstates 69 and 64.

Harmonie may be home to active oil wells and has the usual trappings of a modern state park, but it feels wild. Its large size (sixth in the state), distance from population centers (annual visitation is only about 167,000), and long border with the Wabash River all contribute to this feeling. It's also rugged; the uplands are cut by many streams. Nature preserves anchor the north (Wabash Border, 255 acres) and south (Harmonie Hills, 335 acres) ends of the park. The dense forests and rugged topography create a haven for a variety of mammals, birds, reptiles, and amphibians.

Even though it's bordered by a major river, Harmonie's water-oriented activities are limited. The once-popular Olympic-sized pool was retired and removed. Swimming in the Wabash is prohibited but you are allowed to fish and the park has a boat ramp on the river.

One of Harmonie's biggest attractions is its trail system. In addition to its nearly nine miles of hiking-only paths, Harmonie also has routes catering to horseback

Walking the banks of the Wabash River is a special treat at Harmonie.

riding and mountain biking. In recent years, volunteer crews have carved the twisting cycling routes out of the woods in the southwest corner of the park. The main trailhead is at Sycamore Ridge; there are routes for riders of every skill level.

Harmonie offers two options for staying overnight in the park. The centrally located, all-electric campground has 200 sites. Trails 2 and 5 end in or near the campground, so it's a convenient spot for hikers. Adjacent to the campground are 11 family cabins that sleep up to eight people and offer all the comforts of home, including air-conditioning.

If you can't stay in the park, there are other lodging options in the area. New Harmony, a popular tourist destination, has an inn and conference center that is just 10 minutes away. Mount Vernon, 12 miles south, has a locally owned hotel as well as a grocery store and other amenities. Grayville, Illinois, 18 miles north, has chain motel options next to Interstate 64.

Hiking Harmonie

With its large land area, rugged topography, and beautiful, mature forests, Harmonie seems tailor-made for hikers. Unfortunately, the park has an underwhelming hiking trail network in need of signs and maintenance. Despite these negatives, Harmonie is still a worthwhile hiking destination, offering eight trails totaling almost nine miles. Most follow the beds of former roads, which provide wide paths and good footing.

Trail 4 is the park's best; a significant portion of its length was purpose-built for hiking, and it passes through a beautiful forest. The west side of Trail 5 is both scenic and interesting, but the former loop has been cut by the removal of the Big Harmonie Pond dam.

All routes except Trail 3 connect directly or by short road segments if you're looking to piece together a long (up to 9-10 miles) hike. The centrally located campground is a nice starting point for an extended jaunt, but the Wabash River Picnic Area and Cherry Hill Shelter are both good noncamping trailhead options.

Trail Running

Some of the trail features that detract from hiking might be considered a positive for runners. The wide, gently sloping trails have good footing and lend themselves to speedy passage through the woods. Trails 1, 2, and 4 link together nicely for a five-mile route with plenty of climbs, shade, and scenic interest. The other trails are runnable but short.

There are other ways to pursue running at Harmonie. The mountain bike trails are especially attractive. With 20 contiguous miles of nicely engineered route available, it's possible to put together challenging runs of various lengths.

The park's roads offer another option for runners—especially those who enjoy mixing dirt and asphalt sections. From the campground, two miles of dedicated bike lane run alongside the park road. North of Rush Creek, the bike trail departs on its own paved right-of-way for another mile, to the former site of the swimming pool.

TRAIL GUIDES

Trail 1

Rating: ★★　　　　　　　　　　**Configuration:** Loop
Distance: 1.0 miles　　　　　　　**Difficulty:** Easy

Tour: Part of this loop includes a walk down the road in the Youth Tent Area but because the facility is lightly used, you'll probably have it to yourself. The remainder of the trail is a mixed bag but worth exploring. If you're not camping with a youth group, park at the Cherry Hill Shelter. Head south across the park road and turn left on the trail, which is just inside the forest edge. This section initially shares its pathway with Trail 4, which soon turns off to the north. It's an underwhelming stretch—just a wide, mowed, grass path that rarely ventures far from the road. After turning south, the trail soon emerges from the forest into the parklike camping area. Turn right and follow the pavement, continuing straight when the road turns into two graveled tracks. Past the pit toilets a Trail 1 marker points in the woods and the route enters its most scenic section. A huge stair-and-bridge system crosses a pretty valley, dappled with sunlight in the summer. A trickling stream and abundant birds add to the ambience. The trail returns to your starting point just beyond the edge of the valley.

Trail 2

Rating: ★ ★ ★   **Configuration:** Y-Shaped
Distance: 1.5 miles   **Difficulty:** Moderate

Tour: This trail is a nice walk on its own but also serves as an important connector from the campground to the Wabash River and Trail 4. If you're camping, the trail starts adjacent to Site 194. If you're not camping and want to get the most out of this route, park close to the main road at the Wabash River Picnic Area. Follow the tree line on the left/east and cross the road. An "Authorized Vehicles Only" sign marks Trail 2's start on a service road; Road Brook flows quietly to your left. Soon you encounter an old but charismatic structure—Maude's Barn, named for a former resident—obviously still in use. Stay straight at a junction and bridge (you'll return on this later) and continue past the Trail 4 connector. Trail 2 climbs gently up a retired road through a beautiful valley, crossing the stream a couple of times. After a left turn the trail steepens and climbs the final 100-vertical-feet to its temporary end at the campground entrance. Turn left and walk the length of the main campground road, turning left again when you see a "Sites 167-200" sign. The marked restart of Trail 2 is on the right just before the road's end. The trail, back on another former road, starts descending immediately. The forest is dense and wild feeling; the land drops off into deep valleys on both sides. After a sharp left turn, cross the bridge over Road Brook you passed earlier and turn right to return to your car.

Trail 3

Rating: ★ ★   **Configuration:** Loop
Distance: 1.0 miles   **Difficulty:** Moderate

Tour: This is the first trail encountered upon entering Harmonie, and it is isolated from the rest of the path system. In its short length Trail 3 visits both bottomland and upland forests while passing through a state nature preserve. Past the gatehouse, take the second

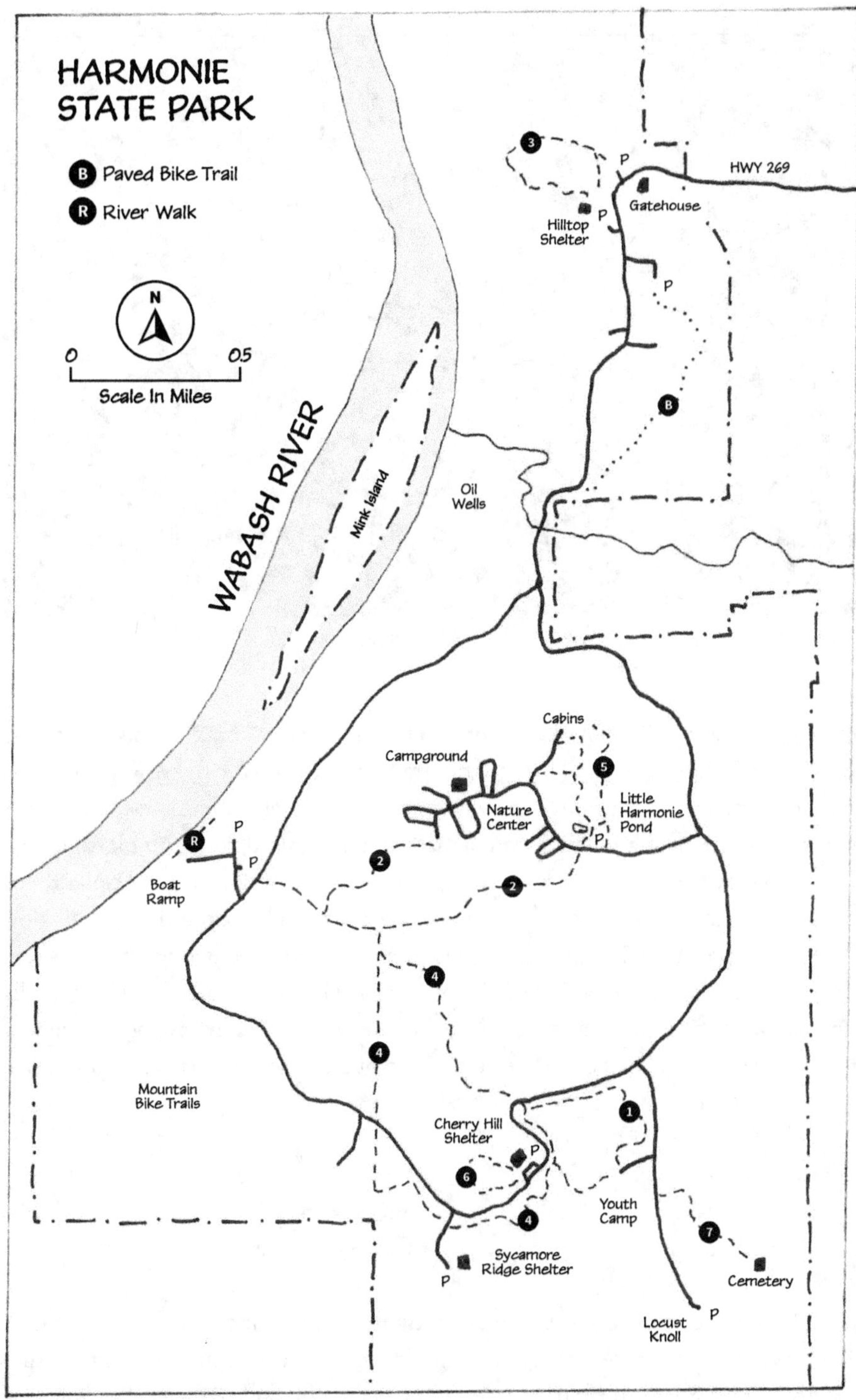

HARMONIE STATE PARK
B Paved Bike Trail
R River Walk
N
0
0.5
Scale In Miles
WABASH RIVER
Mink Island
Oil Wells
HWY 269
Gatehouse
Hilltop Shelter
B
Cabins
Campground
Nature Center
5
Little Harmonie Pond
P
2
2
R
P
P
Boat Ramp
4
4
Mountain Bike Trails
1
Cherry Hill Shelter
P
6
Youth Camp
4
7
Sycamore Ridge Shelter
P
Cemetery
Locust Knoll
P

Massive trees and spring wildflowers are scenic highlights along Trail 4.

right and park at the Hilltop Shelter lot. Go behind the restrooms to find the trail (it looks like a road), turn left, and look for the Trail 3 markers on the right. What becomes a narrower trail descends through the woods toward the Wabash but stops short of the river and turns right at a junction with a marked horse trail. If you're up for exploring, the horse trails can be wet but offer two loops that venture a mile south and closer to the river. Back on Trail 3, cross a small bridge and start the climb back to the upland. Now in the nature preserve with a rugged ravine to your left, the many huge trees—beech, oak, and more—catch your attention. Humanity intrudes at the end of the climb in the form of a white water tower, a service road, and the usual mix of invasive plants you find in disturbed areas. The trail continues to the road but look for a path to the right, which stays in the woods and offers a shortcut to your car.

Trail 4

Rating: ★ ★ ★ ★   **Configuration:** Loop
Distance: 2.5 miles   **Difficulty:** Moderate

Tour: Trail 4 is comprised of three distinctly different segments but together they add up to provide the nicest hike at Harmonie. Follow the parking and start instructions for Trail 1 but turn right after leaving Cherry Hill and crossing the road. The first section stays close to the pavement—but usually not too close and vehicle noise isn't a problem. Upon reaching another road—Sycamore Ridge access—turn right to find the restart to Trail 4. (Turning left takes you to the shelter and the trailhead for the mountain bike network.) The trail follows the road for a distance, turns left into the woods, then turns right onto a wider trail running due north. This former road, utilizing periodic cuts and fills, proceeds arrow-straight for six-tenths of a mile. After crossing the main park road, Trail 4 enters Harmonie Hills Nature Preserve, which while not old growth forest is still *old*. Huge trees, a dense overhead canopy, and—in spring—abundant wildflowers characterize the rest of the hike. After roller-coastering through the woods (including a couple of stiff climbs), Trail 4 turns right on a purpose-built hiking trail. (Staying straight on the old road connects you with Trail 2.) The next three-quarters of a mile is the most delightful hiking in the park. Following the north edge of the nature preserve, the trail skirts large trees and deep valleys, bird calls sounding from the dense canopy. After reaching and crossing the road again, turn right. This roadside stretch, shared with Trail 1, is a letdown after the recent jaunt through the forest but it ends quickly as Cherry Hill comes into view.

Trail 5

Rating: ★ ★ ★　　　　　　　　**Configuration:** Double Point to Point
Distance: 0.75 miles　　　　　　**Difficulty:** Moderate

Tour: Ignore the Harmonie property map: Trail 5 is not a loop, and Big Harmonie Pond is now dry. But though this trail's glory days are behind it, the route is still worth exploring. Park in the lot to the right of the campground control hut and walk over to the interpretive signs. There are no trail markers (they are rare on this route) but you'll see the graveled path leading to Little Harmonie Pond. After pausing to look for waterfowl and wildlife, continue to the right, then left to cross the small earthen dam. Beyond this point, Trail 5 is a narrow path winding through a dense forest—a true hiking path and a pretty one at that, though in need of some TLC. Soon, observation decks and side paths appear, looking at and leading to…nothing. This is where Big Harmonie Pond used to be. Eventually, you reach a T-intersection and find the first "Trail 5" sign. Both directions lead to unmarked trailheads at different points in the Family Cabin area. Turning right takes you as far as you can go along the former pond before a fence directs you up a stair to Cabin 10. Beyond the fence you can see the old path, which quickly peters out. Retrace your steps back to Little Harmonie Pond and recross the small dam, turning left on the far side. There is no sign, and it might be tall grass but keep going—an overgrown bridge soon confirms you're on the trail. Turn left upon reaching a wide, grassy path (another former road). This part of Trail 5 is

A pipevine swallowtail butterfly visits a milkweed along the River Walk.

straight, nondescript, and poorly maintained, but easy to hike. It eventually veers left then quickly withers into nothing. Crawl through some brush and you'll find yourself on the edge of the washed-out dam; the former pond, to the left, is sprouting tall grass and tree saplings. Turn around to retrace your path to the car.

Trail 6

Rating: ★   **Configuration:** Loop
Distance: 0.75 miles   **Difficulty:** Easy

Tour: The Harmonie property map shows Trail 6 as a loop *around* Cherry Hill Shelter; it actually winds through the woods to the west of the shelter. Park at the Cherry Hill picnic area and walk behind the shelter and to the left. Just beyond the swing, you'll see an overgrown "Trail 6" marker next to a wide path. The route is a flat, nondescript, mowed trail through a pretty forest. There are no highlights of note, and your walk will be over relatively quickly, ending just south of where you started. Trail 6 is a nice, post-picnic stroll after eating too many hot dogs, but it doesn't warrant a special stop for hikers.

Trail 7

Rating: ★ ★ **Configuration:** Point to Point
Distance: 0.5 miles (1-mile round trip) **Difficulty:** Easy

Tour: You can hike Trail 7 as an extension of Trail 1 by connecting along a quarter mile of the Locust Knoll Picnic Area access road. Or you can simply park on the wide shoulder along the west side of the road. The trailhead is marked by a misspelled "Edmonds Cemetary" sign. The trail starts in a young forest and soon passes a junction with a horse trail. The woods mature as you walk, and the trees grow larger and more beautiful. The small, shaded burial plot is partially surrounded by a fence. There appear to be two graves, but closer inspection reveals remnants of three crumbling gravestones memorializing Henry Edmonds' three wives: Elizabeth, Sarah, and Sarah, who all died between 1847 and 1853. Edmonds farmed this land until his death in 1863; he had moved to the area from North Carolina around 1815. There is speculation that Henry is also buried in this plot. Retrace your steps to return to your car.

River Walk

Rating: ★ ★ **Configuration:** Point to Point
Distance: 0.25 miles **Difficulty:** Easy
(half-mile round trip)

Tour: This isn't exactly a hike but it's a must-do activity for any visit to Harmonie State Park. The Wabash follows a long section of the park's western boundary and is a big, impressive, and beautiful river. Drive to the Wabash River Picnic Area, park near the vault toilets, and walk toward the river, angling to your left. The shaded path isn't marked but is gravel covered and readily visible. It sits just steps from the water when the river is running bank full, so provides amazing views; keep your eyes open for waterfowl and other highlights. The trail ends at the boat ramp; turn around and return to your starting point. As you walk upstream, Mink Island is in full view; though only accessible by boat, the large island is part of the state park. As a bonus, continue along the water past the picnic area to find a narrow unofficial trail through the woods. It ends about 100 yards later in a grove of huge sycamores along the banks of Road Brook. Pause and look for wildlife, wood ducks, and other interesting birds before returning to your car.

8

Indiana Dunes State Park

I used to live in "The Region" of northwest Indiana, so Indiana Dunes was my home state park for several years. Because the park sits in the middle of one of the country's most biologically significant landscapes—the dune country on the south shore of Lake Michigan—it is not a stretch to argue that it is the most important property in the Indiana State Park system. Plus, it's by far the most popular, hosting about 2 million visitors each year.

But ecological significance and visitor statistics were the last things on our minds several years back when my son, Kendal, and I contemplated where to go for a winter trail run. Being midweek just a couple of days after Christmas, we figured we could avoid crowds and see some great sights at Indiana Dunes. We wouldn't be disappointed.

To get some perspective on how special this area is, consider that Indiana Dunes *State Park* is surrounded by Indiana Dunes *National Park*. Though the national park is much larger, the state park protects what many feel is the most exceptional section of the remaining dunes landscape.

On that December day, we parked at the lot near Wilson Shelter. This central location is a popular starting point for hikers and trail runners because it connects easily with several routes and avoids congestion at places like the beach and Nature Center. Our plans were modest; we were going to run Trail 9 and only cover about 4 miles.

But there is nothing modest about Trail 9, one of the most scenic hiking paths in Indiana and a serious challenge. It has killer climbs and descents, twists and turns galore…and then there's the sand. Hiking the dunes is often a "two steps forward one step back" proposition as you sink and slip on hills. But on this day, the conditions were in our favor—snowless, sunny, and cold. The sand was frozen underneath but soft on top, perfect for running.

We took off on Trail 8 from the north end of the parking lot and crossed a long boardwalk. This path eventually becomes part of the route for the popular 3 Dunes Challenge, which involves trekking up and down the trio of highest points in the park. But we were just using it to connect with Trail 9.

Amazing views of Lake Michigan abound from the dunes traversed by Trail 9.

The first two miles on Trail 9 were a pleasant cruise through the woods with a couple of easy climbs. The trail follows a swale in the lee of the main dunes and runs roughly parallel to the shore of Lake Michigan. To our right was another, lower dune. On the far side of the lower dune and out of sight was Trail 10, which runs parallel to Trail 9 for a distance and is a nice alternative route along the edge of the Great Marsh.

After swinging north, we descended to a low point along the edge of Furnessville Blowout and the scenery changed dramatically. The big lake opened in front of us and the sound of waves rolling into shore filled the air. We paused briefly to enjoy the scene then muscled into a short but steep climb out of the blowout and to the top of the lakefront dunes.

For the next several minutes, we picked our way through the trees while listening to the waves lap at the shoreline of the expansive blue lake to our right—one of the best trail sections in Indiana. Before getting too comfortable, though, we had to make a tough climb in the softest sand of the day to the top of the dune above Beach House Blowout. It was a grind, but at the top we were rewarded with a priceless view: seemingly endless Lake Michigan to the north and the expansive dunes and forests of the state and national parks everywhere else. You could make out small signs of humanity, but it was easy to imagine being in the middle of a vast wilderness.

As we descended from the dune top, Kendal and I were given an exhilarating reminder of how wild this place was. We fell into a quiet, effortless rhythm moving downhill on the almost-perfect sand, rounded a sharp corner, and found ourselves with an unexpected running partner—a coyote who was casually loping along Trail 9 in the same direction. Remarkably, he didn't hear us for several seconds and the three of us ran together in unison. Then, realizing he wasn't alone, he abruptly switched into a fast gear we lacked, turned off the trail, and was soon out of sight. We stopped briefly, laughing and stunned by what had happened, then started up again, feeling lucky to be alive and energized by a great day in an Indiana state park.

Indiana Dunes History

Entire books have been written about the struggle to preserve the Indiana Dunes, and the establishment of the state park is just a small—and relatively early—chapter in that tale. There were many good reasons for preserving the Dunes, but one of the most significant was the area's contributions to science and human understanding of the natural world. Research conducted in the Dunes around the turn of the 20th Century supported the growth of a new branch of science—ecology—and gave the area notoriety on a global scale.

Henry Chandler Cowles, "America's first professional ecologist," rightfully gets most of the credit for sharing the Indiana Dunes with the world, but other colleagues of his at the University of Chicago played important roles, too. One was noted botanist John Merle Coulter, who had been part of the 1872 Hayden survey of Yellowstone and first wrote about the Dunes in an 1879 edition of the *Botanical Gazette*. He later encouraged graduate student Cowles to use the Dunes as a site for his research on plant succession.

Cowles first visited the Dunes in 1896, taking the train to Dune Park. (Visitors in the 21st Century can still use this stop on the South Shore Line as Indiana's only means of traveling by rail to a state park. It's only a one-mile walk or bike ride to the Indiana Dunes gatehouse.) The station lay just south of the most active dunes, which were moving rapidly inland and encroaching on the inland marshes and forest. It was the perfect landscape to explore his concept of "plant succession" and became the focal point of Cowles' research for years to come.

Thanks to Cowles' work, ecology blossomed as a science, and the Dunes came to be known as "the birthplace of ecology." Yet even as Cowles was studying the Dunes, they were coming under attack from expanding industrial development. In 1906, United State Steel purchased 6,000 acres of Dunes country running along seven miles of Lake Michigan shoreline and started developing the city of Gary. There were some who envisioned Indiana's full stretch of shoreline as home to ports and industrial plants rather than one of the world's most biodiverse natural landscapes.

Cowles was part of a group of forward-thinking Chicago scientists, artists, and social reformers who started the effort to save the Dunes. Cowles, along with settlement house leader Thomas Allison and landscape architect Jens Jensen, helped launch the Prairie Club and later the National Dunes Park Association, organizations that were critical to the future state park. Initial efforts focused on establishing a national park; Stephen Mather, the first director of the National Park Service, was a proponent. The effort was stymied by a variety of factors, including local opposition, the country's focus on World War I, and the fact that all the park property would have to be purchased—previous national parks had been established on public land.

By 1917, establishing an Indiana Dunes State Park looked to be a more promising avenue. This shift in strategy was buoyed by the efforts of Richard Lieber, the first Indiana Conservation Commission chairman and the man widely recognized as the "father of Indiana state parks." Lieber began his efforts to preserve the Indiana Dunes in earnest in 1919, eventually getting the support of local business and political entities as well as conservation and civic groups. In 1923, the Indiana legislature passed, and the governor signed, legislation establishing Indiana Dunes State Park, covering 2,182 acres and three miles of shoreline in Porter County.

Unfortunately, the legislation provided no money for purchasing the property. Lieber, a successful businessman before becoming a conservationist, was up to the task of raising the necessary funds—but it wasn't easy, and for two years no money was forthcoming. Lieber changed things in 1925 by wooing newly elected Governor Edward Jackson, convincing him to visit the Dunes. Jackson was swayed by his visit and channeled $200,000 of state money toward purchasing the first 120 acres of land.

The park's high point, Mt. Tom, on Trail 8 and the route of the 3 Dune Challenge.

The deed was delivered to the state and the park dedicated with a simple ceremony on August 29, 1925.

On July 1, 1926, the first admission fees were collected, and 62,880 people visited the park over the next three months. The money was earmarked for additional land purchases. Meanwhile, corporate benefactors, including U.S. Steel and Sears Roebuck, provided their own large gifts. By 1932, the state was able to complete the final purchases of the Indiana Dunes property and Lieber had achieved his dream of establishing "the greatest state park on the American Continent."

Indiana Dunes Today

Indiana Dunes State Park is in northwest Indiana, roughly 150 miles from downtown Indianapolis. Because of their location, the Dunes are more connected to Chicago. It's less than an hour drive from the Chicago Loop and practically in the back yard of the city's sprawling south side suburbs.

The Indiana Dunes region is a fascinating mix of contrasts. The territory is still anchored by a large swath of wildlands centered on the state park and including intermittent chunks of the national park along Lake Michigan and a short distance inland. Together, the two parks protect more than 17,000 acres. The national park is much larger but more broken up. It also lacks a piece of preserved big dunes as expansive as the state park.

Much of the rest of the Dunes country has been heavily modified or completely obliterated. The region is crisscrossed by multiple busy roads, railroads, and power lines. Upscale housing enclaves—Ogden Dunes, Dune Acres, and Beverly Shores—have been carved out of the dune forests. Most jarring are the vast industrial complexes, home to massive steel mills, ports for huge ships, and coal-fired power plants. Suburbia seems to be encroaching on the parks from different directions, and a decaying city is just a few miles away.

Yet despite civilization pressing in from all sides, Indiana Dunes State Park feels remarkably wild, and its closeness to millions of people is a good thing, because it offers easy access to a quality outdoor recreational experience. Swimming is probably the most popular activity at the park. The beautiful beach is free (other than the park entrance fee) and protected by lifeguards during the summer months. The recently restored Dunes Pavilion offers a restaurant, event space, and a place to change.

Aside from the Pavilion, the park is relatively undeveloped and focuses on nature-based activities. In fact, nearly 1,600 acres of the property has been set aside in two state nature preserves.

The Dunes sit at an unusual, overlapping junction of north and south and east and west, offering habitats friendly to a wide variety of species that don't often live near each other. As a result, the Dunes are incredibly biodiverse and home to many

Trail 2 crosses the Great Marsh on a half-mile-long boardwalk.

species designated as threatened or endangered. Wildflowers are a special draw, with more than 1,100 flowering plant species living in the Dunes. Birders are also fond of the state park because it is an important stopover for migrating species; more than 350 species have been observed in the area.

Indiana Dunes is popular with campers. The park has a 140-site main camping area (all have electrical hookups) as well as a youth tent camping area. The main campground offers easy access by trail to the park's many hiking resources. Camping is also available at the national park's Dunewood Campground, which is on U.S. Highway 12 six miles east of the state park gatehouse.

If you're not planning to camp at the park, nearby Chesterton offers lodging, restaurant, and retail options and serves as the gateway to the park.

Hiking Indiana Dunes

Indiana Dunes has more than 16 miles of marked hiking trails. Most of the hiking is centered on the routes closest to the beach, campground, and Nature Center; these can get especially crowded on weekends. One particularly popular hike is the 3 Dune Challenge, which covers 1.5 miles and requires climbing Mt. Jackson, Mt. Holden, and Mt. Tom, the three tallest sand dunes in the park. The hike follows Trail 8 north from the Nature Center and requires 552 feet of total climbing. Your reward for finishing is a free sticker; there is also 3DC clothing available to purchase.

Escaping the busy trails in the western part of the park can provide hikers with a wilderness-quality experience. Trails, 2, 9, and 10 see less traffic and traverse some of the best scenery. Another overlooked route is Trail 3 through Dunes Prairie Nature

Preserve, which is isolated from the main network but travels through a unique environment noted for its prickly pear cactus and late spring wildflowers.

Trail Running

Indiana Dunes is a popular destination for the trail running community. Most runners focus on the Wilson Shelter area as a base of operations. From here, you have easy access to Trails 2, 9, and 10 (the latter two connect via a short section of Trail 8) and can put together runs in all directions of various lengths and difficulty.

The easiest run is a three-mile Great Marsh loop, going out on Trail 2, crossing the marsh boardwalk, and returning on Trail 10. The most challenging is any route incorporating Trail 9, which is beautiful but has several tough dune climbs. The longest simple loop is on Trail 10; it includes a long stretch along the Lake Michigan beach. Close the loop using Trail 7. Total length is about six miles.

TRAIL GUIDES

Trail 2

Rating: ★ ★ ★ ★					**Configuration:** Point to Point
Distance: 3 miles					**Difficulty:** Easy

Tour: Trail 2 is a beautiful—and flat—walk through the woods and across a large marsh. It is an outstanding spring route for seeing wildflowers and migrating birds but worth walking year-round. Wet weather is not kind to this trail. The forested sections can get muddy, and the half-mile boardwalk has a history of flooding, though it was rebuilt and elevated in 2020. The west end of Trail 2 starts near Southwest Shelter. Park near the paved bike trail and start hiking east until the paved trail reaches the bridge over Dune Creek. The start of narrow, dirt Trail 2 is across the road to the right. The path follows the south side of a stream and wetland for the next half mile. This part of the trail is pretty but feels neglected. Things change when you cross the road near Duneside and Wilson shelters. Many hikers prefer parking in, and walking from, this area. East of the shelters, Trail 2 widens and enters an especially beautiful forest in the southern part of Dunes Nature Preserve. It winds northeastward through trees and ferns, crossing several small streams, before swinging left (north) and onto the boardwalk across the Great Marsh—one of the most unique stretches of trail in Indiana. Take your time and enjoy the flooded forest, flowers, birds, and great views in every direction. After the marsh, Trail 2 Ts at Trail 10, where hikers have many options for creating a loop. The shortest is to turn left, follow Trail 10 to Trail 8, Wilson Shelter, and take a short walk down the road to Trail 2.

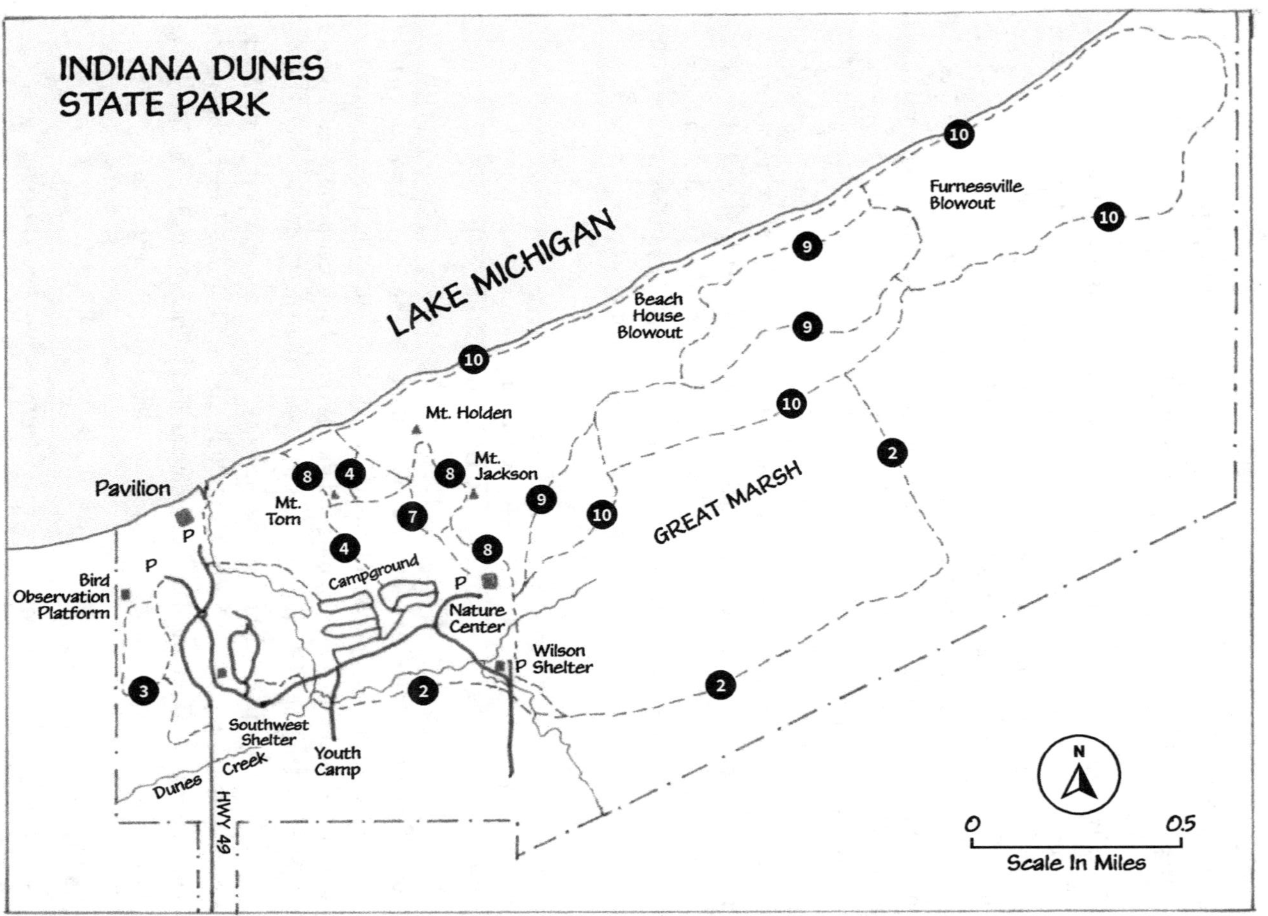
INDIANA DUNES
STATE PARK
LAKE MICHIGAN
Furnessville Blowout
Beach House Blowout
GREAT MARSH
Mt. Holden
Mt. Jackson
Mt. Torn
Pavilion
Bird Observation Platform
Campground
Nature Center
Wilson Shelter
Southwest Shelter
Youth Camp
Dunes Creek
HWY 49
N
0
0.5
Scale In Miles
P

Trail 3

Rating: ★ ★ ★   **Configuration:** Lollipop
Distance: 1.0 miles   **Difficulty:** Moderate

Tour: Trail 3 is unlike any other path in the park and offers hikers lessons in natural history as they traverse its route. Despite being close to the busiest part of the park, few people take the time to explore Dunes Prairie Nature Preserve. After the gatehouse, go to the parking lot accessed by the third exit from the roundabout. Climb the steps to the bird observation platform (which offers great views of landscapes and birds) and the start of Trail 3. Navigate the loop in either direction, taking your time and staying on the lookout for unique plants and birds. Spring wildflower blooms are exceptional and prickly pear cactus are a pleasant surprise. As you travel away from the lake, note the changing mix of plant life and the transition to trees—illustrating Henry Cowles' concept of plant succession. Take the time to explore the side trail at roughly the midpoint of the loop. It takes the succession lesson even further while traversing a beautiful, well-established oak forest. The detour is just under a half mile each way; the path ends at the main road near the park office. After retracing your steps, finish the hike by navigating the remaining section of loop.

Trail 4

Rating: ★ ★ ★   **Configuration:** Point to Point
Distance: 0.75 miles   **Difficulty:** Challenging

Tour: Trail 4 runs from the campground to Lake Michigan. It is the shortest trail in the park but important because it forms one leg of the 3 Dune Challenge. It also offers campers easy access to dune climbing and the big lake. If you aren't camping, park near the Nature Center and hike out the opposite (west) end of the lot. When you reach the campground, stay to the right to access the start of Trail 4, which departs to the northwest near the Campground Shelter. The climb up Mt. Tom takes you to the highest point in the park. Continue past the summit as Trail 4 briefly joins Trail 8. Turn left at the next two junctions to reach the lakeshore, where Trail 4 Ts with Trail 10.

Trail 7

Rating: ★ ★ ★   **Configuration:** Point to Point
Distance: 1.1 miles   **Difficulty:** Moderate

Tour: Trail 7 is perfect for people with limited time or who want a shorter and easier trek through the dunes. Park at the Nature Center lot; the trail departs to the left (northwest) of the center, which has water, restrooms, and interesting interpretive exhibits. The sandy trail through the woods has two climbs and two junctions with Trail 8. The first junction leads to Mt. Jackson; the second is at high point of the hike and sits between Mt. Holden and Mt. Tom. After the second junction, Trail 7 makes a steady descent to Lake Michigan. Trail 4 joins for the final section. At the lake, take some time to explore the beach and enjoy the amazing views before making the return trip. Alternatively, turn left (west) on the beach to create a challenging loop by taking Trail 8 to the top of Mt. Tom then back down to Trail 7.

Trail 8

Rating: ★ ★ ★ ★　　　　　　**Configuration:** Point to Point
Distance: 1.5 miles　　　　　　**Difficulty:** Challenging

Tour: Trail 8 is a must-do route for many visitors to Indiana Dunes State Park but much of the trail is a slog-and-slide up and down the open sand faces of big dunes. Nonetheless, there's a lot of satisfaction in completing the route, plus some incredible views. Trail 8 departs north from the Wilson Shelter parking lot, first crossing the boardwalk/bridge over Dunes Creek at the outlet of the Great Marsh. Trails 9 and 10 depart to the right, then the connector to the Nature Center goes to the left; this is where you enter the 3 Dune Challenge route. The first climb is just a gentle warmup for the following scramble up Mt. Jackson, which has grades of more than 15 percent. The payoff at the top of is an amazing view in all directions. The next climb is Mt. Holden, slightly higher and even closer to the lake. On your descent to the southwest you cross Trail 7 before reaching the 101 stairs that ease your climb to the hike's high point on Mt. Tom. Many people follow the long stairway down Trail 4 to finish the 3 Dune Challenge, but Trail 8 departs on a sand path to the north, continues to the lakefront, where it intersects with Trail 10. Turn right on the beach to navigate a return loop via Trail 7 or left to walk the last stretch of Trail 8, which ends at the swimming area.

Trail 9

Rating: ★ ★ ★ ★ ★　　　　　　**Configuration:** Lollipop
Distance: 3.75 miles　　　　　　**Difficulty:** Challenging

Tour: Trail 9 offers the park's best hike and one of the top trail experiences in Indiana. Beautiful forests, amazing dunetop vistas, and great opportunities for wildlife watching abound. Plus, the traffic is less than you'd expect in such a popular place. Park at the Wilson Shelter lot and start your hike north on the Trail 8 boardwalk. Take the first junction to the right to access Trail 9. For nearly two miles you take a gentle roller-coaster ride through a lovely forest in the lee of the main line of tall dunes along the lake. A lower dune line also rises to your right. Two junctions in this stretch allow an easy connection to parallel Trail 10. Stay right when you reach the Trail 9 fork (later, you'll be returning from the left). Trail 9 eventually swings left (north) along the edge of Furnessville Blowout, revealing the big lake in front of you; it's a short side trip to the water's edge. The trail turns west/left then makes a steep climb to the top of the lakefront dunes. The next three-quarters of a mile is sublime as you wind around trees and up and down the dunes with the huge lake and its lapping waves to your right. The spell is broken briefly when you turn left and start a challenging slog in soft sand to the top of Beach House Blowout, but the payoff is 360 degrees of fantastic views. On clear days, Chicago is visible to the west over Lake Michigan, and a seemingly endless forest unfurls to the south. After a steep descent down the back of the dune and a couple of short climbs, you return to the section of Trail 9 you followed on your outbound trip.

Trail 10

Rating: ★ ★ ★ ★ ★   **Configuration:** Partial Loop
Distance: 5.5 miles   **Difficulty:** Moderate

Tour: Trail 10 offers one of the longer hikes in the Indiana State Park system, especially if you close the loop using one of the several routes available. It's also noteworthy for being relatively level (just one dune climb of any consequence) and visiting the quiet, east end of the park. Wilson Shelter is the best place to park and start. Go north on Trail 8, cross the boardwalk, and turn right when you reach the junction with Trail 10. This level, forested path skirts the north side of the Great Marsh for nearly three miles. Along the way you pass two junctions with Trail 9 and one with Trail 2; the latter takes hikers on a boardwalk across the marsh. After crossing a boardwalk and passing through Paradise Valley, the path reaches the eastern boundary (the land beyond is national park) then turns west and climbs the flanks of Mount Morse before dropping to Lake Michigan. From here, the route follows a long and sometimes lonely stretch of beach; it's more than two miles before you encounter junctions with Trails 4/7, and 8. Trail 10 ends at the latter but both offer return-loop options including a rugged reverse trek on the 3 Dune Challenge. For a longer but flat option, follow Trail 8 along the beach to the swimming area and turn inland along Dunes Creek. Hike along the edge of the parking lot and the paved hike/bike trail. Follow it to Southwest Shelter and the start of Trail 2, which takes you back to Wilson Shelter.

9

Lincoln State Park

I consider myself a serious history buff, have long been interested in Abraham Lincoln, and have visited important Lincoln sites in Illinois and Washington, D.C. Yet despite my interest, I had never until recently explored the 16th president's important Indiana connections at Lincoln State Park and the adjacent Lincoln Boyhood National Memorial. One beautiful fall day, I resolved to fill this experiential gap.

I parked at the state park's Abraham Lincoln Bicentennial Plaza, the perfect trailhead for the hiking tour I had in mind—six miles visiting key Lincoln sites at both the national memorial and state park. After exploring the bicentennial plaza, I walked north on a forest trail, crossed Highway 162, and entered the national memorial.

The trail took me to the visitor's center, which unfortunately was closed. Instead, I walked through a long plaza to the Trail of Twelve Stones, one of the most unusual historic tributes I've ever encountered. Scattered along the woodland path were a dozen rocks from important locations in Lincoln's life. Most were what you'd expect: a stone from the front porch of the house where Lincoln died and a large rock from the Gettysburg battlefield. Others prompted head-scratching: a stone from the building where Lincoln first saw a printing press? Regardless, I found myself looking forward to each mini-monument and wished there were more when I reached the end of the trail.

Next came the Boyhood Nature Trail, which traverses land once owned and farmed by the Lincoln family. Today this is young second-growth forest—nothing like the old growth wilderness that Abe and his father had to clear with axes after they arrived in 1816—but it was still fascinating to consider that the future president grew up here. As I walked, I could see farms and railroad tracks just beyond the forest edge. Much had changed in the past two centuries.

Returning to the main path, I soon reached the living history farm and preserved original Lincoln cabin site. The replica farm was attractive, but quiet; budget cuts had undermined its "living" aspect. The cabin site was an eye-opener. The building's fireplace and foundation had been reproduced in brass. Though the Lincolns later

Abraham Lincoln Bicentennial Plaza near Trail 2 honors our 16th president.

replaced this cabin with larger dwellings, it was still impressive to consider a family of four squeezed into this tiny space and scratching a living out of the wilderness.

A short walk south took me to the pretty cemetery containing the grave of Abe's mother, Nancy Hanks Lincoln. Her death in 1818 was a blow for young Abe but not unusual—early death from disease and injuries was commonplace among pioneer families. After the family moved to Illinois the marker disappeared and the cemetery was swallowed by vegetation, but in 1879 the tombstone was erected by area residents. It took years of work, but eventually the site was protected, maintained, and evolved into the two adjacent parks I was exploring.

After the national memorial, I returned to the state park and continued my search for Lincoln history. Walking south from the bicentennial plaza, I made my way to Trail 5 and Lincoln's Neighborhood Walk. Navigating the looped route clockwise, I passed through a beautiful bottomland forest with many large trees. I suspected that this semiwild area looked nothing like what it did when Abe frequented the somewhat-civilized Little Pigeon Creek Community 200 years ago.

I soon encountered an important place in Lincoln history: the Noah Gorden mill site. Though nothing remained of the pioneer corn-grinding operation, this was where young Lincoln was kicked into unconsciousness by his uncooperative horse and "apparently killed for a time."

To my left, on the far side of a tall fence and locked gate, was a modern-day monument to the president: Lincoln Amphitheater. The popular outdoor venue was built for productions of Lincoln tribute musicals but today thrives thanks to classic rock cover-band concerts. It was quiet on this day, and I hiked on, wondering if Abe would approve of—or even understand—this odd way of celebrating his legacy.

At the end of the forest loop, I reached the state park's historical highlight: Little Pigeon Baptist Church and Cemetery. Abe's father, Thomas Lincoln, built parts of the original church in 1821. The plain white building in front of me was the church's third iteration, dating only to 1948. In the cemetery behind the trim structure was the gravestone for Sarah Lincoln Grigsby, Abe's older sister, who died in childbirth in 1828.

I strolled around the quiet burial ground, which was bathed in late afternoon sun. I paused for a time in one corner of the plot and examined the headstones. All were emblazoned with names and dates that identified these as people who had lived and worked alongside the future president—amazing to consider. While he left this little-known Indiana outpost in 1830, bound for Illinois and future fame, these mostly forgotten citizens had stayed behind and done their part for America, diligently transforming the wilderness into a union worth saving.

Lincoln History

Lincoln is Indiana's most historically significant state park. The property was home turf for the nation's celebrated 16th president and his family from 1816 to 1830. The state park preserves his sister, Sarah's, grave along with other sites that were important to the future president, who lived here from ages seven to 21.

Abe was born in Hardin County, Kentucky, in 1809, two years after Sarah. His father, Thomas, was hard-working, active in community affairs, and a landowner. Unfortunately, he fell victim to Kentucky's chaotic land laws, three times losing property to unclear title claims. He gave up on Kentucky and moved his family to the newly minted state of Indiana, which promised clear title to government-owned property thanks to the Land Ordinance of 1785. Thomas also felt more at home living in an antislavery state.

The family settled on 160 acres near Little Pigeon Creek and started clearing the land for farming. The area, covered with oak-hickory forest, was undoubtedly pretty, but it wasn't the best for farming. This corner of Indiana was skipped by glaciers during the last Ice Age and has only a thin layer of soil over sedimentary bedrock—sandstone, shale, limestone, and coal.

Life was challenging in the young state. In 1818, Abe's beloved mother, Nancy, died of milk sickness, contracted by drinking milk contaminated when the cow ate poisonous white snakeroot. A year later, Thomas married a widow—Sarah Bush Johnston—with three children. She became a nurturing stepmother to Abe and a capable manager of a large and growing household supported by farming and Thomas' carpentry business.

Meanwhile, young Abe grew tall, strong, and adept with both an axe and plow. He was also developing intellectually and socially. Though his formal schooling was limited, his parents encouraged his passion for reading; books were the primary source of his education. In 1828, young Lincoln was hired by James Gentry, the community's leading citizen and owner of its general store, to take a flatboat full of produce to New Orleans. While there, he witnessed a slave auction, an experience that forever changed him. Working occasionally at Gentry's store, an important community gathering place, exposed Lincoln to many viewpoints and fueled his growing interest in politics.

Sadly, 1828 also brought another tragedy to Abe's young life. His sister, Sarah, who in 1826 had married Aaron Grigsby and moved to her own cabin two miles to the south, died while giving birth to her first child. Sarah and her stillborn baby are buried in Little Pigeon Creek cemetery; the grave is not far off Trail 5.

Not long after Sarah's death, in 1830, Thomas sold his property and moved the family, including Abe, to Illinois. Despite many good years in Indiana, the elder Lincoln was lured by the promise of fertile—and easier to clear—prairie land, as well as an escape from the milk sickness that was still threatening the people of Little Pigeon Creek.

Though the Lincolns' Indiana story ended with their move west, Abe's unlikely journey to becoming one of America's greatest presidents fueled an interest in his life that continues to this day. Yet for more than 40 years, the Lincoln property was ignored and decayed, leaving few signs of a previous homestead. In 1871, four Cincinnati businessmen, hoping to capitalize on the late president's fame, bought the property and platted an all-new town, which they named Lincoln City.

For a time, the new town grew and prospered, even becoming an important railroad center. In 1879, located residents located Nancy's grave, erected a tombstone, and convinced the businessmen to donate a half-acre of land around it to Spencer County. A cemetery grew around the grave, and the county later purchased another 16 acres of land. It became a popular park, though maintaining the property was an issue. In 1907, the state assumed oversight of the park and, in 1925, transferred the property to the Department of Conservation.

Meanwhile, fortunes in Lincoln City fell, initiated by a major fire in 1911 and accelerated by the decline of passenger train service. As the town emptied out, interest increased in preserving and expanding the area's Abraham Lincoln heritage. In 1929, Frank Ball—one of the brothers who founded the hugely successful glass canning jar company—bought 30 acres in the area, including the Lincoln cabin and farm site. He deeded the property to the state, which used it to create the Nancy Hanks Lincoln State Memorial.

Desiring to create an even more significant tribute to the president's mother as well as develop recreational resources, the state continued acquiring land south of the Lincoln farm, including the former Little Pigeon Creek community that was central to the Lincolns' lives. In 1932, the property was dedicated as Lincoln State Park.

Trail 1 circumnavigates Lake Lincoln, a popular destination for boaters and fisherman.

From 1933 to 1941, Civilian Conservation Corps crews built out much of the park infrastructure we see today. The largest project was building the dam for Lake Lincoln, but the CCC also built roads, trails, shelters, and the ranger cabin. They also planted trees and undertook erosion control on the played-out former farmland.

In 1962, the Nancy Hanks Lincoln State Memorial was transferred to the federal government and became the Lincoln Boyhood National Memorial. The National Park Service expanded the site to 200 acres by purchasing most of the remaining Lincoln City property. Despite this transfer of property, the state park has grown since its founding through new land acquisitions. Today, it covers 2,029 acres, making Lincoln the 13th largest in Indiana.

Lincoln Today

Lincoln State Park is in southwestern Indiana, 146 miles from Indianapolis. Its relative isolation from major population centers contributes to the fact that the park ranks only 19th in popularity, counting just 267,000 visitors in 2023–2024. But people who make their way to Lincoln are usually surprised by how much it has to offer—a nice mix of history and outdoor recreation, with a little live music thrown in for good measure.

Not surprisingly, Lincoln family history is the star, with highlights including the Bicentennial Plaza, the "Neighborhood Walk" along Trail 5, and the Little Pigeon Baptist Church and grave of Sarah Lincoln Grigsby.

While on the Neighborhood Walk, it's hard not to notice the large performance venue lying to the west: Lincoln Amphitheatre, which opened in 1987. For its first four years, the tribute musical *Young Abe Lincoln* was the amphitheater's only offering, but starting in 1992 popular musicals were also staged. COVID-19 and other challenges threatened the facility's future, but a renovation and expansion (to 2,200 seats) completed in 2025 cemented its place as a top outdoor performance venue. Today, Lincoln Amphitheatre is best known for a robust lineup of classic rock tribute bands and other concerts.

In addition to history and live music, outdoor recreation is also popular at Lincoln State Park. Lake Lincoln is the most popular amenity for many visitors, and the 58-acre reservoir is known for its fishing, swimming, and boating. In 2025, the DNR drained Lincoln Lake to both repair the dam and improve fishing. It may take a couple of years, but the lake promises to be an even better resource after the project. The park is also a stop on the Indiana Birding Trail and has a nature center south of the lake that offers a variety of summertime interpretive programs.

There are multiple options for overnighting in the park. Campers can choose from a variety of 269 sites in three different areas, all north of the lake. The options include 150 full-electric sites, 88 nonelectric sites, and 31 primitive sites, which cater more to tent campers.

The Blue Heron area, just east of the lake, has 10 all-season cabins that each sleep up to six people. The Pine Hills area, near the Nature Center, has 15 rustic (no heat or plumbing) group cottages that sleep anywhere from four to 16 people.

Outside the park, there are multiple lodging options just minutes away, including a Christmas-themed hotel in Santa Claus (three miles east), a local motel in Dale (four miles north), and chain hotels at the I-64 interchange (six miles north).

Hiking Lincoln

Lincoln State Park doesn't offer any spectacular hikes, but it offers several very good ones, making it a great trail destination. There are about 12 miles of numbered routes along with connector segments and hikeable service roads. The footpaths are generally wide, well-signed, and nicely maintained. All the trails are linked; it's possible to park in one spot, start walking, and cover every trail at Lincoln without moving your car.

Lincoln has a couple of nice options for building a long (five-plus mile) hike. On the east side of the park, Trails 1, 2, and 3 connect in multiple ways. One suggested route is to park at Lakeside Shelter and walk straight north on the connector to Trail 2, which makes a two-mile arc in the park's northeast corner. Hike the fire tower route (Trail 1) and Trail 3 before returning to your car via Trail 1's water-level route. On the west side, park near Spring Shelter and head west on Trail 6 to Weber Lake, where there are a couple of junctions with Trail 4. Follow that latter route on a loop out and back from the Gentry Home Site in the northeast corner of the park.

Trail Running

Lincoln is an outstanding trail running destination and well known despite its relative isolation. Don't be surprised to encounter other runners when you are plying its paths.

The shady forest trails and rolling terrain—without being too steep or technical—add to Lincoln's running appeal. Every numbered path offers a good run, but my favorites are Trails 1, 4, and 6. Trail 1 has a wide and level bed (except on the fire tower side trail) and great lake views. I've encountered the local high school cross country team training on this route. Trail 4 has a challenging but engaging roller-coaster profile. Trail 6 is a pretty journey to and around Weber Lake; connect with Trail 4 to create a longer loop.

TRAIL GUIDES

Trail 1

Rating: ★ ★ ★ ★   **Configuration:** Loop (with side trail)
Distance: 1.5 miles   **Difficulty:** Easy (Moderate on fire tower route)

Tour: Trail 1 circumnavigates Lake Lincoln, staying close to the water's edge much of the time. As a result, this hike is both highly scenic and relatively easy—except for the side trip to the fire tower. Campers have direct access to this trail, but non-campers should park by Lakeside Shelter or in the large beach lot. Walk west toward the boat ramp to pick up Trail 1, which begins by crossing the dam. After the spillway bridge, the path passes the first junction with Trail 3 (to the right), makes a sharp left turn, and follows the shoreline not far from the nature center. Beyond the camp, the trail moves inland and passes the second Trail 3 intersection and the side path to the fire tower, a fun but challenging detour. The short, steep climb leads to the historic metal tower, which has some decent views to the northwest but is largely obscured by mature trees. After your climb, either return the way you came to hike all the shoreline route or continue on the detour trail down a series of stairs to a second junction with the main trail. After passing the junction with Trail 2, Trail 1 sticks close to the water for the rest of its route around the lake's upper end. On the lake's north shore, Trail 1 passes the family cabins and electric campground before crossing a small bridge and petering out near the beach parking lot.

Trail 2

Rating: ★ ★ ★ ★   **Configuration:** Partial Loop (complete with Trail 1)
Distance: 3 miles   **Difficulty:** Moderate

Tour: Trail 2 wanders aimlessly through the woods on Lincoln's east side before connecting with Trail 1 near the lake's upper end. My favorite trailhead is Bicentennial Plaza, which has vault toilets and water. Follow the trail north and turn right at the first marked junction onto a twisting path. The second-growth forest has patches of pines mixed in, a product of the CCC era. The area is shaded and smells lovely, but the path is root covered and requires attention for good footing. The trail eventually swings to the right, straightens, and for a half mile follows railroad tracks that cut through the park property. After crossing a small bridge, a highlight appears on the left—a pretty pond, the remnant of a coal mine strip pit. Savor the scene and keep an eye (and ear) open for birds, which are plentiful here. The trail turns sharply to the right and starts the first of two steep climbs up an eroding pathway. En route to the top a shortcut connector to the campground, cabins, and Trail 1 departs to the right. After a long, steady descent—all the way hugging the park boundary—Trail 2 turns west, crosses a languid stream, and ends at Trail 1. Turn left and follow the shore of Lake Lincoln across the dam until you reconnect with Trail 2 near the boat ramp.

Trail 3

Rating: ★ ★ ★   **Configuration:** Point to Point
Distance: 1.7 miles   **Difficulty:** Moderate

Tour: Trail 3 has two endpoints on Trail 1, so it's a logical side trip off that route. If you wish to hike the route by itself, park at the nature center and backtrack on the access road to Trail 3's west end near the spillway bridge. No matter which direction you approach it, Trail 3 is a hefty climb (about 150 feet) followed by a similar descent. The route passes through Sarah Lincoln's Woods Nature Preserve, named in tribute to Abe's older sister who is buried a short distance away. The counterclockwise hike from the west end makes a steady ascent up an eroded trail through a forest with occasional persimmon trees; fallen fruit covers the path in early autumn. You enter the nature preserve, which protects a rare oak barren ecosystem, near the top of the climb. It's a drier forest than seen in other parts of the park and is attractive in all seasons. The

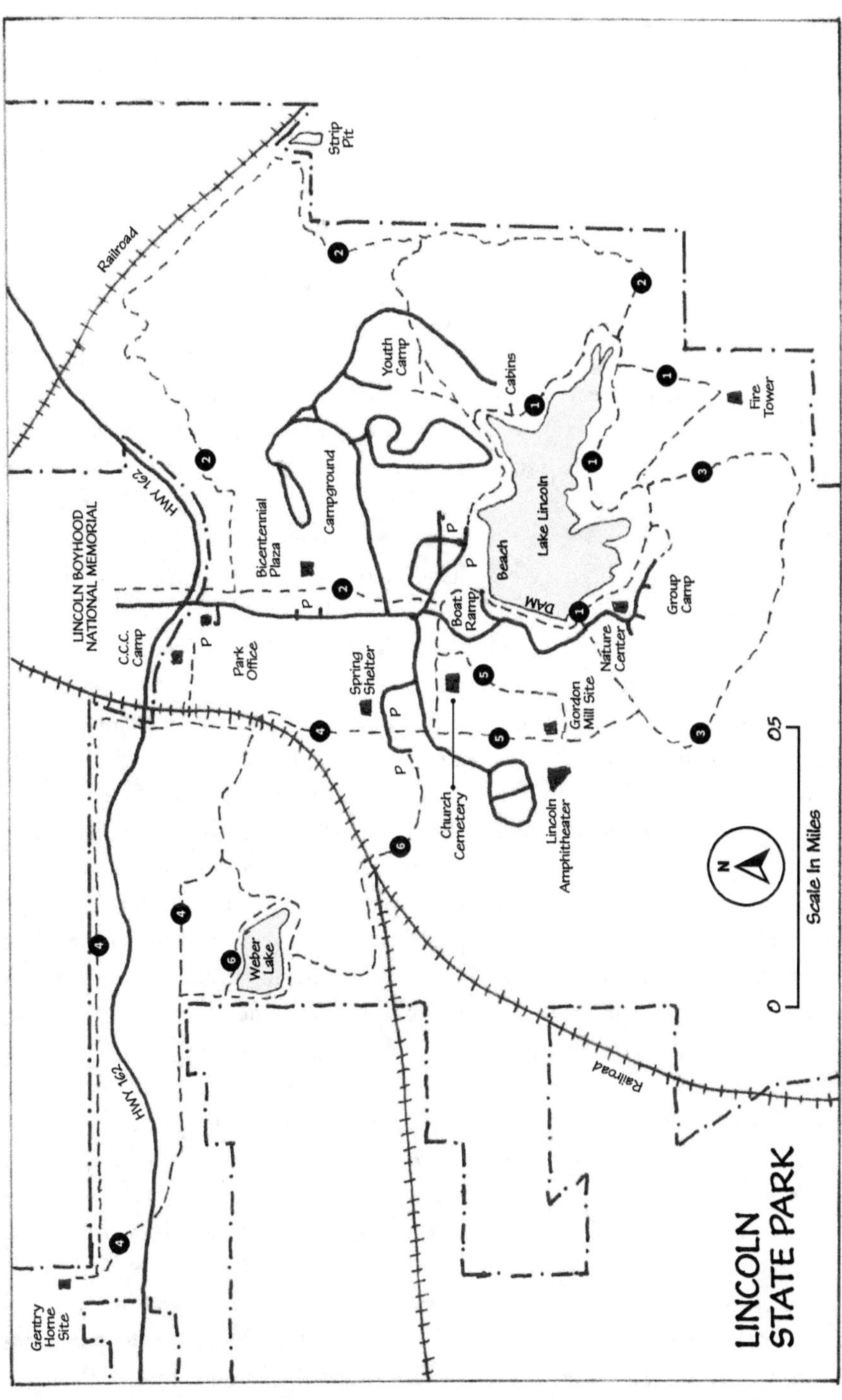

Strip Pit
Railroad
Youth Camp
Cabins
Fire Tower
HWY 162
Campground
Bicentennial Plaza
LINCOLN BOYHOOD NATIONAL MEMORIAL
Lake Lincoln
Beach
DAM
C.C.C. Camp
Park Office
Boat Ramp
Spring Shelter
Group Camp
Nature Center
Gordon Mill Site
Church Cemetery
Lincoln Amphitheater
Weber Lake
HWY 162
Railroad
Gentry Home Site
N
Scale In Miles
O5
O
LINCOLN STATE PARK

eastbound descent is easier than the climb thanks to trail repair and steps created by erosion-control timbers. The route ends at Trail 1. Turn left along the lake to complete a loop to your vehicle or turn right to visit the fire tower and/or hike the long way around Lake Lincoln.

Trail 4

Rating: ★★★　　　　**Configuration:** Lollipop
Distance: 3.7 miles　　　　**Difficulty:** Moderate

Tour: This route follows a roller-coaster profile through the northwest corner of the park, passing the home site of James Gentry, one-time employer of Abe Lincoln. The trail officially begins at a junction with Trail 5 just south of the amphitheater road, but Spring Shelter is a more efficient starting point. Trail 4 heads north into the woods just beyond the playground west of the shelter. The loop starts after the trail crosses railroad tracks; turn left to navigate it clockwise. After a quarter mile you encounter the first of two junctions with Trail 6—paths to pretty Weber Lake, a nice side trip. Trail 4 continues west on a continuous up-down-up profile through the woods, interesting and not too challenging, and probably a very old roadbed. After encountering a gravel county road, the trail follows and crosses Highway 162 to a small parking lot. The Gentry Home Site—today just an open area with a picnic table—is a short distance beyond. Trail 4 turns east from here, closely hugging the park's northern boundary in a thin strip of land between the highway and private farmland. Nonetheless, it's a pretty stretch, rolling like the rest of the trail and featuring some remarkably large trees. Views of barns, grazing cows, and farm ponds beyond the forest add interest. The trail ducks beneath the highway at an overpass for the rail line and follows the tracks back to the start/end of the loop and the return path to your vehicle. Along the way, you pass a side path across the tracks to Lincoln's historic CCC camp. It's interesting to visit though easier to access from the park office.

Trail 5

Rating: ★★★　　　　**Configuration:** Lollipop
Distance: 1.0 miles　　　　**Difficulty:** Easy

Tour: This pleasant walk through the forest probably doesn't look much like it did when Abe lived here but it offers a nice mix of nature and history. NOTE: Ignore any directions that start from the amphitheater; the gate to the trail from there is locked. Instead, park near Lakeside Shelter, walk west on Trail 1 to the boat ramp, then turn north on joint Trail 5/Trail 2. Turn left at the first junction and cross the park road to reach the start of the Trail 5 loop. Turn left and travel clockwise, saving

A state right-of-way marker just south of where Trail 4 passes under Highway 162.

the church and cemetery for last. The next quarter mile winds through a gorgeous bottomland forest, dotted with huge trees, along Buckhorn Creek. After crossing a long boardwalk, you reach the site of the home and mill owned by Noah Gorden, a prominent landowner and businessman during Lincoln's time here. Just beyond, the Lincoln Amphitheater looms on the far side of a tall fence. The trail turns north on a former road, navigating a steep downhill with a long ADA-friendly ramp system. Trail 5 turns right at a junction with the start of Trail 4 then reaches Little Pigeon Baptist Church. Abe's older sister, Sarah, is buried in the cemetery behind the church; her grave has a large, modern marker. Take time to explore the eastern/oldest half of the cemetery before returning to the trail and the walk to your vehicle.

Trail 6

Rating: ★ ★ ★   **Configuration:** Lollipop
Distance: 1.8 miles   **Difficulty:** Easy

Tour: Trail 6 is an pleasant walk through an unremarkable forest, but it has a big payoff at the end: Weber Lake, a wonderful oasis with a great story. Until 1958 it was a coal mine strip pit but was later acquired by the park and rehabilitated. It's the perfect place to include fishing, bird watching, or a picnic as part of a hike. Park at the lot just beyond Spring Shelter; you'll see the trailhead and large interpretive panels on the right. Throughout the walk you'll encounter these panels, which tell the fascinating story of turning a coal mine into thriving, nature-rich lake. The trail is wide, flat, and graveled. It crosses an active rail line, turns north, and delivers you to a fishing dock on the lake's south shore. Turn right to circle the lake counterclockwise; frequent openings offer great water views—watch for waterfowl, wading birds, and bald eagles. The mowed track passes a junction with a side path to Trail 4, crosses a levee on the lake's east end, then circles around its north shore. When the mine closed in the 1950s there was a steep headwall in this area. Today, it is gently sloped and forested, and it's hard to imagine massive excavating machines working here. After passing a second side path to Trail 4, Trail 6 passes the west and south shore before returning to the fishing dock and the route back to your vehicle.

10
McCormick's Creek State Park

Just before midnight on March 31, 2023, an early season tornado hit McCormick's Creek State Park with devastating results. The twister touched down at the park's western boundary near the White River and followed a destructive path to the northeast. The campground took a direct hit and, tragically, two campers were killed. Fortunately, most of the 50 people at the campground that night heard storm sirens and took shelter in a concrete-block bathhouse that was damaged but saved their lives.

After destroying the campground, the tornado tore through the heart of Wolf Cave Nature Preserve, an idyllic woodland and home to the eponymous landmark. The preserve is one of best-loved destinations in the Indiana state park system, but its once-dense canopy of mature hardwoods was leveled in a matter of seconds.

* * *

McCormick's Creek is a special place for me. It was the first Indiana state park I ever visited and, once I moved to Indianapolis, it became a regular hiking and trail running destination for me. In 2023, just a couple months before the tornado, my wife and I celebrated a milestone birthday by staying two nights at the park's Canyon Inn. We were rewarded with two warm winter days that allowed us to hike all over McCormick's Creek.

I was deeply saddened by the news of the tornado. I understand that storms like this are a natural phenomenon and was heartened by the DNR's forward-thinking attitude about the damage. Yes, they would rebuild the campground and salvage the trees that had fallen in that part of the park. (Some were milled into lumber used to restore the historic mill flume at Spring Mill State Park.) But in the nature preserves they were only planning to clear trails and remove snags that appeared to be dangerous. Otherwise, the downed trees and brush—up to ten feet deep in some spots—would be left to decompose according to nature's leisurely timetable. McCormick's Creek would be an ongoing demonstration of the healing power of nature.

McCormick's Creek, with the falls in the distance, accessed by Trail 3.

Regardless of this ray of light in an otherwise sad situation, I couldn't bring myself to visit the park. I knew that one of my favorite hikes was forever altered, or at least for the remainder of my life. But as the second anniversary of the tornado approached, I changed my mind. It was time to witness the destruction firsthand and see how nature was faring.

Two years and one day after the storm, I parked my car near Pine Bluff Shelter and started hiking west on Trail 8. The paved trail was the start of an improvised hike on Trail 5, a large portion of which (along with the primary trailhead) was still closed. I steeled myself for what lay ahead. Forest soon gave way to logs, stumps, brush, devastation. I was overwhelmed.

After taking a minute to compose myself, I moved forward and started taking in my surroundings, which I had hiked through many times before—but today looked nothing like I remembered. The landscape was dominated by a ghost forest of standing trunks that had been stripped clean of limbs. Many trees had just toppled, their dirt-covered root wads standing out as light-brown mounds among the trunks and brush.

The most jarring sight was the stumps and trunks cut into log length by chain saws. It resembled a clearcut, but the intent had been very different—to open and make the area safe for future passage. I was thankful for the effort that had gone into reopening this trail.

As I adjusted to the new landscape, I started to see—and hear—signs of hope and regrowth. Spring wildflowers were emerging everywhere and small trees that had survived the storm were showing their first leaves. Birds were calling from every direction: titmice, chickadees, cardinals, towhees, and especially woodpeckers, which thrive in disturbed environments liked these. The storm had caused an explosion of life fueled by the death of the large trees—nature's natural cycle.

Soon I crossed a bridge and seemingly passed back in time two years: I had entered a section of the nature preserve that had escaped the tornado, the beautiful forest intact. Twin Bridges and the bottom entrance to Wolf Cave appeared ahead. Litten Branch flowed to my right, passing below a scenic rock wall and a forest hillside covered with emerging wildflowers: twinleaf, cutleaf toothwort, and the first May apple sprouts. Some of the best sights along the trail had been saved.

After making an obligatory visit to the cave's upper entrance, I reached the end of the trail's open section. Turning around, I started my return trip; my hike back into the storm zone wasn't as jarring as before. Listening to the birds and searching for new wildflowers, I realized that I had already found the positive in what had happened. "I need to see this place in the summertime," I told myself as I soaked in the sun and strolled contentedly back to my car.

McCormick's Creek History

McCormick Creek was Indiana's first state park—but that wasn't the original plan. Richard Lieber, the first Indiana Conservation Commission chair, intended to launch the system with Turkey Run. When he ran into snags finalizing that property's acquisition, he changed plans. The first small section of McCormick's Creek was purchased, and it was dedicated as the first Indiana state park on July 4, 1916, as part of the state's ongoing centennial celebration.

The property contained within McCormick's Creek's borders had a rich and varied journey to becoming a state park. With geologic features—the canyon, waterfall, caves, sinkholes, and more—anchoring the park's popularity, it's appropriate to explore how the rocks underlying the park came to be. About 250 million years ago, the area was covered by a warm, shallow sea. As sediments accumulated at the bottom of the sea, they were compressed over millions of years into three distinct layers of limestone, visible at different places in the park.

Over time, the rock layers were lifted by tectonic forces of the earth's crust, covered with glaciers, then scoured by water rushing off the melting ice. The result was the deep, rugged canyon of McCormick's Creek. Water flowing *through* the limestone dissolved the rock away, creating sinkholes, caves, springs, and other features that are visible as you hike. This landscape is known as karst topography. McCormick's Creek sits at the north end of a narrow but active karst zone that runs southeast into Kentucky.

Humans eventually made their way into what is now the state park. Native tribes, including the Delaware, Miami, and Potawatomi, hunted and camped in this area. The first white property owner was the park's namesake, John McCormick, a Revolutionary War veteran who acquired a parcel as payment for his military service on September 1, 1816. Ironically, McCormick never may have visited the property, which passed to his daughter and two sons when he died in 1837.

Thomas and Hudson McCormick both operated mills on the creek, though neither venture was successful because of unpredictable and intermittent streamflow. Daughter, Nancy, meanwhile, fared better: she and husband, Jesse Peden, and later their son, Tom, farmed about 100 acres near modern-day Trail 9. Remnants of the Peden house, barn, and spring house can be explored while hiking the trail. Nancy is credited with naming Wolf Cave thanks to the (likely apocryphal) legend of her being chased by wolves while returning from either a trading trip to Spencer or doing laundry in the creek.

Several other early settlers established homesteads in the park and tried to scratch out a living as farmers. Houses were located near Beech Grove Shelter (built by Artemus Pratt), the falls (Sidney Hendrick), falls overlook parking lot (Marion

Laymon), and the campground (Harrison Bean). A schoolhouse was located near the site of the stone arch bridge.

With limestone becoming popular in building construction, a quarry was established on what is now the park property in 1878. It grew quickly and employed up to 75 men at a time. At its peak, what become known as Statehouse Quarry was surrounded by a small village of 13 buildings and served by a spur from the railroad line on the opposite bank of the White River. Huge limestone blocks were cut from the quarry, hauled out by rail, and used to build the foundation and basement of the Indiana capitol building. Despite its initial success, the operation lasted just two years because the rail bridge was knocked out repeatedly by river flooding. The owners finally gave up and let nature take back the quarry site. Hikers can see it today with a short side trip off Trail 2. The remnants of the rail bridge are visible during low water just downstream of where Trail 7 meets the White River.

About the time the quarry closed, the area caught the attention of Indianapolis physician, minister, and entrepreneur Frederick Denkewalter. He visited while recovering from sunstroke and was impressed by the healing power of the natural setting. He purchased 90 acres of land, including an old farmhouse on the site of modern-day Canyon Inn that he converted into a sanitarium. It was a hit with visitors looking for a place to rest and recuperate, part of a national obsession with the reputed healing properties of mineral-rich waters. Denkewalter expanded the old farmhouse twice, adding large porches and beautifully landscaping the surrounding grounds. He also bought more property, eventually accumulating 374 acres, quit his medical practice, and became a full-time resort manager.

Denkewalter died in 1914, and his family planned to sell the property at auction. This development concerned local citizens; the canyon and its environs had become a popular recreation destination during the sanitarium era. Enter Richard Lieber, who was looking for a place to establish a state park and saw a promising opportunity at McCormick's Creek. Lieber helped Owen County raise its portion of the purchase price and convinced state leaders to contribute the rest of the money. After the land acquisition was finalized, the Indiana state park system was formally launched on July 4, 1916.

The small park at dedication was a far cry from the much larger property we visit today. Expansion by purchasing adjacent homesteads and farms continued until 1951, when the area around what is now Deer Run Shelter was added and the park reached its current 1,961 acres. Significant changes were made from 1933 to 1935, when Civilian Conservation Corps Company 589 lived and worked in the park. In less than two years, the young men built the gatehouse, many of the trails, the fire tower, and the beautiful Stone Arch Bridge. The CCC Recreation Hall, still standing near the start of Trail 2 is the only building remaining from the worker's camp.

Nature is already rebounding along Trail 5 from the devastation of the 2023 tornado.

The former sanitarium became the Canyon Inn and over the years was remodeled, new brick siding added, and new wings built—but all resting on the original farmhouse foundations. Today, the building is a beautiful and comfortable lodge and, with great access to trails, a popular place for hikers to stay. The inn was also a favorite of Richard Lieber, who passed away while staying there in 1944.

McCormick's Creek Today

McCormick's Creek is about a 60-mile drive from downtown Indianapolis and a half-hour northwest of Bloomington. The proximity to population centers and excellent scenery make it popular. Prior to the 2023 tornado it was attracting more than 600,000 visitors annually, eighth most in the park system. It may take a few years and lots of rebuilding to return to these levels, but it will happen. To avoid summer weekend crowds, consider visiting early mornings, weekdays, and in the cold-weather months, when McCormick's Creek is still a great hiking destination.

Enjoying nature is by far the No. 1 activity at McCormick's Creek. The spring wildflower bloom is one of the best in the state. The park is a noted stop on the

Indiana Birding Trail and popular with birders year-round. Wildlife lovers will encounter species that are typical of Indiana forests, including white-tailed deer, red fox, and raccoons. Fishing is allowed in the White River, with smallmouth bass and channel catfish popular quarry.

More civilized activities are also popular at the park. The Olympic-sized swimming pool is open from Memorial Day to Labor Day, and tennis, volleyball, and basketball courts are all located near Canyon Inn. Horseback trail rides are offered at the saddle barn, which was closed for renovation in 2025 but scheduled to reopen in 2026.

McCormick's Creek has many options for an overnight stay inside the park. The campground remained closed in 2025 but is being rebuilt and upgraded. It will likely reopen in 2028. The park also has 16 family cabins in the southwest corner of the park, including the newer and large Sunset and Centennial cabins. Trails 1 and 2 both start in the cabin area.

The lodging highlight at McCormick's Creek is historic Canyon Inn, which has 76 rooms, a quality restaurant, and ample rustic but comfortable lounging areas. The inn is centrally located for hikers and offers easy access to most of the trails.

If you don't stay in the park, your best bet for overnight lodging is to explore one of the many options in Bloomington. Spencer, just two miles west of the park, has many charms, including several restaurants and a microbrewery.

Hiking McCormick's Creek

Before the 2023 tornado, McCormick's Creek was one of the premier hiking destinations in the Indiana state park system. The tremendous and varied scenery has always been a big draw, but the park also has some of the best-maintained trails in the state.

Post-tornado, things have changed on many routes. As of 2026, Trails 6, 7, and 10 were fully closed and Trails 5 and 8 partially closed, with no public timetable for reopening. The closed routes will likely reopen when reconstruction work on the campground is completed. Keep track of current trail status by visiting the DNR's McCormick's Creek website and downloading the most recent trail map, on which open and closed routes are clearly marked.

Is McCormick's Creek still worth visiting? Absolutely! It is one of the best places to hike in Indiana. Most of the park's trails were untouched by the storm, and others have been cleared and reopened to hiking. All the trails in McCormick's Cove Nature Preserve, in the southwest corner of the park, are open, providing multiple routes through one of Indiana's most beautiful forests. Popular Trail 3 to and through the canyon is open and as stunning as ever. Many people ignore Trail 9 but now is a good time to explore this pretty loop with a history lesson, as it passes near the Peden Farm site.

Trail Running

McCormick's Creek is a popular trail running destination. My son was introduced to the park when his college cross country team held summer training camp at the park; its hilly trails were a good test for the young runners.

The north trails—5, 6, 7, and 8 surrounding the campground—comprise my favorite running route, more than six miles with connector sections. At this writing, these trails are mostly closed but expect them to reopen with the renovated campground. Pine Bluff Shelter is a good starting point if you're not camping.

The south trails —1, 2, 3, 4, and 10—are more scenic but challenging. Trails 1, 2, and 4 comprise a hilly, forested loop about three miles long. Add distance with Trails 3 and 10. Both have long segments on the bed of McCormick's Creek and are arguably not run friendly, especially if the water is high. Walk them if you must—while enjoying some of the best scenery in the state.

TRAIL GUIDES

NOTE: *The following guides were written with a nod to the past and an eye to future. Some descriptions use information acquired during pre-tornado hikes. This book was published with the hope that all the trails will eventually reopen, and the information provided will remain valid. Regardless, check the McCormick's Creek website or visit the park office to determine a trail's status before you plan to hike it.*

Trail 1

Rating: ★ ★ ★   **Configuration:** Loop (using road)
Distance: 0.5 miles   **Difficulty:** Moderate

Tour: Trail 1 starts and ends at two different places in the Family Cabin Area. The nearest public parking is at the Friendly Recreation Area. From there, walk along the edge of the road toward the cabins. To walk the loop counterclockwise, pass the first Trail 1 access and start on the second one, just before Sunset Cabin. The trail takes a relatively straight path downhill from the road, paralleling a ravine on the left. The trail turns abruptly, goes down into the ravine, then immediately starts climbing out of it. The steep uphill will slow you down but take time to appreciate your surroundings. McCormick's Cove Nature Preserve includes many large trees and in the spring the forest floor is carpeted with wildflowers. The short hike ends all too quickly at the access you passed earlier in the Family Cabin Area. Turn right on the road to return to your car or consider extending your hike by turning left to find the start of Trail 2.

MCCORMICK'S CREEK STATE PARK

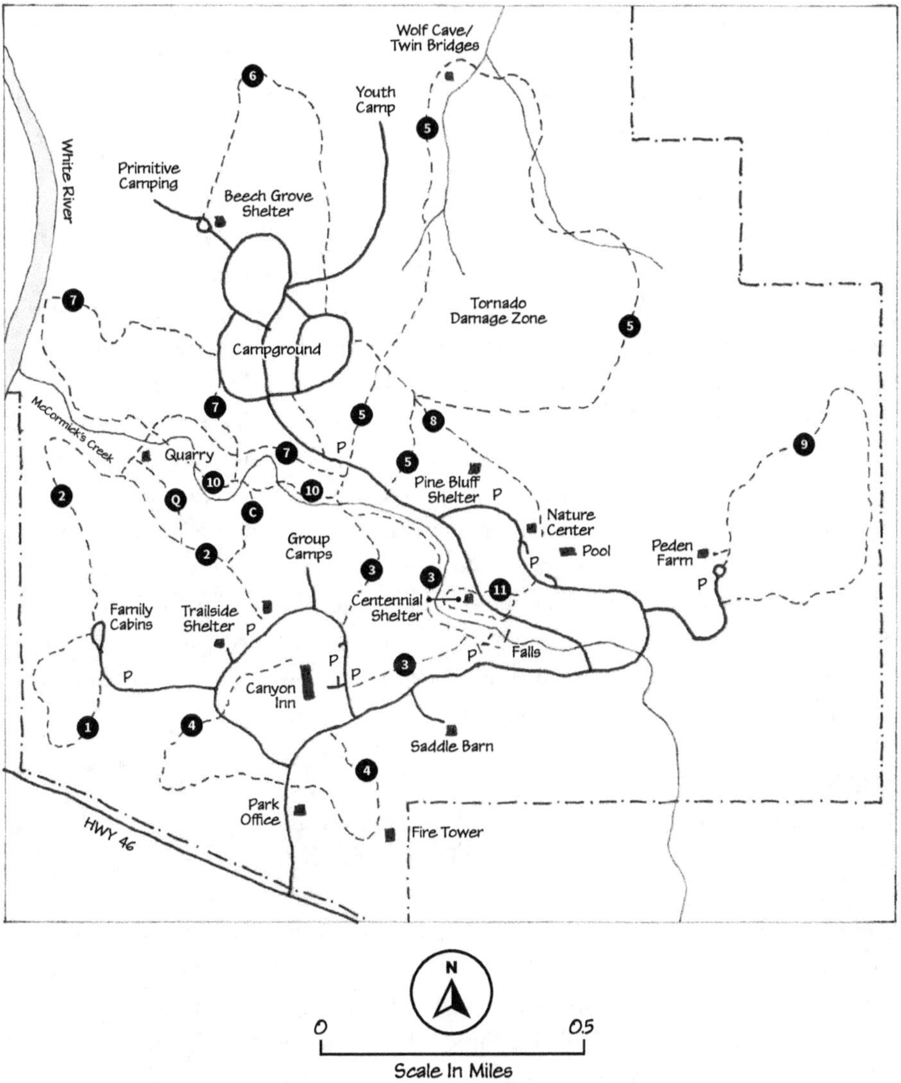

Trail 2 (plus Quarry Loop)

Rating: ★ ★ ★ ★   **Configuration:** Point to Point
Distance: 1.0 miles   **Difficulty:** Moderate
(plus .25 miles on Quarry Loop)

Tour: Trail 2 is a great hike for exploring both natural and human history. Start next to Trailside Shelter, north of Canyon Inn, parking near the preserved CCC Recreation Hall. The trailhead is on the west side of the shelter. Trail 2 descends steadily from the ridgetop into a deep valley. A connector trail to the right (noted as "C" on the map) leads to Trail 10; this route was still closed in 2026. Large hardwoods appear, a sign you have crossed into McCormick's Cove Nature Preserve. The first Quarry Loop trail (noted as "Q" on the map) departs to the right after about a quarter mile. Continue past it and turn right at the second Quarry Loop sign. A short walk takes you to a jumble of huge moss-covered rocks and a small pond—the remains of the quarry. Trail 10 (still closed in 2026) connects here and makes a water crossing to the opposite bank of nearby McCormick's Creek. Returning to Trail 2, the path enters a wet riparian forest dominated by sycamores of all ages. This also marks the edge of the damage zone from the 2023 tornado, which clipped the north end of the nature preserve. The trail has been cleared and opened, but there are no plans to remove the massive sycamores felled by the storm. Not far from the White River (just out of sight) Trail 2 turns abruptly southward and starts climbing, a relentless 200 feet in just a half mile. Soon, cabins appear on the ridge above you; the trail passes between two structures and ends abruptly at the road. You can turn around and retrace your steps, turn right to access Trail 1 (next to Sunset Cabin) or follow roads for a half mile back to your car, turning left at the intersection.

Trail 3

Rating: ★ ★ ★ ★ ★   **Configuration:** Loop
Distance: 0.8 miles   **Difficulty:** Challenging

Tour: Trail 3 is short but offers some of the most spectacular scenery in Indiana. Park in the lot on the right across from the Canyon Inn. Start at the trailhead down the road, next to the stone restroom. As you walk through the open woods, the faint sound of the falls portends highlights ahead. The trail turns abruptly and drops down a 116-step staircase that deposits you at the bottom of McCormick's Creek Canyon next to an intersection with Trail 10 (still closed in 2026). Turn right to stay on Trail 3, which follows a limestone ledge along the water. The creek dances its way downstream next to you, cascading over low drops and around rocks on its way to the White River. Steep, rocky bluffs rise overhead in some areas; dense forests come to

The quarry, just off Trail 2, that supplied stones for the Indiana capitol building.

the water's edge in others. The trail turns right, away from the water, and passes near a small stone shelter. An unofficial trail, passable in low water, follows the creek to the falls. Instead, follow the official Trail 3 up a staircase to the blufftop for an elevated perspective on the canyon. Continue straight, passing two side trails to the right, to reach the stairs back to canyon. Before descending, follow the side trail ahead to an elevated viewpoint of the falls. The twisting concrete staircase drops you on a big slab next to the water. You have a nice view of the falls but may be tempted to get closer, which will require some rock-hopping. Returning to the top of the stairs, turn right. Walk past the wide staircase and take the second left, marked with a Trail 3 sign. This short climb takes you back to the parking lot.

Trail 4

Rating: ★ ★ ★ ★　　　　**Configuration:** Loop
Distance: 1.4 miles　　　　**Difficulty:** Moderate

Tour: This is great hike for Canyon Inn guests because both ends of the path are a short walk from the front entrance. If you're not staying at the inn follow the parking instructions for Trail 3. Walk out the inn access, turn right on the main park road, and look to the left for the Trail 4 start. After a short downhill section, the trail climbs though a hardwood forest on, then parallel to, a service road. After the surroundings shift to a mature pine plantation, the fire tower makes an appearance through the trees. The 86-foot tower, built in 1935, looks rickety but it's quite sturdy thanks to a 2018–2019 restoration. The climb to the top is fun but the rejuvenated forest limits the view. After the tower, Trail 4 winds downward through the woods to a road crossing adjacent to the park office. The path continues its downhill course on the hillside of a narrow valley with a small stream; note the remnants of a deconstructed boardwalk that mark Trail 4's former water-level path. The trail enters McCormick's Cove Nature Preserve, hits its low point, turns sharply right, and starts climbing. The surroundings are gorgeous, punctuated by large hardwoods and wildflowers in spring. The path steepens, using switchbacks to gain elevation. Civilization returns as Trail 4 crosses a road and follows the forest edge next to a large, grassy recreational field. Turning back into the woods, the trail passes multiple sinkholes, indicative of the area's Karst topography. Canyon Inn appears through the trees to the right; the trail ends near the swimming pool at the north end of the building.

Trail 5

Rating: ★ ★ ★ ★ ★   **Configuration:** Loop
Distance: 2.0 miles (full loop)   **Difficulty:** Moderate

Tour: Trail 5 was long known as the path to Wolf Cave as well as one of the most beautiful woodland hikes in Indiana. The March 2023 tornado changed this route dramatically, leveling most of the trees in Wolf Cave Nature Preserve. As of 2026, only a portion of the trail had been cleared and reopened. The original trailhead (small and lacking a toilet) is located on the main park road near the campground. The new access, via Trail 8, has always been a better option. Park at the Pine Bluff Shelter lot; Trail 8 is on the far side of the grassy area, near the vault toilet. Go left (northwest) into the woods. Sinkholes can be seen on either side of the trail. The trees are soon replaced by open skies, stumps, logs, and debris as you enter the storm zone and turn right at the junction with Trail 5. (Turning left from here, when allowed in the future, takes you to the park road and the Wolf Cave parking lot.) For a short distance the trail passes through remnants of the original forest before turning into the heart of the storm zone and making several small-stream crossings. A bridge marks the edge of the storm zone and a return to the beautiful riparian forest that was only minimally impacted by the tornado. Soon, the trail's best-known highlights—Twin Bridges and the lower entrance to Wolf Cave appear on the left. To your right is a beautiful scene: Littens Branch flowing northward below a low rocky wall. Follow the wide, stepped trail up the hill to reach to top entrance to Wolf Cave. Crawling through the cave is allowed, if you're so inclined. As of 2026, Trail 5 was blocked beyond here, but it continues south for another mile to the parking lot, along the way crossing Trail 8 again.

Trail 6

Rating: ★★   **Configuration:** Partial Loop
Distance: 0.6 miles   **Difficulty:** Easy

Tour: Trail 6 is a simple near loop with both ends in or near the campground; a quarter mile of road walking turns it into a full loop. The trail and campground were severely damaged in the 2023 tornado; both remained closed in 2026. Trail 6 starts behind the CCC-era Beech Grove Shelter, which sits between the main campground and the primitive camping area. The path heads downhill through the forest on a straight, wide course. At the edge of the cutover bottomlands that make up the nondescript northern corner of the park, the trail turns right/east to stay in the woods and climb back to the uplands. After crossing the road to the youth tent area, the trail ends in the campground between sites 19 and 20. Turning right takes hikers back to Beech Grove Shelter; turning left leads to the start of Trail 8 and alternate access and parking options.

Trail 7

Rating: ★★★   **Configuration:** Lollipop
Distance: 1.8 miles   **Difficulty:** Moderate

Tour: Trail 7 is the park's only path to the While River. Unfortunately, part of the trail lies in the tornado damage zone and remained closed as of 2026. The trail starts across the road from the Wolf Cave parking area, the trailhead for Trail 5. Head west along the blufftop with a steep drop into McCormick's Creek Canyon to your left. After a tenth of a mile a connector path to the campground departs to the right and the trail starts its descent into the canyon. After climbing a short rise, the trail reaches a junction. To the left is a long stairway connector down to Trail 10 in the canyon bottom. To the right is the campground via the Trail 7 loop. Stay straight for the direct route to the river along the north bank of the creek. Another connector with Trail 10 departs to the left and crosses the creek to the Old Quarry and Trail 2. Note that this is a challenging crossing, impassable when the water is high. As Trail 7 breaks out into the bottomlands and turns away from the creek it passes through the tornado damage zone before reaching and following the White

River for a short distance. Turning away from the river, Trail 7 climbs out of the valley, reenters the storm damage zone, and joins a service road for part of the trip. (The road provides access to a wastewater treatment facility that has been on your right for the last half mile.) Trail 7 temporarily ends in the campground; turn right and follow the road a short distance to access the remaining section of the loop trail back to the start.

Trail 8

Rating: ★★   **Configuration:** Point to Point
Distance: 0.7 miles   **Difficulty:** Easy (ADA Accessible)

Tour: Trail 8 is a utilitarian, ADA accessible path that allows campers to access important park amenities like the Nature Center and pool. The western third of the trail was in the path of the 2023 tornado and closed as of 2026, though the remaining open section took on a new role as the only way to access Trail 5. Day hikers interested in walking the full path should park at the north end of the pool lot. Trail 8 starts by the concession stand, passes behind the Nature Center, and continues as a straight, level path near Pine Bluff Shelter before entering a beautiful forest dotted with sinkholes. As of 2026, the trail ended at the first intersection with Trail 5, which continues to the right/north. Trail 8 proceeds to the northwest, toward the campground, now clearly visible with the forest cover gone. Trail's end comes shortly after the second intersection with Trail 5.

Trail 9

Rating: ★★   **Configuration:** Loop
Distance: 1.2 miles   **Difficulty:** Easy

Tour: Trail 9, located in the east side of the park and isolated from the main trail network, is overlooked by most day hikers. Scenically, it pales in comparison to most McCormick's Creek trails, but it's an easy, pleasant walk with an interesting history lesson. Drive past Deer Run Shelter and park in the lot on the right by the trailhead. The route passes through a variety of landscapes, including mature forests with occasional sinkholes and young woodlands on former farmland. Trail 9 intersects twice with the bridle trail, which temporarily was opened to hiking in 2025 when the saddle barn closed for maintenance. After the second bridle trail intersection, look for the sign and narrow path to the historic Peden farm site. Exploring the stone remnants of the house, barn, and spring house is a worthwhile side trip. Trail 9 ends on the access road just north of the parking area where you started.

Trail 10

Rating: ★ ★ ★ **Configuration:** Point to Point with connectors
Distance: 0.7 miles **Difficulty:** Challenging

Tour: Trail 10 is a beautiful path at the mercy of McCormick's Creek, limiting its use when the water is high. As of 2026, the trail remained closed. It lies outside the tornado damage zone, but key connector paths were closed after the storm. Once Trail 10 reopens, its best access is from the Wolf Cave parking lot. Cross the road and turn left where Trail 7 turns right and descend the large wooden stairway into McCormick's Creek canyon. At the bottom, an alternative access from Trail 3 on the south bank is available during low water. (This is a good place to gauge whether the remainder of Trail 10 will be passable.) Turn right and follow the creek downstream. Though the canyon is shallower here than near the falls upstream, it's still beautiful, with low rocky bluffs and dense forest. After the first of four stream crossings, another trail intersects from the left. It goes uphill and connects with Trail 2 near its start, creating an opportunity for a return loop using another connection by the Quarry. After the second creek crossing, a large stairway from Trail 7, connects on the right. Going straight up from here leads to the west side of the campground. Trail 10 leaves the creek temporarily, cuts off a meander with a straight route up and over a low ridge, crosses the water again, tops a second rise, and goes across the water one last time before approaching its end point. From here, hikers have three options: turn around retrace your steps upstream; turn right and use Trail 7 for a return loop to your car; or turn left, cross the creek by the Quarry, and use the Trail 2 return loop mentioned previously.

Trail 11

Rating: ★ ★ **Configuration:** Lollipop
Distance: 0.5 miles **Difficulty:** Easy (ADA Accessible)

Tour: Even as some trails remained closed by damage from the 2023 tornado, McCormick's Creek added new mileage in 2024 with the help of funding from the state and the local community foundation. Trail 11—aka the Echo Canyon Trail—is an ADA accessible loop around Centennial Shelter with an extension to the Redbud Shelter and Nature Center. Park either at Centennial Shelter (the official starting point) or near the Nature Center The short trail, protected by new fencing, hugs the blufftop and offers views into the chasm also known as McCormick's Creek Canyon.

11

Mounds State Park

At just 290 acres, Mounds is Indiana's second smallest state park; only Falls of the Ohio covers less ground. But within its small footprint, Mounds packs a rich and fascinating human history—one dating back more than 2,000 years. For that fact alone, Mounds is worth a visit. Throw in a beautiful natural environment, an excellent trail system, and other visitor amenities, and you realize that Mounds is an often-overlooked little jewel of the state park system.

My wife, Tari, and I made the drive from Indianapolis to Mounds a few years ago to enjoy a couple of hours on the trails. We parked at the lot by the Pavilion, not far from the Visitor's Center. Before hiking, we took a short tour of the center, a recommended stop on your first trip to Mounds. The exhibits provide a nice overview of the park's rich human and natural history, which you experience first-hand as you explore the trail system.

We departed on the path leaving the southwest corner of the Pavilion parking lot, turned left onto Trail 2, and navigated the boardwalk through the pretty, forested glen behind the Visitor's Center. The segment ended at Trail 1; the Great Mound, the park's best-known feature, was directly in front of us. We followed the trail to the left to find interpretive signage and the entry point to the center of the mound.

The Great Mound is fascinating, especially when you consider it has survived two millennia—including two decades in the middle of an amusement park! As we stood in the middle of the doughnut-shaped mound, we imagined Adena people gathering for religious ceremonies based on celestial observations of the night sky. Then we thought about the fact that a century ago a children's train ran around the mound and a roller-coaster was standing nearby—mind-boggling.

After exploring the mounds, we followed signs directing us to the White River and discovered a connector heading down the bluff to Trail 5. This wide, level, gravel-covered path follows the riverbank for about a mile. It's arguably the park's hiking highlight, offering great views.

The boardwalk to the center of the Great Mound is accessed by Trail 1.

After traveling just above the water for about a half-mile, Trail 5 turned inland then made a steep climb to the blufftop. We were rewarded with impressive viewpoints that are especially good when the leaves are off the trees. Beyond this point, we crossed the main park road and climbed northeastward as part of a loop near the campground. At an intersection with Trail 4, we turned right, using a boardwalk and stairs to cross a beautiful, forested valley with a small stream.

After hiking along the opposite side of the valley, we recrossed the road and retraced our steps —downhill this time—on the steep section of Trail 5. Then we turned left on Trail 3 for the return trip to our car. Trail 3 is a network of parallel forest paths between the White River blufftop and the main park road, so it offers multiple trip options.

The route we chose on the fly ended up being a pleasant three-mile journey. We also realized that we had covered less than half of the park's trail mileage and still hadn't visited all highlights. A return visit to Mounds State Park was definitely in our future.

Mounds History

The human history at Mounds State Park can be traced back more than 2,000 years. The property contains the remains of ten earthworks—the "mounds" of the park's name—that were constructed by indigenous people who once lived in eastern Indiana. Researchers have determined that this part of the state once contained 300 such earthworks. Only 100 remain (most have been destroyed by farming and excavation) and Mounds is one of only two sites that remain relatively unharmed.

Archaeologists have conducted intensive studies at the Mounds earthworks and trace the first activity to around 250 BC. The ditch and embankment that now make up the Great Mound—which is as wide as a football field is long—were constructed in stages, starting around 160 BC. The park's earthwork construction has been tied to the so-called Adena people, named for an archaeological site in Ohio. Adena culture thrived from about 500 BC to 100 AD.

While we will never know for sure, the mounds' purpose was likely ceremonial. The Great Mound and nearby structures align with several important celestial events, including the summer and winter solstices. It appears that the mounds were used as ceremonial sites for a relatively short time, then fell into long-term disuse. About 500 years after the Adena, people from the Hopewell culture (named for another Ohio archaeological site) were living in the area and used the Great Mound as a burial site.

Fast forward to the 19th Century. In 1849, pioneer Frederick Ronnenberg acquired 600 acres, including the land on which the state park sits, and began farming the northern part of the property. He protected the Great Mound and other earthworks on the south end of the property and in 1853 built a beautiful brick farmhouse nearby; it still stands and is periodically open for tours.

Three decades later, an improbable boom-and-bust cycle started that forever changed the world around the Great Mound. In 1876 the huge Trenton natural gas field was discovered in eastern Indiana. A decade later the first commercial well was drilled, soon followed by countless others. Once-sleepy towns like Anderson, just a few miles west of the Ronnenberg farm, were transformed overnight. Factories sprouted, lights illuminated every corner (day and night), and seemingly needless flames flickered everywhere. The resource seemed inexhaustible and brought incredible wealth to the area.

The now-prosperous residents of eastern Indiana started looking for recreation, and the Mounds soon caught their eye. At first just a popular daytrip destination, entrepreneurs had other plans. In 1897 the Indiana Union Traction Company purchased the southern part of the Ronnenberg property and built an interurban railroad and station to transport patrons to the area. The company then started developing an amusement park around the earthworks. The park included a two-story pavilion with restaurant, skating rink, boat docks, bowling alley, shooting gallery, merry-go-round, and, just west of the Great Mound, a 41-foot-tall roller-coaster called Leap the Dips. A miniature railroad, popular with children, circled the Great Mound. Round trip train fare from Anderson cost a nickel and included admission to the park.

Trail 4 uses a long boardwalk to cross a pretty valley south of the campground.

By 1912 gas reserves started to play out and eastern Indiana faced an uncertain economic future as businesses dependent on the cheap fuel closed or moved away. For a time, the Mounds amusement park stayed open, but visitors dwindled. Indiana Union Traction suspended rail service in the early 1920s. By 1923 the park was silent—but as one era closed on the Mounds another was just beginning.

Interest in keeping the property open as a park was high and the Madison County Historical Society started raising money with that goal in sight. In 1926 the organization purchased the land and deeded it to the county, which in turn gave the property to the state on the condition that it become a state park. The state was happy to comply, and Mounds State Park was dedicated on October 7, 1930.

Mounds Today

Mounds State Park is located 47 miles northeast of downtown Indianapolis, an easy one-hour drive via Interstates 70, 465, and 69. The park packs a lot into a small area and history takes center stage. Plan to stop at the Visitor's Center for a good introduction. While there, inquire about interpretive naturalist programming, which is available year-round. During the warm months, tours of the Ronnenberg House are also offered.

Trail 5 is a wide, level pathway in this beautiful stretch along the White River.

The White River forms the park's western boundary, and it is probably its most underutilized resource. Fishing is good in this area, especially for smallmouth bass and channel catfish. There is a canoe/kayak launch at the north end of the park but no rentals are available. At least one local outfitter offers float trips that pass through the park.

Mounds is a noted stop on the Indiana Birding Trail and welcomes a wide variety of migrators, especially in April/May and September/October. The forested corridor along the river is also a haven for mammals. Deer, red fox, squirrels, and more will delight wildlife watchers.

Camping is the only option for an overnight stay at Mounds. The main campground, in the far northeast corner of the park, is all electric and offers 75 sites. There is also a small tent area for youth groups. The campground connects to Trails 4, 5, and 6 for hikers. For non-campers, Anderson offers several hotel options near the interchanges on Interstate 69.

In recent years, Mounds has gained fame for its large, drive-through holiday light show. The Mounds' Friends group coordinates the event, which is an important fundraiser. In 2023 more than 4,500 cars paid for the privilege of driving past 67 displays set up in the park campground.

Hiking Mounds

Despite its relatively compact size, Mounds has a varied and challenging 6-mile trail network that can keep day hikers entertained for several hours—especially if they take the time to absorb the history of the area as they navigate the paths. Many of the pathways are not traditional point-to-point trails. Instead look at the park as having a web of walking paths that, when pieced together in different ways, offer hikers a variety of routes.

Parking for hikers is not an issue, nor is deciding where to park. There are a half-dozen lots spread out along the length of the main park road, and walkers can easily jump on a trail from any of them.

Trail Running

Despite its limited network of paths, Mounds is a favorite of central Indiana trail runners. The routes offer good footing, enough hills to make things interesting (but not too challenging), and connectivity allowing runners to easily piece together a length of trail that suits their needs for any outing. The DINO trail running series offers an annual race at Mounds in March with 5K and 15K distances and the Run the Mounds race in November has 5K and 5-mile distances.

TRAIL GUIDES

Trail 1

Rating: ★ ★ ★ ★

Distance: 1.0 miles

Configuration: Multiple Loops

Difficulty: Easy

Tour: Park near the visitor's center and start your trip inside to immerse yourself in the history of the area. After viewing the exhibits, depart to the south and walk past Bronnenberg House on the paved path leading to Trail 1, a mile of looped pathways through an open woodland at the south end of the park. Note that the southernmost trails are labeled 1A, while the northern loop is 1B. As you walk in this area, take your time to soak in the sights, sounds, and history. Multiple interpretive signs provide context. Indiana native trees are also marked, providing a natural history lesson as well. The focal point of Trail 1 is the Great Mound, but three other earthworks—including the uniquely shaped Fiddle Back Mound—are encountered as you walk. Keep your eyes open for signs of more recent human use—crumbling concrete and other partially hidden structures that mark the location of the amusement park and interurban station that occupied this site a century ago. Trail 1 connects with both Trail 2 and Trail 5 (in two places) if you want to extend your hike to other areas of the park.

Trail 2

Rating: ★ ★ ★

Distance: 0.5 mile

Configuration: Point to Point

Difficulty: Moderate

Tour: Trail 2 is short, beautiful, and dominated by long stretches of boardwalk/stairway. Its primary purpose is to take hikers to other trails in the park. Access by parking at the Pavilion; Trail 2 departs from the far west corner of the lot. This access path Ts at roughly the midpoint of the main trail. Turning right takes you to a stairway that descends sharply to Trail 5 and the White River. Going left from the T-intersection, Trail 2 navigates a beautiful, wooded ravine (mostly on boardwalk and stairs) that features a small, spring-fed creek. This section feels wild, but you can see the back side of the Visitor's Center above you. The path ends at Trail 1. Turning left at the intersection leads quickly to the Great Mound, while turning right follows a meandering loop that eventually passes between both Great and Fiddle Back mounds.

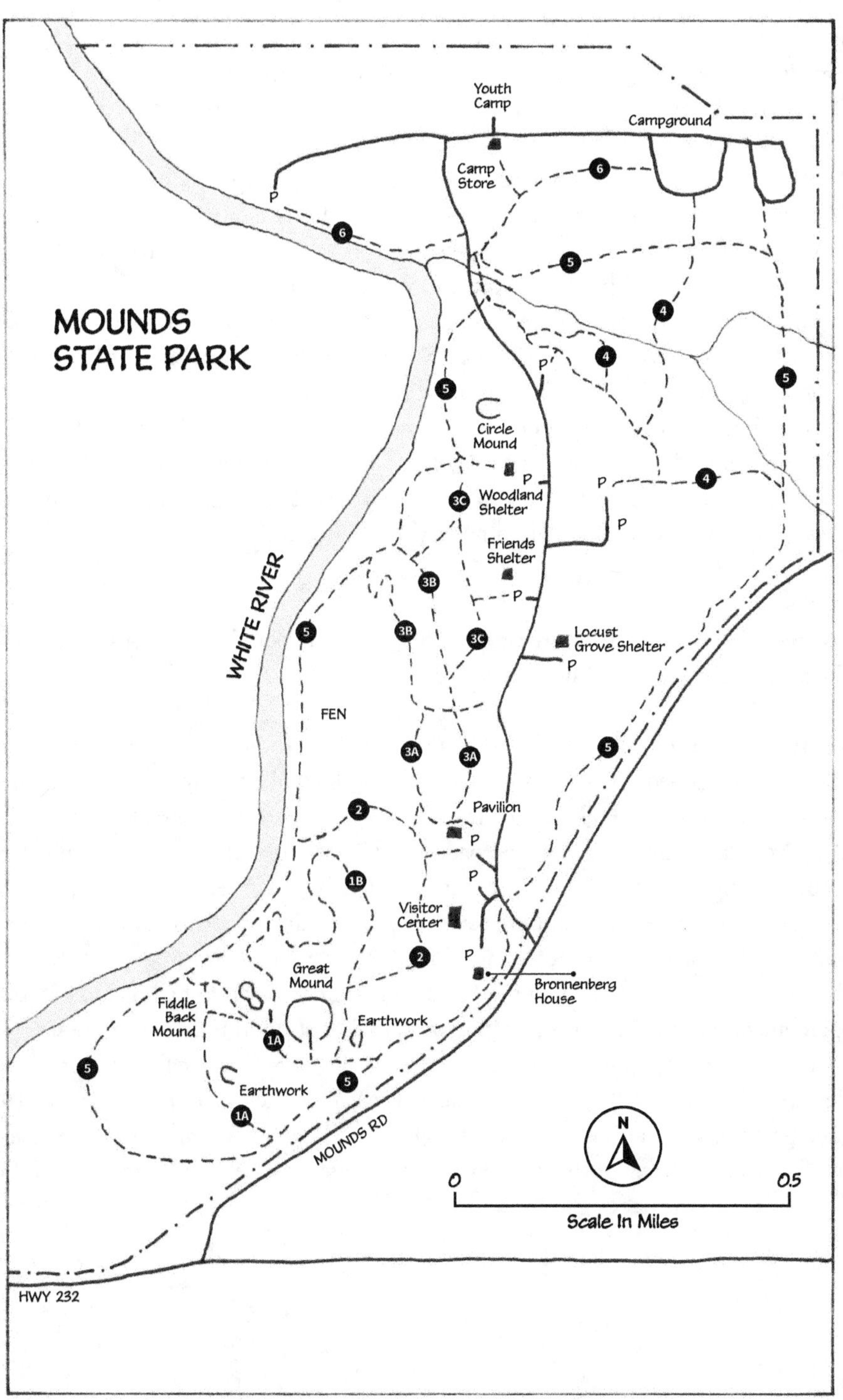
Youth
Camp
Campground
Camp
Store
P
6
6
5
4
4
5
MOUNDS
STATE PARK
5
Circle
Mound
P
P
3C
Woodland
Shelter
4
P
Friends
Shelter
WHITE RIVER
3B
P
Locust
Grove Shelter
5
3B
3C
P
FEN
3A
3A
5
2
Pavilion
P
1B
P
Visitor
Center
P
2
Great
Mound
P
Fiddle
Back
Mound
Earthwork
Bronnenberg
House
5
1A
5
Earthwork
1A
MOUNDS RD
N
0
0.5
Scale In Miles
HWY 232

Trail 3

Rating: ★★★   **Configuration:** Multiple Loops
Distance: 0.9 mile   **Difficulty:** Moderate

Tour: Trail 3 is laid out as a series of interconnecting loops—with sections labeled 3A, 3B, and 3C—that traverse the forest above the White River. It's a great place to find wildflowers in the spring and birds year-round. To access, pass the Pavilion on the main road and park at the next lot you encounter on the left. For a pleasant circumnavigation of the outer loop, take the connector out of the back of the lot and turn left on Trail 3A. After passing behind the Pavilion, the trail swings back north; to your left is the Mounds fen, a groundwater-fed wetland. Turn left at the junction with Trail 3B and descend to the river and a short overlap with Trail 5. Trail 3C soon joins; continue along the river until Trail 3C swings to the right and uphill. The trail turns back south and passes behind two shelters before ending back at Trail 3B. Turn left to return to the connector leading to the parking lot.

Trail 4

Rating: ★★★   **Configuration:** Y-Shaped with Loop (Longer loops with Trail 5)
Distance: 0.7 mile   **Difficulty:** Moderate

Tour: Though short, Trail 4 offers a quality hiking experience as it climbs in, out of, and along a wooded ravine with a small stream. The trail also offers multiple connections to Trail 5 that can be used to create loop routes. Park at the first lot on the right after Woodland Shelter (across the road from Circle Mound). A popular 1-mile loop incorporating part of Trail 5 departs from the northeast corner of the lot. At the first junction you can follow an optional side loop by turning left. This narrow and pretty path travels in and out of the ravine while circling back to the parking lot. Back on the main trail, you an encounter a major junction; turning right leads to the pool (permanently closed) and a connection to Trail 5. Instead, turn left onto the stairway leading in and out of a beautiful, not-too-deep valley, a great place for birds and wildflowers. After climbing up the other side, turn left at the junction with Trail 5 (the campground is just a short distance straight ahead) and start a roller-coaster descent of the ravine. Turn left at the first intersection, cross the creek, and turn left to follow Trail 4 back to the parking lot.

Trail 5

Rating: ★ ★ ★ ★ **Configuration:** Loop
Distance: 2.5 miles **Difficulty:** Moderate

Tour: Trail 5 is a fun route if for no other reason it takes you near just about every highlight in Mounds State Park. It's also easy to navigate: the path is wide, firm, and graveled in many spots, and the climbs and descents are reasonable. These features make it especially popular with runners. You can park just about anywhere, but I like to park near the Visitor's Center, hop on Trail 5 near the gatehouse, and travel the loop clockwise. After passing Bronnenberg House and the Great Mound area, the trail turns right and descends to the White River. The next mile is my favorite stretch of trail in the park, as you walk along the river, sometimes just above the water (yes, it can flood). At one point, off to your right, the trail passes a fen, a rare (in Indiana) type of groundwater-fed wetland. After climbing to and following the blufftop for a while, Trail 5 crosses the park road (watch the signs; this section is confusing) and skirts just south of the campground before turning right to follow the park boundary. You might hear airplanes nearby—that's because Anderson Municipal Airport is just north of the park. The final stretch of Trail 5 is straight, level, and shaded but not wild, with houses and Mounds Road off to your left.

Trail 6

Rating: ★ ★ **Configuration:** Point to Point
Distance: 0.4 mile **Difficulty:** Moderate

Tour: Trail 6 is a convenient route for campers wanting to access the White River on foot. Day hikers can park at the canoe access at the far north end of the Mounds main road, but the lot is small. The lot across from Circle Mound offers more parking; follow Trails 4 and 5 to access Trail 6. From the canoe access, Trail 6 follows the river for its first half then joins the road for a short distance. Turning left off the road, hikers encounter Trail 5 and a connection to the rest of the park's paths. Turn left, then left again, to stay on Trail 6, which climbs to the campground. Along the way a side trail departs to the left for the camp store and youth tent area. Complete a loop back to the canoe access by turning right at the first campground road, right when you reach the start of Trail 4, and right again at the junction with Trail 5.

12
O'Bannon Woods State Park

O'Bannon Woods is a conundrum for hikers. It is wild, rugged, and crisscrossed with miles of trails. But most of those trails are focused on horseback riding and mountain biking. Walkers are "welcome," but as I've noted elsewhere in this guide, horses and cyclists aren't always the best trail companions.

An added irony is that O'Bannon Woods is home to the Adventure *Hiking* Trail (AHT), one of Indiana's few backpacking-focused paths. A short section of the challenging 25-mile loop passes through the state park, but most of the trail lies in the surrounding Harrison-Crawford State Forest.

I'm not a backpacker but am intrigued by the AHT. For several years, I've been kicking around a plan to use the O'Bannon Woods campground as base for a one-day traverse of the AHT. The fastest known time for the loop is just under five hours, but I envision a run-walk of 10-12 hours. There are challenges to consider: the trail is rugged (think lots of rocks and roots) and has nearly 4,000 feet of elevation gain. Plus, it's notoriously dry, meaning you must carry water and stash refills at road crossings.

My son and I day-hiked a short section of the AHT a few years ago. I was surprised by its ruggedness, but it didn't deter me from my plan. I thought I needed a better trial so recently hopped in my car at 5:30 AM and started driving south. Nearly three hours later, I reached Pioneer Cabin, a small shelter on the southeast edge of O'Bannon Woods next to the AHT.

My plan was an out-and-back run/hike along the AHT route through the park to the campground. The sign at the trailhead told me this would be 1.6 miles—but I've learned to take posted and property map distances at O'Bannon Woods with a grain of salt.

My run started with a climb; the campground sits nearly 300 feet higher than Pioneer Cabin. The woods were quiet (I never encountered another person during my outing), and the hardwood forest was open and dry.

By late summer, the stream near the CCC Ghost Trail dwindles to small pools.

Within the state park, the AHT is identified as the "Adventure Trail," likely because it's also a mountain bike route maintained by Hoosier Mountain Bike Association. At one point the trail seemed to disappear. It took me a couple of minutes searching and scrambling over loose limestone before I retrieved the path. This section also lacked signage and tree blazes. I discovered later that this segment was a new layout dating from 2024. It was scenic and apparently eased the uphill climb but also extended the length beyond the posted 1.6 miles.

Even with my eyes glued to the challenging trail, I couldn't miss movement in the open forest valley to my left—a whitetail doe. She navigated the parallel draw much more deftly than me and soon vanished out of sight. The trail swung to the north and started switchbacking in earnest to gain altitude. I plodded along as best I could until more movement, this time above me, caught my attention. It was a big whitetail buck. He paused along the trail about 30 yards uphill, eyeing me warily, but was soon on his way.

I passed a junction with the Breeden Ridge mountain bike trail, then an obviously well-used horse trail joined in. Tiptoeing through road apples, I finally reached the point next to the Horsemen's Electric Campground where the AHT turned sharply left on its own path. This was my turnaround. My phone said I'd covered 2.5 miles, a distance it confirmed on the return trip.

The downhill run back to the car was nearly as challenging as the uphill. The rocky footing mostly kept my speed in check, and I worked hard to place my steps on stable ground as opposed to loose rock and gravel. Descending demanded more concentration than climbing.

But the weather was glorious, and sunlight dappled the mostly shaded forest floor. A hooded warbler called repeatedly from the trees above. The trail smoothed out; I picked up speed and was feeling fine…right up until that root caught my right toe. My last view before impact was of my airborne iPhone. Fortunately, there was a nice layer of leaves next to the path to cushion my face plant. After finding my phone in the brush, I resumed my run.

I slowed my pace, kept my eyes on the trail, and made it back to Pioneer Cabin without further incident. I had completed five challenging trail miles in 80 minutes and felt good. But I was sobered as I considered my AHT test run: I had covered only the equivalent of 20 percent of the AHT. Could I repeat this tough run/hike four more times in one day?

On this day, it didn't matter. After a short rest, I was back on a nearby trail, this time traveling at hiking pace but still enjoying the glorious late summer weather. As I walked, I thought, "What exactly is an *adventure*?" It dawned on me that sometimes it's a grand plan you explore in your mind, but often it's just a matter of getting out of the house to run or walk down a simple path through the woods.

O'Bannon Woods History

Established in 2004, O'Bannon Woods is one of Indiana's youngest state parks. But unlike Prophetstown, launched that same year and created from newly acquired land, O'Bannon Woods is the product of renaming an existing state recreation area—the culmination of a long, meandering journey not unlike a hike on one of the park's trails.

Limestone is the dominant geologic feature at modern-day O'Bannon Woods. It was formed 340 million years ago from sediments accumulating at the bottom of a shallow, warm sea. Today, that limestone is everywhere: on the surface, where it appears in numerous outcrops and stream bottoms; and underground, beneath a thin layer of soil, where the Mississippian Period bedrock extends downward for hundreds of feet.

Even underground limestone has a profound effect on what happens on the surface, especially at O'Bannon Woods. The park lies in the Indiana karst region, an area extending to the northwest beyond Bloomington. The limestone in a karst landscape has been dissolved extensively by water, creating sinkholes, underground streams, and caves. And it is a pair of caves, Big and Little Wyandotte, that first drew attention to this area.

The larger cavern was discovered around 1798 and initially known as Saltpeter Cave, thanks to the potassium nitrate that covered its floor. Early settlers mined the chemical compound, a constituent of traditional gunpowder. The property around the caves was purchased by Henry Peter Rothrock in 1819 for farming, timber, and as the site for a mill. He showed little interest in the caverns, which had to be fenced off to keep cows out. By 1850, the Rothrock family realized that the caves offered a business opportunity and started providing guided tours. Exploration confirmed that Big Wyandotte has more than nine miles of passageways, several very large rooms, many rare formations, and a large bat population.

Apart from the cave, the land covered by the modern-day park was used for timber, crops, and grazing. While trees grew well, the thin soil, steep slopes, and dry conditions made farming difficult. The karst topography contributes to the arid nature of the land. Many streams run dry except during periods of heavy rain. Most have sinkholes in their valley bottoms that drain water from the surface to underground passageways.

By 1932, the southern Indiana economy was in crisis thanks to the Great Depression. The state, looking to revive local fortunes, began purchasing depleted and eroded farmland with the idea of developing it for other uses. Harrison-Crawford State Forest—at the time an ironic name because few trees remained on the land— was established and over time grew to more than 24,00 acres in its namesake counties.

The Depression offered another resource that helped jumpstart the new property: cheap labor. In 1934, the Civilian Conservation Corps Company 1556 set up camp near Corydon and started work on roads, reforestation, and structures In Harrison-Crawford before being moved to another assignment. They were replaced by Company 517, a rare (for Indiana, at least) all-Black group. Its headquarters were established deep in the state forest, in an area now occupied by the O'Bannon Woods group camp. Company 517 worked at Harrison-Crawford for three years, then moved north to South Bend. A third CCC company worked briefly in the area in 1941. The CCC legacy lives on today in the form of essential infrastructure, including roads, bridges, trails, and a variety of structures, such as the fire tower and Shelter 2.

In the early years, recreation was secondary at Indiana state forests; growing trees for timber was the priority. But in the late 1950s, attitudes in the state shifted. Harrison-Crawford established four recreational areas (including a boat landing on the Ohio River), built ponds, and managed the property as a destination for camping, hunting, fishing, canoeing, hiking, horseback riding, and other outdoor sports.

A major gap in the property was filled with the 1966 purchase of 4,000 acres from the Rothrock family. The acquisition not only added the Wyandotte Caves to

The Adventure Hiking Trail climbs through a dry forest toward the campground.

Harrison-Crawford it provided critical protection to a long stretch of the pristine Blue River, which today sets the western boundary of O'Bannon Woods.

Efforts to create a recreation-focused preserve within the confines of the timber-focused state forest started in the early 1970s. An early proponent was State Senator Frank O'Bannon, who was part of a prominent political family from nearby Corydon and loved canoeing and birdwatching in the area's woodlands. His efforts to establish a state park were rebuffed but he successfully helped the Indiana Department of Natural Resources get $2.5 million to build out what became known as Wyandotte Woods State Recreation Area.

Frank O'Bannon was elected governor in 1996 and re-elected four years later. Sadly, he suffered a massive stroke in September 2003 and passed away—as of this writing, the last American governor to die in office. In November 2004, as a tribute to the popular governor, Wyandotte Woods was renamed O'Bannon Woods and dedicated as a state park. At that time, some aspirational plans were laid out for the property, including building a new state park inn. Over the next two decades, actual changes were more modest, but O'Bannon Woods remains popular with horseback riders, mountain bikers, and hikers who enjoy its growing trail network.

O'Bannon Woods Today

O'Bannon Woods is deep in southern Indiana and nestled against the Ohio River. Depending on the route you take, the distance from downtown Indianapolis is 140 miles and driving time is about two and a half hours. Louisville is the closest big city—35 miles east of the park.

O'Bannon Woods covers 2,294 acres, size-wise in the middle of Indiana state parks. But this is misleading. Unlike some properties that are hemmed in by small towns, farms, or housing developments, O'Bannon Woods is surrounded by Harrison-Crawford State Forest, a vast, rugged woodland tract. This helps O'Bannon Woods feel bigger and wilder than other state parks. It also makes things confusing for trail users, because hiking, mountain biking, and horseback routes flow between the two properties and boundaries aren't marked. In fact, some of O'Bannon Woods' popular hiking trails—as identified on the official property map—are actually in the state forest.

Horseback riding is popular at O'Bannon Woods. The park has two horsemen's campgrounds, which are the jumping-off points for a 64-mile network of bridle trails that cover both the state park and state forest.

Mountain biking is also popular, and trail mileage is expanding. One online resource tallies 59 miles of rideable trails on public lands in this area. The state park recognizes seven bike-and-hike routes within its boundary that cover more than 15 miles.

Beyond trails, O'Bannon Woods is best known for its cave tours, which are offered on weekends and holidays from Memorial Day to Labor Day. The Little Wyandotte tour is short (about 45 minutes), easy, and open to all ages. The Big Wyandotte tour is a rugged, two-hour hike during which participants must wear headlamps, climb stairs, and scramble over challenging terrain. The payoff is seeing an amazing subterranean world complete with huge rooms, beautiful formations, and even an underground "mountain." The caves are in a separate park unit, three miles west on Highway 62 past the Highway 462 turnoff to the main park.

Water-based sports are also available at O'Bannon Woods. Shore fishing is possible in the Ohio River but there is no boat ramp. The Blue River is a highly regarded canoeing and fishing stream (with rental and shuttle services available), but access is limited to sites outside the park, in the state forest and to the north.

History buffs will enjoy a visit to the Nature Center and attractions near it. Directly behind the building, visitors will find a replica pioneer farmstead intended to show how people lived in the area in the 1830s. A large barn at the site contains a preserved hay press, built in 1850 and once a common device on area farms. Powered by oxen (which the park keeps on the farm), the huge presses were used to create hay bales that could be transported by riverboat to customers in nearby cities.

After touring the farmstead, visitors should explore the animal exhibits in the Nature Center. Nature study is a popular pastime at O'Bannon Woods, which has diverse mix of flora and fauna. The park is home to a variety of mammals and is a stop on the Indiana Birding Trail.

Camping in O'Bannon Woods is the best way to take advantage of the park's rich trail resources. In addition to the group and horsemen's camps, the park has a large, all-electric campground with 239 sites for RVs and tents. Visitors seeking more comfort for their overnight stay should consider Corydon, about 10 miles east, a full-featured tourist destination with plenty of hotel, restaurants, and retail options.

Hiking O'Bannon Woods

O'Bannon Woods State Park is covered with a rich network of trails, but hiking seems to be less popular than horseback riding and mountain biking. As a result, few trail miles are hiking-only routes; most are shared with horse and/or bikes, including the Adventure Hiking Trail within the park boundary.

This state park is one of the few in Indiana that I will soften my stance about not hiking on biking trails. Some of the hike-and-bike routes at O'Bannon Woods get ample foot traffic and offer a quality hiking experience. Plus, if the biking-focused volunteers weren't building and maintaining these trails, the routes wouldn't get much attention. A quality shared path is better than no trail at all—just be patient with your fellow trail users who are on bicycles or horseback.

One problem at O'Bannon Woods is that many of the hiking-focused trails are isolated and/or located just outside the park in the state forest. Expect some driving between trailheads if you want to fully explore the area's trails. Things are different around the centrally located campground, where you can connect bike-and-hike paths to create long and varied routes through the forest.

Trail Running

Because mountain biking trails tend to make good running routes, O'Bannon Woods is arguably a better destination for running than hiking. None of the hiking-only paths in and near the park are particularly well-suited to running, so focus your attention on the bike trails.

The Fire Tower and Group Camp trails both start from a large parking area just past the gatehouse. Linking those routes with the Potato Run Trail forms a loop of about seven miles. The campground is the focal point for most of the park's mountain bike trails, so it's a good running base. If you're not camping, park at the lot adjacent to the control station. Potato Run departs across the road to the south. From here you can follow it to Breeden Ridge, Rocky Ridge, Fire Tower, and even the AHT to create loops of varying lengths. In addition to the campground, inside the park you can access the AHT at Pioneer Cabin for out-and-back runs.

TRAIL GUIDES

The letter designations (Trail A, etc.) below conform to what you find on the O'Bannon Woods property map. On the ground, the hiking trails (Trails A-G) are identified by names not letters. Trail crossings, signs, and blazes are all abundant but confusing, because they use varying colors, symbols, and names or abbreviations to identify hiking, mountain biking, and horse trails. Pause at junctions to ensure you are, in fact, following your intended route.

Trail AT: Adventure Hiking Trail

Rating: ★ ★ ★
Distance: Inside park— 4.5 miles; Total—25 miles

Configuration: Point to Point (in park)
Difficulty: Challenging

Tour: This guide covers only the short AHT section within the park boundaries (identified on signs as "Adventure Trail"). Refer to online resources, including the O'Bannon Woods website, for information on the full 25-mile route. Inside the state park, the AHT is a combined bike-and-hike trail. In 2024 a large section was relocated/extended, so mileages might not agree with what you find online. The best strategy for day-hiking this segment is an out-and-back from Pioneer Cabin, located along the main park road near the Ohio River. Parking is limited to a gravel pull-off parallel to the road. Enter the trailhead on the west side of the road (the trail near the shelter goes east into Harrison-Crawford State Forest) and start climbing—you'll gain 300 feet over the next 2.5 miles. The maturing second-growth forest provides plenty of shade, even in the summer, and the limestone outcrops offer scenery—and a challenge. In addition to tough footing, the trail is faint in some rocky areas and signs and blazes (green and white squares) are limited. After working through several switchbacks, the path joins a more established, better-marked trail for the remainder of its route. Near the campground, a well-traveled horse trail joins for a short stretch; watch your step and be alert for riders. The AHT makes a sharp left as you approach the Horsemen's Campground and follows a right-of-way established in 2021. From this junction, the hike's high point, the trail descends to a usually dry ravine, which has a waterfall when the stream is flowing. The trail climbs back up to a ridge above the Blue River before reaching the park boundary at the Old Forest Road. Either turn around and retrace your steps or continue another mile and turn right at the Fire Tower Trail, which you can use as an alternate route back to the campground and a connection to the AHT.

Trail A: Fire Tower/Rocky Ridge Bike and Hike

Rating: ★ ★ ★   **Configuration:** Lollipop
Distance: 2.4 miles   **Difficulty:** Challenging

Tour: The Rocky Ridge section lives up to its name, forming part of a quality hiking/running route. The trailhead is next to Site 35 in the Class A campground. If you're not camping, park in the visitor lot by the gate and walk to the trailhead. The sign says, "Rocky Ridge," but officially you're starting on the Fire Tower Trail, which descends steadily on a narrow, loose path winding through trees and limestone outcrops. Pass the first Rocky Ridge junction and continue to the second, turning left at the "Loop" sign. This segment is a switchback, continuing its descent into the ravine you've been following. The trail bottoms out in a dry creek bed, then crosses and follows the waterway to the right for a quarter mile. A sharp left marks the start of a long climb back to the top. Halfway up, Breeden Ridge Trail, a popular mountain biking route, joins from the right. Turning right here connects with the Adventure Hiking Trail and an alternative return to the campground. After crossing a small bridge near the head of the ravine, Rocky Ridge makes a final uphill and rejoins the Fire Tower Trail; turn right to return to the campground.

O'BANNON WOODS STATE PARK

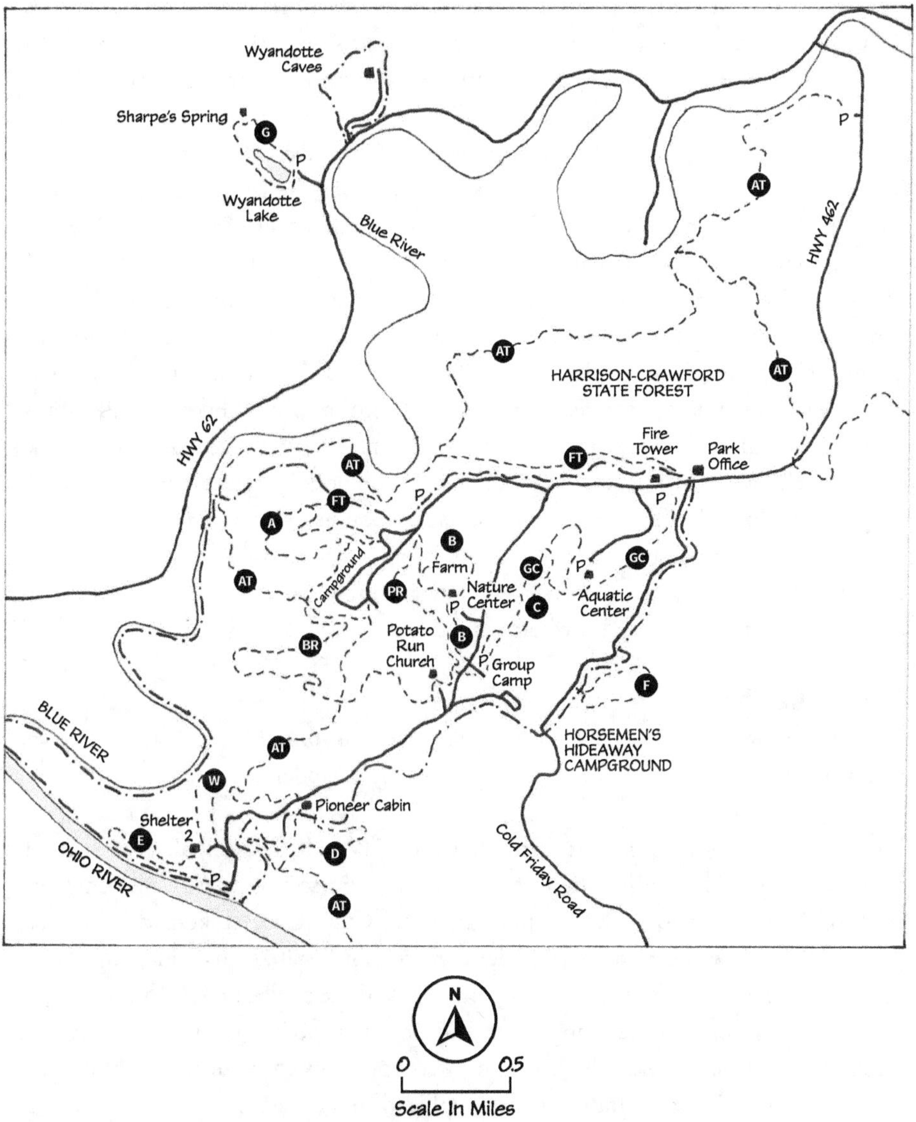

Trail B: Tulip Valley

Rating: ★ ★ ★ **Configuration:** Loop and Two Connectors
Distance: 2 miles **Difficulty:** Loop—ADA Accessible; Connectors—Moderate

Tour: This is the longest hiking-only path within the park boundary. It is varied, scenic, and serves multiple purposes. Park in the large lot near the Nature Center. The wide, level, and accessible trail, which is covered with a layer of crushed limestone, crosses a small, covered bridge and enters the woods at the west end of the lot. The half-mile stub to the Group Camp soon departs to the left. This pleasant forest path offers a connection to the CCC Ghost Trail in addition to the camp. Back on the main loop, the winding path climbs gently through an attractive, mature forest. Signs identify the various tree species, interpretive panels add interest, and benches provide plenty of places to rest. Near the halfway point, the unsigned campground connector departs to the left through a split-rail gate. This quarter-mile trail is a stiff climb, but at the top you can reach connections with the several bike-and-hike trails. The main Tulip Valley loop descends from the junction, crossing many boardwalks before reaching a small wetland area. An observation deck and blind offer opportunities to watch for wildlife, especially birds. As the loop nears its end, it passes through a replica pioneer homestead from the 1830s, complete with oxen. A large barn (open only limited hours) contains a preserved hay press built in 1850. The trail ends at the opposite end of the parking lot where you started.

Trail C: CCC Ghost

Rating: ★ ★ ★ **Configuration:** Lollipop
Distance: 1.25 miles **Difficulty:** Moderate

Tour: This short, scenic trail pays tribute to the 517th CCC Company, an all-Black unit headquartered near this site in the 1930s. It has a section that is hike only, but most of the route follows the Group Camp and CCC Ghost bike-and-hike trails. The latter is a new route that was under construction in 2025. Its wide, engineered roadbed took over part of the hike-only trail. Park at the trailhead, which is along the main road just north of the group camp. Turn right at the first intersection, with the Group Camp Trail, to enter the hiking-only section. This charming segment has just the barest hint of a trail winding its way uphill through a dense forest with numerous limestone outcrops. When the trail passes close to the parallel dry creek bed, take some time to investigate. The limestone layers are gorgeous, forming a series of cascades on the occasions water is flowing. Back on the main route, the spell of the wonderful hike is broken near the half-mile mark when the new bike trail, bulldozed through the woods, appears. Turn right to reach the aquatic center, left to continue on the CCC Ghost Trail, or turn around if you want to stay on a hiking-only path. The new bike trail continues for about a quarter mile to the stream bed, crosses, and soon intersects with the Group Camp Trail. Turn left on this more rustic route to follow the west side of the dry creek bed back to your starting point.

Trail D: Cliff Dweller

Rating: ★★★   **Configuration:** Loop

Distance: 1.75 miles   **Difficulty:** Moderate

Tour: This loop gives you a nice introduction to the O'Bannon Woods landscape but, ironically, most of the route lies outside the park in Harrison-Crawford State Forest. It also shares three quarters of a mile with the Adventure Hiking Trail (AHT). The Cliff Dweller Trailhead is at the Pioneer Cabin; there is limited parking at a pull off along the main park road. To hike the loop clockwise, enter the woods right behind the shelter and immediately start downhill. At the bottom, you cross the usually dry, rocky bed of Potato Run, turn left, and start climbing parallel to the waterway. It's a steady uphill for a half mile from here, with the trail switchbacking to gain elevation. The path is narrow and rocky, demanding your attention to ensure good footing, but the surroundings are beautiful. Unfortunately, you may notice signs of logging. This forest is timber-focused and trailside trees have been cut in recent years. Logging

Near Shelter 2, the River Bluff Trail offers exceptional views of the Ohio.

typically happens in the winter, and signs will notify you of any activity. After about a mile, the AHT joins from the left and the combined routes follow the top of a steep ridge above Potato Run then descend to the waterway. After crossing, it's just a short climb back to Pioneer Cabin, where Cliff Dweller ends. The AHT crosses the road and continues towards the campground.

Trail E: Ohio River Bluff

Rating: ★ ★ ★ ★ **Configuration:** Loop
Distance: 1.5 miles **Difficulty:** Challenging

Tour: The Ohio River is in sight for most of the length of this enjoyable hike, which shares part of its path with a horse trail. Drive to the end of the main road and park by the riverside shelter and the trailhead. Head west down the wide, flat trail (a shared horseback route) through a pretty bottomland forest. The diverse scenery will keep your head turning: To the left are glimpses of the river, to the right steep limestone bluffs. After a half mile, the horse path continues straight while the hiking trail turns right and starts climbing a narrow trace up a low ridge. The forest is dense and filled with some of the park's oldest and largest trees. Views of the river are screened but the atmosphere is exceptional. As the climb continues, limestone outcrops increase and soon you're on top of the rocky bluffs you gawked at from below. At the top of a final steep climb you emerge from the forest near Shelter 2, which has amazing river views. The trail restarts on the far side of the grass. It's all downhill from here but be cautious—the many limestone steps are treacherous when wet. On reaching the road, turn right and follow the pavement back to your car.

Trail F: Post Oak-Cedar Nature Preserve

Rating: ★ ★ ★ **Configuration:** Loop
Distance: 0.8 miles **Difficulty:** Moderate

Tour: This trail lies in Harrison-Crawford State Forest but in a nature preserve that abuts the east side of O'Bannon Woods. It's off the beaten path and doesn't get much visitation, so expect to have the trail to yourself. To reach the trailhead, turn south on Cold Friday Road—near the gatehouse—and drive one mile to the small parking lot on the left. Turn left at the start and hike the loop clockwise. It's a self-guided nature trail with numbered signs along the way; a brochure, available online, explains the highlights as you venture through two distinct habitats. The first section climbs up a higher, drier slope dominated by post oaks and red cedar. The area is marked by limestone outcrops and periodic grassy openings featuring prairie plants. When the trail turns and starts descending, the vegetation changes with the elevation. Soon the faint path is alongside Potato Run, which is often dry. Nonetheless, the habitat here is wetter, with ferns in the understory and sycamore and black walnut trees overhead. After a short climb out of the valley, the trail delivers you back to the start.

Trail G: Sharp's Spring

Rating: ★ ★ ★   **Configuration:** Loop
Distance: 1.4 miles   **Difficulty:** Moderate

Tour: This trail is entirely on state forest land but near the state park's Wyandotte Caves unit. The trailhead is on Highway 62, three miles west of the Highway 462 turnoff to the main park. Hike the loop counterclockwise, following the east/right shore of small Wyandotte Lake. Above the lake, the path follows the inlet stream through a sometimes-swampy forest. A small tributary may be a challenge to cross when the water is high. Just beyond, a horse trail enters, which can leave the rest of the route rough and muddy in places. Any challenges will be forgotten when you reach Sharp's Spring, which emerges with gusto from a hole at the base of a limestone wall. After pausing to take in the pretty scene, cross the stream and follow the trail through the woods on the Wyandotte Lake's west shore. If the water is low, you may be able to cross the dam to return to your vehicle. If not, follow the trail below the dam and over a culvert containing the outlet stream to the access road; turn left to reach the parking area.

Trail W: Whitetail Deer Trail

Rating: ★ ★   **Configuration:** Loop
Distance: 0.9 mile   **Difficulty:** Moderate

Tour: This mysterious route is not shown on the park property map and incorrectly routed on a popular online resource. But it's there to be stumbled upon, near Shelter 2. Park at the end of the shelter access road; the trailhead is marked by a large sign. The trail is a simple loop through an open, upland forest. It travels nearly straight to the bluff above the Blue River and swings right to follow a valley back toward the start. The trail emerges from the woods on the access road; turn right and follow the pavement to your vehicle. Whitetail Deer is a nice add-on to the Ohio River Bluff Trail, which crosses the Shelter 2 picnic area.

OTHER BIKE-AND-HIKE TRAILS

Trail BR: Breeden Ridge

Distance: 2.8 miles

Notes: This up-and-down route wraps around the west side of the campground but must be accessed from other trails. It departs from the Rocky Ridge Trail just west of the Class A section, crosses the AHT twice, then ends at the Potato Run Trail southeast of the campground.

Trail FT: Fire Tower

Distance: 3.1 miles

Notes: This was O'Bannon Woods' first bike-and-hike trail, though for most of its distance it lies outside the state park. Fire Tower starts at the parking lot north of the main road just past the gatehouse and ends next to campground Site 35. Along the way it shares right-of-way with the AHT and Rocky Ridge Trail. It is less rocky and rugged than some of the park's other routes.

Trail GC: Group Camp

Distance: 3 miles

Notes: This route starts at the parking lot south of the main road just past the gatehouse and extends to the Group Camp. It is downhill most of the way, descending 500 feet in the process. It connects with both the hike-only and bike-and-hike sections of the CCC Ghost Trail and the south end of Potato Run Trail.

Trail PR: Potato Run

Distance: 1.1 miles

Notes: This route runs uphill from the Group Camp to the main campground, where it shares a trailhead and short section with the Tulip Valley Trail. Despite its big climb, Potato Run is considered the easiest of O'Bannon Woods' bike-and-hike trails.

13

Ouabache State Park

Driving north through dense fog on Interstate 69, I wasn't convinced this was the best day for a trail run at Ouabache State Park. But by the time I pulled up to the gatehouse, the fog had burned off, replaced by a bright blue sky.

I owed Ouabache a full day of exploration. My previous visit to the park was on the last leg of a longer trip to other parks. I drove around, hiked a couple of miles and, feeling tired and unimpressed with my surroundings, left for home.

Now, with my full attention on Ouabache, I parked near the "Iron Mike" statue celebrating the Civilian Conservation Corps and laced up my trail runners. I ran down the park road a short distance and turned left to start a counterclockwise circuit of Trail 5. This route, which circumnavigates the northeastern half of the park, was the perfect reintroduction to Ouabache. Throughout its six-mile length, Trail 5 shares pathway with the park's four other marked trails and passes several landmarks of note.

Trail 5 quickly established the character it would retain for most of its length: wide, winding, shaded, and with good footing. It was mowed grass in sections and covered with crushed rock elsewhere. Even though it had rained the previous day, the path was firm. I couldn't have asked for a nicer running route.

Soon, campsites from Campground B came into view on the left. Taking a quick detour, I scanned the tree-shaded area and concluded that it would have been a nice place to set up my tent.

After the campground, Trail 3 joined from the left and the combined paths entered the prettiest chunk of forest in the park. Interpretive signs identified tree species, of which there was an impressive variety. The birds were also varied—and numerous. Their calls echoed through the woods.

Trail 2 soon replaced Trail 3 and accompanied Trail 5 on a northward trek next to the park boundary. The forest in this area was younger and scruffier and included many pine trees, planted during the property's game farm era, which started in the 1930s. Suddenly, I was startled by a reddish-brown flash ahead: whitetail! The deer hadn't made a sound while crossing the trail, but its spring coat stood out brightly

Trail 1 encircles the bison enclosure, offering views of Ouabache's top attraction.

against the green underbrush. It waited quietly off trail without moving, waiting for me to pass.

I continued until I could see a large fence in the distance: the bison enclosure. Ouabache's biggest attraction may be its herd of the animal featured on the state seal—which no longer roams free in Indiana. Joined by Trail 1, I followed the fence line to the right. A crowd appeared, the first people I'd seen on the trail since I started. They were enjoying a view of Ouabache's newest star, a baby bison born six days earlier. The light-colored calf and its dark brown mother were just 10 feet beyond the fence.

Trail 5—joined by Trail 4—took a sharp right away from the fence and into the woods. The area was a mixed forest but attractive, with many pines interspersed throughout. I considered how few invasive plant species I'd seen compared to other parks. Invasives are a constant challenge at all Indiana state parks, and the unwanted plants have the upper hand at many properties. Clean pathways like the ones I was enjoying at Ouabache are often a sign of a strong volunteer force.

As if on cue, I rounded a sharp corner and nearly ran into the back of a small off-road vehicle operated by two volunteers, one younger and one older. They were hauling a load of crushed rock down the trail, filling in low spots as they encountered them. I stopped to chat for minute, grateful for the break, but I also wanted to say "thanks." In this era of shrinking budgets, volunteers like this pair make it possible for me to have a fun and safe day on the trails.

I ran onward into Ouabache's northwest corner and entered the low-maintenance zone, beyond where the volunteers had been able to work this year. The grass on the trail was tall, and the honeysuckle and multiflora rose encroached from both sides. I was reminded just how important those volunteers are.

The trail turned east, and the gatehouse came into view through the trees to my right. Trail 4 joined again from the left and the path continued through the woods until an earthen berm appeared: the Kunkel Lake dam. I followed Trail 4 for the short side trip to the top of the long, low dam, which encircled the southern half of the small reservoir. Fishermen ringed the impoundment, which looked more like a suburban retention pond than a state park lake.

Returning to Trail 5, I crossed the outlet stream bridge and followed a tree line off trail and through the grass back to Iron Mike, my car, and a few minutes rest. But I wasn't done—Ouabache had more to offer, and I wasn't going to waste the beautiful weather. I soon switched to hiking gear and returned to the trails at a slower pace, relishing another great day in an Indiana state park.

Ouabache History

Ouabache—the French spelling of "Wabash"—not surprisingly has a history influenced by the important river that sets the park's southern boundary. The Wabash rises in Ohio, 59 miles above Ouabache State Park. Near the park, the stream is wide and shallow, with many limestone rocks visible in the clear water—the "water over white stones" in the Miami language that was translated into its French and English names.

The Miami people had a long history of living along the upper Wabash River. They were farmers, growing corn and other crops, but also hunters; bison were a key food source.

The river was an important travel route for French trappers, linking the Great Lakes and the Gulf of Mexico with the help of an eight-mile portage between the Wabash and Maumee Rivers. The Miami controlled the portage but had a strong relationship with the French, even fighting alongside them against the British—though they eventually sided with the British against the insurgent Americans.

With settlers from the new country pressing west, it was inevitable that the Miami would be displaced from their ancestral home. The land occupied by the park was ceded to the United States in the 1805 Treaty of Grouseland, but members of the tribe maintained a foothold in the new state of Indiana until they were finally removed to western reservations by the 1840s.

The first white settlers in the vicinity of the park can be traced to 1829. More followed and population in the area grew thanks to the productive farmland. Wells County was formed in 1837 and Bluffton, just a couple miles west of the park, was named the county seat a year later.

Fast forward nearly a century and the future parkland largely had been cleared of its dense forests and farmed until the soil was depleted and eroding. A contemporary source described the property as a "useless, expensive eyesore." On top of that, the country had fallen into a Depression and rural areas like Wells County were struggling with the economic downturn.

Enter two Wells County lawyers with a different vision for the property along the Wabash. In 1933, newly elected Indiana governor Paul McNutt appointed Virgil Simmons commissioner of the Department of Conservation and Kenneth Kunkel as director of the Division of Fish and Wildlife. Friends and Bluffton residents, the two men envisioned a beautiful park on north bank of the Wabash; soon they had possession of a thousand acres of depleted farmland and a workforce assigned to improve it.

In 1935, Civilian Conservation Corps Company 1592 set up shop in the newly minted Wells County State Forest and Game Preserve. The young workers, supervised and taught by local skilled craftsman, started building the infrastructure that is so familiar in the modern park, including buildings, shelters, trails, and roads. The CCC workers dug—by hand—the basin of Kunkel Lake (named by Simmons in honor of his friend). They also built the fire tower in 1939. Interestingly, the 100-foot structure, still a park highlight and recently renovated, was never used for spotting fires. Its purpose was purely recreational. Company 1592 was finally reassigned to another location in January 1941, but they left the park ready to host thousands of visitors for decades to come.

The park that became Ouabache first focused on trees and wildlife. The CCC crews planted thousands of trees—the maturing pine and hardwood forests that make today's park so beautiful—and raised countless nursery trees for planting on other properties. Raising game animals was another priority, so important that the park became known as the country's "greatest wildlife laboratory." Early photos show acres of pens south of the lake containing thousands of pheasants, quail, rabbits, and raccoons raised at the farm and shipped around the country to replenish depleted game animal populations.

And then there are the bison. They were never raised as game animals at Wells County State Forest, but rather as a novelty to be viewed by visitors. The first bison arrived in 1936—extras from a small herd at Pokagon State Park that could trace its lineage to wild animals from Yellowstone National Park. Today, Ouabache maintains a herd of no more than a dozen animals, who loll around their 20-acre fenced enclosure, safely entertaining visitors awestruck by their enormous size.

The game farm was phased out and in 1962 the park was renamed Ouabache State Recreation Area. The new name became a source of contention that remains today. Locals proudly say "o-BOTCH-ee" and that has become the most common pronunciation. Adding confusion, an early map identified the park as "Quabache," and even today some old timers call it "qua-BOTCH-ee." The property was renamed again in 1983, becoming Ouabache State Park.

Ouabache Today

Ouabache State Park is located in northeast Indiana about 115 miles from downtown Indianapolis. The park is much closer to Fort Wayne; Indiana's second-largest city is only 28 miles north.

At 1,104 acres, Ouabache is Indiana's third-smallest state park, but it attracts more than 300,000 visitors in a typical year, ranking it 17th. The park has a decidedly different vibe from other state parks. It feels less wild and more "civilized"—not surprising for a property that was pasture and row crops a century ago and spent its first 25 years as a game farm.

Ouabache is loved by the local population and well cared for. It is one of Indiana's cleanest and best-maintained state parks and appears to have one of its most active Friends volunteer groups. Even in the modern tight-budget era, the park is adding new amenities and programs while doing a good job of maintaining what it already has.

The park has a lot to offer visitors beyond hiking. The bison exhibit may be Ouabache's most popular attraction. Bison are native to this part of the state but were extirpated by the early 1800s. As of this writing, eight animals were living at the park, including calves born in both 2024 and 2025.

Climbing the 106 steps to the top of the fire tower is another Ouabache tradition. The tower—nicely renovated in 2019 thanks to $80,000 raised in just six months by the Friends group—offers tremendous views of the park and surrounding environs. Though it covers just 25 acres, Kunkel Lake acts as the attractive centerpiece of Ouabache State Park and is the source of several activities, including fishing, boating, and swimming.

Ouabache is one of a handful of Indiana state parks that you can ride to on a paved bicycle path. The Rivergreenway Trail starts two miles west of the park in downtown Bluffton. Its route follows a pretty stretch of the Wabash before connecting with the park's paved bike trail, which runs an additional 2.7 miles to the Youth Tent Campground.

Ouabache has a seasonal interpretive naturalist service but currently no nature center. That is about to change. As of 2025, the park was in the design stages for building a new visitor's center that will incorporate a nature center and a permanent home for its many programs.

A special treat at Ouabache is the park's popular holiday light show. Organized by the Friends group and an important fundraiser, the drive-through attraction is open nightly for most of December. All the sites in Campground A have light displays, as do the entrance gate, fire tower, and other structures.

For visitors wishing to overnight in the park, Ouabache offers two adjacent campgrounds on the east side of the property totaling 124 all-electric sites. The campgrounds offer easy access to hiking, with Trails 2, 3, and 5 passing nearby.

Ouabache does not have an inn or cabins. If camping is not your thing, a short trip to Bluffton is your best option for an overnight stay. There are a few national hotel chains represented, along with the restaurant and retail choices you'd expect to find in a town of 10,000 people.

Hiking Ouabache

The hiking opportunities at Ouabache are enjoyable but modest. There are five numbered trails; total mileage is listed at 12.75, but that is misleading. All the trails share routes in various places putting the length of unique trails at less than nine miles.

On the positive side, the trails are well maintained and connect nicely. It's easy to improvise a long hike without much advance planning. Throw in all or part of the paved bike trail, a pleasant 2.7-mile walk through a riparian woodland, and hikers can easily stay entertained for a full day at Ouabache.

Hike Trail 4 around Kunkel Lake to reach fishing spots and great viewpoints

Trail 5 is the park's signature hike, because it covers the most ground and hits many of the park's highlights. If you only have time for a short hike, consider following Trail 4 around its Kunkel Lake loop or making a loop of Trails 2 and 3, which pass through Ouabache's prettiest forests.

Trail Running

Ouabache State Park is an outstanding destination for trail runners. The flat, well-maintained pathways flow nicely through forests providing shade even on midsummer days. If you love hills, rocks, and gnarly challenges you might be disappointed. But if you're looking to just cover lots of ground in a relaxed, beautiful setting, get ready to be rewarded.

The signature run is Trail 5, about six miles in length, but because all routes interconnect it's easy to start adding mileage. A logical extension from Trail 5 is a side trip around Kunkel Lake on Trail 4, accessible from either the dam or the bison enclosure.

Another option for runners is to take advantage of the paved bike path, which parallels the main park road (but is nicely separated from it) from the western boundary to near the youth tent campground. Consider running the bike trail west to the gatehouse, then crossing the road to jump on Trail 5. Want an even longer run? Just west of the park, the bike trail connects with the pretty Rivergreenway paved trail and follows the Wabash for another two miles into Bluffton.

TRAIL GUIDES

Trail 1

Rating: ★ ★
Distance: 1.0 miles

Configuration: Loop
Difficulty: Easy

Tour: As a hiking experience, Trail 1 is ho-hum, but it offers a great family-friendly animal-watching opportunity by circling the bison habitat. Park in the lot next to the fire tower; the bison enclosure is across the road to the north. Trail 1 is a wide, graveled path that follows the tall fence around the enclosure. It's an easy walk and the only place in the park where you're almost guaranteed to see other people. Bring your binoculars if you want a good view of the huge animals. While they are sometimes next to the fence, they are often lolling in the distance under trees or near the pond. If you want a longer hike, follow Trail 4—the mowed path—south out of the parking lot for a circuit around nearby Kunkel Lake. Before you leave, take the time to climb the fire tower, which offers nice views of the park in all directions.

Trail 2

Rating: ★ ★ ★ **Configuration:** Loop
Distance: 1.25 miles **Difficulty:** Easy

Tour: Trail 2 passes through Campground A before heading off into the woods in the northeast corner of the park. If you're not camping, follow the main road to the T-intersection just past the park office. Turn left, then take the first right; the trailhead is at the far end of the parking lot. For a counterclockwise circuit, take the trail that crosses a boardwalk and enters the woods. The path drops you into the campground; turn left and follow the paved road to Trail 2's exit into the forest between two split-rail fences. Trail 3 soon joins from the right, which offers a great option for a longer and prettier hike. Continuing straight, you encounter a combo intersection; turn left to stay on Trail 2, now joined by Trail 5. The path closely follows the eastern park boundary, passing through a scrub forest with many tall pines. The trees, nearly 100 years old, have shallow roots that frequently cross and jumble the trail. The path swings to the southwest and eventually reaches a wide-open T-intersection. Turn left to stay on Trail 2. Look to the left as you follow this straight, mowed-grass section back to your car. Hidden in the woods are seemingly misplaced tennis and basketball courts, still in use and outfitted with lights, accessible by a narrow connector.

Trail 3

Rating: ★ ★ ★ ★ **Configuration:** Loop with Connectors
Distance: 1.5 miles **Difficulty:** Easy

Tour: Trail 3 starts at connector paths from the northeast and southeast corners of Campground A. If you're not camping, follow the access directions for Trail 2. After leaving the campground, turn right at the first intersection onto the Trail 3. This path loops through an extension of the park property and juts eastward toward Highway 301. It's not remote—you can see farms beyond the trees—but it feels wild. This is the park's most mature forest visited by a hiking trail. The trees are large; the birds are many. Many trailside trees have identification markers; QR codes take you to a website with more info on each species. (Yes, you can get a cell signal here.) At the first intersection you can follow Trail 3 (along with Trail 5) on a pleasant quarter-mile stub eventually connecting to the campground. Back on the main loop, enjoy the walk to a junction where Trails 2 and 5 depart to the right. Take this turn if you'd enjoy adding another mile to your walk or stay straight to retrace your original path back to your vehicle.

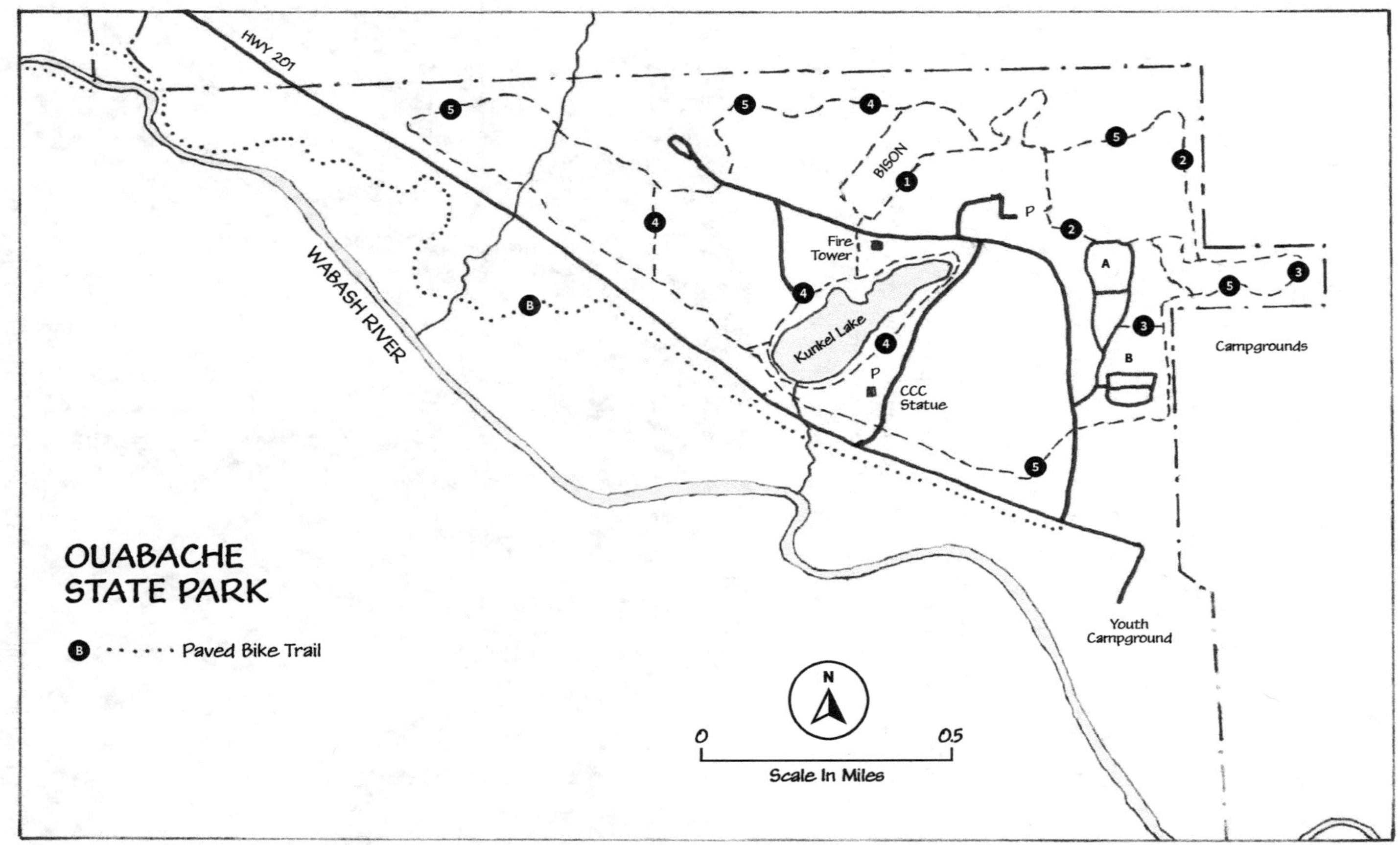
HWY 201
WABASH RIVER
BISON
Fire Tower
Kunkel Lake
CCC Statue
Campgrounds
Youth Campground
OUABACHE
STATE PARK
Paved Bike Trail
N
0   0.5
Scale In Miles

Trail 4

Rating: ★ ★ ★   **Configuration:** Double Loop

Distance: 3 miles   **Difficulty:** Easy

Tour: Trail 4 takes in several of Ouabache's highlights while scribing a figure-eight route. Follow the access directions for Trail 1 and start your hike across the road. Turn left at the bison enclosure and follow the wide, graveled path along the fence, keeping your eyes open for the big mammals. On the north side of the enclosure, Trails 4 and 5 depart to the left. The forest here is scrubby, with many pines mixed in. After crossing the park road, you encounter a T-intersection. Turn left to stay on Trail 4 then turn left again at the next intersection. Follow Trail 4 when it breaks off to the left and climbs the low Kunkel Lake dam. Turn left to fully circumnavigate the lake or right if you don't mind cutting off a quarter-mile portion. Going left, take in the views along the lake's north shore, which you should follow even when the trail encounters grassy sections with no signage. The fire tower comes into view about the same time as a mowed path enters from the left. You can turn and cut your hike short, but why?

Climbing the restored fire tower offers a good workout and great park views.

The remaining walk around the lake is easy and pretty. The next section passes by wetlands and crosses the inlet stream before turning south. On the lake's south side, you pass the boat ramp/rental, the beach, and in warm weather many fishermen and geese. Follow the path you previously walked on the north side back to the parking lot side trail and your car. Before leaving, take a few minutes to climb the fire tower for a splendid panoramic view of the park.

Trail 5

Rating: ★ ★ ★   **Configuration:** Loop
Distance: 6 miles   **Difficulty:** Easy

Tour: Trail 5 gives you a little bit of everything that Ouabache has to offer. It's pretty in many places, but monotonous in others. Conveniently, it passes near the campgrounds, Kunkel Lake, and the bison enclosure. The parking lot east of the lake near the "Iron Mike" CCC memorial is a good place to park. There are vault toilets and drinking water. Walk down the park road a short distance and turn left on Trail 5 for counterclockwise navigation of the loop. The first section passes through a young forest, crosses a road, and soon passes close to Campground B. Just past the campground, Trail 3 joins and the path winds through a gorgeous, mature forest—the prettiest stretch of trail in the park. Trail 2 joins for a while, passing through a younger, more-open forest with many pine trees. Trail 2 leaves and eventually Trail 1 joins for a short pass by the north end of the bison enclosure. Departing to the right into the woods with Trail 4, Trail 5 crosses the park road then goes it alone into Ouabache's northwest corner. This is the trail's most remote section. It also tends to be overgrown, mushy, and plagued by invasives. After passing the gatehouse, Trails 4 and 5 team up until reaching the Kunkel Lake dam; take a short side trip to see the lake. After crossing the bridge over the outlet stream, it's a short walk through an open section to your starting point.

14
Pokagon State Park

The Indiana State Park Challenges are popular—and until recently I wasn't aware of how popular. Thirteen parks feature some type of Challenge, and four properties have two different Challenges. Most of the Challenges are centered on hiking, though two are for paddlers and five Centennial Challenges (celebrating a park's 100th anniversary) require driving and walking. Participants photograph waypoints along the Challenge routes to prove completion. Upon showing their photos to staff at a designated location, participants are rewarded with a free sticker.

My eyes were opened to the allure of Challenges by a hiker named Steve from Fort Wayne. I encountered him on the trail multiple times during my year of revisiting Indiana's state parks, and he explained that completing the Challenges was his hobby. "I love stickers!" he professed, but I could tell that he also loved hiking.

Steve considered Pokagon his "home" state park and said that he'd already collected 50-plus Hell's Point Challenge stickers in 2025 and was shooting for at least 75. During an on-trail conversation in Charlestown, I told him that in his honor I would hike the Hell's Point Challenge in the fall.

A couple of months later I was setting up my tent in Pokagon's campground and looking warily at the cloudy sky. The afternoon forecast declared just an *8 percent* chance of precipitation. To buoy my spirits the sun finally broke through the clouds as I departed for the Challenge's start at Pokagon's nature center.

The initial section of the eight-mile hike was easy, following a paved bike trail with the first swatches of fall color brightening the palette around me. The first waypoint was a reproduction of a historic overpass built by the Civilian Conservation Corps in 1936. County Road Bridge, which is used to reach private homes on Lake James, started as a wood structure, was converted to concrete in 1953, then was restored to its original design in 2000.

The bike trail ended, and I followed Trail 4 for a short distance before turning left on a Trail 2 spur near the amphitheater. Periodic Hell's Point Challenge signs eased my wayfinding through the route's many junctions.

A long staircase eases the climb to the top of Hell's Point on Trail 3.

Spring Shelter was the next photographic waypoint. The small structure was built by the CCC in 1936. During construction, crews found a spring just downhill and added piping to keep the artesian well flowing freely. I enjoyed a generous drink of the cold water ("tested regularly for purity," a sign assured me), which I thought was a necessary part of the Challenge.

My luck ran out after I turned onto Trail 3 and the rain started falling. Feeling optimistic, I'd left my jacket back at camp. Fortunately, there was a dense forest canopy overhead, so I took refuge beside a big oak tree until the shower let up.

The Challenge turned onto Trail 7 and the sun popped out as I entered one of my favorite places at Pokagon. In 1991, a project here removed drain tiles from former farmland and returned the area to its historic self—a wetland. I snapped my Challenge picture, watched wood ducks paddle across the pond, and enjoyed the colors of early fall prairie flowers.

Next up was a jaunt on Trail 8 back to Trail 3 and a climb to the Challenge's name-sake landmark, my next photo stop. Contrary to its name, Hell's Point's is not a fiery furnace but rather a pleasant, shady place to rest. Maybe the moniker comes from the steep climb to the top (84 steps up wood stairs) but even that is modest compared to what you find in other parks.

Trail 9 takes the Challenge on a side loop around Hawk Hollow. The first stretch boasts some of the park's biggest trees—which provided me shelter when the skies opened again for an even longer shower. When the rain finally let up, I kept plugging along and soon found myself with a great view…of Interstate 69. Until the late 1990s, this had been the site of the Pokagon Motel. After it closed, ACRES Land Trust spearheaded a project to raise money and acquire the property for the park.

The hike turned away from the highway and returned to the woods before reaching the next Challenge photo location: the CCC Dams. Though difficult to see in the now-dense woods, work crews built—by hand—several stone dams in this area to slow erosion on what, in the 1930s, was cutover land.

Soon I was back on Trail 3 and crossing a marsh on a boardwalk through a narrow hallway of tall cattails. Back on dry ground, a side trail led to the final photo waypoint, Lake Lonidaw. A boardwalk reached to the edge of open water on the beautiful kettle hole, which was ringed by cattails and water lilies. Back on the trail, I passed the Potawatomi Inn, reconnected with the bike path, hiked past the saddle barn, and eventually found myself back where I started.

Inside the nature center, the staffer checked my photos and cheerfully handed me a reward sticker. I asked her if she knew Steve—of course she did. It turns out that he had surpassed his original goal and completed 103 Hell's Point Challenges! I smiled, happy that Steve, and so many other hikers, were having fun in their own way in Indiana state parks.

Pokagon History

Geologically, Pokagon State Park is one of the youngest landscapes in Indiana, the product of massive glaciers advancing south from Canada then retreating again. It's hard to imagine, but 24,000 years ago, about two-thirds of the state was covered with a mile-thick sheet of ice. Then, the earth started to warm, and the ice melted. The last part of Indiana freed from the glacier was the northeast corner, where Pokagon lies, just 14,000 years ago.

Pokagon lay near the collision zone of two expansive ice lobes. As they melted, massive ice blocks broke off and formed lakes, like Lake James, which sits on Pokagon's western boundary. Smaller ice blocks became kettles, some of which have filled in and today are just depressions in the landscape. Deeper kettles today are wetlands or ponds, like Lake Lonidaw, common throughout the park.

Melting glaciers also left more vertical features. Cracks in the ice, called crevasses, collected sand and gravel that were left behind as ridges, like the one along Trail 7 west of the restored wetland pond (a kettle). Melting holes in the ice sometimes collected sand, gravel, and rocks that would form a steep-sided hill, called a kame—like Hell's Point, on Trail 3.

In the wake of the Ice Age, humans were naturally drawn to this landscape. Artifacts found in Steuben County, where Pokagon is located, indicate that people have frequented the area for at least 10,000 years. When the first white explorers reached this area in the 1600s, the Potawatomi were the resident tribe, though they are thought to have migrated from their original homeland north of Lake Huron.

The westward spread of white settlement led to conflict with the native tribes in the late 1700s and early 1800s. A series of treaties conveyed large swaths of land to the U.S.; Pokagon was acquired in an 1826 land purchase sealed by the Treaty of Mississinewas. The first white settlers followed in the 1830s and Steuben County was organized in 1837.

Meanwhile, congress' passage of the Indian Removal Act in 1830 had paved the way for states to force native people off their lands so that they could be acquired by incoming settlers. One Potawatomi band resisted. Led by Leopold Pokagon, the group converted to Catholicism, purchased land, and lived an agrarian lifestyle not unlike that of the incoming whites. The charismatic and savvy Pokagon used the U.S. legal system to protect his tribe's rights. Later, Leopold's son, Simon, became a well-known writer and advocate for native rights, a celebrity who met with presidents and hobnobbed with the nation's social elites. Today, the Pokagon Band of Potawatomi is a federally recognized tribe with its main office in Dowagiac, Michigan.

Back in Steuben County, the rugged landscape east of Lake James had been largely cleared of trees and converted to farmland, but it wasn't well suited to its new role. The soil was rocky, and the area dotted with hills that eroded easily and wetlands that

Historic Spring Shelter is a good spot to grab a cold drink along Trail 2.

were difficult to drain. It was a challenging place for a farmer to make a living—but it was an excellent place to establish a recreation area.

A 1923 report by the Indiana Department of Conservation first suggested the area east of Lake James as suitable for a state park. In 1924, Conservation Commission Chair Richard Lieber visited Steuben County to urge the local Chamber of Commerce to act. Excited by the idea, they moved quickly, raising $35,000 and purchasing the 580-acre Thomas Failing property. The land was gifted to the state of Indiana in December 1925, and Lake James State Park was established.

In 1926, the park expanded to 700 acres and the property renamed Pokagon State Park, honoring Leopold and Simon and celebrating the area's native heritage. Also in that year, construction began on the Potawatomi Inn, which opened in May 1927 as a 20-room facility built largely with materials gathered from the park property. The inn was expanded and renovated multiple times over the next century and today is a 137-room retreat complete with a conference center, restaurant, indoor pool, and wide frontage on Lake James, including a beach.

The Great Depression provided a resource that would forever change Pokagon: the Civilian Conservation Corps, which worked in the park from 1934 to 1942. Company 556 built all the roads, many of the trails, and several important structures. They also rehabilitated the landscape by planting thousands of trees and building erosion control dams like the ones along Trail 9.

The CCC's best-loved legacy was something crews built for their own entertainment in the winter of 1935: the toboggan run. It started as a single, curving track kind of like a bobsled run. The next year crews straightened the track to make it faster. The park, capitalizing on the popularity of the toboggan run with the public, has expanded the facility over the years. Today, sleds ride two refrigerated tracks departing from a 30-foot tower and reach speeds of 40 mph before stopping near the inn. The toboggan run is arguably Indiana's best-known winter attraction and is ridden by thousands of people each year.

Pokagon Today

Pokagon is in far northeast Indiana, 170 miles from downtown Indianapolis. The park is less than 50 miles north of Indiana's second-largest city, Fort Wayne. Modern-day Pokagon has grown to 1,260 acres but still ranks among Indiana's smallest. Pokagon's small size hasn't limited its popularity: 741,000 people visited in 2023–2024, ranking the park fifth overall.

Many people consider the toboggan run to be Pokagon's must-do attraction. From Black Friday through about March 1, the facility is open weekends, many holidays, and over the winter break. The sleds are rented by the hour. If the snow cooperates, visitors can also rent snowshoes, providing an alternative way to explore the park's trails.

Lake James, at 1,200 acres Indiana's fourth largest natural lake, is another big draw for visitors. Much of the lake's shoreline is privately owned and lined with houses and cottages, which makes the state park's public access and lack of development so valuable. Pokagon has two swimming beaches, which are open from Memorial Day to Labor Day, and a rental concession where visitors can hire fishing boats, pontoon boats, paddleboats, row boats, kayaks, and stand-up paddleboards. Lake James has a high-quality fishery with largemouth and smallmouth bass, walleye, and northern pike among the most-prized species.

Other popular park activities include horseback riding (on saddle barn horses only), bird watching, and biking. Cyclists can use the 1.6-mile paved path or follow Highway 727 east from the gatehouse to a connection with the Steuben County Multipurpose Trail for a seven-mile ride to Angola.

Options abound for overnighting in the park. The previously mentioned Potawatomi Inn has a classic lodge feel but offers exceptional comfort and great amenities. Hikers can jump on Trails 1 and 3 just steps from the inn. Not far away are eight historic "inn cabins" (recently renovated) and four larger "cabin suites."

Pokagon has a large camping area with six different units offering a variety of options, including youth camping and group camping. The campgrounds were even more expansive in the past but downsized over the years to better fit the park's relatively small footprint. Campgrounds 1, 3, and 4 have a combined 200 electric sites. Campground 2 has 73 non-electric sites and is a welcoming facility for tent campers. The campgrounds connect directly with Trails 2 and 4.

Outside Pokagon, there are multiple national hotel chain options nearby along Interstate 69, both north and south of the park. Angola, just a few miles south, is a college town (Trine University) and regional commerce center.

Hiking Pokagon

For its small size, Pokagon has outstanding hiking resources, including nearly 14 miles of numbered trails as well as various connector paths and 1.6 miles of paved recreational path. Everything connects, so it's possible to park at one location and hike all the park's trails without getting in your car again. None of the trails are rugged (despite what the official property map says about Trail 9) and all are well-maintained. Signs and on-trail locator maps are common.

Trail 3 is Pokagon's most versatile route, acting as hub on the park's east side with Trails 2, 7, 8, 9, and 6 spoking off on their own lollipop or loop routes. (In fact, the latter four of this group lack their own trailhead and can only be reached by first hiking Trail 3). On the west side, closer to Lake James, Trails 1, 5, and 4 can be pieced together for their own four-mile-plus loop. The variety of routes that you can create by linking together path segments is key to Pokagon's attractiveness for hikers.

Trail Running

Pokagon is an exceptional trail-running destination, boasting a nicely networked mix of paths, good footing, and a rolling topography without too many challenging hills. One of my favorite routes, about nine miles in length, follows the main loop of Trail 3 clockwise from Potawatomi Inn and includes side trips on Trails 2, 7, 8, and 9 as well as a detour on Trail 6. Trail 2 offers fleeting glimpses of Snow Lake and Trail 7 circles a beautifully restored wetland. By the end of the run, you will have visited all of Pokagon's primary habitats.

TRAIL GUIDES

Trail 1

Rating: ★ ★ ★   **Configuration:** Point to Point
Distance: 2 miles   **Difficulty:** Easy

Tour: This path serves as a connector between important park locations (inn, nature center, and beach) but has scenic value as well. From the inn, walk down to Lake James and turn right/west after the beach volleyball courts. The shoreline is public here and side trails go left to the water or right to the cabins. Beyond the first connector to the

POKAGON STATE PARK

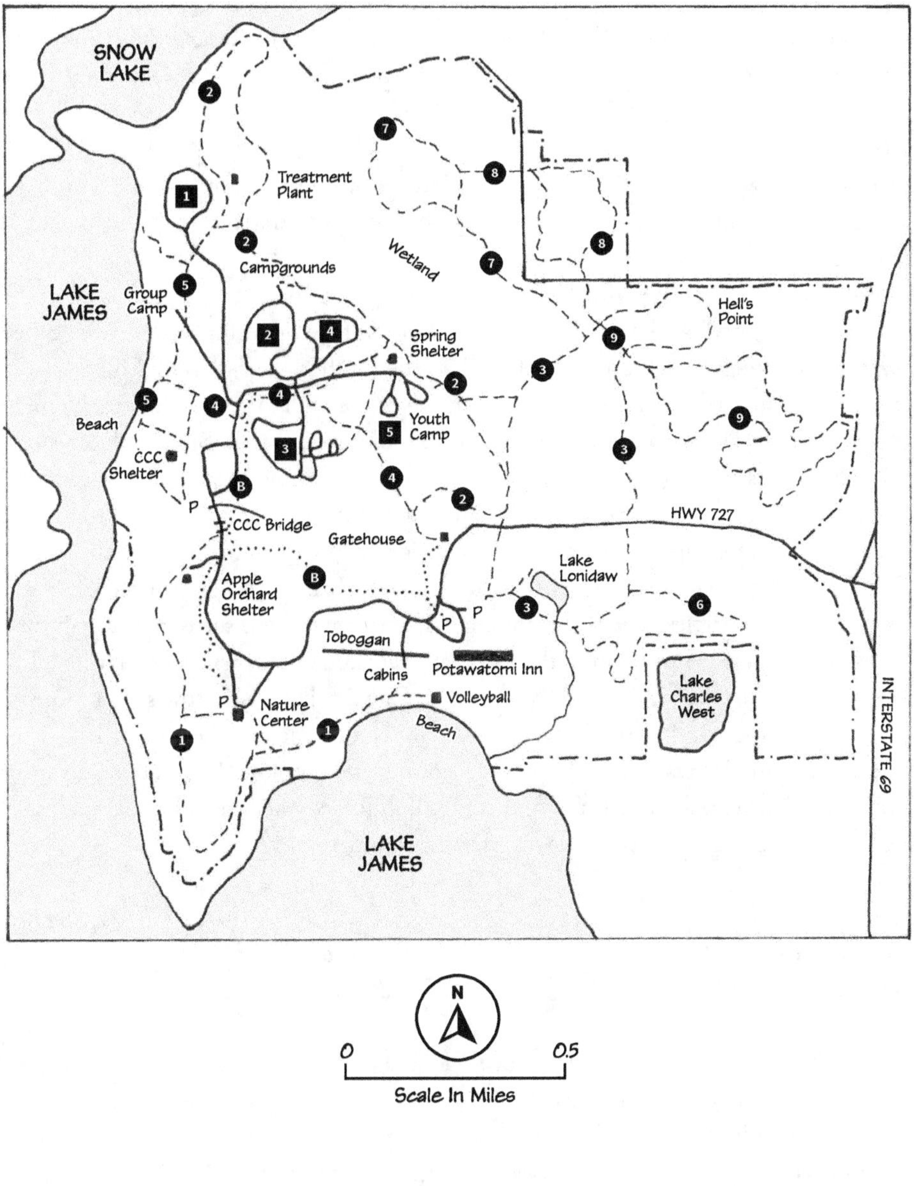

nature center, the shoreline is privately owned; houses and cabins are visible, especially when the leaves are gone. Turning north into a young forest, you pass two more side trails to the nature center before angling through the Apple Orchard picnic area. The trail ends at the park road near the historic County Road Bridge. Turn right on the paved recreational trail then left at the next intersection for a more direct route to the inn parking lot or right to create a return loop past the nature center.

Trail 2

Rating: ★★★

Distance: 2.2 miles

Configuration: Lollipop

Difficulty: Moderate

Tour: This route starts (with Trail 4) near the gatehouse, but parking is limited there. Instead, park at the inn lot and walk west on the connector to the paved bike path. Turn right to reach the start of Trail 2. The southern half of Trail 2 is wooded, rolling, and pretty but shares its route with the bridle path. Things change at Spring Shelter, a nice place for a break and a drink from the artesian well. Beyond the shelter, Trail 2 departs north (right) from the bridle path, following the edge of a wetland in Potawatomi Nature Preserve before entering a beautiful mature forest. The path travels near the campground; connectors periodically depart to the left. You soon hear an odd mechanical noise in the woods; it's the park's sewage treatment plant, which Trail 2 encircles. The plant noise fades, and you start to see blue through the trees: Snow Lake. Unfortunately, the banks are high and overgrown, access is difficult, and views are limited when the leaves are out. Trail 2 follows a narrow strip of forest between Campground 1 and the treatment plant before reaching the start of Trail 5 at the plant's gate. It's really a gravel access road, but keep walking for about 100 yards until Trail 2 takes a sharp left turn and climbs uphill to a junction with the outbound route. Retrace your steps back to your starting point.

Trail 3

Rating: ★★★★★

Distance: 2.2 miles

Configuration: Loop

Difficulty: Moderate

Tour: Featuring beautiful second-growth forests and glacial country wetlands this route is Pokagon's signature trail. It also provides the only access to Trails 6, 7, 8, and 9. The trailhead is in the northeast corner of Potawatomi Inn's main parking lot, near the electric vehicle charging stations. Turn left at the main trail to hike the route clockwise. After crossing Highway 727, Trail 2 and the bridle path join from the left and share the right of way for a short distance before departing again. Back on Trail 3, you soon encounter a third connection with Trail 2; to your left beyond this junction

Lake Lonidaw is a short, easy walk from Potawatomi Inn via Trail 3.

are the Potawatomi Nature Preserve wetlands. Left turns to Trails 7 and 8 and a right turn to Trail 9 follow, before Trail 3 begins its one big climb (only about 100 feet of elevation gain). At the top is Hell's Point and an observation deck. The view is limited, but the hardwood forest is beautiful. Don't be surprised by vehicle noise—the park boundary and a county road are nearby. From Pokagon's high point, Trail 3 makes a steady half-mile descent past a second junction with Trail 9 to a boardwalk across a marsh. After recrossing Highway 727, Trail 6 departs into the woods to the left. Beyond a second junction with the Trail 6 loop, Trail 3 crosses a long boardwalk through a gorgeous wetland, which in summertime is rich with cattails, wildflowers, and calling birds. Take a right turn after the boardwalk to reach one of Pokagon's signature viewpoints: Lake Lonidaw, a glacial kettle hole surrounded by cattails and lily pads. After returning to the main trail, your starting point soon appears through the trees to your left.

Trail 4

Rating: ★ ★　　　　　　**Configuration:** Point to Point
Distance: 1.4 miles　　　　**Difficulty:** Easy

Tour: This nondescript trail provides access to some of Pokagon's key points of inter-est. Park at the inn and follow the directions for Trail 2; Trail 4 departs to the left after sharing space with the bridle path for a short distance. After a quarter mile it rejoins the bridle path, departs to the left, skirts the north edge of Campground 3, and passes the amphitheater. Trail 4 parallels the main campground road then joins the paved bike path for a short distance. As you approach the campground control station, look for the Trail 4 restart across the road to the right; follow the dirt path into the woods. At a T-intersection, Trail 4 splits and you have a choice. Turn right then left to join Trail 5 on a lakefront walk to the beach. On the south end of the beach follow the trail angling uphill through the woods to Trail 4's end, marked by a sign. Or, back at the T, turn left for a more direct upland route to the same endpoint along the edge of the picnic areas and past the beautiful CCC Shelter.

Trail 5

Rating: ★ ★ ★   **Configuration:** Point to Point
Distance: 0.7 miles   **Difficulty:** Moderate

Tour: Trail 5 is a curious, short route that feels more like an extension of Trail 2 than its own path. It begins where Trail 4 ends—near the beach—but the park hasn't provided a Trail 5 sign to tell hikers. Park in the beach lot (first left after the County Road Bridge). The hike starts at the Trail 4 sign, following the angled, stepped path down to the beach, offering a pretty lake view year-round. You finally encounter a Trail 5 marker at the beach's north end as you follow the dirt path into the woods. Lake James stays in view for a time, and side paths provide more access to the water, but the path soon turns inland, and Trail 4 departs to the right. Trail 5 continues through the woods and over two paved road crossings. After the second it follows a gravel road—the sewage treatment plant access—passes a right-hand junction with Trail 2 and ends unceremoniously at the plant's chain-link gate. A narrow, dirt path restarts to the left: this is Trail 2, which, with Trail 4, offers a loop option for your return trip.

Trail 6

Rating: ★ ★ ★   **Configuration:** Loop (with Trail 3)
Distance: 0.7 miles   **Difficulty:** Moderate

Tour: Trail 6 is a beautiful, short hike close to the inn. The route offers a pleasing mix of wetlands and forest—some of the wettest hardwood plots in the park, with more ferns and mushrooms than you'll see elsewhere. Follow the parking and access instructions for Trail 3, but turn right on the main loop. Trail 6 starts just beyond the boardwalk over the Lake Lonidaw outlet marsh. The first stretch transitions from wetlands to second-growth forest. To your right, water—and houses—soon come into view. This is Lake Charles West, private and just beyond the park boundary. As the trail swings back to the west, it passes through one of Pokagon's most pleasing woodlots. The area is wet—there are more wetlands to the right—and has a gorgeous mix of large living trees, ferns, and fungus-covered dead trees. Take your time to look at the interesting details all around you. Trail 6 ends all too quickly when it returns to Trail 3.

Trail 7

Rating: ★ ★ ★ ★   **Configuration:** Lollipop
Distance: 1.8 miles   **Difficulty:** Moderate

Tour: Trail 7 runs through a restored landscape—former farmland in which drain tiles were removed and fire used to promote native species. The result is a hike (or run) that is a feast for the eyes, a mix of water, flowers, grasses, and trees and home to a diversity of birds and other wildlife. Follow the parking and access directions for Trail 3; Trail 7 departs to the left three quarters of a mile north of the trailhead. After an initial drop, Trail 7 makes a steady climb through the woods to the start of both the restored prairie/wetland area and its loop; turn left. An interpretive panel explains how the land you're about to hike through was restored. You pass through a pleasant mix of tall grasses, shrubs, and young trees until finally reaching an outstanding viewpoint above the pond's northwest corner. Continue around the loop, which offers

Trail 1 starts near the Potawatomi Inn beach on the shore of Lake James.

more wetland and prairie views from a variety of angles and passes a junction with Trail 8, before reaching the return path back to Trail 3.

Trail 8

Rating: ★ ★   **Configuration:** Lollipop
Distance: 1.0 miles   **Difficulty:** Moderate

Tour: Trail 8 traverses a square of land cut off from the main park by a county road running along two sides. Much of this area looks like recovering farmland. Follow the parking and access instructions for Trail 3; Trail 8 breaks north just past the Trail 7 junction. The first stretch passes through a beautiful, mature second-growth forest, which continues for a time past the road crossing. Turn left at the loop junction; the trail turns north and enters a mix of grassland, sumac, and young oaks. Turn right at the next intersection to stay on the loop; left connects to Trail 7. The Trail 8 loop continues through open ground to Pokagon's eastern boundary. A junction here used to connect to the Beechwood Nature Preserve trail, but in 2023 owner ACRES Land Trust closed that property to visitors. It may reopen in the future, providing a nice add-on to this hike. Beyond the junction, Trail 8 returns to mature woods for the remainder of its loop back to the Trail 3 connector.

Trail 9

Rating: ★ ★ ★   **Configuration:** Lollipop
Distance: 1.7 miles   **Difficulty:** Moderate

Tour: Trail 9 is a varied and interesting loop on the park's east side, offering both scenery and history. Follow the parking and access instructions for Trail 3; Trail 9 departs to the right just past the Trail 7 junction. Trail 9 re-crosses Trail 3 (after its journey to Hell's Point) then reaches the start of its loop. Turn left and wind your way through one of the prettiest stretches of forest in the park. After crossing a wetland on a boardwalk and making a short climb, Trail 9 pops out of the woods and onto a low ridge overlooking Interstate 69. The trail turns south and skirts a grassland that was once the site of the popular Pokagon Hotel, which operated from the 1950s to the 1990s. Soon it's back into the woods and after a quarter mile a short side trip to a viewpoint (mostly grown over) of the CCC Stone Dams, built in the 1930s to control erosion. After a short climb, Trail 9 switchbacks down to a boardwalk through a wetland before climbing back up to the loop's starting point. Turning left at the first Trail 3 junction offers a different return option to the inn.

15
Potato Creek State Park

My son, Kendal, was visiting a few years back when we decided to drive to Potato Creek—a state park neither of us had visited—for a trail run. Arriving at the gatehouse we grabbed a property map. We didn't know the park, but the northeast quarter of the property looked like a logical place to link together Trails 4, 2, and 1 for a decent-length run. We drove to the lot for Trail 4 and as we parked did a double take at what lay next to the trailhead. A cemetery in the middle of a state park? We decided to get moving now but check out the graveyard later.

After passing the cemetery, Trail 4 followed the shore of Worster Lake, the reservoir that serves as Potato Creek's centerpiece. We paused at the first gap in the trees to take in the view across the 327-acre body of water. It was quiet and the shoreline undeveloped.

Back on the trail, we soon left the lake but a small building in the woods caught our attention. An interpretive panel explained that this was a restored springhouse, the kind used to chill and preserve food in the days before electricity and refrigerators. The constantly running water remained 50 degrees year-round and created a small pond that was brimming with life, a nice spot for a break.

Trail 4 made for an easy, scenic run. The path gently climbed up the wooded valley of a small tributary, with periodic views of the stream and small wetlands it created. We arrived at a junction with a wide, straight trail and turned left. This was the connector to Trail 2. In addition to numbered footpaths, Potato Creek is crisscrossed with remnant farm roads like the one we were running, noted as "CT" on the property map.

We passed by the first junction with Trail 2—to the left—but took the second one, to the right. The trail passed through a mature forest, but a wetland, the Swamp Rose Nature Preserve, lay to our right. Arriving at the edge of the marsh, we found a heavily overgrown viewing platform just off the trail. Without much to see, we pressed on.

Potato Creek is a relatively level and marshy park, but its northeast corner has a pair of hills and Trail 2 climbs both. After the viewing platform, we bounded up a long wooden stair that marked the start of the first climb. Muscling up a section of

This Trail 3 observation deck, on an arm of Worster Lake, is great for birding.

steep, rutted path, we topped out at Steam Boat Hill, elevation 883 feet, though there was no sign to mark our victory.

We quickly gave up our elevation, winding down the back side and bottoming out at an unmarked connector path. Trail 2 immediately started climbing again, though this section was less steep and not as eroded. At the summit, a sign announced "Vargo Hill Elevation 885 Feet" but an overgrown viewing platform offered no view. After a short break, we kept running.

The trees were young here—some of this area was cropland until the park was established in the 1970s—but it felt wild. We scared up a couple of whitetails, adding to the atmosphere, but soon the spell was broken. Vehicle noise turned our attention to a nearby road visible beyond the park's northern boundary—a reminder that Indiana's fourth largest city, South Bend, was just 10 miles away.

Reaching a junction with Trail 1, we turned left on a short connector back to Trail 2, which was overgrown in this area and followed a rickety boardwalk over a marsh. Things soon improved with a climb to higher ground and a patch of woods filled with large, old trees.

Returning to the connector we'd run earlier, we soon turned left at the junction with Trail 4. We were getting tired, but this new section of trail provided a breath of fresh air. It followed the small stream up a scenic valley, highlighted by a pleasing mix of big trees, trailside glacial erratics, and pops of color from interesting mushrooms.

The last mile moved by quickly. Scenic highlights dwindled in the young forest and the downhill route encouraged a quick pace. Soon we were back at the car—but what about that cemetery?

It turns out that Porter Rea Cemetery has a fascinating history. Established in 1854, it was a rare integrated burial ground from before the Civil War. Free Blacks were buried alongside their white neighbors. Forgetting the miles we had just put on our legs, Kendal and I wandered quietly among the graves, fascinated by the tale they told. It was another reminder that Indiana state parks have a human story every bit as powerful as their natural history.

Potato Creek History

Like other state parks in Indiana, Potato Creek has a landscape shaped by glaciers, but this one is relatively young: The last ice melted away just 12,000 years ago. The land is gently rolling and doesn't drain particularly well but it supports rich plant and animal communities that have long attracted humans to the area.

The Potawatomi were the last native tribe to live in the future park and were present when the first white settlers arrived in the early 1800s. One legend about how Potato Creek got its name points to settlers observing native people digging and using for food a potato-like tuber that grew in the wetlands. The Potawatomi were forced out of Potato Creek after the federal Indian Removal Act of 1830, which directed that all native people in this area move west of the Mississippi River.

This sad development opened the door for a remarkable but little-known chapter in Indiana history. In 1837, Samuel Huggart, a free Black man originally from Virginia, purchased 80 acres of land just east of the current park. (A historical marker along Highway 4 marks the location.) This was an area that had been settled by a community of anti-slavery Quakers, who were welcoming to Black neighbors. Samuel likely moved to the area in 1848 with his younger brother, Andrew. In this growing community, white and Black neighbors lived together peacefully, doing business with each other, even attending the same church.

The Huggart brothers expanded their landholdings and business, and Andrew become a prominent citizen in the area. In addition to being a successful farmer and shoemaker, Andrew was the first Black man to serve on a jury as well as run for public office in Indiana. In 1849, he helped found the Olive Branch School, which served both Black and white students—illegal in pre-Civil War Indiana.

The era of interracial harmony was short-lived—many of the area's Black residents, searching for jobs and economic opportunity, moved away by the 1880s. But memories of their time at Potato Creek remain in the historic Porter Rea Cemetery, in which both Black and white residents were buried.

Farming remained Potato Creek's primary occupation into the 20th Century, but in the 1930s the area was touted as a potential recreation destination. A local conservation club thought it was a good place to build a dam, create a lake, and surround the water with a state park. The idea's most ardent supporter was club member and self-taught naturalist Darcey Worster. In addition to surveying and mapping the site himself to confirm its worthiness for a reservoir, Worster hand-crafted insect figurines, which he sent to Indiana legislators to "bug" them about establishing a state park.

Worster's unique lobbying had an impact. In 1939, the Department of Conservation announced that a lake would be built on the site. But World War II intervened, delaying the project for years.

The park project came back to life in 1964, but along with it came local opposition. The proposed property affected 110 different landowners, many of whom were opposed to a state park. Other sites were considered and rejected, and the opposition waned, opening the door for the Department of Natural Resources to announce the new park in 1968. Land acquisition started in 1969, which is now recognized as Potato Creek's birth year. Things moved slowly at first, hampered by an unsupportive governor and families unwilling to sell their land. Eminent domain was used, and feelings were hurt. There is still some anger 50-plus years later.

Development began in earnest in 1971, and there was a lot of work to be done. In addition to building infrastructure, including roads and a dam, many old structures had to be razed or relocated. The first visitors were allowed into the park in 1974. By 1977, nearly $6 million had been spent on South Bend's new state park and it was formally dedicated by Governor Otis Bowen on June 6 of that year.

Potato Creek Today

Potato Creek State Park is a 145-mile drive north of Indianapolis, but just minutes away from South Bend. This proximity to a population center has made it a popular recreation destination: in 2023–2024 Potato Creek attracted 694,000 visitors, sixth most in the park system.

Potato Creek is Indiana's fourth-largest park, covering 3,840 acres. It squeezes a wide variety of activities into this area. Water sports, thanks to Worster Lake, take center stage. The lake is a popular fishing spot, with largemouth bass, bluegill, and black crappie among the most sought-after species. The lake has two boat ramps and in summer watercraft can be rented from a livery on the north shore, near the swimming beach.

Bicycling is also popular at Potato Creek thanks to a 7.7-mile, beginner-friendly mountain bike trail and a paved 3.3-mile recreational bike path. A rental shop offers bikes that can be used on either trail. Horseback riding is the primary activity in Potato Creek's southeast quadrant. A day use area and a 70-site horseman's campground provide access to nearly seven miles of bridle trails.

Trail 4 climbs a pretty valley alongside a tributary of Worster Lake.

Trail 4 hikers pass a historic integrated cemetery established before the Civil War.

Even though much of Potato Creek was logged and previously farmed, restoration efforts have resulted in a diverse, natural-feeling landscape—a pleasing mix of forests, wetlands, and prairies that is home to a rich flora and fauna. Potato Creek is a noted stop on the Indiana Birding Trail, with opportunities for viewing a wide variety of species. Bald eagles are common, and two osprey nesting sites can be found in the park.

The biggest news from Potato Creek is the construction of its new inn—Indiana's first built from the ground up since 1939. It will offer beautiful views from Worster Lake's south shore (an area previously occupied by the Whispering Winds shelters), feature 120 rooms, and boast loads of amenities. It is not expected to open until at least 2027.

Until the inn opens (and after), you have a couple of other options for overnighting in Potato Creek. The park has 17 family cabins that sleep up to eight people and are available year-round. Potato Creek also has a large campground, with 287 electric sites spread across five loops. Connector paths link to Trail 1 and most of the hiking trail network.

Outside the park, the nearest lodging options can be found on the edge of South Bend in the vicinity of U.S. Highways 20 and 31. Closer to Potato Creek, the towns of North Liberty and Lakeville offer gas stations, restaurants, and places to buy supplies.

Hiking Potato Creek

For its size, Potato Creek has relatively modest hiking resources. It's also impacted by a lack of trail connectivity. There are eight numbered or named trails covering 10-plus miles of pathway. In addition, there are at least four miles of connector trails, which aren't signed but are shown on the property map. The numbered/named trails are in good shape and nicely signed.

In the northeast quarter of the park, Trails 1, 2, 4, and various connecting trails link well, affording the opportunity for long hikes in a scenic setting. This network connects to the campground, or you can hike it from the Nature Center on the west and Porter Rea Cemetery on the east. Total walking distance would be more than seven miles on the three linked loops.

The park's other hiking-only trails are all isolated and require a drive-then-walk strategy to access them. Trail 3 is the best of the other trails and worth a visit. Another walking resource to consider is the park's 3.3-mile paved bike path, which offers access to areas on the west end of the lake and below the dam.

Trail Running

Potato Creek has a lot of potential for trail running. Most of the trails are wide and the footing is good. Trails 1, 2, and 4 plus various connectors create a network in Potato Creek's northeast quadrant that is very friendly to runners. By repeating loops—plus using connector segments for variety—it's possible to put together an enjoyable 13 or 14-mile run on these paths.

The other hiking trails are runnable, but short and isolated from each other. Potato Creek is a big park, which means enduring long road stretches to link them together. A better option is to run the park's paved bike path, which has a southern terminus near Trail 3 and a northern terminus near the beach. From the beach, you can run Trail B to the campground and various road or footpath connections to Trails 1 or 5.

TRAIL GUIDES

Trail 1

Rating: ★ ★ ★   **Configuration:** Loop
Distance: 2.2 miles   **Difficulty:** Moderate

Tour: Trail 1 is accessible from the campground (via a connector path) but non-campers should park at the nature center. Follow the "To Trails" sign to an interpretive panel explaining the short Nature Center Trail and how it connects to Trail 1. As you start walking you pass a small pond and an observation deck with a view of Worster Lake. After swinging north, Trail 1 joins the right-of-way of the Old Peppermint Road, which was inundated by the lake. Trail 1 departs to the right at a large, odd sign extolling the route's virtues. The trail drops to a shoreline overlook of a marshy arm of the lake, passes an unmarked connector road, and turns north. Trail 2 joins from the right then departs in the same direction a quarter mile later. Trail 1 makes a sharp left, passes the north end of the connector encountered previously, then meets its first mountain bike trail crossing. This area has some older trees and a scattering of pines. Continuing west, the path crosses a paved access road then the campground connector departs to the right. Turn left and follow the "To Nature Center" sign. The route ends in a large picnic area; the nature center and your vehicle should be visible on the far side of the playground.

Trail 2

Rating: ★ ★ ★   **Configuration:** Loop (Lollipop using Trail 1)
Distance: 2 miles   **Difficulty:** Moderate
(3.9 miles round trip via Trail 1)

Tour: The property map calls this route "Rugged" but there isn't much in the way of technical challenge. Trail 2 must be accessed by other routes. Follow the guide for Trail 1 and turn right at the first junction with Trail 2. The initial stretch is overgrown, marshy, and includes a rickety boardwalk. Things improve as the trail climbs into a mature forest with large trees, rocks, and—in the spring—plenty of wildflowers. The trail Ts at a former road; turn left. (A right takes you to Trail 4.) Trail 2 departs to the right from the old road, descends, and makes its closest approach to Swamp Rose Nature Preserve, a large wetland in the northeast corner of the park. A trailside viewing blind once looked onto a small pond but now is overgrown. A large wooden staircase departs from the viewing deck and starts the first big climb of the day, to the top of Steam Boat Hill. The summit is unmarked, and the trail drops immediately, passes a connector trail junction, and starts an easier climb to the next high point. Vargo Hill is only two feet taller but warrants both a sign and a viewing platform—also overgrown. Continuing, it's a steady quarter mile downhill to the junction with Trail 1. Turn left to return the way you started or go straight for a longer return route on Trail 1.

Trail 3

Rating: ★ ★ ★ ★   **Configuration:** Loop
Distance: 1.0 miles   **Difficulty:** Moderate

Tour: This one-mile walk traverses a beautiful mature forest and offers views of Worster Lake. Park in the Quaking Aspen picnic area. The wide trail starts just beyond

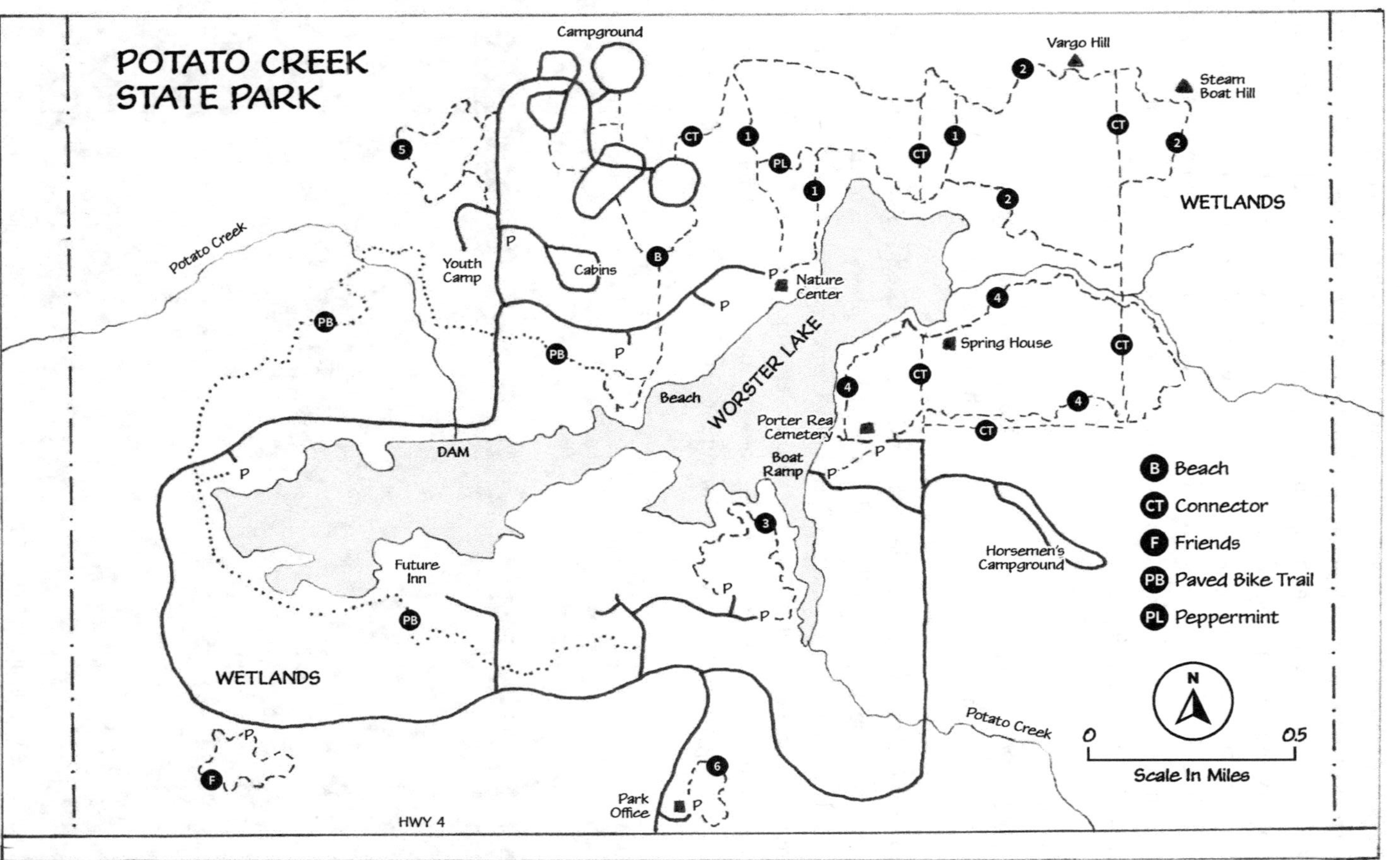
POTATO CREEK STATE PARK
Campground
Vargo Hill
Steam Boat Hill
WETLANDS
Youth Camp
Cabins
Potato Creek
Nature Center
Spring House
WORSTER LAKE
Beach
Porter Rea Cemetery
Boat Ramp
DAM
Future Inn
Horsemen's Campground
WETLANDS
Potato Creek
Park Office
HWY 4
B Beach
CT Connector
F Friends
PB Paved Bike Trail
PL Peppermint
N
0   0.5
Scale In Miles

the easternmost lot. The path quickly reaches an overlook of the Potato Creek arm of the reservoir before turning inland and winding among large trees. It's a lovely forest; wildflowers are plentiful in the spring. A V-shaped boardwalk/bridge crosses a small tributary and offers a bench for a short rest. At its halfway point, the trail descends a steep hill, crosses a boardwalk, and reaches a viewing platform by a marshy bay with open water in the distance—a great spot to look for birds. Resuming your hike, you begin a gentle climb back to the uplands. The trail emerges from the forest on the north side of the picnic area.

Trail 4

Rating: ★ ★ ★ ★ ★   **Configuration:** Loop
Distance: 2.5 miles   **Difficulty:** Moderate

Tour: If you only have a couple hours to visit Potato Creek, this is the hike to do. It explores an especially beautiful part of the park and passes two interesting historical sites. Park by one of these sites, Porter Rea Cemetery. Trail 4 skirts the south and west sides of the cemetery then the path closely follows the shore of Worster Lake. Periodic openings offer commanding views across the water. After turning inland and passing through an attractive, mature forest the path returns to the water in a

Worster Lake is a popular destination for boaters, fishermen, and swimmers.

marshy area with a viewing platform—a good place to look for water-loving birds. Continuing, the trail passes a small building in the woods: a reconstruction of the Shrader Springhouse. It's a pretty spot, with a small pond and a bench. The trail starts climbing the valley of a small tributary—at one point there's a viewing platform over a small pond—then intersects with the connector to Trail 2. Cross this wide path and continue up the valley, which only seems to get more beautiful, with pretty stream views, glacier-deposited boulders, big trees, and colorful mushrooms. Eventually the path exits the mature forest for a scrubby younger one, crosses another connector trail, and enters a downhill straightaway for the last half mile to the parking lot. Don't forget to tour the cemetery, which dates to 1854 and was integrated—very rare for pre-Civil War America.

Trail 5

Rating: ★
Distance: 1.0 miles
Configuration: Lollipop (two access options)
Difficulty: Easy

Tour: This forgettable trail is disconnected from others in the park but can be reached by a short roadside walk west from the campground. If you aren't camping, park at the visitor lot adjacent to the campground office and walk north along the entrance road; you'll see the trailhead on your left. The loop is a simple mowed path through a scrubby young forest with dense undergrowth. A pine plantation and summertime trailside flowers offer some interest. A side trail departs toward the campground. A quick trip down this stub reveals a historic highlight: an old stone wall, a ghostly remnant of a former farmstead.

Trail 6

Rating: ★ ★ ★
Distance: 0.5 miles
Configuration: Loop
Difficulty: Easy

Tour: It would be easy to miss this short hike—which is located *before* the gate-house—but make a point to stop. Park by the Visitors Center, which is just off Highway 4. The trail departs from the east side of the lot and immediately deposits you into a different world. The path winds through a marshy forest, with several large trees and small pools of water standing nearly year-round. In the summer, it's a rich, green world, with mosses, ferns, and lush undergrowth. At the back side of the loop you encounter a large pond, complete with a viewing platform. It's a little overgrown, but still a good place to see herons, wood ducks, and other water-loving birds. The trail ends on the north side of the parking lot.

Friends Trail

Rating: ★ ★   **Configuration:** Loop
Distance: 0.75 miles   **Difficulty:** Easy

Tour: As the name implies, this trail was developed by the Friends of Potato Creek. It isn't much of a hike but offers a good way to enjoy the wetland-rich southwest corner of the park. Turn left at the intersection past the gatehouse and drive a mile to the parking area, which is on the left. Follow the mowed trail to the right through the dense undergrowth until you reach the first viewing platform. This is the best of the three viewpoints, so take your time to scan the adjacent pond for interesting bird life. Continue along the path to the next platform, which has a nice bench but is distant from the water. The final stop is a modest platform, but it has a decent view of a small pond.

CONNECTING TRAILS

The northeast quadrant of Potato Creek is crisscrossed with unmarked hiking paths, many of which are shown on the official property map. Together, they represent at least four miles of walking paths separate from the hiking trails. Some are former roads that predate the park; others are utilitarian paths, connecting one popular site with another.

B Trail: This Y-shaped connector provides a direct path from two of the campground loops to the beach and mountain bike trailhead.

CT Trail: This isn't one trail but many—the property map denotes at least 10 "CT" segments. Many are former roadways, meaning they are arrow-straight and might even have a crumbling layer of thin asphalt as a base. They are valuable for linking trails and are runner friendly.

PL Trail: This is a designation for segments of Old Peppermint Road, which shares a route with parts of Trail 1 and makes connections just north of the Nature Center.

16
Prophetstown State Park

Summer—when the prairie flowers are blooming—is the best time to visit Prophetstown State Park. Unfortunately, one particular summer had offered mostly hot, humid, and stormy weather. When a break in the heat wave appeared, I hit the road and crossed my fingers that the cool weather would hold for a few hours at least.

After driving to the north end of the park road, I hopped out and walked to a nearby scenic overlook. I was immediately reminded why this was the best time to visit Prophetstown. Spreading out in front of me was an expansive restored prairie. A small stream meandered through the grassland. Pops of white, yellow, pink, and purple—wildflowers in bloom—decorated the broad green palette. I couldn't wait to explore the trails that cut through this inviting landscape.

I took off at a gentle jog down a paved bike trail. After crossing the dam holding back a small but pretty pond, the trail turned right. I followed Trail 3 down a two-track graveled path through the heart of the restored prairie. Interspersed among the tall grass were cone flowers, milkweed, black-eyed Susans, Joe-Pye weed, and Queen Anne's lace. Butterflies and bees flitted around the flowers. Field sparrows called all around me.

The trail turned left and entered a green hallway bordered by tall, dense plants typical of river bottomland. A glance to the right through a thin spot in the vegetation revealed a flash of water. I ran until I reached a side trail and followed it to the banks of the Wabash River. This was the third state park I'd visited that year that bordered Indiana's beloved home stream, and all offered different experiences. Upstream, Ouabache State Park barely acknowledges the river's existence and doesn't run a marked trail to its banks. Harmonie State Park, near the river's junction with the Ohio, embraces the Wabash with a picnic area and short trail.

At Prophetstown, nearer the river's midpoint, the Wabash is accessible but isolated from the main part of the park. This area tends to flood but on this day the river, well within it banks, was a scenic highlight not a threat. Just upstream of where I was standing, the Tippecanoe River added its clear water to the muddier Wabash. The

Summer wildflowers bloom in abundance in restored prairie along Trail 3.

next stretch of my run followed the Tippecanoe through a bottomland forest, and I stopped briefly to enjoy a view of the smaller, shallower tributary.

My run took me to another junction with the paved bike path, which I followed. The pavement ended at a river overlook and Trail 4 continued as a wide dirt path paralleling the Tippecanoe through a bottomland forest. The trail departed the trees for a long, mowed stretch along the forest's edge. The grassy area to my left looked like recovering agricultural land in need of restoration.

Back in the trees I crossed a small bridge and reached an unmarked T-intersection, the beginning of a loop. I followed the riverside leg to the right until it turned inland, marking the start of my return trip. It was a good place for a break, so I walked to the water's edge.

This wasn't a wild place—there were small houses lining the far bank of the Tippecanoe—but it was *alive*. In the silty shallows I could see tracks left by raccoons and herons. The air was filled with small mayflies, emerging from the water to enjoy their brief adult life. Splashes from midriver caught my attention. Small fish, probably creek chubs, were voraciously grabbing mayflies trying to escape to the open air. I imagined larger fish, including smallmouth bass, likely hovering just downstream, ready to enjoy a chub meal.

Turning away from the lively river, I resumed my run, completed the loop, and soon was back on the bike path. I exited the pavement on a mowed path through the prairie then followed Trail 3 into the woods.

The narrow trail was beautiful here, roller-coastering along a hillside and winding past huge sycamores, oaks, and other trees; it felt like I had entered a completely different state park. After crossing the second of two large, new-looking bridges, I scanned uphill ahead of me and saw I wasn't alone: a whitetail doe, startled by my approach, was frozen in the middle of the trail. For a moment, we considered each other from a distance, then she decided it was time to move on.

I continued my run, reveling in the wildness, until I saw a well-worn side trail and decided to explore it. I emerged from the woods in a subdivision filled with suburban McMansions. Nature's spell was broken. Back on Trail 3, it was a short distance back to my car. My trek was over, and it had been a great one.

Looking later at a map of the area, I realized that the gorgeous, forested section of Trail 3 ran just yards away from the edge of an 18-hole golf course. Initially, I felt a sense of letdown, but I reconsidered. In modern-day Indiana we have to grab, restore, protect, and cherish pieces of nature—like Prophetstown State Park—wherever we can find them.

Prophetstown History

Dominated by prairies and gentle, rolling plains, Prophetstown has a different look than most other Indiana state parks. The park can thank glaciers and rivers—relatively recent geographic forces—for shaping its landscape.

Prophetstown was covered by a thick sheet of ice during the final push of the Pleistocene glaciers. The ice scoured the landscape and laid down a thick layer of deposits as it melted away to the north, starting about 22,000 years ago. Sometime between 17,000 and 14,000 years ago, a catastrophic flood scoured a wide, new valley—home to the modern-day Wabash River, which makes up the southern border of the state park.

Over time, the Wabash and its tributary, the Tippecanoe River, eroded away more of the glacial deposits, leaving three distinct terraces. The floodplain along the rivers is the lowest terrace. The middle terrace lies west of Harrison Creek and constitutes most of the park's land. And the upper terrace tops the hill north of the fishing pond.

Historically, the Wabash in this region formed a dividing line between the deciduous hardwood forests to the east and the vast tallgrass prairies to the west. The earliest surveys reveal a mix of forests and prairies along with wetlands in the areas that became part of the park.

Thanks to its rich soil, abundant plant and animal resources, and proximity to navigable rivers, Prophetstown has attracted humans for thousands of years. A variety of native tribes traveled through and lived in the area, and French traders were common visitors. The French built a major trading post, Fort Ouiatenon, just downstream on the Wabash, west of modern-day Lafayette. Over time, the fort became a conflict point for native tribes battling first with the British and later Americans, who took over the installation and ultimately burned it. Yet removing the fort, did not end the conflict, which came to a head in the early 1800s.

Charismatic Shawnee leader Tecumseh, seeing the Americans as an existential threat to native people, began recruiting and unifying tribes for a military stand against the onslaught of white settlement. Aided by his spiritual leader brother, Tenskwatawa (known as "The Prophet"), Tecumseh began massing his resistance at Prophetstown, a large settlement established in 1808 within the modern-day park. There, people from 14 different tribes lived and prepared for battle, drawing the attention of the U.S. government. Indiana Governor William Henry Harrison was directed to assemble militia in 1811 and proceed to Prophetstown.

The troops camped near modern-day Battleground on November 6 in advance of a meeting with Tenskwatawa scheduled for the next day. It never happened. Instead, the native forces attacked and were repelled in what today is known at the Battle of Tippecanoe. The natives escaped but the U.S. forces burned the village. The Shawnee later returned and partially rebuilt Prophetstown. Tecumseh, who was on a recruiting trip during the battle, supported the British during the War of 1812 and continued fighting the Americans until he was killed in 1813 at the Battle of the Thames.

In the wake of the Battle of Tippecanoe and Indiana statehood in 1816, settlers streamed into the area around Prophetstown and Lafayette grew into an important center for transportation and trade. What would someday become a state park was for many years farmland. The property attracted little attention until the late 1980s. The Department of Natural Resources was looking to site a new park along the Wabash River, and the Prophetstown property fit the bill, especially when considering the area's historic resources. In 1991, the legislature approved $900,000 for planning and land acquisition, starting a process that took more than a decade to complete. Eventually, with enough land in hand and infrastructure completed, the park was opened and dedicated in 2004.

It took considerable work to turn Prophetstown into a valuable recreational resource. A trailer park had to be removed, farm buildings were torn down, and fence rows ripped out. Significantly, agricultural lands had to be reworked into something more natural after nearly two centuries of domestication. Much of the park is restored prairie, which required plant removal, native replanting, and ongoing fire management. Up to 500 acres of the park are managed with controlled burns each year. Invasive plants are an ongoing challenge.

The Tippecanoe River glides past Trail 4 on its way to joining the Wabash River.

One interesting aspect of Prophetstown is that it's scheduled to keep growing. It's currently listed at 2,000 acres, while the original plan called for 2,770 acres. The property map shows three large plots noted as "Future Park Area." In a recent interview, the park manager mentioned excitement about the large parcel adjoining the park's west side, which as of 2025 had an active gravel quarry. This operation could shut down, and the land conveyed to the state as early as 2030. The addition contains gravel pit lakes that someday could provide boating, fishing, and other water-based recreation.

Prophetstown Today

Prophetstown State Park is a convenient and beloved resource for the Lafayette/West Lafayette metro area. It's also easy to reach from Indianapolis, just 70 miles and a 75-minute drive via I-65.

Prophetstown has a varied mix of activities available in addition to hiking. One of the most popular is visiting the Farm at Prophetstown, a living history operation preserving a 1920s-era working farm. The 125-acre homestead is leased from the state and operated by an independent nonprofit. Visitors can tour the buildings, get an up-close look at the animals, and even purchase food items (in season) grown at the farm.

An earlier era of history is preserved at the Native American Village, a collection of five buildings that pay tribute to Prophetstown in 1808 (which was not located at this site, by the way). The replica structures are relatively new—they were constructed for filming a documentary—but are in poor shape. Access is restricted to some of the buildings (for security reasons) and the interpretive signage is limited. The village is a quarter mile walk from the Visitors Center, or a half mile walk from the farm. The park is exploring plans to relocate an expanded version of the village to a more accessible site near the Circle of Stones, a monument to the 14 tribes that lived at historic Prophetstown.

The park is also known for its large aquatic center with a pool, water slides, and a lazy river. Fishing, both in the pond and in the two rivers, is also popular. Mountain biking isn't allowed on Prophetstown's trails, but road cyclists make good use of the park. A five-mile paved bike path, roughly paralleling the main park road, runs from the gatehouse to a Tippecanoe River overlook near the start of Trail 4.

Focusing attention on the natural resources may be the best way to appreciate Prophetstown. The prairie areas are expansive, beautiful, and unique for 21st century Indiana. Summertime offers a riot of color when the flowers are blooming—and with flowers come the insects, butterflies, and birds that are attracted to them.

The campground was one of the park's original features when it opened and it remains popular today. There are 110 sites; half are electric only and half are full

The Farm at Prophetstown is a popular stop after hiking the Village Trails.

water/sewer/electric. The campground is in what used to be a Christmas tree farm. A few spruce and pine trees remain but most have replaced with native hardwoods. For hikers, the campground offers multiple access points to Trail 1.

The park has no inn or cabins, but as long as long as you're not trying to find a room on a Purdue football or basketball weekend, you will find ample hotel options in Lafayette/West Lafayette.

Hiking Prophetstown

Prophetstown has five numbered/named trails, which together offer more than 12 unique miles of hiking. In addition, there is a five-mile paved biking/hiking trail running through the heart of the park that connects with the four numbered trails at multiple locations.

The four numbered trails are best hiked as joined pairs. Trails 1 and 2 can be combined for a loop—or better yet, a figure 8—hike of four or five miles. This route is primarily prairie but offers sections through scrub woods, past a pond, and alongside a unique wetland type called a fen; 134 acres in this area has been set aside at Prophetstown Fen Nature Preserve.

Trails 3 and 4 naturally go together, in part, because you must hike either the bike path or Trail 3 just to get to the start of Trail 4. The full Trail 3/4 loop-plus-out-and-back covers nearly seven miles and offers tremendous variety. It visits restored prairies, big rivers, bottomland forests, wetlands, and mature upland forests.

Prophetstown can be hiked year-round but varies greatly by season. The prettiest time is summer when the prairie flowers are blooming, but autumn offers expansive views (especially of the rivers) after the leaves fall. Spring is also inviting but river flooding can close parts of Trails 3 and 4.

Trail Running

The Prophetstown trail system offers an exceptional running resource. All the trails—including the paved bike path—are run-friendly. The park is the domain of the mowed path. Footing is good and hills are gentle. The views are exceptional and always changing. It's a place where the miles seem to roll by with relatively little effort.

The general openness is something that runners will have to consider before visiting Prophetstown. There is minimal shade in the prairie area and sunny, summer days can be brutal. Wind is also a challenge. All the trails have long open stretches with few breaks. Finally, there's the water. Flooding can close Trails 3 and 4 in the spring, and after rains it's easy to find soggy conditions throughout the part.

Because the numbered trails and the paved bike path all connect, putting together a run of whatever length pleases you is easy. My favorite is the Trail 3 and 4 run, just under seven miles. For something longer, consider a tour of all four numbered trails, 11-12 miles depending on how you manage Trails 1 and 2. The Village Trails are also another nice running resource, offering almost three miles of mowed prairie paths.

TRAIL GUIDES

Trail 1

Rating: ★ ★ ★   **Configuration:** Loop (with spurs to campground and aquatic center)
Distance: 2.25 miles   **Difficulty:** Easy

Tour: This is the first trail you encounter along the main park road and arguably the best for exploring the restored prairie. It connects directly with the campground, but if you aren't camping, park at the Bobolink Shelter lot. To hike the trail counterclockwise, follow the sign to the left of the vault toilet. The first section passes through a young scrub forest that was once part of a Christmas tree farm. The trail breaks out onto a mowed path through the prairie, which in the summer will be festooned with blooming flowers. After a left turn, Trail 2 departs to the right, continuing along the fence line. Follow Trail 1 northwest past the Blazingstar Shelter, cross the park road, and start a gentle descent toward Harrison Creek. The prairie gets even more beautiful with many milkweeds appearing along the trail. At a T-intersection near a small grove

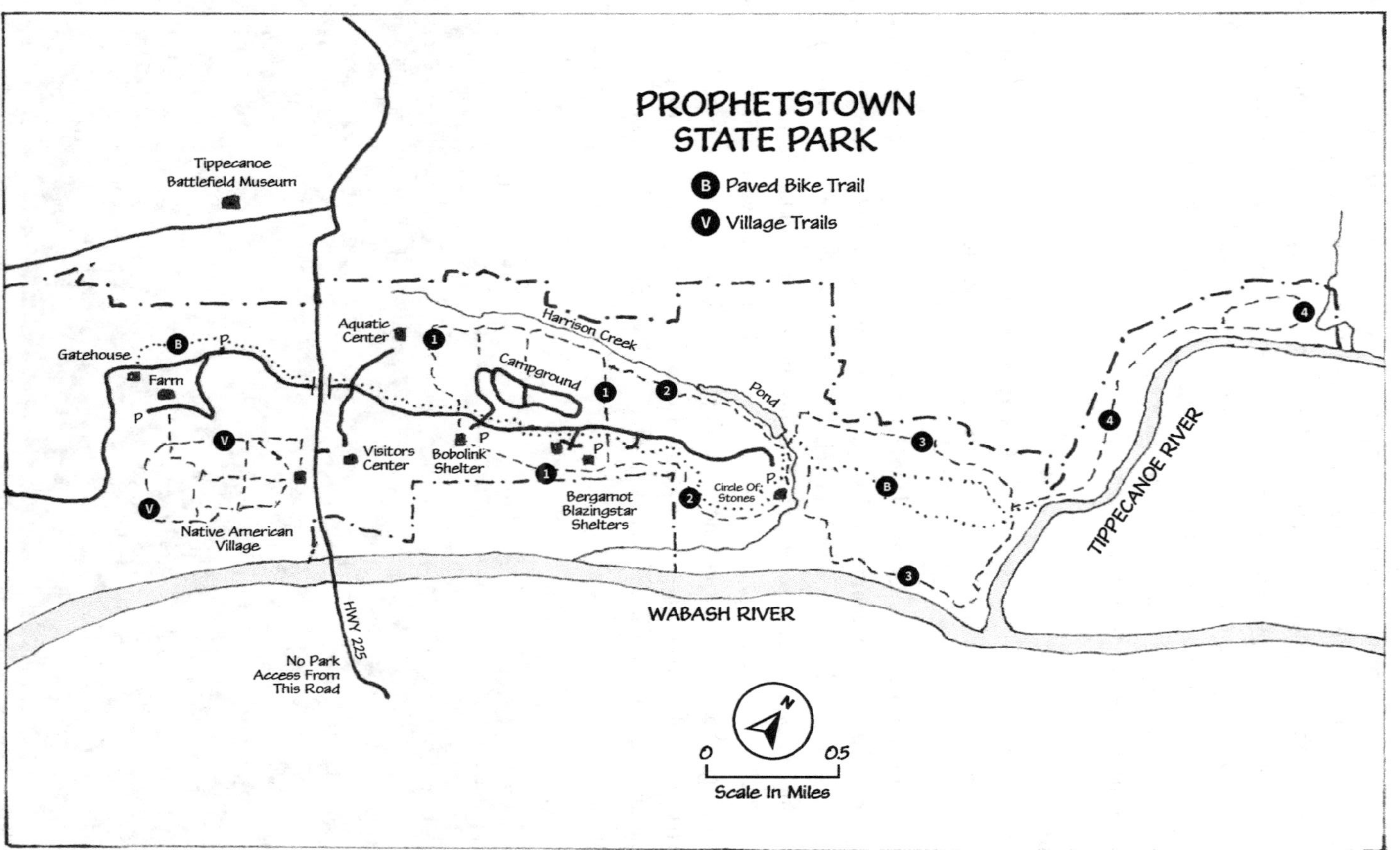
PROPHETSTOWN
STATE PARK
B Paved Bike Trail
V Village Trails
Tippecanoe Battlefield Museum
Gatehouse
Farm
Native American Village
Aquatic Center
Visitors Center
Bobolink Shelter
Bergamot Blazingstar Shelters
Campground
Harrison Creek
Pond
Circle Of Stones
HWY 225
No Park Access From This Road
WABASH RIVER
TIPPECANOE RIVER
N
0
0.5
Scale In Miles

of trees, Trail 2 appears again from the right; turn left to stay on Trail 1. This area is part of a fen, an alkaline, groundwater-fed wetland with a unique mix of plants. It can be wet here in the spring. Skirting the north side of the campground, continue hiking straight past two campground access trails and an unmarked aquatic center spur to the right. After hiking through some scrub woods, you'll reach an area that in 2025 was undergoing invasives removal, obliterating the trail. Follow the prairie edge to the right until you reach a wide trail opening. After crossing the bike path and main road, you return to the Bobolink Shelter area.

Trail 2

Rating: ★★★   **Configuration:** Loop (with part of Trail 1)
Distance: 1.9 miles   **Difficulty:** Moderate

Tour: Most of Trail 2 roughly follows Harrison Creek and passes through some unique and scenic environments. Park in the lot at the northern terminus of the park road. From the lot, walk to the left on the paved bike trail, and turn off on the concrete path leading to an overlook. Just before the wooden deck, follow the Trail 2 sign onto the dirt path. The trail swings right and follows the winding creek above a gorgeous wet prairie—the result of a restoration made possible by Indiana Department of Transportation mitigation funds. The trail continues into a narrow riparian woodland, a beautiful stretch offering views through the trees of prairies

Trails 2 and 3 pass alongside the Fishing Pond, a small impoundment on Harrison Creek.

and ponds. Trail 2 climbs out of the valley to the restored upland prairie, parallels the bike path for a while, then follows a fence line to a T-intersection with Trail 1. Technically, Trail 2 ends here, but turn right and follow Trail 1 to a second T near a stand of sycamores. Turn right to return to Trail 2. To your left are the upper reaches of Harrison Creek and a scenic fen. Soon the park's small-but-pretty Fishing Pond appears. Follow its bank to a junction with the paved bike path and a quick uphill trip to your vehicle.

Trail 3

Rating: ★ ★ ★ ★   **Configuration:** Loop
Distance: 3.5 miles   **Difficulty:** Moderate

Tour: This scenic route explores several unique habitats; by the time you finish the full loop you feel like you've hiked multiple trails. Park at the north end of the main road and walk to the left on the paved bike trail. After crossing the Fishing Pond dam, follow the Trail 3 markers down a two-track gravel path. The trail passes through a gorgeous, flower-rich prairie, the result of a restoration project funded by Indiana DOT. Soon the prairie is replaced by the tall, dense plants of a river bottomland. In summer, the Wabash is out of sight to your right; it's much more visible in fall and winter. In a half mile you'll reach an easy river access point, with side trails to the confluence of the Wabash and Tippecanoe. Trail 3 turns left and enters an open bottomland forest along the Tippecanoe. As you emerge from the trees, the paved bike path reappears. To the right, it becomes Trail 4. Instead, stay straight on the mowed path through the prairie, which soon dives into a narrow opening in the trees and transforms into a winding forest trail. This pretty section looks unlike any previous part of the path. It's a remnant of mature forest hemmed in by prairies and a golf course. Despite the proximity to civilization, this section feels wild and remote, with bridges, large trees, and expansive views of the nearby grasslands. The path climbs and descends multiple times, in the process bouncing over rocks and roots—authentic hiking. On emerging from the woods, Trail 3 rejoins the pavement, passes the pond, and returns to your starting point.

Trail 4

Rating: ★ ★ ★   **Configuration:** Point to Point (with short loop)
Distance: 3.4 miles   **Difficulty:** Easy
(out and back from Trail 3)

Tour: Trail 4 follows a long, narrow slice of land along the Tippecanoe River that feels like an add-on to the main park. The area is not wilderness, but it's remote, which adds to its appeal. Park at the lot at the far end of the main road and walk the paved bike trail to its end, where Trail 4 begins as a wide dirt/mowed path following the Tippecanoe. After passing through a bottomland forest the trail pops out of the trees and follows the edge of a former agricultural field that hasn't yet been restored to prairie. Numerous side trails offer periodic access to the river. After returning to the woods and crossing a small footbridge, the trail reaches an unsigned T-intersection, the start of a loop. Continuing to the right offers nice views of the river. Just before a small tributary (beyond which the park border lies), Trail 4 turns inland through a grove of huge sycamores. After following the loop back to its beginning, retrace your steps to the paved bike path. You have four options for returning to your car: the paved path, either leg of Trail 3, or a parallel gravel bike trail that branches off just past the Trail 3 intersection.

Village Trails (V)

Rating: ★★

Configuration: Network

Distance: 2.8 miles

Difficulty: Easy

Tour: This interconnected web of mowed pathways allows hiking and running through the restored prairie in the vicinity of Prophetstown's replica Native American village. Drive to the parking lot for the Farm at Prophetstown; the Village Trails start to the right of the restrooms you pass on the drive in. Hike down the mowed path to the interpretive sign. All three routes leaving from this spot eventually reach the village, but for the most direct path turn left and follow the fence line towards a large woodlot. Take the second right turn and follow the path that angles eastward through the tall grass. The "village" is a collection of historically correct replica buildings constructed for filming a documentary. They re-create representative structures that were likely present at Prophetstown (though not at this site) in 1808. The Visitors Center is a short walk from the village, or you can return to the farm using either of two mowed paths that enter from the south.

17
Shades State Park

Shades is an outlier in the Indiana state park system because it is relatively undeveloped and feels wild and untamed. It's also exceedingly beautiful, with old-growth forests, spectacular rock formations, and one of the state's prettiest streams. It also offers the value of its relative anonymity. Despite ultra-popular Turkey Run being 11 miles away, Shades attracts fewer visitors than all but one Indiana state park.

Looking for a relatively people-free experience surrounded by autumn colors, I drove to Shades for a late October weekday camp-and-trail adventure. Following a night in the tent, I planned to rise early the next morning for a trail run to Pine Hills Nature Preserve. After some rest, I'd hit the trail again, this time with my fishing gear, in a quest to catch some smallmouth bass in Sugar Creek.

I arrived at the near-empty campground with enough daylight to set up the tent and cook some dinner. After eating and cleaning up, I stayed warm next to a crackling fire before snuggling into my winter-weight sleeping bag.

I was up just after sunrise, focused on warming up with oatmeal and hot coffee, my breath visible in the cold air. It took me a while to convince myself that this run was going to be fun, but soon I was heading east on the Backpack Trail to the heart of the park and a connection with Trail 10. This route is flat and nondescript—largely forgettable in a park blessed with amazing trails—but its purpose became clear as I reached the pavement of Highway 234. On the far side was the entrance to Pine Hills Nature Preserve.

Technically part of Shades but isolated from the main park, Pine Hills was Indiana's first nature preserve, established in 1969. Old-growth forest and beautiful rock formations highlight the 470 acres. Frankly, running the double-lollipop trail isn't easy. Climbing up and down the rocks to reach the Devil's Backbone, then crossing the narrow rock formation with 100-foot drops on both sides can put a little wobble in your legs. But any trip, fast or slow, through this natural gem is worth the effort.

After navigating the trail, stopping to gawk at the sights, and not getting totally turned around (the trails aren't well marked), I reversed course and returned to my

Trail 4's upper ladder helps hikers navigate a sandstone notch in rugged Frisz Ravine.

campsite for brunch and a couple hours of rest. As eager as I was to start fishing on Sugar Creek, I knew it was pointless until the sun rose higher and the stream warmed up.

In the early afternoon, I donned my fishing vest and wrapped my neoprene waders over my shoulders. Rod in hand, I followed the Backpack Trail west on a two-mile hike to Sugar Creek. The trail is flat compared to other Shades routes, but it winds pleasantly through dense woods, scrub forest, and occasional open areas. The trail's primary destination is Shades' backpack camp, which looks like a traditional tent campground lacking vehicle access.

I passed the campground and continued down a wide, steep path to the canoe camp and access, which made overnight float trips on Sugar Creek possible. But on this day, no campers were present. I was going to have this little slice of semi-wilderness to myself.

I donned my waders, stashed my hiking boots, and rigged my rod. I waded to the middle of the creek, shuffled a short distance downstream, and started casting at the base of the sandstone bluffs that lined the far bank. It didn't take long before I hooked and released a footlong smallmouth.

Lost in the rhythm of casting, reeling, shuffling, I suddenly had a sensation that I wasn't alone. From behind me came a *Stomp!* followed by a loud snort. I pivoted my head and saw that a massive whitetail buck had crept up behind me. He was standing on a sandbar at the water's edge, not 20 feet away. I had intruded on his turf; he was not happy.

I love wildlife and this was one of the biggest deer I'd ever seen. Nonetheless, I wasn't overjoyed by his presence. I'd walked a long way to get here, and the fish were biting! I tried to ignore him, but he stood on the shore snorting, pounding the ground, and looking menacing. Could I talk my way out of this? "I'm not here to bother you," I told him. He was unmoved.

The possible danger finally hit me; water wasn't going to stop this deer if he decided to charge. I gently began moving away, shuffling downstream. Eventually, the buck turned, walked upstream, then picked up speed. Within a couple of minutes, he was out of sight.

Maybe I should have stopped to contemplate my brush with dangerous nature but there were fish to catch. Over the next couple of hours, I landed about a dozen bass while exploring a section of Sugar Creek I'd never visited before. My only brush with civilization was when a pair of kayakers appeared and quietly floated by. We barely exchanged a greeting. I think we were all a little disappointed to encounter another human during an otherwise near-perfect immersion into the best nature can offer.

Shades History

Shades' journey to becoming a state park was long and convoluted—not surprising for a property that was once known as "The Shades of Death."

The area's dense forests inspired "shades," but the roots of the "death" part of the moniker are unclear. The name may have taken hold thanks to a series of events that started before white settlers arrived in this area, which was once home to competing bands of Piankashaw and Miami people. One unsubstantiated legend suggests that in the 1700s there was a pitched battle in the area of modern-day Shades State Park that left 600 fighters dead.

Though unlikely, this story may have contributed to white settlers avoiding the area. A more plausible explanation was the area's rugged topography, which made farming and logging difficult. One person who did try settling in the area, Moses Rush, came to a violent end in 1836. His wife, tired of Moses' drunkenness and abuse, put an axe through his skull. A jury acquitted her after a short trial, but the Shades of Death nickname took a deeper hold.

Another sensational murder happened in February 1865 right outside the park's current boundaries. Milton Wineland mistakenly thought his father, Fred, had willed the family farm to his cousin, Benjamin Vancleave. Milton ambushed the pair and killed them with two blasts from his shotgun. Milton's mother offered a $1,000 reward for his capture—dead or alive. Six months later he was shot and killed near Montezuma, about 30 miles southwest of Shades, trying to cross the Wabash River in a small boat.

Despite the history of violence, Shades of Death became a popular tourist destination, in part, because of mineral springs deep in the park's ravines that had first been identified by surveyors in 1819. By the late 1800s, the area attracted students from nearby Wabash College, as well as visitors from both Indianapolis and Terre Haute.

In the late 1880s, the Indianapolis medical community, spurred by interest in the purported healing properties of mineral springs, took notice. In 1886 a group calling itself the Garland Dells Mineral Springs Association bought a 65-acre property at Shades. A year later they built Dell House on the site of modern-day Dell Shelter and started to develop the area as a health resort.

Around 1890, amidst rumors that a sanitarium, served by an electric tramline connected to the railroad at nearby Waveland, would be constructed, the property's name was changed to Garland Dells. While these grandiose plans never materialized, the area remained popular with visitors.

In 1909, Joseph Frisz, a Terre Haute grocer and the man now remembered as "The Father of Shades," purchased stock in Garland Dells. By 1914, he had bought out his partners and gained complete control of the resort. Though he was very much an entrepreneur, Frisz also proved to be a preservationist, diverting roads and keeping the area's forests largely intact. He also worked to grow the park, buying adjacent properties until he had amassed nearly 2,200 acres.

Frisz also developed places for his visitors to stay and play while they enjoyed the area's natural wonders. The original Dell House eventually became a 40-room inn. The property also included 14 cottages, a pavilion with a theater and dance hall, and riding stables.

Frisz died at the park in November 1939 and willed the property to his family. They struggled to manage the resort and put it on the market, hoping to find someone willing to preserve the land as a park. The state was interested but could not raise the necessary purchase funds, about $300,000. Meanwhile, timber companies were pushing the Frisz family to sell about 1,300 acres of prime forest so that they could log. The heirs, lacking better options, were listening.

In 1947, things came to a head. Deadlines for the state to purchase the property came and went. The Indiana Chapter of the American Legion intervened and requested an option to purchase while it launched a "Save the Shades" campaign. The situation looked bleak when the Legion's option expired, but a reprieve came when the Arthur Baxter Foundation of Indianapolis purchased the property and held it until the fundraising was completed. Jumpstarted by nearly $80,000 from the Legion and $11,500 raised by Indiana schoolchildren, Save the Shades generated $262,000, enough to purchase the property. More than 10,000 people showed up to celebrate the dedication—and official renaming—of Shades State Park on April 16, 1948.

Shades Today

Shades covers 3,082 acres straddling the line between Parke and Montgomery counties. It is located about 60 miles west of downtown Indianapolis. Despite its proximity to the state's biggest city, Shades feels remote, and is noted by local astronomy buffs for its dark-sky status.

Modern-day Shades State Park is a far cry from its resort-era predecessor. Despite protests from people who preferred the old park (including some of Joseph Frisz's descendants), Shades has taken a much different direction under state ownership. In fact, Shades is something of a wild sibling to its more refined and amenity-laden sister park, Turkey Run.

Consider lodging. The old Garland Dells Inn finally fell into such a state of repair that it was closed in 1965 and torn down three years later. Shades also lacks cabins, and its main campground is decidedly tent-centric—all 101 sites are non-electric. It's also unique in that it offers backpacking and canoe campgrounds. The additional park amenities are limited, just some picnic areas and a couple of playgrounds for kids.

Nature takes center stage at Shades, with waterfalls, rocky ravines, and old-growth forests among the highlights. The eastern 470 acres of the park is Pine Hills Nature Preserve, which was dedicated in 1969 as Indiana's first nature preserve. This beautiful

Follow Trail 2 down a long stairway to Steamboat Rock and amazing views of Sugar Creek.

corner of Shades contains rare native stands of white pine and hemlock trees, which mix in with jaw-dropping natural landforms to create a must-visit landscape.

Birdwatching is popular at Shades, and a variety of mammals abound in the property. Sugar Creek offers outstanding fishing and is popular for floating. Multiple outfitters offer canoe, kayak, and tubing trips through the park, complete with shuttle service.

Camping is the best way to experience Shades, but there are other options if you need more civilized lodging. The inn at Turkey Run State Park is just 11 miles west of Shades. Crawfordsville, home of Wabash College, offers several hotels, especially near I-74, that are about a 25-minute drive from the park.

Hiking Shades

In addition to amazing scenery, Shades' primary drawing card is the park's outstanding 12-mile trail system. "Trail" or "path" might not be the best descriptors for the hiking routes, many of which simply follow the rugged, rocky, log-strewn streambeds at the bottom of the park's ravines. After heavy rains, some of the routes are impassable thanks to high water. Even experienced hikers will appreciate a pair of boots or sturdy trail runners when visiting the park.

Shades' trails are an up-and-down affair. Trails 1 and 2 have long, steep stairways, Trails 4 and 5 utilize ladders, and nearly every trail demands a challenging slog out of Sugar Creek valley.

Though the individual trails are relatively short, not everyone is going to enjoy—or be physically able to handle—hiking in Shades. The easiest trails in the park—6, 9, 10, and the Backpacking Trail—are among the least scenic, but still worth hiking.

One attraction for many Shades hikers is completing the Department of Natural Resources' official Six-Ravine Challenge. The designated 4.42-mile route follows segments of Trails 1, 4, 5, 6, 7, 8, 9, and the Backpack Trail and requires photos for documenting your journey. After finishing your trek, show your photos to staff at the Shades gatehouse or Turkey Run Nature Center to obtain an official completion sticker.

Trail Running

Only the four "easy" trails mentioned in the previous section offer a traditional running experience—as opposed to rock scrambling and ladder climbing. Nonetheless, I've run all the trails and once encountered the Wabash College cross country team practicing in the park, so it's a legitimate running destination.

The Backpack Trail offers the best pure running route. It's a five-mile round trip, nicely shaded and offers a good level of technical challenge. Trail 10 and Pine Hills together offer a nice run, especially if you skip the Devil's Backbone, or are content to carefully walk/climb that scenic obstacle. Add some interest on your return trip by taking a connector to the upland section of Trail 2. Round-trip length is 5-6 miles.

Trail 6 is my favorite of the ravine routes for running. Combine it with the upland loop of Trail 1, the non-ravine (moderate) sections of Trails 4 and 5, and part of Trail 9 for a short but hilly route. You can extend your run with another loop using the upland sections of Trails 7 and 8, returning on the Backpacking Trail.

TRAIL GUIDES

Trail 1

Rating: ★ ★ ★ ★   **Configuration:** Double Loop
Distance: 0.75 miles   **Difficulty:** Moderate

Tour: Trail 1 gets the most traffic at Shades, so hike it early in the day. Start from the small lot near the pond; Trails 1 and 6 depart together to the north. Navigation can be tricky, but stay straight on the boardwalk when Trail 6 turns left. Take the stairs into the Devil's Punchbowl then follow the trail down the streambed into a gorgeous sandstone canyon. Follow the trail stub to see Silver Cascade Falls (amazing but the viewpoint is limited) then climb out of the canyon on steep stairs to reach the upland loop. Turn right to pass Inspiration Point (overgrown) and access Prospect Point, which has a spectacular overhead view of Sugar Creek and its valley. Continue around the loop to a three-way junction; right connects to other trails and far left returns to Prospect Point. Take the middle path to staircase bridges above Devil's Punchbowl, a connection to Trail 6 up Fox Ravine, and a return to your car.

Trail 2

Rating: ★ ★ ★ ★ ★   **Configuration:** Lollipop
Distance: 1.25 miles   **Difficulty:** Challenging

Tour: Trail 2 might be the best short hike in Indiana, and it gets less traffic than other Shades trails. Park near Dell Shelter; the trailhead is at the forest edge to the north. The first section winds gently downhill through an open forest of tall hardwoods, including many huge beech trees. At the loop, turn left, and navigate a set of stairs across a small ravine. Soon you encounter a huge, steep, and sometimes slippery stairway that descends almost to the banks of Sugar Creek. At the bottom, take a minute to walk to the water's edge for a beautiful scene: the creek, Steamboat Rock, and massive sycamore trees. Return to the trail and start rock hopping up Pearl Ravine, which in the summer is rich green with moss, ferns, and dense stands of jewelweed. It takes some concentration to keep your feet dry, but the footing is generally stable and the rock-hopping entertaining. Small but pretty Maidenhair Falls appears halfway up the ravine, which starts to close in and transform into a twisting sandstone canyon. The trail eventually climbs a stairway at the top end of the ravine and returns to a relatively young forest that matures as you hike. Two connectors to Trail 10 depart to the left; use them to create an extended route to Pine Hills. At the end of the Trail 2 loop turn left to return to your car.

Trail 4

Rating: ★ ★ ★ ★   **Configuration:** Loop
Distance: 0.625 miles   **Difficulty:** Challenging

Tour: Hikers will encounter two ladders as they navigate Frisz Ravine, named after the one-time owner of the area. I recommend hiking the loop clockwise so that you travel up the ravine. Park at the Hickory Lot, start hiking on the paved connector trail leaving the east end and turn left at the first junction. Pass the Trail 5 and first Trail 4 intersections before turning right and following wide, graveled Trail 4 down to Sugar Creek. The short section in the creek bottom is beautiful, with huge sycamores and side paths to the water. After this relatively easy introduction, the trail gets challenging: you hop rocks, pick through mud, and climb ladders as you work your way

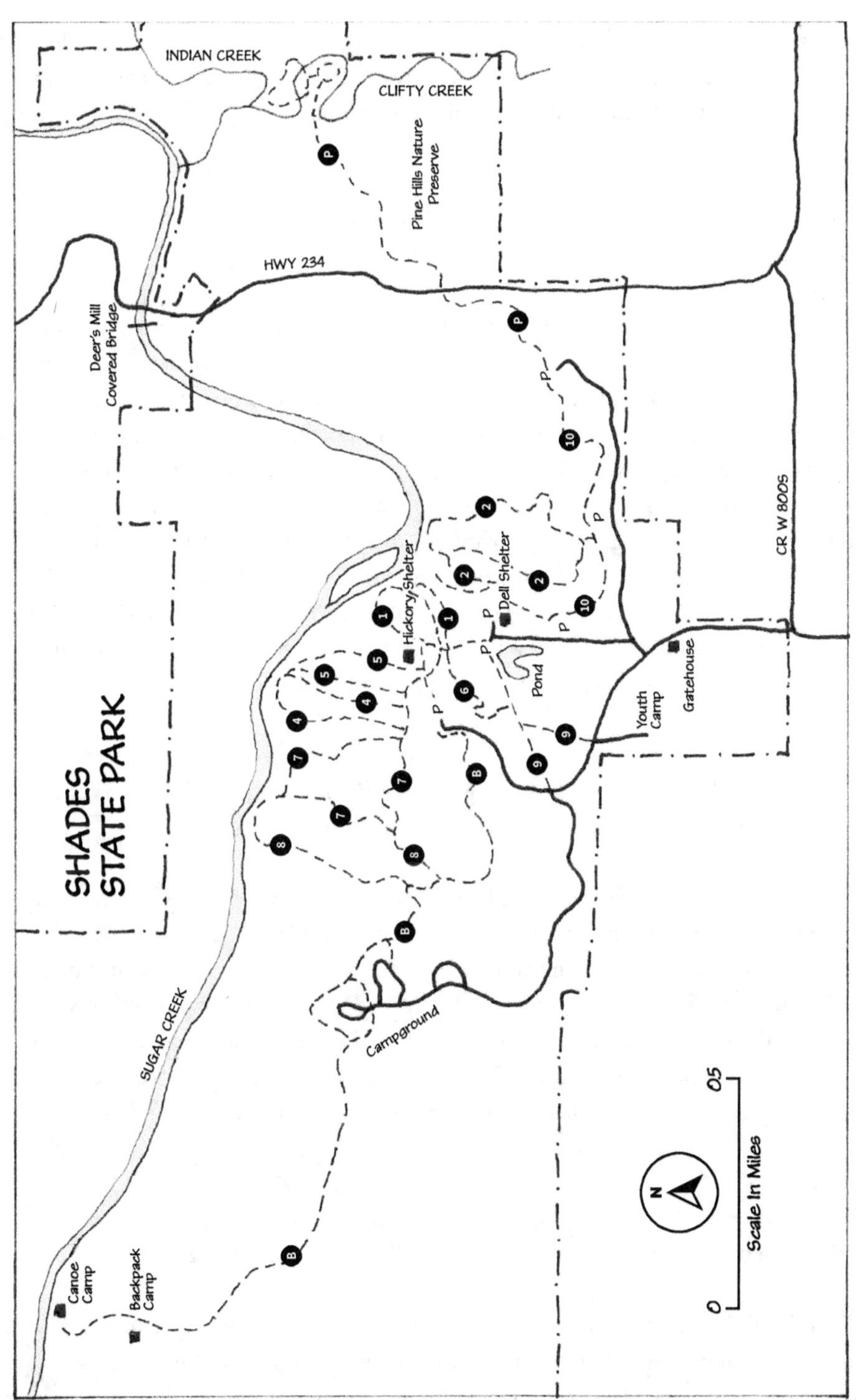
INDIAN CREEK
CLIFTY CREEK
Pine Hills Nature Preserve
HWY 234
Deer's Mill Covered Bridge
CR W 800S
SHADES STATE PARK
SUGAR CREEK
Hickory Shelter
Dell Shelter
Pond
Youth Camp
Gatehouse
Campground
Canoe Camp
Backpack Camp
N
Scale In Miles
0   O5

back to the top. July and August are prime for hiking this and other ravine trails. The footing is usually drier, and the ground covered with dense stands of green jewelweed bushes dotted with beautiful orange and yellow blooms.

Trail 5

Rating: ★ ★ ★ ★ **Configuration:** Loop
Distance: 0.75 miles **Difficulty:** Challenging

Tour: This trail is adjacent to Trail 4 and very similar. Like all the ravine trails, you can hike it in either direction, but I recommend walking up the creek bed (clockwise in this case). Follow the parking and starting instructions from Trail 4 but turn right at the Trail 5 intersection. This forest path is steep and uses staircases and step structures to move safely downhill. As you walk, look to your left to see Frisz Ravine and Trail 4 below you and to your right to see your return route on Trail 5. At the bottom, near Sugar Creek, Trail 5 swings to the right and up Kintz Ravine. (Turning left takes you to Trail 4.) Trail 5's uphill climb starts off easily but gets steeper and harder as the ravine narrows, requiring rock hopping and climbing over fallen trees. Near the top, a short ladder scales a narrow cleft in the sandstone wall. The trail emerges from the forest behind the restroom near Hickory Shelter. Turn right to return to your car or left to access Trail 1.

Trail 6

Rating: ★ ★ ★ **Configuration:** Partial Loop (use Trail 9 to complete)
Distance: 0.5 miles **Difficulty:** Moderate

Tour: Trail 6 is a nice add-on to Trail 1 and easy enough that most people can walk it. But though it's easier than typical Shades ravine scrambles, Trail 6 has some technical features that make it interesting and a good trail running route. Park by the pond; the trail departs to the northwest in conjunction with Trail 1. The paths split just above the Devil's Punchbowl, with Trail 6 going left and up the streambed. Red Fox Ravine is pretty and gentle but requires a little rock-hopping to keep your feet dry. Trail 6 eventually ends at Trail 9. Turn left and walk past the pond to reach your car.

Trail 7

Rating: ★ ★ ★ ★ **Configuration:** Loop
Distance: 0.875 miles **Difficulty:** Challenging

Tour: Trail 7 lacks ladders but is probably the most rugged of the ravine trails, with large rocks and downed trees adding to the challenge of working your way up a narrow canyon. Follow the parking and hiking instructions for Trail 4, then turn left on Trail 7 before descending into the valley. Take the first right to hike the loop in the preferred counterclockwise direction. Follow the trail downhill through a beautiful hardwood forest, punctuated by an occasional staircase. At the bottom, the trail turns left and follows Sugar Creek for a short distance. The trail turns left into the mouth of Kickapoo Ravine and starts heading upstream. (It's a little obscured but Trail 8 starts here and continues ahead along Sugar Creek.) Take your time on this beautiful section as you pick your way around rocks, over trees, and through the mud. At the top of the ravine, Trail 8 departs to the right, while following Trail 7 takes you back through the woods to your starting point.

Trail 8

Rating: ★ ★ ★ ★ ★ **Configuration:** Partial Loop (Use Trail 7 to complete)
Distance: 0.75 miles **Difficulty:** Challenging

Tour: For me, Trail 8 ranks behind only Trail 2 and Pine Hills among Shades' hikes. The trail takes more work to access, so hikers often skip it. This is a mistake, because Shawnee Canyon offers a beautiful and peaceful setting plus a somewhat easier ravine to navigate. It's a favorite spot to stop, relax, and listen to the birds and trickling stream. You have two options for hiking Trail 8. The first is to follow the directions for Trail 7 then go straight at the mouth of Kickapoo Ravine to reach the bottom end of Trail 8. At the top of the ravine, the route intersects with the Backpacking Trail. Turn left to stay on Trail 8. Alternatively, create a lollipop route by hiking the Backpacking

Trail 2 ducks beneath ancient sandstone layers as it climbs Pearl Ravine.

Trail from Hickory Parking Lot and turning right at the second Trail 8 junction. Close the loop by turning right (shorter but harder) or left (longer but easier) when you reach Trail 7.

Trail 9

Rating: ★ ★   **Configuration:** Y-Shaped
Distance: 0.5 miles   **Difficulty:** Easy

Tour: In a few Indiana Parks, a trail like this would be a standout, but at Shades it's largely forgettable. Trail 9 connects the youth camping area and the main campground road to Trails 1 and 6 and thus the full network of paths. Trail 9 is flat and passes through a beautiful stretch of forest, so it's worth a visit.

Trail 10

Rating: ★ ★   **Configuration:** Point to Point
Distance: 1.5 miles   **Difficulty:** Easy

Tour: Trail 10 offers an easy hike (and a nice trail running route if you're so inclined), but its most important purpose is providing access to Pine Hills Nature Preserve. The trail starts near Dell Shelter, which has an adjacent parking lot, and follows the forest's edge in the southeast corner of the park. The path is especially pretty in the summer when flowers are blooming in the adjacent restored prairie and butterflies are common. Along the way you pass two wide side paths, which connect to Trail 2. Eventually, you'll reach a modern vault toilet and the Pine Hills parking area, where the trail turns north into a second-growth woodland. After a pleasant, winding (and sometimes muddy) trip through the forest, Trail 10 ends at Highway 234. The stair-style gate into the nature preserve is visible across the road.

Backpack Trail (B)

Rating: ★ ★ ★   **Configuration:** Point to Point
Distance: 2.5 miles   **Difficulty:** Moderate

Tour: The Shades Backpack Trail is the only way to reach Shades' backpack campground, which offer seven sites on a first-come first-served basis. The trail is also an essential connector for hikers staying at the drive-in campground and for anyone trying to reach Trail 8. It's also my favorite trail run route in the park. Park at the Hickory Lot and hike back out the access road a short distance to reach the start of the Backpack Trail. It's a beautiful, winding route through a classic Shades forest though somewhat technical (thanks to tree roots) and prone to muddiness after heavy rains.

Trail 8 joins the route for a short distance before departing to the right in the middle of a streambed. Hikers soon encounter the first of three marked connector trails as the route skirts the campground. The path soon passes a utility line and through a sometimes-scrubby forest before reaching the backpacker camp. Stay to the right, on the main trail, which becomes a wide and steep path leading down to the canoe camp, Sugar Creek, and a scenic ending for your outbound hike.

Pine Hills Trail (P)

Rating: ★ ★ ★ ★ ★   **Configuration:** Double Lollipop

Distance: 2.7 miles   **Difficulty:** Very Challenging

(including Trail 10 from parking area)

Tour: This is one of Indiana's top destination hikes, especially if you add a trip to Trail 2 (via Trail 10) to your itinerary. Reach the parking lot by turning right immediately after the gatehouse and following the road to its end. Take Trail 10 north from the lot, cross Highway 234, and enter Pine Hills Nature Preserve via the stairstep gate. The trail starts as a pleasant but unremarkable hike through a second-growth forest but changes abruptly at the vertical edge of Clifty Creek valley. Turkey Backbone is the first highlight, with steep drop-offs on both side of the narrow trail. The path descends an eroded stretch through an aromatic hemlock grove, goes down a steep staircase, and deposits you at a T-intersection on the valley floor. The path is overgrown, disorienting, and lacking signs in key places, but turn right at all intersections to stay on track. As you circumnavigate the first loop, the path passes Mill Cut Backbone and a tall, eroding rock wall called The Slide. Take the first right to reach the second loop; turn right again and cross Clifty Creek (this unsigned turn is easy to miss but look for the trail with wooden steps on the far bank). You'll be facing a steep wall, but the trail works its way up through the rocks. At the top is the intimidating Devil's Backbone, just 6 feet wide and with a 100-foot drop on both sides. On the far side, the trail returns to the creek but in the meantime be prepared for some climbing, scooching, and a tricky hike down. Back on the valley floor, Honeycomb Rock, a pockmarked sandstone wall, towers over the confluence with Indian Creek, where the trail makes a sharp left. One more forested section and another Clifty Creek crossing returns you to the start of the loop. Turn right to reach the staircase out of the valley and your route back to the parking lot.

18
Shakamak State Park

A few years ago, I was driving west from Indianapolis with a brand-new Indiana State Parks pass burning a hole in my wallet. There's something about a fresh pass and the first park visit of a new year that really gets your outdoor juices flowing. It was mid-January, the sky clear, and the sun shining brightly. Four inches of snow—freshly fallen overnight—covered the ground.

My destination was Shakamak State Park, but first I had to pass through Coalmont. The tiny burg's name hinted at what originally drove the economy in this corner of Indiana: coal, though few signs of the industry remained in what was standard Midwestern farm country. But that's part of the attraction of a destination like Shakamak, which has a rich history hidden just below the surface.

Driving into Shakamak, the forested parkland offered quite a contrast to the surrounding farm fields. I parked near Tulip Shelter, bundled up, and started walking down the trail. My footsteps were the first in the light, fluffy snow.

My plan was relatively modest. Because this was just a stop en route to visiting family in southern Illinois, I only had a couple of hours for hiking. Circumnavigating Lake Shakamak, the middle-sized of the park's three reservoirs, was about a four-mile walk using Trail 1.

From this starting point, Trail 1 immediately heads west across a long causeway that is in fact the dam for Lake Shakamak, which was to my right. To my left was Lake Kickapoo, the largest of the park's three bodies of water. An interpretive marker on the dam explained that the structure originally was built as a valley-crossing fill for railroad tracks serving a nearby coal mine. I pressed on, eager to escape the biting wind.

At the far end of the dam, I paused to watch two ice fishermen, seated on buckets, intently at work in one of Lake Kickapoo's frozen arms. The lake is one of the better fishing holes in southwest Indiana. Not seeing much activity, I returned to my hike, followed the trail into the woods, and found a welcome respite from the cold breeze.

Dogwoods bloom along Trail 1, with Lake Shakamak in the background.

The fluffy snow was just deep enough to make hiking more work than usual. It also made the trail more challenging to follow. Nonetheless, I made good progress picking my way through the trees.

After encountering two shelters, crossing the main park road, and passing near the park's family cabins, the trail returned to the water's edge, where it would stay for much of the remainder of its course. Lake Shakamak has a relatively small main pool connecting four long arms. Trail 1 hugs the shoreline on all four arms, affording hikers cross-water vistas on one side and dense woods on the other. It also offers a smorgasbord for wildlife watchers: in warm weather seasons, turtles, fish, and waterfowl in one direction and woodpeckers, warblers, and a variety of small mammals in the other.

Though I was the first human on Trail 1 that morning, I was far from the first creature: the fresh snow was overrun with an abundance of tracks. Squirrels and rabbits were expected visitors but soon turkey sign appeared, the three-toed marks and scratchings of a small flock working its way through the woods.

More exciting were the predator signs. A straight-line set of dog-like tracks joined the trail for a while before departing. This was likely a coyote, and I encountered two more similar runs of these tracks before my hike was over. I wondered whether this was a single animal roughly following my same route, or maybe three different coyotes out hunting in the fresh snow.

Other than the squirrels, I never saw any of the track-makers in person, but that didn't dampen my enthusiasm. Plus, the birds in the forest offered a constant symphony of calls and a feast for the eyes. In addition to the woodpeckers (downy and red-headed), I heard and/or saw blue jays, chickadees, nuthatches, and other species.

As the hike continued, my temperature increased, and I had to shed a layer. I also had to slow down and watch my footing. Tree roots are a constant tripping hazard on Trail 1, especially when they're buried under the snow. The boardwalks crossing upper creek arms also had to be navigated carefully. I never went down, but I had a little scare when I hit one at full stride and discovered a layer of ice under the snow.

Late in the hike I encountered two junctions with Trail 2 but left that side trip—which visits the site of a former coal mine—for a future visit. The final stretch of Trail 1 passes near the nature center and a large swimming pool, a popular park amenity in the summer months.

As I passed the dormant boat ramp and ended my hike at the parking lot, I resolved to return to Shakamak. Since that first hike, I've visited several times, introducing my wife and son to the park, tenting at the campground, and running and/or hiking all seven numbered trails. With an amazing history, a diversity of landscapes, and great views of woods and water, Shakamak is a must-visit Indiana destination for outdoor enthusiasts.

Shakamak History

Southwest Indiana is coal country. The landscape from roughly Terre Haute to Evansville is dotted with several working mines and countless abandoned ones. Together, the active mines yield enough product to consistently land Indiana among the nation's top ten coal-producing states.

It's unusual to make a connection between coal mining and recreation-friendly outdoor landscapes, but Shakamak State Park owes its existence to a coal mine. In fact, in the early 1900s, two mines were operating within or near the boundaries of the current park. One of them, the Golden Knob Mine, was in what is now the park's northeast corner.

The Golden Knob owners built a railroad spur from the main line at Jasonville west to the mine. The spur was later extended to the Badder's Mine, just to the west. This subsequent track construction required a massive earthen fill across Johnson Hollow. A five-foot culvert in the fill allowed water to drain from the hollow. The rail line operated for just five years, from 1903 to 1908, but allowed trains to haul 155,000 tons of coal out of the mine. Then the coal played out, the mines closed, the railroad was abandoned, and the land reverted to public ownership.

Fast forward nearly two decades. Some local citizens decided that the railroad fill had the potential to serve as a dam—a popular idea in an area starved for lakes and public parks. The concept gained traction, and a state study concluded that the fill would be an effective dam. The resulting lake would serve as the centerpiece of a proposed new state park. To further support the idea, land was donated by Clay, Greene, and Sullivan counties; the proposed park's boundaries encompassed slices of all three.

Despite some snags raising the $150,000 needed to develop the property, Shakamak State Park was established in Fall 1929 as Indiana's seventh state park. The name is a Kickapoo word meaning "river of the long fish," a reference to the nearby Eel River.

Work over the next few years brought the founders' vision to life. First, Johnson Hollow was cleared (by hand) of trees and the lakebed dredged. When the culvert was capped, 56-acre Lake Shakamak started to fill. In 1931, construction started on Indiana Highway 48, providing a reliable road connection to the park. In 1933, a Civilian Conservation Corps company started a variety of improvements to the park and built a dam for 49-acre Lake Lenape.

In the years that followed, Lake Shakamak gained national attention thanks to the construction of a 32-foot-tall high-diving platform. Starting in 1934 and continuing over the next two decades, the park hosted a variety of regional and national swimming and diving events. The diving tower remained a noted feature of the park until it was finally torn down in the 1990s.

In the 1960s, the focus of the park went a different direction with the development of 290-acre Lake Kickapoo. The lake quickly gained a good reputation for fishing; Shakamak State Park is considered a prime destination for catching largemouth bass along with a variety of panfish species.

Shakamak Today

Shakamak State Park is located 85 miles southwest of downtown Indianapolis. The nearest town, Jasonville, is located on Highway 48 just a few miles east of the entrance gate. It's a good place to find gas, groceries, and restaurants.

The current state park covers 1,766 acres and offers visitors a variety of recreational opportunities, especially on or in the water, which covers more than a quarter of the park's total area. Swimming is still popular but allowed only in the park's large pool, located on the southeast shore of Lake Shakamak. All three lakes have boat ramps and rental craft available (rowboats, paddleboats, and kayaks). Inquire at the entrance gate about rental offerings. The two smaller lakes are especially attractive for kayakers and standup paddleboarders.

As mentioned earlier, Shakamak is also a great destination for wildlife and bird watching. Waterfowl are a main attraction on the lakes during spring and summer, while woodpeckers, owls, and a variety of perching birds are often encountered in the woods. Migrating warblers are a special treat in the spring.

Most of Shakamak's hiking occurs in woodland environments. The forests are second growth but mature and feature a variety of hardwood and pine trees. In the spring wildflowers carpet the forest floor.

A turtle basks in the sun on Lake Shakamak, not far from Trail 1's shoreline path.

The large campground includes 164 electric and non-electric sites and is located between Lake Lenape and the east arm of Lake Kickapoo. It offers easy access to trails 4 and 5.

If camping isn't your style, Shakamak offers a nice selection of 22 cabins, including 19 in its family area. All the cabins are in the northern part of the park near Lake Shakamak and offer easy access to either Trail 1 or 2 and, thus, the rest of the trail system. If the cabins are all booked, motels can be found in Linton (12 miles) and Sullivan (16 miles).

Hiking Shakamak

With pleasant and varied scenery, 13-plus miles of trails, and a fairly contiguous system, Shakamak State Park is an attractive hiking destination. The trails are well marked and nicely maintained; technical challenges are minimal.

One interesting feature at Shakamak, particularly on the park's original hiking paths—Trails 1-4—is the outsize quantity of wooden stairs, bridges, and boardwalks. The structures ease hill climbs, shorten the traverse of lake arms, and help keep your feet dry in the many wet spots. All are numbered, with the first digit representing the trail and the next two the structure number, e.g. 101, 102, etc.

Shakamak is off the beaten path and gets light trail traffic compared to other state parks. Almost every hike offers a nice mix of woods and waters and a laid-back vibe that encourages you to take your time and really appreciate your surroundings.

Looking for a wilderness experience? This isn't the park for that. On the other hand, it's easy to find solitude at Shakamak. Trails 4 and 5, in particular, have quiet, little-traveled sections that feel a long way from civilization.

Trail Running

Shakamak State Park is one of my favorite Indiana trail-running destinations. The hills are manageable and most of the routes are tree-covered, so you can find shade on warm summer days. Waterside sections provide interesting sights and a cooling effect.

The trails also connect nicely, allowing long runs without too much repetition. Once, using the campground as a base, I mapped out and ran a 15-mile loop that traversed almost every trail section along with a few connector road segments.

Trail runners looking for a good introduction to the park should focus on Trails 1 and 2, which can be combined into a double loop of about 6 miles. Because of tree roots, stairs, and boardwalks, these are the most technical routes, but they are also the most scenic.

Trail 5 is also a good running route, and you usually have it to yourself. Treat it as an out-and-back, starting from either end, or create a loop (approximately 5.5 miles) using campground roads, Trail 4, Trail 3, the Pedestrian Path, Trail 1 (across the dam), and the park road west of the Lake Shakamak dam. You can easily lengthen this run by incorporating side trips on Trails 6 and 7.

TRAIL GUIDES

Trail 1

Rating: ★ ★ ★ ★ ★   **Configuration:** Loop
Distance: 3.95 miles   **Difficulty:** Moderate

Tour: Trail 1 is Shakamak's premiere hike and one of my favorite trails in Indiana. The official start is on the northeast side of the swimming pool lot (see the description for Trail 2), but I prefer parking near Tulip Shelter and circumnavigating the lake clockwise. From the shelter, head west on the paved trail crossing the Lake Shakamak dam. The views from the dam (of both Lake Shakamak and Lake Kickapoo) are outstanding but at the west end you encounter one of the trail's confusing spots. Continue straight past the small structure and onto the road, then look for the trail turnoff to the right. You soon reach two shelters and the trail briefly disappears; continue straight through the grassy area and the trail starts again at the woods' edge. After crossing a paved road and passing some of the family cabins, you encounter the lake and the trail will take on its most familiar form, closely following the shore and the arms of the reservoir. Periodic bridges, boardwalks, and stairs ease the passage and keep you out of marshy spots. One of the most pleasant parts of the hike is the constantly shifting perspective. For long sections you feel nearly surrounded by water with the open part of the lake looming ahead. Then you reach the tip of a peninsula, turn left, and start a section that takes you towards the woods. At the head of the third lake arm, you encounter the first junction with Trail 2. Beyond the intersection, the easternmost section of Trail 1 is scenic but has some challenging footing thanks to erosion and aging stairs and steps. After crossing a large bridge and passing the second junction with Trail 2, turn right to follow the lakeshore behind the log cabin, Pool Shelter, and past the swimming pool. You'll eventually reach the final section through the woods, over a small creek, and back to the boat ramp and Tulip Shelter.

Trail 2
Rating: ★ ★ ★ ★   **Configuration:** Partial Loop (Full Loop with Trail 1)
Distance: 1.5 miles   **Difficulty:** Moderate
(2.1 miles as loop)

Tour: This trail passes a former coal mine that was active around the turn of the 20th century. Today, an interpretive sign marks the site, but nature has reclaimed the space to such a degree that it's hard to imagine a mine ever existed here. The area is now a maturing hardwood and pine forest traversed by a fun up-and-down partial loop connecting at two places with Trail 1. Park at the large swimming pool parking lot and look for the "Trails 1 and 2" sign on the northeast side of the lot. Once on the path, go straight before the large bridge to stay on Trail 2. The narrow trail climbs a tributary valley away from the lake, crosses the main park road, and turns north into the woods, periodically climbing up and down stairs. Eventually road noise from nearby Highway 48 intrudes but it's still a great walk in the woods. After passing the former mine in the far northeast corner of the park, the trail swings west then southwest and you recross the main park road near Cabins B, C, and D. Trail 2 ends at the junction with Trail 1. To return to the parking lot, go left and follow the scenic, shoreline-hugging trail to your starting point.

Trail 3
Rating: ★ ★ ★   **Configuration:** Loop
Distance: 1.4 miles   **Difficulty:** Moderate

Tour: Trail 3 offers the perfect one-hour introduction to Shakamak State Park. After entering the gate, turn left and park at the first lot you encounter on the left. The trail departs from the south edge of this parking lot. The route is pleasant and wooded and

SHAKAMAK STATE PARK

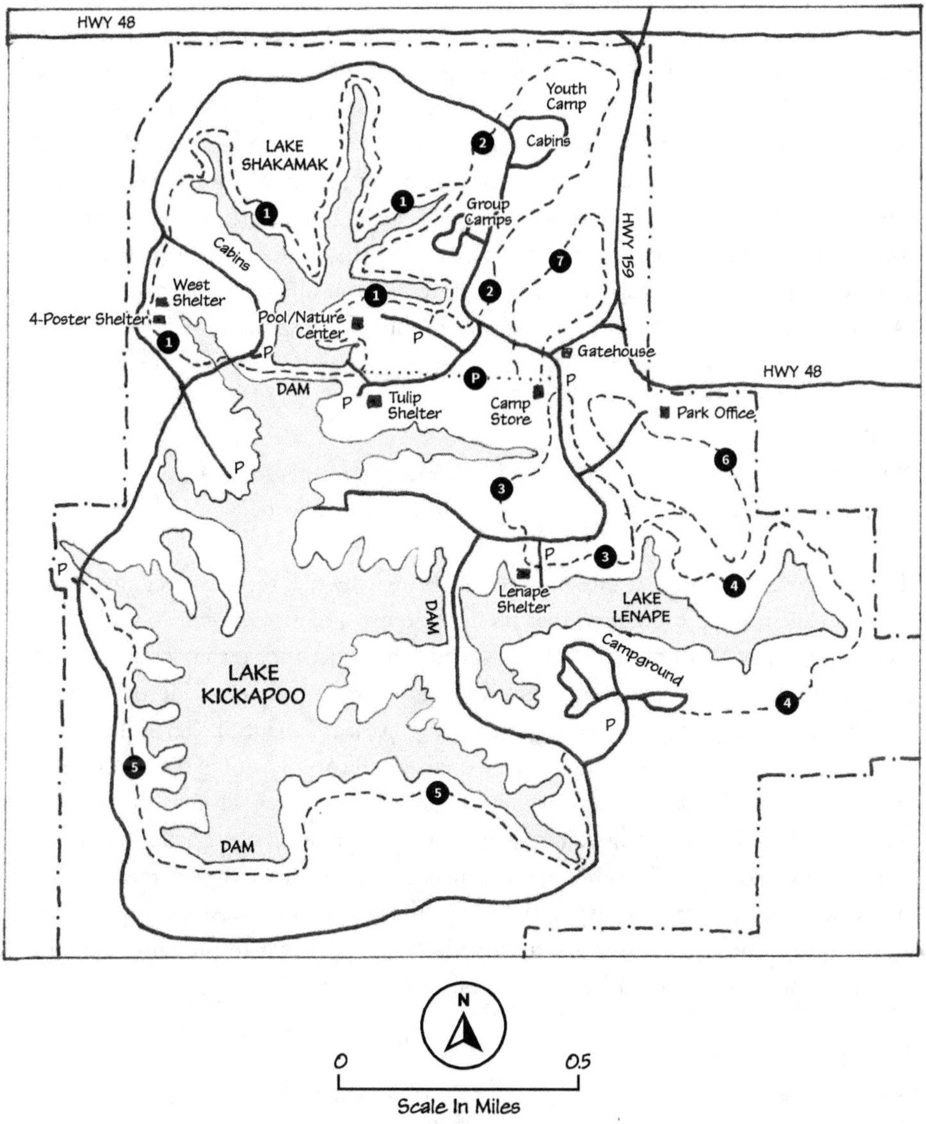

requires navigating several staircases. At the quarter-mile mark cross the road leading to the park office; turn left to reach the first access to the Trail 6 loop, which you'll encounter twice more on the next stretch of trail. After crossing Trail 6 and covering another quarter mile you reach a combo junction with Trail 4, which heads left/east up a staircase toward the campground, and Trail 6, which goes uphill in two different directions. Stay straight on Trail 3, following an arm of Lake Lenape; soon you cross the "covered bridge," which offers a shaded bench for a quiet break. Occasional lake views appear to your left as you pass huge trees, cross more bridges, and climb periodic stairs en route to the Lake Lenape boat ramp and Lenape Shelter. Boasting a large parking lot, picnic tables, and vault toilets, this area is a nice starting point for hiking Trails 3, 4, and 6. Crossing the ramp road, Trail 3 turns back north, crosses the main park road, and passes through an attractive forest surrounding an eastern arm of Lake Kickapoo. The path ends near the camp store (open during the summer) across the park road from your starting point.

Trail 4

Rating: ★ ★ ★ ★   **Configuration:** Point to Point
Distance: 1.6 miles   **Difficulty:** Moderate

Tour: This densely forested and, in some places, marshy trail roughly circumnavigates Lake Lenape but be forewarned that it's not a loop—unless you want to walk about two miles of pavement on the main park road. The good news is that it's a great out-and-back hike from the campground. The trail starts on the east side (nonelectric area) near the playground. If you're not camping, park at Lenape Shelter and hike east on Trail 3. You connect with Trail 4 after a quarter mile or so, turning right and climbing the "401" staircase at the junction. As you work your way around the lake you encounter boardwalks, bridges, and stairs that ease elevation changes and keep you out of the wettest areas. This trail has a rich variety of trees, dense undergrowth, and many birds including waterfowl on the lake in the warm months. At the upper end of Lake Lenape, the trail turns south then west. The final stretch to the campground is wider and straighter than earlier sections but just as pleasant.

Trail 5

Rating: ★ ★ ★   **Configuration:** Point to Point
Distance: 2.2 miles   **Difficulty:** Moderate

Tour: Trail 5 was built in 2017 and receives minimal traffic. As a result, it's easy to find yourself alone on this path. The trail is easily accessed from the campground, with its eastern end located near the campground entrance. The other access is from

Tulip trees reach for the springtime sky alongside Trail 2.

a parking lot at its terminus on the west side of Lake Kickapoo. Starting from this latter trailhead, Trail 5 follows the highly irregular shoreline south, winding through a young forest that offers lake views through the trees without going to the water's edge. The path parallels the main park road, but traffic is light in this area. Across the road is a tract of restored prairie. Trail 5 takes on a completely different character as it crosses the grassy expanse of the dam; fine lake views open to the north. On the far side of the dam, the trail returns to the woods—in this section, more mature hardwoods. The attractive pathway winds along and around an eastern arm of Lake Kickapoo before finally reaching its endpoint. From here adventurous hikers can walk into the campground to Trail 4 and continue to Trail 3, the Pedestrian Path, Trail 1, and the main park road to create a loop of 8-11 miles depending on how much of Trail 1 you include.

Trail 6

Rating: ★★　　　**Configuration:** Loop
Distance: 1.08 miles　　　**Difficulty:** Easy

Tour: Trail 6, which passes through a mixed hardwood and pine forest, was at one time Shakamak State Park's bridle trail. As a result, the pathway is wide, gently rolling, and has a firm (in places grassed or graveled) surface. Today, it is designated as multiuse trail open to hiking and biking. It's also a nice surface and terrain for running. Unfortunately, Trail 6 lacks a formal trailhead. The best way to access it is via Trail 3. Park at either the Camp Store or Lenape Shelter and follow the eastern leg of Trail 3 to one of the Trail 6 intersections. From the Camp Store lot, reach the first Trail 6 access by turning left at the road to the park office and walking a short distance along the shoulder. From Lenape Shelter, follow Trail 3 east for a quarter mile to the intersection with Trails 4 and 6.

Trail 7

Rating: ★　　　**Configuration:** Loop
Distance: 1.7 miles　　　**Difficulty:** Easy

Tour: Trail 7 is the flattest trail in park and winds through a mixed hardwood and pine forest. The multiuse path has a firm surface and is open to both hiking and biking. Park at the lot just past the entrance gate and across the road from the camp store, near which the paved Pedestrian Path starts. Trail 7 intersects with the Pedestrian Path at two places; use a section of pavement to complete your loop.

19
Spring Mill State Park

My wife, Tari, recently suggested a springtime weekend getaway to hike and enjoy wildflowers. Spring Mill quickly came to mind. Our previous visit there was brief and we had barely scratched the surface of the park's myriad hiking opportunities. Another reason for choosing Spring Mill was to stay at the park's historic inn, which had just reopened after nearly two years of renovation. Plus, our selected days included the park's Wildflower Weekend, so we knew we could enjoy at least one guided hike with a naturalist.

We reached the park in late afternoon and proceeded straight to the inn. After checking in and lacing up our boots, we hiked out the front entrance and onto Trail 3, our primary target for the day. We also had an interesting side trip planned.

Immediately, we were surrounded by trees, blooming wildflowers, and—off to our right in the bottom of a canyon—the sound of flowing water. The weather was summerlike, sunny and 80 degrees; it didn't take long to work up a sweat.

We passed the first intersection and entered Trail 3's main loop. Being early spring, the tree crowns were faint green, showing the first hint of leaves. Redbuds waning on the bloom added periodic pops of pink to our surroundings, including on the trails, which were littered with their fallen petals. The blues, purples, yellows, and whites of wildflowers completed the color palette.

At the second intersection we turned right and started a side trip on Trail 4, descending a long, steep staircase into the canyon. The stream that had been entertaining us with its gurgling since the start of the hike greeted us at the bottom. We followed it upstream on a sturdy new walkway that ran alongside. Apparently, this route used to be a challenging, rocky, and often wet scramble.

Soon we reached the stream source and the purpose of our side trip: Donaldson Cave. Named for eccentric Scotsman George Donaldson, who in the late 1800s owned, loved, and passionately protected this beautiful area, the cave is one of the park's most popular attractions.

Flowers bloom in the garden at Spring Mill's Pioneer Village.

The cave has two openings: the lower "wet side," from which the stream gushed; and the higher "dry side," which we explored. Using flashlights and headlamps, we worked our way through the main chamber, enjoying the 20-degree temperature drop from the warm spring day outside. Relishing the cool air but eager to get back to the forest, we left deeper cave exploration to others and retraced our steps out of the canyon and back to the Trail 3 loop.

Though Spring Mill's caves get more attention, the park's real treasures may be its forests. This became clear as we crossed the park road on Trail 3 and started winding through trees and around sinkholes in the Mitchell Karst Plains Nature Preserve. The number of *big* trees—oak, hickory, maple, beech, and tulip poplar—was impressive, and their size seemed to increase as we worked our way around the loop.

The trail turned eastward, crossed the entrance road, and continued another half mile to its next highlight. Bronson Cave is a just a short side trip down a stairway and proved the perfect place for a break. Enjoying cold water and a snack on the bench, we listened to the bird songs while watching emerging caddisflies flutter over the cave's stream. Tari pointed out fern fiddleheads poking through the leaf litter on the forest floor. Giant trees reached for the skies all around us.

Not far down the trail, we encountered another of Spring Mill's big draws: Twin Caves. The two caverns are connected by a stream (the same one that flows through both Bronson and Donaldson Caves). In summer, a small dam above the lower cave is closed, creating a pool in the upper cave that visitors can explore on a guided boat trip.

The far side of the Twin Caves parking lot marks Trail 3's entry into one of the most ecologically significant places in Indiana: Donaldson's Woods Nature Preserve. Another legacy of the previously mentioned Scottish preservationist, the 145-acre preserve contains one of the state's few remaining old-growth forests. As we hiked, we were astounded by our surroundings. The trees were huge, the wildflowers more varied, and the bird songs more plentiful than what we had seen previously on our hike—and we had already seen some of the best environments our state park system has to offer.

As we took our time walking through Donaldson's Woods—gazing upward toward the tops of the enormous trees, stooping to get a close look at interesting flowers, and taking multiple pictures—we couldn't help but think about the special people who had helped preserve this amazing slice of nature. From George Donaldson to "Father of Indiana State Parks" Richard Lieber to multiple generations of park staff and volunteers…it was their vision, hard work, and love of nature that made it possible for us to have these incredible experiences. We gave a quiet thanks to all these heroes and continued our walk through the woods.

Spring Mill History

The history of Spring Mill begins in the bedrock that underlays the entire park. Formed at the bottom of a warm sea more than 300 million years ago), the rock today is known as Salem Limestone. It gained fame as a building stone, fueling a quarry industry that dominated the local economy for many decades.

Over time, water started to work its magic on the landscape, first by eroding sediment and exposing the limestone. Then, rainwater started infiltrating cracks and eating away limestone, leaving underground caverns, sinkholes (formed when caverns collapse), and subterranean river systems—the elements of the karst topography that gives Spring Mill its distinctive personality.

Samuel Jackson, Jr., a Canadian who had served in the U.S. Navy during the War of 1812, explored southern Indiana in 1814, looking for somewhere to build a grist mill. When Jackson encountered the little valley surrounded by forests and carved by a stream gushing steadily out of a limestone cavern (today known as Hamer Cave), he knew he had found the right place to settle.

Jackson built a small mill and a cabin for his family and soon had a thriving business grinding corn grown by nearby settlers. Despite his success, he moved to Pennsylvania in 1817 and sold the property to brothers Thomas and Cuthbert Bullitt, prosperous landowners and developers from Louisville. Though the Bullitts owned the property for just six years, they left an indelible mark on the little valley by building a three-story mill. Constructed using limestone quarried nearby, the mill's huge wheel, 24 feet in diameter, was powered by water diverted from Hamer Cave.

Soon a village blossomed in the valley, as more settlers arrived and new businesses sprang up around the mill. In 1823, the Bullitts sold out to another set of brothers, William and Joseph Montgomery, who lived in Philadelphia. Yet Spring Mill kept growing, with a distillery, tavern, and sawmill among the new enterprises.

After the death of the Montgomery brothers, Spring Mill was sold for the bargain price of $7,000 in June 1832. The new owners were yet another set of brothers, Hugh and Thomas Hamer, who already lived in Spring Mill and knew it well. Hugh had been the Montgomery's miller since 1925, and Thomas was his assistant.

The next two decades, with the Hamers in charge, were Spring Mill's heyday. Eventually, about 100 people lived in the village, which had a post office and was a regular stop on the Louisville-Terre Haute stagecoach line. In the 1850s, railroads bypassed the rugged Spring Mill valley for routes that crossed in nearby Mitchell, and the little village's fortunes changed forever. The mill finally closed in 1892, and the village emptied and fell into ruin.

During the village's later years, an important personality was living in the blufftop woods just a short distance away. George Donaldson, a wealthy and eccentric

Scotsman, arrived in 1865 and bought a sawmill and cabin located near the cave now bearing Donaldson's name.

Donaldson loved nature and was committed to protecting this beautiful piece of southern Indiana. For the next 17 years, he shielded his property from vandalism, poaching, and logging. Even after moving away, Donaldson refused to sell his land, but his 1898 death in Scotland started a legal battle over the title that raged for years. Eventually, the State of Indiana became owner, and a legislative act directed the sale of the property to the University of Indiana in 1915.

It was about this time that Richard Lieber was launching the Indiana state park system. Local boosters had a strong case for establishing a park at Spring Mill, but it took until 1927 for the project to get off the ground. That year, Indiana University donated the Donaldson tract to the Department of Conservation and Lawrence County contributed another 539 acres abutting the west side of the land around the cave.

The final piece of the puzzle was 300 acres owned by Lehigh Portland Cement Company, property that included Hamer Cave and Spring Mill. The village was a ruin—just the crumbling mill plus five other abandoned buildings. Regardless, Richard Lieber saw this area as the crown jewel of the new park. What if it could be restored as a tribute to Indiana's early settlers? Lieber sold his vision to Lehigh Portland Cement, which conveyed the land to the state (while keeping water rights) for just $1. The new park was established in 1927, though not yet ready for visitors.

Restoring the village was the top priority for the new park, and work on the mill started in 1928. Two years later, the mill building (but not grinding equipment) and office, apothecary, and post office had been restored. The park officially opened on June 15, 1930, and nearly 15,000 people visited that first season.

A new water wheel was built in 1931, and other buildings were moved to or reconstructed in the park in subsequent years. In 1933, the Civilian Conservation Corps arrived and over the next seven years dramatically changed the look of the park. In addition to helping with the village restoration, Company 1536 built the dam creating Spring Mill Lake, as well as trails, fences, bridges, picnic areas, and shelter houses.

In 1939, a beautiful limestone inn was built on the blufftop above the Mill Creek valley. The 71-room lodge has been renovated twice during its history, most recently in 2024, and is a comfortable, centrally located base for exploring the park.

Spring Mill Today

Spring Mill is located 89 miles south of downtown Indianapolis. The park is less than an hour's drive from Bloomington and a 75-minute drive to Louisville, Kentucky. The park packs an amazing variety of activities and amenities into a relatively small land area—only 1,358 acres. The park is also popular: in 2023 Spring Mill hosted 665,000 visitors, ranking it seventh in the state park system.

A sturdy walkway keeps hikers dry as they access Donaldson Cave from Trail 4.

In addition to hiking, what is there to do at Spring Mill? What are you interested in—history, spelunking, nature study, water sports, cycling? You can indulge your passion for all those things and more at Spring Mill. The Pioneer Village is the park's biggest draw, with a three-story limestone grist mill and 20 other restored structures—many staffed by costumed interpreters—that take visitors back to the earliest years of Indiana history.

If your interest is space-age history, Spring Mill also delivers, as the only state park with a museum dedicated to an astronaut. Virgil "Gus" Grissom, born and raised in nearby Mitchell, Indiana, was one of the original Mercury Seven and the second American in space. He died in a tragic fire during testing for the Apollo I mission. You can learn all about his fascinating life at the Virgil I. "Gus" Grissom Memorial adjacent to the park gatehouse.

The caves are another special attraction at Spring Mill, and two are open for exploration. Donaldson Cave, accessible by Trail 4, can be entered year-round without special permission. From Memorial Day through mid-October, there is a guided boat tour into Twin Caves' upper cavern. Boats float about 500 feet into the cave before turning around.

Spring Mill is a popular destination for nature lovers. Nearly half of the park— 643 acres—has been dedicated to three state nature preserves: Mitchell Karst Plains;

Donaldson Cave; and Donaldson's Woods, which contains a 67-acre tract of old growth forest, a rare resource in Indiana. Wildflowers are a special treat in the spring, and the park is a popular stop year-round on the Indiana Birding Trail.

Spring Mill Lake offers fishing and boating but not swimming. Swimmers have access during the summer to an Olympic-sized outdoor pool in the east end of the park. The pool is also the place to rent a bicycle for exploring Spring Mill's beginner-level mountain bike trail or its dedicated bike/hike lane on the park's main loop road.

There are two options for overnighting inside the state park. Renovated Spring Mill Inn has 71 rooms and is an excellent choice for hikers, with direct access to Trails 1 and 3. There also is a campground in the northeast corner of the property with 175 electric and 44 full hookup sites. Unfortunately, the campground requires a walk along the road to reach the trail system.

The closest lodging outside the park is a few miles away in Mitchell, where a couple of small, local motels can be found. Bedford, 15 miles north, has several national chain lodging options.

Hiking Spring Mill

Spring Mill has just nine miles of hike-only trails, but it's one of the best collections of walking paths in Indiana. The routes are varied and beautiful, the network connects well (except for one short, isolated route), and the trails are generally in great shape—many are wide, gently rolling, and covered in crushed limestone.

Individually, none of the park's trails is very long; Trail 3 covers the most ground, about 2.5 miles. This makes Spring Mill a great place for a quick-stop day hike or, alternatively, a park where you can piece together multiple trails for a longer, varied route. The centrally located Trail 4, which connects with several other paths, is the perfect centerpiece for a longer hike.

Trail Running

Despite its small size and steep hills, Spring Mill is popular running destination. Many runners ply the park's winding main road, which includes a paved bike/hike lane and a long stretch of one-way traffic to improve safety.

The trails are a different story. Yes, there are some healthy climbs and long staircases with sketchy footing, but much of the trail network flows nicely and feels like it was made for running. Two routes are standouts: Trail 3 and Trail 7.

Trail 3 is beautiful and offers a great running surface—wide, generally free of roots and rocks, and in many places covered with crushed limestone. The trail rolls nicely through one of Indiana's prettiest forests, gently curving around sinkholes and huge trees.

Trail 7 is a similar type of running route but flatter and faster. The forest is beautiful, but you probably won't encounter many hikers; this is an underappreciated corner of the park. For a quality longer run, start at Tulip Poplar Shelter, navigate the Trail 7 loop then proceed to Trail 4. Turn right (east) and run to the Trail 3 connector path. Navigate the Trail 3 loop then retrace your route on Trails 4 and 7 to the starting point. Total mileage: about seven—and with minimal hills.

TRAIL GUIDES

Trail 1

Rating: ★★   **Configuration:** Lollipop (when fully open)
Distance: 0.375 miles   **Difficulty:** Moderate

Tour: Trail 1 wraps around the back side of Spring Mill Inn and sends paths downhill in two directions: northeast to Trail 5 and west to Trail 4. It also has a water-level path along the south shore of Spring Mill Lake connecting these two intersections. As of 2025, ongoing construction had closed the trail near the inn as well as the arm to the northeast. If you're not staying at the inn, leave your vehicle in the facility's two-story parking structure. A sign between the parking lot and the inn's west wing marks the start of Trail 1, which switchbacks down the steep hill behind the inn. The stream from Donaldson Cave greets you at the bottom. Turn left to reach the bridge crossing stream to Trail 4. Turn right on Trail 1 to reach the junction with Trail 5.

Trail 2

Rating: ★★   **Configuration:** Point to Point
Distance: 0.5 miles   **Difficulty:** Moderate

Tour: Trail 2 offers a safe and efficient pedestrian connection between Pioneer Village and the lake. It passes through an upland forest and provides elevated views of Mill Creek valley. Park at the large Pioneer Village lot; Trail 2 starts north of the lot on the opposite side of the park road and begins with a challenging uphill climb. The trail is wide and covered with crushed limestone; it probably started as a utility right of way. The path levels out and you soon encounter one of the park's lesser-known historic structures: the restored Red Cross Cabin, was owned by Dr. Joseph and Enola Gardner, two of the original members of the American Red Cross. Stay to the right (south) of the cabin to reach the paved path/driveway that marks the final stretch of Trail 2, which

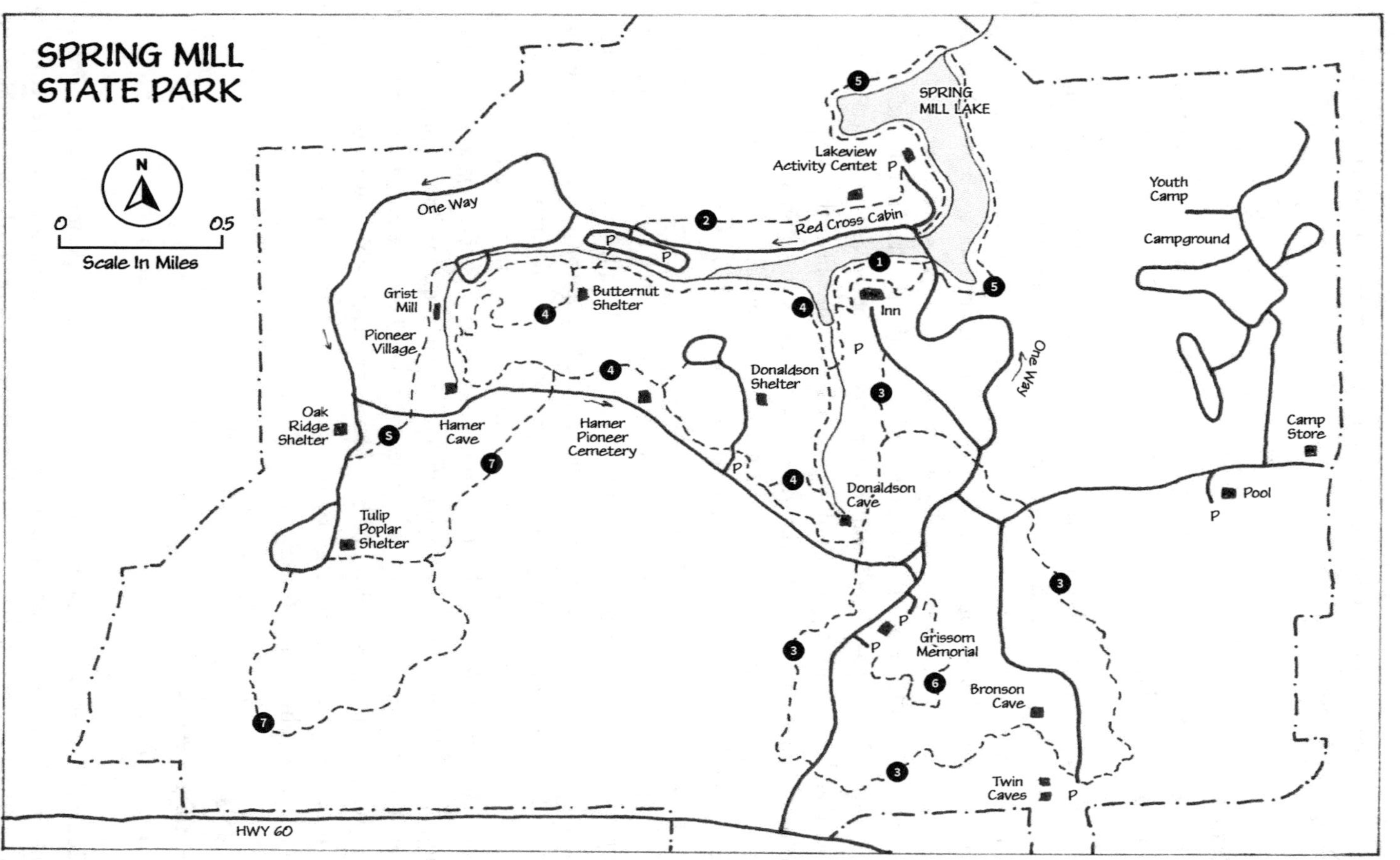

SPRING MILL STATE PARK
N
0
0.5
Scale In Miles
SPRING MILL LAKE
Lakeview Activity Center
P
One Way
Red Cross Cabin
P
P
Inn
P
One Way
Grist Mill
Butternut Shelter
Pioneer Village
Donaldson Shelter
Donaldson Cave
P
Oak Ridge Shelter
S
Hamer Cave
Hamer Pioneer Cemetery
Tulip Poplar Shelter
Grissom Memorial
P
P
Bronson Cave
Twin Caves
P
Youth Camp
Campground
Camp Store
Pool
P
HWY 60

ends near the Lakeview Activity Center. Trail 5 is found on the far side of the center, along the lakeshore.

Trail 3

Rating: ★ ★ ★ ★ ★   **Configuration:** Loop (plus two connector stubs)
Distance: 2.5 miles   **Difficulty:** Moderate

Tour: Trail 3 passes through three state nature preserves (Donaldson's Cave, Mitchell Karst Plains, and Donaldson's Woods) and immerses hikers in some of the most memorable natural features in Indiana. Start at the inn parking structure; Trail 3 departs just beyond the south end, following the ridgetop above Donaldson Cave and its outlet stream, which you can hear as you walk. Turn right when you reach the main loop, go straight past the fork connecting to Trail 4, and cross the park road. What was already a nice hike gets even better as you enter a gorgeous woodland filled with big trees and sinkholes. Road noise mars the experience some-what as you go farther south but the scenery remains amazing. The trail turns left (east), crosses the entrance road, and continues toward Bronson Cave, which is a short side trip down a wooden staircase. No entry is allowed but take time to rest on the bench and listen to the stream burble through the cave, which is technically a collapsed sinkhole (also known as a karst window). After a short climb out of the sinkhole, you reach a parking lot and the trail's next highlight: Twin Caves. During summer, this area will be busy when the park offers popular boat tours of the upper cave. Regardless of how many people are around, take a few minutes to walk down the stairs to the caves; note that the stream connecting them is the same one you just saw at Bronson Cave. Trail 3 resumes on the far side of the parking lot, enter-ing one of the most ecologically significant areas in Indiana: Donaldson's Woods, a rare tract of old growth forest. The trees are bigger here, the undergrowth (includ-ing wildflowers) more varied, the birds more abundant—this is what untrammeled nature looks like. After two more road crossings, you'll reach the start of Trail 3's loop; turn right for a short walk back to the inn.

Trail 4

Rating: ★ ★ ★ ★ ★   **Configuration:** Loop
Distance: 2 miles   **Difficulty:** Challenging

Tour: For sheer variety, it is hard to beat Trail 4, which packs multiple historical and natural highlights into just two miles of hiking. Park at the Pioneer Village, cross Mill Creek and turn left, hiking Trail 4 along the south shore of the creek, which soon transitions into an upper arm of Spring Mill Lake. The trail swings south and starts following the rocky, gurgling outlet stream from Donaldson Cave. Trail 1 from the inn crosses a bridge and connects from the left. Just beyond the bridge lies George Donaldson's small stone monument to ornithologist—and fellow Scotsman— Alexander Wilson. Soon hikers reach an important junction. Trail 4 turns right and follows a long, steep staircase out of the valley, but hikers are encouraged to stay straight on the sturdy walkway to Donaldson's Cave. The cavern has two openings; people are welcome to explore the "dry" opening to the right, though you'll need a decent headlamp or flashlight. After spelunking, retrace your steps to the stairway and start climbing. At the top, the Trail 3 stub goes left; go right (and through the parking lot) to stay on Trail 4. You soon reach another historical highlight, Hamer Cemetery. Take a few minutes to walk around to the gate in front and explore the graves, which date back to the first half of the 19th century. Back on the trail, you soon pass the intersection with Trail 7, a great woodland side trip if you have time. Trail 4 reaches the upper end of Mill Creek valley, turns right, and starts downhill. In the valley, you can see the flume and the historic mill it serves. Water from the creek, which emerges from Hamer Cave, is shunted into the flume to power the mill's huge wheel. After passing the small quarry that provided building stones for the mill, the trail descends a staircase and reaches a junction with a stub to the Pioneer Village. Save that highlight for later and stay on Trail 4, climbing up and around a low ridgeline offering occasional views of the village buildings. Before ending, Trail 4 gently descends a pretty valley that is a riot of wildflowers in the spring and has two CCC-era picnic areas. At trail's end, turn left to return to the restored Pioneer Village, which has a fascinating history and is worthy of an hour or two of exploring.

Trail 5

Rating: ★ ★ ★ ★ **Configuration:** Loop
Distance: 1.0 miles **Difficulty:** Moderate

Tour: Limestone is the dominant geologic feature in Spring Mill and Trail 5 may be the best place to see the fascinating interplay of rocks and trees that shape the park's forests. Early spring, when wildflowers bloom in huge numbers, may be the best time to hike here. Park at the Lakeview Activity Center (Nature Center) lot and walk around or through the building to the trail on the lakeshore. Turn left, passing the boat ramp and entering the woods along the lake's northwestern arm. The forests in this area have a mix of younger trees than other parts of the park. Large, moss-covered limestone boulders dot the landscape, in the spring decorated with limestone-loving red flowers like fire pink and columbine. Watch your footing because unlike other park paths, this route is narrow, twisting, rocky, and root covered. Forest and lake

Massive, ancient trees abound in the old growth forest section of Trail 3.

views entertain as you work your way to the dam and cross a bridge over the outlet stream. The trail stays mostly elevated above the lake after the dam, then turns into a valley to cross a small tributary. (This bridge was washed out by a 2025 flood, but the rock-hop crossing is simple in low water.) Finish your Trail 5 hike by crossing the lake on the park road bridge and following the marshy shoreline back to the Lakeview Activity Center.

Trail 6

Rating: ★ ★
Distance: 0.25 mile

Configuration: Loop
Difficulty: Easy (ADA accessible)

Tour: This short trail is a nice companion to the Virgil I. "Gus" Grissom Memorial and the perfect place to take people who might not be up to a full hike on Spring Mill's other trails. After entering the gate, turn right into the Grissom Memorial and park; the trail starts at the northeast corner of the lot. The paved path winds gently through the woods with sinkholes visible through the trees. There are a couple of places to sit, rest, and enjoy the beautiful surroundings. The path ends at the far end of the parking lot.

Trail 7

Rating: ★ ★ ★   **Configuration:** Loop with Stub
Distance: 1.75 miles   **Difficulty:** Easy

Tour: Trail 7 is the perfect place for an easy-hiking, woods-and-wildflowers experience—without the crowds you might encounter in other parts of the park. Follow the one-way road all the way around the park to the turnoff for Oak Ridge and Tulip Poplar shelters. Drive past the former and park at the latter, near the start of Trail 7. Hike into the woods on the wide, nearly flat trail, a nice running route. The trees in this part of the park are younger and smaller than the giants along Trail 3, but the forest is still beautiful. There also is more bird activity; woodpeckers are especially abundant. After a quarter mile, the trail forks. The path to the left is a half-mile walk to a junction with Trail 4. Treating that pretty section as an out-and-back side trip is encouraged. Once back on the main loop, continue to work your way south, then west. The trail ends back at the shelter access road. Turn right and walk a short distance along the road back to your car.

Stagecoach Trail

Rating: ★ ★   **Configuration:** Point to Point
Distance: 0.5 miles   **Difficulty:** Moderate

Tour: The Stagecoach Trail offers a short lesson in Spring Mill's transportation history. It starts in the Pioneer Village and runs south, ending at the Oak Ridge picnic area and playground. The wide path, as the name explains, was once part of the stagecoach and wagon route between New Albany and Terre Haute. In the village, hike uphill past the grist mill on the paved road. Continue out of the village on the now-unpaved trail, which curves to the right and climbs a steep valley to bluffs above. Turn around to return—or turn left on the access road to reach the start of Trail 7, which you can use along with Trail 4 to create a loop back to village.

20
Summit Lake State Park

Summit Lake isn't the first place that serious Indiana hikers think about when considering destinations, but the park has a half-dozen interesting trails worth exploring. The trails are disconnected but laid out along the spine of the main park road. I developed a plan to cover the whole network in one outing. Starting in the north, I would run each trail, then venture onto the park road to the next trail. Run trail, run road, repeat. When I finished on the south end of the park, I would simply turn around and run back to my car.

I drove to Summit Lake on a weekday September morning. It was foggy, overcast, a little bit drippy—perfect running conditions. Because of the weather, not many other visitors were at the park.

After parking in the small lot that served as the trailhead for Trails 1 and 5, I took off down the path, staying right at intersections. Trail 5 was my first destination; it's also my favorite path in the park, winding through a beautiful little upland forest.

The path broke out into open prairie and Trail 1 joined from the right. I continued forward, following the edge of a brush line until turning right at the second junction with Trail 1. This mowed path winds through tall grasses near arms of Summit Lake. Occasional side trails take you to the water's edge and great views across the lake. One arm is filled with flooded timber and a good place to watch waterfowl.

After repeating the short forest-edge overlap with Trail 5, I finished the loop, passed my car at the trailhead, and ventured onto the park road for a short run to the beach access road and Trail 3. This firm, wide path is deemed ADA accessible. It winds through a forested peninsula before reaching the shores of Summit Lake. The fog had burned off and the reservoir's beautiful 800-acre expanse opened to my right as I ran. A couple of fishing boats were visible in the distance.

My next destination was Sunset Shelter and Trail 6, a short out-and-back on a small peninsula. Like the beach trail, the path offers great lake views and shore access for fishermen and picnickers.

A Summit Lake fisherman appears through a hole in the brush alongside Trail 3.

Back on the park road I passed the entrance road and veered to the right at Harvey Shelter to reach Trail 4. This short self-guided nature trail looped through a prairie, scrub forest, and small wetland, providing a lake view before returning me to the shelter and park road.

The road curved west and passed the campground control station. During the warm-weather months, vehicle traffic beyond this point is limited to campers. A parking area is available for non-campers and visitors who want to proceed on foot.

The entrance to Trail 2 was a left-hand turn opposite the campground. The path was a twisting route through the trees with frequent visits to lakeshore, offering nice views and frequent waterfowl sightings. But like the park's other hiking routes, Trail 2 ended relatively quickly and dropped me back on the park road for the 1.5-mile run back to my car. A wilderness adventure? No, but definitely a varied and fun day on the trails.

Summit Lake History

Summit Lake and its surrounding state park is a relatively new recreation area—the state park was dedicated in 1988—but it was a project that took several decades to bring to fruition.

Much of the credit for the existence of Summit Lake goes to Ralph Harvey, the longtime U.S. congressman from Mount Summit who lived most of his life in a farmhouse overlooking the Big Blue River not far from the current state park. Harvey farmed his property, but the Purdue grad also taught agriculture and science at the local high school. He gravitated to politics, serving a decade on the Henry County Council followed by five years in the Indiana House.

In 1947 Harvey was elected to the U.S. Congress, filling a vacancy in Indiana's 10th District created by the death of Raymond Springer. Harvey served until 1966, except for two years when he temporarily lost the seat (1959–1960).

Harvey is probably best remembered for his support of critical civil rights legislation and his role in promoting the use of U.S. agricultural products to feed hungry people around the globe in the wake of World War II. But his work on lesser-known legislation paved the way for the construction of Summit Lake.

Harvey was thinking about the possibility of building a reservoir on the Big Blue River when he helped craft and pass the Watershed Protection and Flood Prevention Act of 1954. There was interest in building a lake for recreation purposes in Henry County, but the cost without federal support would have been prohibitive. Unfortunately, the government at this time was focused on huge flood control projects, not building small, local lakes.

The 1954 legislation changed things dramatically. It created the U.S. Department of Agriculture's Small Watershed Program, which helped communities and private landowners conduct surveys, develop plans, and build structures—i.e. dams—that would control flooding, lessen erosion, and trap sediment while protecting water resources. And if these projects created a local recreational opportunity? That was okay, too!

With a tool in place to make their dreams a reality, Henry County lake proponents got to work, but it was a slow process. In 1966, the Big Blue River Conservancy District (BBRCD) was formed and began formulating a project that included flood control, waterway improvement, and recreation. Its official (and less-than-romantic) name: Structure 20, Summit Lake. Construction of the dam, paid for primarily with federal funding, started in 1974. Sadly, the lake's champion, Ralph Harvey, wasn't around to celebrate this milestone. He had passed away at his winter home in Florida three years earlier.

The dam was completed in 1980, the floodgates closed, and the new lake started filling. Soon an 800-acre lake beckoned boaters, fishermen, and other outdoor enthusiasts. Initially, the area was known as the Big Blue Recreation Area and managed by the conservancy, but the plan for years had been to entice the state of Indiana into taking over the property and developing it as a state park. That goal was realized when BBRCD sold the property to the state as part of a $250,000 lease-purchase agreement. The land and lake were transferred, and Summit Lake State Park was officially dedicated on January 9, 1988.

Summit Lake Today

Summit Lake State Park is located 59 miles east of downtown Indianapolis. The nearest community of any size is New Castle, the seat of Henry County, nine miles southwest.

Vernal pools near Trail 5 resound with the calls of frogs seeking a mate.

Trail 1 offers numerous access points for viewing Summit Lake's abundant waterfowl.

The park covers 2,680 acres, but almost a third of that area—835 acres—is the surface of Summit Lake. In addition, large sections of the park are taken up by wetlands as well as the dam, designated natural areas, and other areas deemed off-limits to human access. As a result, only a relatively small area in the south and southeast sections of the park is dedicated to dry-land activities.

Understandably, the focus at this state park has always been the lake, which is relatively deep (maximum of 47 feet) and has a lot of natural cover. Fishing is a big draw, and the lake has a reputation for being one of the best angling spots in eastern Indiana. The state park ensures lots of access for shore fisherman but also provides two boat ramps and a rental concession in the warm-weather months with rowboats, kayaks, and canoes.

Summit Lake offers two kayaking trails, which together form the park's all-water 2 Kayak Trail Challenge. Trail 1 leaves the north ramp and explores bays at the upper end of the lake, while Trail 2 from the south ramp visits bays and islands closer to the dam.

Summit Lake also boasts an amazing variety of bird life. The eBird app lists 269 identified species at the park, a mixture of forest, grassland, and water-loving birds.

Camping is the only option for an overnight stay at Summit Lake. The campground, located at the far south end of the park adjacent to the lake, has 114 sites, all with electric hookups. Trail 2 offers the only easy access to hiking from the campground. Other trails must be reached by a long walk or a short drive on the park road. Noncampers will find the best hotel options in Muncie, about 20 miles north of the park.

Hiking Summit Lake

Summit Lake is a decent hiking destination, but the trails are short and disconnected. Three miles is about the longest hike you can put together at Summit Lake without spending time on the shoulder of a road or repeating long stretches of trail. Instead, consider that the trail network does a good job of supporting other activities, including providing easy access for bird watching, fishing, or picnicking. To get the most out of your experience at Summit Lake, consider taking along a pair of binoculars, a camera, or a fishing rod on your walk. Stop frequently and sit quietly—in the woods, along the prairie, on the lakeshore. The experience will be a feast for your eyes and ears.

Trail Running

All six Summit Lake trails are runnable, but only two connect to each other. Trails 1 and 5 together form a quality loop of about three miles, but if you want a longer run, you'll have to take to the main park road to connect disparate trail segments together.

TRAIL GUIDES

Trail 1

Rating: ★ ★ ★　　　　　　　　**Configuration:** Lollipop
Distance: 1.75 miles　　　　　　**Difficulty:** Easy

Tour: Trail 1 is an easy walk and offers some of the best lake views and birdwatching in the park. To access, turn right on the main road and park at the small, unmarked lot to the right just after the turnoff to the beach. Trails 1 and 5 depart together north from the lot. Stay left at the two intersections where Trail 5 branches to the right. Trail 1 is a wide, mowed path throughout its route; restored prairie (sometimes burned in the spring) sits to the right, the lake to the left. Multiple access points make it easy to reach the water's edge. The trail eventually swings south and follows a long, narrow arm of the reservoir with flooded timber and even more interesting bird life. A Leopold bench marks the intersection with Trail 5. Turn right and follow this stretch of shared trail between the prairie and a line of brushy bushes back to your starting point.

Trail 2

Rating: ★ ★ ★   **Configuration:** Loop
Distance: 1.25 miles   **Difficulty:** Easy

Tour: Trail 2 is another great path for birdwatching, both forest and water-loving species. It starts adjacent to the campground; as you enter, there is a small gravel parking area on the left next to the trailhead. In warm-weather months, when the camp office is manned, non-campers may have to park in the visitor lot and walk in. Trail 2 heads west through a mature forest before reaching the reservoir at the end of the first of the five small peninsulas that this trail visits. Stop and look for waterfowl, which are common in this shallow arm of the lake. The twisting trail turns inland into the woods then back toward the water and the next point, a process that is repeated multiple times around the full loop. The last peninsula ends in a long sand spit that is a common resting place for geese and other water birds. The trail climbs from the lake on a wide grassy section before ending abruptly at the campground road; turn right to return to trailhead.

Trail 3

Rating: ★ ★ ★   **Configuration:** Loop
Distance: 0.9 miles   **Difficulty:** Easy (ADA Accessible)

Tour: Located near the beach, Trail 3 is a beautiful route and friendly to hikers of all ages and abilities. Because the path is wide, level, and covered with fine crushed limestone, it is rated as ADA accessible. Park on the right side and near the entrance of the big beach lot; the trailhead is located on the northeast corner. Trail 3 immediately enters a mature, hardwood forest. Families will appreciate the frequent benches and kid-friendly interpretive signs. As the trail circles around the end of the peninsula, it passes several lake access points with great views; shoreline fishing is also reported to be good in this area. Eventually the path reaches the beach house and swimming area and pavement begins. As you return to the parking lot, pause and scan the small pond to your left for ducks, geese, turtles, and other water life.

Trail 4

Rating: ★   **Configuration:** Loop
Distance: 0.75 miles   **Difficulty:** Easy

Tour: To reach this short trail, turn left on the main park road, pass the access to the south boat ramp, and park near the small building on the right, the naturalist office. The trail starts behind this building and makes a simple loop to the lake's edge and back. In the process, it passes a variety of habitats, including prairie, wetland, and scrub brush.

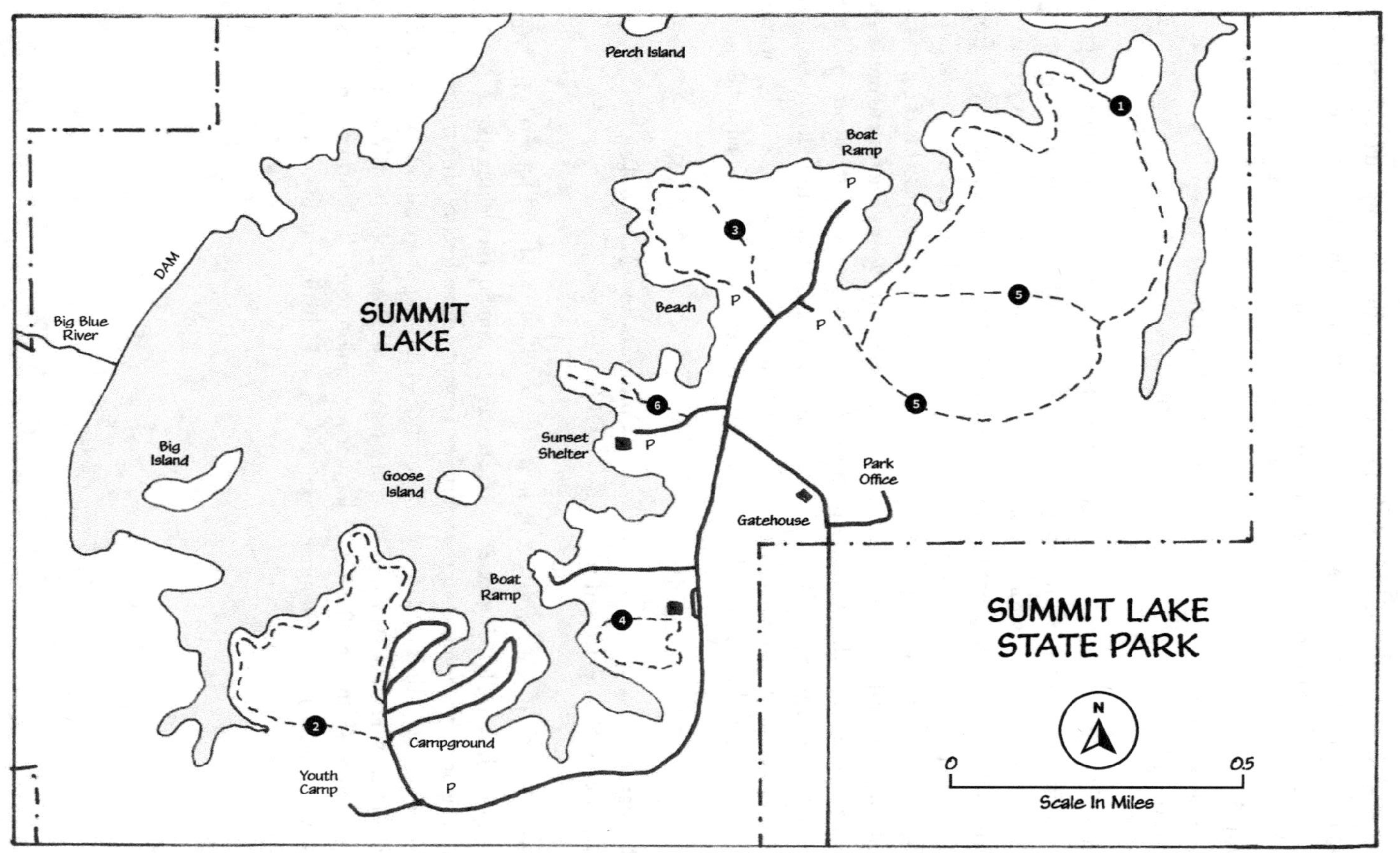
Perch Island
Boat Ramp
DAM
Big Blue River
SUMMIT LAKE
Beach
Big Island
Goose Island
Sunset Shelter
Park Office
Gatehouse
Boat Ramp
Youth Camp
Campground
P
1
3
5
5
6
4
2
SUMMIT LAKE
STATE PARK
N
0
0.5
Scale In Miles

Habitat restoration in 2024–2025 eliminated most of the scrub and made the trail difficult to walk, but the work will replace invasives with native vegetation and deliver an improved experience for both wildlife and humans in the years ahead.

Trail 5

Rating: ★ ★ ★ ★   **Configuration:** Lollipop
Distance: 1.25 miles   **Difficulty:** Moderate

Tour: This hike includes the nicest stretch of trail in the park, passing through an attractive forest dotted with vernal pools that are alive with amphibians in the spring. Follow the instructions for accessing Trail 1; at the first junction, follow Trail 5 to right and up a small hill into the forest. In the early spring you hear the chorus frogs, spring peepers, and leopard frogs before you see any water, but the vernal pools, flooding low-lying trees, soon appear to your right. Periodic pools appear for the next half mile until the trail reaches a brushy, scrub section of the woods, then straightens and widens. An arm of the lake appears through the trees on the right as you approach the junction with Trail 1. Before that, a narrow path leads to a waterside viewpoint, a great place to see waterfowl. Back at the junction, turn left to stay on Trail 5 or consider turning right to follow Trail 1 to create a longer hike with excellent lake views.

Trail 6

Rating: ★   **Configuration:** Point to Point
Distance: 0.5 miles (round trip)   **Difficulty:** Easy

Tour: Trail 6 offers more of a walk to the lakeshore rather than a hike, but it's worth exploring if you're looking for easy route to scenic fishing or picnicking spots. To access, turn right on the main road then turn left toward Sunset Shelter. The trailhead is on the right. The path is a relatively straight shot to the end of a peninsula with multiple lake-access side trails. Much of the trail passed through scrubby invasives—until they were removed during 2024–2025 habitat restoration work. This project promises to deliver a native-rich environment in the future and a better walking experience.

21
Tippecanoe River State Park

I had reached that point in half-marathon training when I was tired of running and bored with the streets and recreational trails near my house. I needed to mix it up a little. Visiting the Indiana state parks website and scanning the list of properties, my eyes locked on Tippecanoe River. "Perfect for a long trail run," I thought.

I'd previously hiked at Tippecanoe River and made a mental note to come back someday and run. The trails are flat, shaded, and connect well. I easily could piece together a 10-plus-mile route that would serve as my next long run—if I could make the time for a trip.

A Monday vacation day from work opened 24 hours for a mini expedition starting late afternoon Sunday. I loaded camping gear in the car and drove to Tippecanoe River, pulling in as the last few RVs were pulling out. It was mid-September, the weather was perfect, and there were only a couple other campers hanging around.

I used the waning daylight to set up camp and light some charcoal in the fire ring. It was dark by the time I cleaned up after dinner, but I already had a nice fire burning. As I settled into my camp chair, the fire crackling in front of me and burgers sitting nicely in my belly, I felt pretty content. It was so *quiet,* something that stands out every time I visit Tippecanoe. Soon I was dozing in my chair.

"*Who cooks for youuuuu!*" screamed a voice not 10 feet overhead. I jumped, wide awake, my heart pounding. A barred owl had settled in the tree above and announced his or her presence. When the owl departed, I realized it was time for bed.

I was up by first light, pulled on my running gear, and made do with a quick, ready-made breakfast. Time was tight, and I needed to get on the trails and get moving.

I jumped on Trail 4, which skirted the southern edge of the campground, took to a road for a short distance, and passed the nature center. I made a detour to the canoe launch to get a glimpse of the park's namesake river. The Tippecanoe, which creates the park's eastern boundary, is wide and shallow in this area. It flowed by silently, moving southward to a meeting with the Wabash.

This pretty picnic spot is just off Trail 5 and near the River Tent Camp.

Back on Trail 4, I entered Tippecanoe River Nature Preserve and the prettiest section of the park. The riparian forest was dotted with oxbow lakes and huge trees; the undergrowth was dense, even in late summer. I stopped briefly to listen; other than occasional bird calls, it was silent.

After making another close pass to the river—in the process scaring a great blue heron, which took off and squawked angrily at me—I followed the path inland to a junction with Trail 5. This route follows the Tippecanoe almost to the northern boundary of the park. It's wide and flat, a perfect trail-running route.

I passed the shortcut turnoff and the Trail 3 connector and continued north on a long stretch that closely follows the park road. The park was so quiet vehicle noise wasn't a problem. In fact, over the course of running 10 miles I never saw another human.

I stopped briefly at the River Tent Camp to rehydrate and enjoy a view of the Tippecanoe at the boat ramp. It was the last time I'd see the river until the northern end of Trail 5.

The next section was pretty but nondescript; the only highlight was passing the youth tent area. Another half mile down the trail, I encountered a junction and first took the right turn, which delivered me to the Tepicon canoe access and a short rest on the banks of the Tippecanoe.

Returning to Trail 5, I climbed the only hill I'd encounter all day and followed the route to its end near Tepicon Hall, built in the 1930s by the Civilian Conservation Corps. While exploring the site of the former group camp, I noticed the start of Trail 8 across the road—an option if I wanted to add another mile or so to the run.

I decided that 10 miles was plenty and started the return trip to the campground, all the while thinking about how alone I felt in this park. South of the youth camping area, the trail jumps onto the park road for a short distance. I turned left on the pavement and was startled to see someone else crossing the road 20 yards ahead—a coyote. We both stopped, frozen by the encounter, silently staring at each other. After a long pause, the coyote decided it was time to depart and disappeared into the forest.

I continued my run, thankful that even in civilized Indiana, we still had places where wildness could find a home.

Tippecanoe River History

The history of Tippecanoe River State Park is one told by glaciers. The thick, moving ice scraped the landscape flat as it moved south. Then, as the ice melted and pulled away to the north—about 12,000 years ago—it deposited a thick layer of sand that today dominates the soil.

The Tippecanoe River rises in the glacial lakes region of northeast Indiana, not far from Chain O'Lakes State Park. It boasts some of the best water quality in the state and supports a highly biodiverse ecosystem, including 54 fish species and 57 mussel species.

Humans have a long history of appreciating and using the river. The stream and its basin are the ancestral home of the Tepicon (or Tippecanoe) Band of the Miami people. The name "Tippecanoe" means "people of the place of the buffalo fish." French voyageurs in search of furs traded with the Miami and maintained a close relationship with them.

After American independence, settlers began moving west, increasing the tension with Native tribes living in the future state of Indiana. The Miami did not participate in the 1811 Battle of Tippecanoe, fought by other tribes near the river's mouth, but they were not immune to its impacts. The Miami bands ceded their lands to the U.S. in a series of treaties; the land now in Tippecanoe River State Park was transferred in 1832.

Settlement followed and Pulaski County was organized in 1839 with Winamac, five miles south of the park, named the county seat. Farming was, and still is, the main economic pursuit in this area, but not all farmers enjoyed the same success. The area north of Winamac, near the river, was prone to flooding in wet months while in dry times the sandy soil couldn't hold water. It wasn't good farmland.

By the Depression, much of the future parkland had been stripped of trees, farmed unsuccessfully, and abandoned. It was perfect for a New Deal program launched in 1934. Recreational Demonstration Areas (RDA) were part of the National Park Service and designed to convert failed farmland into parks that would invigorate rural economies.

The federal government started buying land for the park in 1935. Most of the properties had been foreclosed upon and were held by local banks. Eventually, 7,353 acres were acquired. By the fall, workers employed by the Works Progress Administration started clearing brush and replanting more than one million native trees and shrubs on the property. By 1938, the workers had built a road to the new park—called Winamac RDA—as well as picnic areas, trails, shelters, a campground, and a fire tower. They also constructed two group camps, Camp Tepicon and Camp Potawatomi, each including several small cabins and a central recreation and eating hall. The camps lasted into the 1960s and one of the last vestiges of their existence is preserved Tepicon Hall, now on the National Register of Historic Places.

Without the budget to administer its 46 RDAs during World War II, the National Park Service requested and received legislative approval to turn the properties over to the states. On March 18, 1943, Winamac RDA was transferred to Indiana, becoming Tippecanoe River State Park.

The section of the new state park west of U.S. Highway 35 had a different feel from the area closer to the river and soon became popular for other uses, including dog field trials. In 1959, it was transferred to the Division of Fish and Game and renamed Winamac Fish & Wildlife Area. Tippecanoe River State Park retained 2,785 acres after the split and is the seventh largest park in Indiana.

Tippecanoe River Today

Though located halfway between Indianapolis and Chicago, 120 miles north of Indiana's capital, Tippecanoe River is off the beaten track and gets fewer than 150,000 annual visitors.

The park's dense forests, wetlands, and river make it a draw for wildlife and birds. It is a noted stop on the Indiana Birding Trail and mammal encounters are common, too, with white-tailed deer, coyotes, and river otters among the park's residents.

The Tippecanoe River is shallow and slow-moving near the park and is a popular destination for canoeing, kayaking, and fishing. The park has four canoe access points as well as a primitive tent-only campground geared toward river users. There are no rental services in the park, but Pulaski County has two outfitters offering canoe/kayak rental and shuttle services.

The southern third of Tippecanoe River is geared toward horseback riding. More than 14 miles of trails wind through the woods, climbing up and over low sand dunes and around scenic wetlands. One of the trails passes the park's historic fire tower, which was built by WPA laborers in 1938. It takes 110 steps to climb the tower's 90 feet, but the reward is a nice view in all directions of the forested parkland.

On Trail 4, hikers cross this bridge and enter Tippecanoe River Nature Preserve.

There are multiple options for overnighting in the park. In addition to the youth, river, and horsemen's camps there is an all-electric campground with 108 sites. It connects with Trails 3 and 4, so is a good starting point for hikers.

For people who want a rustic experience but aren't inclined toward sleeping on the ground, Tippecanoe River offers one of Indiana's unique lodging options: Rent-A-Camp cabins. These dozen lodges, located at the north end of the park, are simple 12x16 structures with bunk beds, a loft, and room to sleep six people. They have electricity—meaning lights and the ability to plug in a space heater in cold weather—but cooking must be done outside. Trails 5 and 8 are both nearby, so you can hike from your doorstep.

Outside the park, nearby Winamac offers limited lodging but ample gas, grocery, and restaurant options.

Hiking Tippecanoe River

Tippecanoe River ranks seventh in size among Indiana state parks but counts just four hiking-only paths extending for less than 10 miles. Nonetheless, it's a great destination if you value quiet and solitude. The park ranks 22nd in visitation and you won't encounter many other people on the trails. On top of that, wildlife is plentiful, and the birdwatching is exceptional.

But because the trails wind through a lush river floodplain, they can get soggy, especially in the spring. They also are monotonous—nondescript hardwood and pine forests with dense undergrowth. The river views are nice, but there are relatively few of them.

The best hiking is in Tippecanoe River Nature Preserve—Trail 4 and the south end of Trail 5. There are river views, huge trees, and abundant bird life. Trail 8 offers a glimpse into a different environment as it passes through Sandhill Nature Preserve, including some open areas of prairie and oak barrens.

Tippecanoe also has 14 miles of "Horse/Hiking" trails that dominate the southern third of the park, an area with sand hills and the property's only significant elevation changes. Despite the possibility for some scenic variety, the trails are not appealing for hiking. The routes are soft sand, chewed up by the equine traffic, and dotted with droppings.

Trail Running

Tippecanoe River is an outstanding running destination, arguably better than for hiking. The flat, smooth, and shaded trails are tailor-made for long, relaxing runs, even in summer. The trails connect well, so you can put together interesting circuits of whatever length you prefer. Plus, you will rarely encounter another human being, so you always feel like you have the whole park to yourself.

My favorite run is an out-and-back from the Nature Center combining the east side of Trail 4 with Trail 5. The full round-trip to the north end of the park is about 10 miles but you can shorten that with cutoffs or extend it by adding a loop around Trail 8. Shorter circuits are possible by combining Trails 3 and 4 with the southern part of Trail 5.

TRAIL GUIDES

Trail 3—Homestead Trail

Rating: ★ ★   **Configuration:** Loop with Connectors
Distance: 1.4 miles   **Difficulty:** Easy

Tour: The heart of this route is a long, straight, graveled path through the trees that doubles as a service road. It's a pleasant walk and efficiently connects the main campground with the River Tent Camp on Trail 5 but not a destination hike. If you intend to hike just Trail 3 and aren't camping, take the first left after the gatehouse; the trailhead is less than a half-mile north on the right. Trails 3 and 5 leave the lot together.

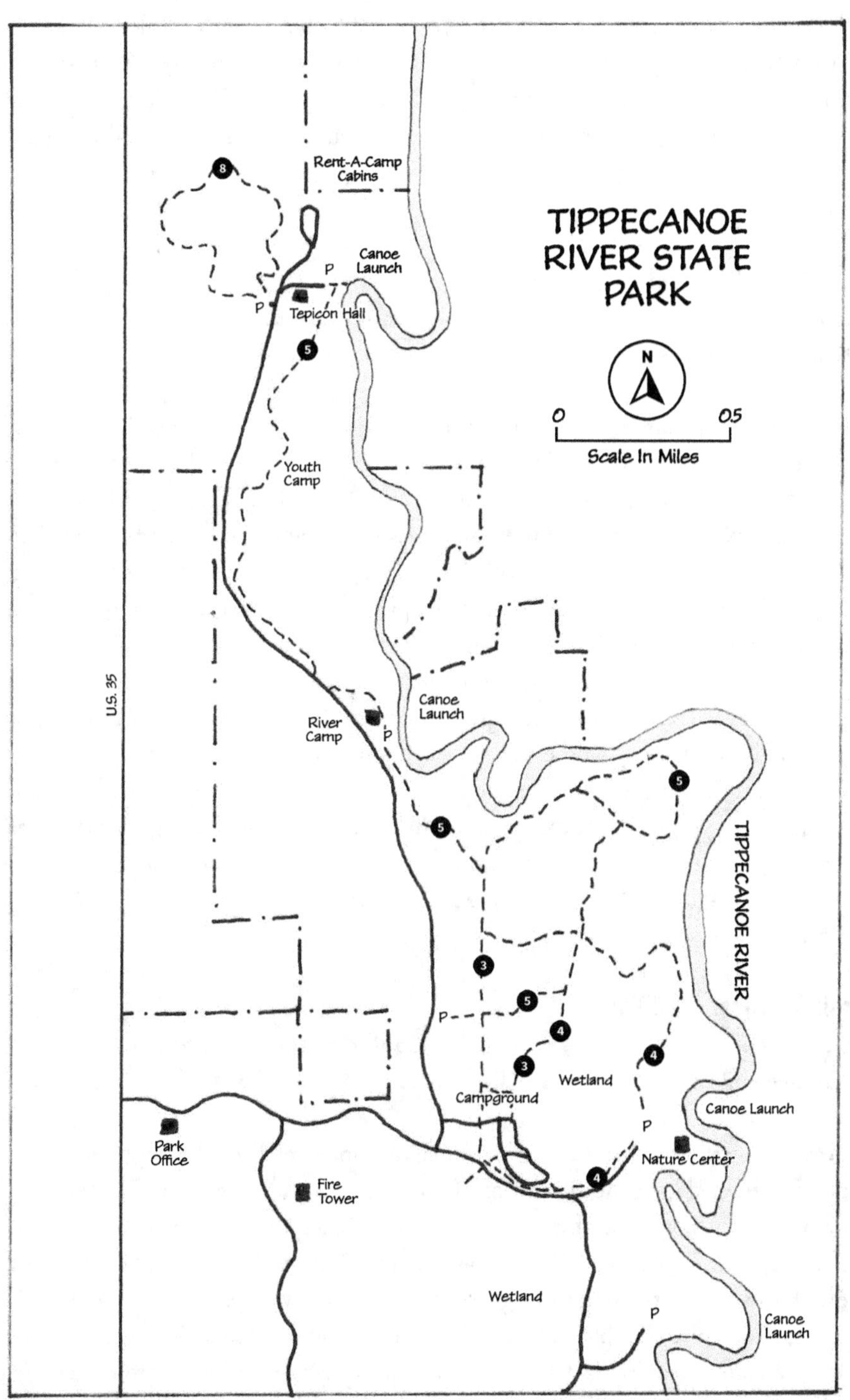

Rent-A-Camp Cabins
8
Canoe Launch
P
P
Tepicon Hall
5
TIPPECANOE RIVER STATE PARK
N
0
0.5
Scale In Miles
Youth Camp
U.S. 35
Canoe Launch
River Camp
P
5
5
3
TIPPECANOE RIVER
5
P
4
3
4
Campground
Wetland
P
Canoe Launch
Park Office
Nature Center
Fire Tower
4
Wetland
P
Canoe Launch

Turn left at the service road, which is also Trail 3. After a quarter mile, turn right to stay on Trail 3. The path heads east through a lush woodland to a right turn at a junction where Trails 3, 4, and 5 combine for a short distance. Keep straight when Trail 5 peels away (back to the starting point) and when a connector to the campground goes to the left. At the next T-intersection, turn right to finish the loop and return to your car.

Trail 4—Oxbow Trail

Rating: ★ ★ ★ ★ **Configuration:** Loop
Distance: 2.3 miles **Difficulty:** Easy

Tour: This trail earns an extra star because it includes the prettiest section of forest, a mature hardwood wonderland with huge trees. Winding around an oxbow lake and through areas subject to flooding, the area feels wild and has a diverse bird population. Park at the Nature Center lot; the trail leaves from the north side. You immediately enter a beautiful forest, with a footbridge marking the boundary of the nature preserve. An interpretive sign notes the oxbow lake on the left side of the path. Farther ahead, stop to enjoy the river—the only place the trail encounters it—then follow the path as it turns inland and winds through the dense woodland. At the edge of the forest preserve, Trail 4 turns left/south, joined by Trails 3 and 5. Continue straight when Trail 5 peels away to the right and a connector to the campground departs to the left. Turn left at the T-intersection onto what looks like a service road. Continue past the campground access road to a left turn just before the main park road. Trail 4 skirts the south edge of the campground before dumping out onto the road. Walk the road's edge, taking a left turn into the Nature Center parking area and your starting point.

Trail 5—River Bluff Trail

Rating: ★ ★ ★ **Configuration:** Point to Point
Distance: 4.2 miles **Difficulty:** Moderate

Tour: The park's longest trail follows a significant stretch of the Tippecanoe River but unfortunately touches it in only four places. Also, "River Bluff" is something of a misnomer. For most of its route, Trail 5 occupies a modest low ridge just above the floodplain. To access Trail 5, follow the directions for Trail 3—they share a trailhead. Head east on the trail through dense woods and walk past the first intersection, a service road that doubles as Trail 3. Turn left at the second intersection onto a pathway shared with Trails 3 and 4, then continue straight when those routes depart at the next junction. Another junction offers a shortcut to the left; instead stay to the right and enter the northern part of Tippecanoe River Nature Preserve. After inscribing a big loop through the woods, the trail makes its first encounter with the river. Continue past the other end of the shortcut encountered earlier, another close pass to the Tippecanoe, and a left-turn connector to Trail 3 to begin the route's long northbound out-and-back. In a half mile you reach the River Tent Camp, which has pit toilets and water. Turn right on the boat ramp road to visit a pretty, open spot on the river, a nice place for a break. North of the camp, the trail leaves the river and closely follows the road, for a short stretch taking to the pavement. The northern section is pretty but nondescript, a mixed pine and hardwood forest, with the Youth Tent Camp as a noted landmark. Near the northern end, the trail hits a T-intersection. Turn right for a short detour to the river at the Tepicon Canoe Access or turn left to finish Trail 5. You immediately climb the single hill of note on the park's hiking-only trails, topping out at the small canoe access parking lot, the end of Trail 5. Continuing for a short distance on the access road takes you to historic Tepicon Hall (built by the CCC), the Rent-A-Camp cabins, and the trailhead for Trail 8.

Trail 8—Bluestem Trail

Rating: ★ ★ ★   **Configuration:** Loop

Distance: 1.2 miles   **Difficulty:** Easy

Tour: Trail 5 has a different feel from the park's other hiking-only trails. Winding through Sandhill Nature Preserve, the path passes a 15-acre prairie interspersed with pin oaks—an oak barrens—and climbs a forested, low sand dune covered with many pines as well as sugar maples, black walnuts, and other hardwoods. After the gatehouse, take the first left turn and drive 2½ miles north to the trailhead, on the left before Tepicon Hall. On the trail, turn left to follow the loop counterclockwise. Initially, the path looks like others in the park until you reach the open oak barrens. Park personnel have worked diligently to remove invasives and maintain prairie grasses and flowers. Returning to the woods, mature pines dominate, and the path is a soft and needle covered. Soon, the trail begins to climb ever so gently—the "sandhill" in the preserve's name. The last section passes near some of the park's Rent-A-Camp cabins. Continue past two connector trails to the left to return to your starting point.

22
Turkey Run State Park

I peered skeptically through the rain-splattered windshield, not convinced this trip was a good decision. The forecast had called for sunny skies, but soon I was enjoying a new meteorological treat: fog. Despite the weather, I pressed on toward Turkey Run State Park, eager to start the day with a hike on popular Trail 3 before it got busy.

The rain had stopped and the fog lifted but it was still cloudy as I passed the gatehouse. I needed more sun to get decent photos on Trail 3's route through deep, narrow canyons. On a whim, I turned right and followed a quiet road through the southeast corner of the park to Newby Gulch picnic area. My new plan was to hike a loop combining sections of Trails 1 and 2. This beautiful, underappreciated area of the park was more open and better oriented for the morning sun—if it planned on showing itself.

Not surprisingly, there was nobody else at Newby Gulch. I departed downhill on the connector to Trail 1, made a sharp right at the junction with Trail 2 and worked my way up the ravine toward Box Canyon.

The gorgeous, rocky environs of this trail are always a surprise to first-time visitors more familiar with the park's better-known hiking routes to the west. As I clambered over the roots of a giant beech then climbed out of the canyon on stairs cut into the rock, the first peeks of sun started to light isolated spots on the sandstone walls.

At the intersection beyond the top of the stairs, I turned left, onto the northern side of the Trail 2 loop, and descended into the upper reaches of Sugar Creek valley, a land of big trees and sandstone outcroppings.

The highlights continued as the trail wound around huge moss-covered boulders surrounded by ferns and wildflowers. A variety of birds called, and the air carried the faint spicy-sweet fragrance of blooming sycamore. Wooden stairs and boardwalks helped me through the most challenging sections but with a drop-off to my left, every step demanded care. Parallel Trail 1 was frequently visible on the creek-side flats not far below.

Trail 6 navigates the spectacular narrows of Turkey Run's namesake waterway.

At Gypsy Gulch, Trail 2 took a turn away from the river and soon I could hear the patter of falling water hitting rocks—a thin waterfall that was likely dry most of the year. The trail cut behind the falling stream, allowing me the opportunity to stand in a moist, shaded alcove while looking out into the now-sundrenched valley, light filtering through huge tulip-poplars and sycamores. The day had shaped up nicely.

I climbed out of the valley and reached another Trail 2 junction, this one near a pond. I turned left and followed a flat, arrow-straight path with the pond to the right. This was Lusk Earth Fill, built by John Lusk, the man most responsible for preserving this amazing forest. The eccentric recluse refused to allow logging on his property but built this earthwork to entice the county to route a new road through his land. For unknown reasons the county laid the road to the east (it follows the current park's eastern boundary), but Lusk's pond remains as a rare still-water habitat in this area.

Beyond the fill, Trail 1 joined from the left. Ahead was the Narrows Covered Bridge and, out of sight on the far bank, the preserved Lusk home. Those would be destinations for another day; instead, I opted for an immediate stroll alongside Sugar Creek.

A realm of huge sycamores, the narrow and winding east end of Trail 1 is unlike the wide and more civilized west end. Here, the undergrowth and stream constantly threaten the path's existence. The dense jewelweed, still low during my spring hike, would nearly cover Trail 1 by late summer. Meanwhile, Sugar Creek scours huge cutbanks with every flood that has forced the relocation of Trail 1 several feet inland. This year's recent deluge and erosion made me think—as I walked very close to a steep bank drop-off—that the last move wasn't far enough.

Past Goose Rock, a movement in a streamside tree caught my attention. A bald eagle, irked by my approach, silently departed its perch and followed a sweeping arc across the water. On the far side of Sugar Creek, it quickly settled in a new tree, leaving me to finish my hike.

And what a hike it had been! It occurred to me that the two-mile loop I had just completed, if located in almost any other Indiana state park, would be considered that park's *best hike*. At Turkey Run, a property blessed with amazing trail riches, it was merely a second-tier route. Yet for me, on an unlikely morning when everything good somehow fell into place, I couldn't imagine being on any other path than this one.

Turkey Run History

The landscape hikers encounter at Turkey Run is unexpected for Indiana; it's rocky, rugged, and crisscrossed by deep, narrow, water-carved canyons. During the Pennsylvanian Period, the land on which Turkey Run now sits was at the bottom of a large west-flowing river bound for an inland sea. As the river slowed while approaching the sea, it deposited a huge amount of sand that over millions of years was compacted and cemented into Mansfield sandstone. The gritty, red-tinted rock, which can be seen at outcroppings in various places in western Indiana, was at one time quarried for making glass.

In addition to sandstone, the Mansfield Formation contains other sedimentary rocks, including thin layers of coal. A coal seam, mined until the 1920s, can be seen along Trail 4 in Turkey Run.

Glaciers were the other geologic force that shaped Turkey Run. The last ice sheet stopped just south of Turkey Run about 20,000 years ago, leaving deposits, called glacial till, that covered up the existing landscape. As the glacier pulled away to the north, its huge volume of meltwater eroded and reshaped the park, grinding out Sugar Creek valley as well as the steep, narrow sandstone canyons.

The Turkey Run region was long inhabited by Native Americans; Kickapoo and Miami villages were located nearby. Captain Salmon Lusk and his wife, Polly, were, in 1821, the first white settlers in what is now the park. Lusk built a grist mill at the Narrows area and his business thrived and expanded; over the years, the Narrows became an important trading site and included a general store and tavern.

In 1848, a catastrophic flood swept away the mill and other buildings. Lusk never rebuilt, but he and Polly continued to live in an opulent residence up the hill from Sugar Creek they had constructed a decade earlier. The house, preserved today and open periodically for tours, is located just steps from Trail 4.

Salmon Lusk died in 1869 and willed the house and 1,000 acres to his son, John. Polly continued to live in the house with John until her death in 1880. John was a noted eccentric and recluse. He lived in the house until his own death in 1915.

John, despite his oddities, loved the Lusk woods and was committed to protecting them. Even though he refused to sell or allow logging on his property, he wasn't opposed to letting others enjoy the area's natural gifts. Starting in the 1880s, the area became a popular destination for nature lovers; it was known as Bloomingdale Glens. Indianapolis, Decatur & Springfield Railroad ran excursions to the site; visitors overnighted in tents. The excursions, eventually taken over by other operators, continued until Lusk's death left the future of the property up in the air.

Richard Lieber, "the father of Indiana state parks," saw the Lusk property as the perfect place to launch his state park project and celebrate Indiana's centennial in 1916. Joined by several other Turkey Run supporters, most notably the journalist Juliet Strauss from nearby Rockville, Lieber convinced Governor Samuel Ralston to form the Turkey Run Commission to raise money to purchase 288 acres of the Lusk woods.

By the April 16, 1916, property auction, the committee had raised $20,000, more than the appraised value. Optimistic park supporters were stunned when Hoosier Veneer Company—which planned to log the land—won the auction with a $30,200 bid. The committee refused to back down and soon convinced Hoosier Veneer to sell the property for $40,200. Carl Fischer and his colleagues at the Indianapolis Motor Speedway generously provided the necessary funds to close the purchase on November 11, 1916. Turkey Run ended up being the second Indiana state park; McCormick's Creek had been dedicated earlier in the year, on July 4.

Change came quickly to the small park. In 1918, the first permanent suspension bridge was built across Sugar Creek, allowing visitors to safely visit Rocky Hollow and other features on the north bank. A year later, construction started on the Turkey Run Inn; the popular lodge was expanded in 1920 and again in 1930. By the latter year, acquisition of adjoining properties had enlarged the park to 1,150 acres. During the 1930s, Civilian Conservation Corps Company 2580 built much of the distinctive infrastructure that remains today, including the gatehouse, picnic shelters, and the saddle barn.

Two of Turkey Run's founders have been memorialized at the park. Juliet Strauss, whose writing played a huge role in building support for the park, died less than two years after its founding. She was honored with a statue placed by the Women's Press Club of Indiana. You can visit it just off Trail 11 south of Turkey Run Inn. At the far end of Trail 11 is a memorial to Richard Lieber, who passed away in 1944 while visiting McCormick's Creek. Lieber's ashes, along with those of his wife and son, are interred at the memorial, a fitting resting place for the man who did so much for Indiana state parks.

Turkey Run Today

Modern-day Turkey Run State Park has expanded to 2,382 acres. The park is 69 miles west of downtown Indianapolis, an hour and 15-minute drive. Despite being relatively isolated, Turkey Run is extremely popular. In 2023–2024, roughly 872,000 people visited, making it the fourth most-popular state park. Its notoriety extends beyond the state's borders. Website *Travel Awaits* recently ranked Turkey Run as the seventh-best state park in the U.S. while *Midwest Living* magazine declared Trail 3 the best hike in the Midwest. This popularity means that hikers should not be surprised by crowds on the most popular trails during the warm-weather months, even on weekdays.

Enjoying nature is at the center of most activities, and it has been this way since the park's founding. Turkey Run was one of three parks to hire state-funded nature guides starting in 1927. Today's interpretive naturalist service is headquartered at the Nature Center, just south of the suspension bridge. Stop in to view the exhibits and get information on trails, programs, and guided hikes.

About two-thirds of the park—the 1,609 acres north of Sugar Creek—is Rocky Hollow-Falls Canyon Nature Preserve. Of this area (near Trails 5 and 9), at least

Trail 2 hugs sandstone walls while working its way up Box Canyon.

285 acres has never been logged, one of Indiana's few remnants of old growth forest. Throughout the park, wildflowers explode in the spring, and a rich variety of birds is present year-round. Not surprisingly, the park is highlighted stop on the Indiana Birding Trail.

Sugar Creek is popular for fishing as well as canoe, kayak, and tubing trips. Private outfitters offer both rental watercraft and transportation on either end of the trip. Horseback rides are available at the saddle barn. The scenic bridle trail winds through the forest near hiking Trail 2.

History buffs will want to make stops at several places in the park. On the east side of the property, the Lusk home (open for occasional tours) and Narrows Covered Bridge are highlights. On the west side, along Trail 11, are memorials to park founders Juliet Strauss and Richard Lieber. The trail also passes the log church, a still-operating house of worship built in 1871 and relocated by Lieber in 1923. Near Sunset Point on Trail 6, visitors will find Lieber Cabin, a log structure dating to 1848, that Richard Lieber purchased and relocated to the park.

Turkey Run offers multiple options for visitors who want to overnight in the park. Turkey Run Inn is the best known. It features 61 rooms, a restaurant, meeting rooms, and plenty of room for recreating and relaxing. Near the inn are five family cabins of various configurations.

Turkey Run has a large, modern campground in the southwest corner of the park; all 232 sites offer electric hookups. The campground has a separate entrance from the main gate, three-quarters of a mile west on Highway 47. There is a short connector from the Twin Oaks loop to Trail 7, so it is possible to hike from the campground.

If there is no room at the inn, Rockville, 10 miles south of the park on U.S. 41, has a few small motels, as well as restaurants, gas, and groceries.

Hiking Turkey Run

Turkey Run is arguably Indiana's top state park for hiking. There are nearly 16 miles of scenic, well-maintained, and highly varied trails. Most individual trails are short, but the paths connect well, allowing countless route combinations of varying lengths.

In thinking about hiking Turkey Run, I break the trails into three zones—southwest, northwest, and east—each with their own preferred parking and access points.

The southwest zone lies near the inn and campground and includes the west end of Trail 1 along with Trails 6, 7, and 11. Park in the inn lot for easiest access. Trails 6 and 7 form a short but tremendously scenic double loop that is a must-hike route.

The northwest zone is the area that comes to mind for most Turkey Run fans: narrow canyons, waterfalls, ladders, and stairs. Park near the Nature Center and follow the trail to the suspension bridge to access this hiking zone. Trail 3 is a must-hike even if it's busy—just be patient. The smart play in this zone is to head west along Sugar Creek to Trail 9, creating a return loop with Trail 5. The crowds dwindle and the trees get bigger; it's a special hike.

The east zone is the quietest and most overlooked in the park. The loop along Sugar Creek formed by the east end of Trail 1 and the north side of Trail 2 is one of the best hikes in Indiana. Trails 4 and 8 north of the creek are part of this zone and a target for a longer hike. Park at either Newby Gulch or Canyon Picnic Areas, which get relatively little use. Cross Sugar Creek at Narrows Covered Bridge or the suspension bridge.

Ice Hiking

Hiking is a year-round activity in Indiana state parks and winter outings can deliver remarkable experiences punctuated by solitude, quiet, and landscapes beautifully altered by ice and snow. Ice creates special challenges—even dangerous conditions—for Turkey Run hikers. Microspikes and trekking poles are must-have gear for hikers venturing onto trails through the ravines.

There's good news if you don't have the right equipment and just want to get a taste of this unique experience. Thanks to funds raised by the Friends of Turkey Run and Shades group, the park purchased a generous supply ice spikes in a variety of sizes (though not for young children). The spikes, which pull on easily over hiking boots, are available for rent at the Nature Center for a modest fee.

Trail Running

Turkey Run is a mixed bag for trail runners. Crowded paths, ladders, stairs, and ravine scrambling make it a challenge to actually run on many trails. But go to the east zone and you'll find some quality routes. Trail 1 is a good run throughout its length but especially in the beautiful, winding creek-side stretch on the east end. North of Sugar Creek, Trails 8, 10, and 12 are wide and generally have good footing. Trail 4 has some challenging sections but much of its route is run-friendly.

Runners are encouraged to park in Turkey Run's "quiet corner," either at Newby Gulch or Canyon Picnic Area. If you park at the latter, follow Trail 2 west then run straight across Lusk Earth Fill to access Trail 1, Narrows Covered Bridge, and trails north of Sugar Creek.

TRAIL GUIDES

Trail 1

Rating: ★ ★ ★ **Configuration:** Point to Point
Distance: 2 miles **Difficulty:** Easy/Moderate

Tour: Though a single path, this route is a tale of two trails. The west end of Trail 1 is wide and flat, a heavily traveled connector between the inn and suspension bridge. The path follows Sugar Creek, but it doesn't get very close to it. East of the bridge, Trail 1 narrows, starts to wind, and moves close to the creek—sometimes very close. Thanks to flood-caused erosion, in some places the trail has been relocated several yards inland. Trail 1 is commonly included as part of other hikes but it's possible to have a pleasant, 4-mile out-and-back stroll exclusively on the path. Start on the north side of the inn, where Trail 1 departs east from Trail 6. The wide path passes recreational facilities, parking lots, and picnic shelters en route to the suspension bridge, where its character changes markedly. The eastern end is beautiful, with Sugar Creek on the left and sandstone outcrops on the right. The sycamore trees are huge, and the wildflowers are plentiful in the spring. You pass a couple of unmarked connectors with Trail 2, which parallels at the base of the bluffs to the right. At the three-quarters mark the trail passes Goose Rock, which is said to resemble a goose's head when viewed from a distance. Near the end there is one challenging scramble up a low rock face, then a formal intersection with Trail 2. Trail 1 ends at the attractive Narrows Covered Bridge. Cross it to reach an intersection with Trail 4 and access to the Lusk Home. Trails 4 and 2 offer alternative return routes that will eventually take you back to Trail 1 or simply retrace your route back to the inn.

Trail 2

Rating: ★ ★ ★ ★ ★　　　　**Configuration:** Loop (plus two access legs)
Distance: 2 miles　　　　**Difficulty:** Challenging

Tour: Relatively few people hike—or even know about—Trail 2, which is one reason why it's one of Turkey Run's top routes. Another reason is amazing scenery on the north side of the loop. Park at Newby Gulch for the easiest access. Follow the steep connector into the creek valley then take the sharp right onto Trail 2. The path immediately starts climbing up a narrow valley then swings left into the sandstone-studded environs of Box Canyon. A stair cut into the rock wall takes you out of the canyon. At the top you intersect with the trail's main loop. Turn left to keep the scenic highlights coming. Trail 2 follows the base of the south bluff above Sugar Creek. Sandstone looms overhead to your right, while the wooded valley is to your left; you catch occasional glimpses of Trail 1 below, near the water. After climbing over rocks and navigating stairs and boardwalks, Trail 2 goes deep into Gypsy Gulch, in the process passing behind a thin (often dry) waterfall. The trail climbs out of the valley and hits another intersection near a pond. Turn left to cross the Lusk Earth Fill and reach a junction with Trail 1 (a recommended return option) and Narrows Covered Bridge. Turn right to return to your starting point via the upland forest route. On this section of the loop, you cross and recross the park road before passing behind Canyon Shelter, an alternative option for parking and access. At the next junction, turn left to retrace your path through Box Canyon and back to Newby Gulch.

Trail 3

Rating: ★ ★ ★ ★ ★　　　　**Configuration:** Loop
Distance: 1.7 miles　　　　**Difficulty:** Very Challenging

Tour: This is the route that people think about when you mention hiking at Turkey Run. It's a nonstop tour of sandstone bluffs, narrow canyons, and dense forests with ladders, waterfalls, and countless other scenic delights. Park near the Nature Center, cross Sugar Creek on the suspension bridge, and turn left. You immediately start working up, around, and through the sandstone bluffs while paralleling the creek; multiple steps and boardwalks ease your passage. Turn right into narrow Bear Hollow and hike up the winding creek bed past moss-covered walls to the double ladder next to a small waterfall. At the top, Trail 5 departs to the left; go straight, climbing a third ladder to stay on Trail 3. The next section is an upstream scramble at the bottom of a wider ravine followed by multiple stairs taking you up and down through a series of heavily wooded valleys. Along the way, you pass two intersections with Trail 10. After the second junction, Trail 3 swings south and descends a rock-bottomed creek

TURKEY RUN STATE PARK

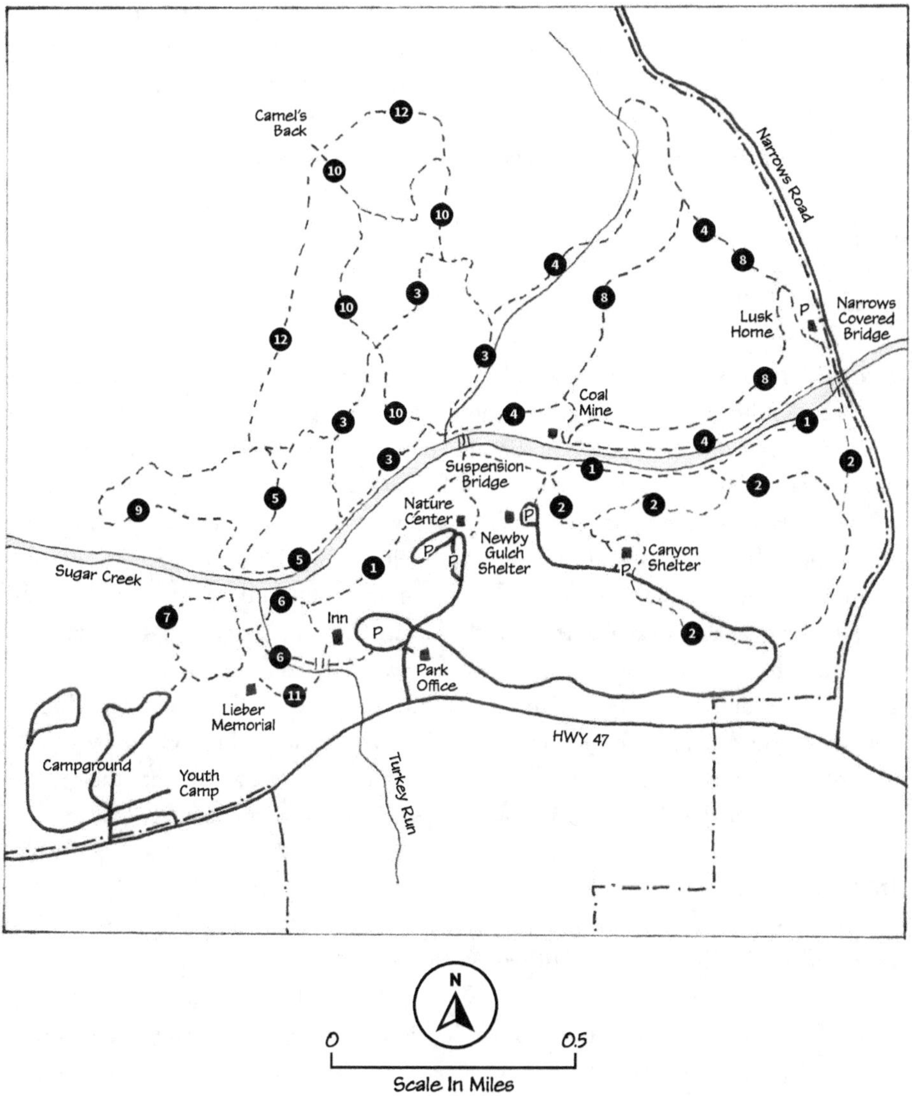

bed, distinctive with its countless thin layers of sandstone. A stair cut into the rock appears on the left. This is Trail 4 which joins Trail 3 for the remainder of its journey. The junction is next to the Punch Bowl, a distinctive formation with a small waterfall. Continuing downstream, the trail enters a narrow chasm in which you're likely to get your feet wet (if they're not soaked already) and you wonder if you're actually following a trail. Tree trunks, towering red-and-green walls, and little sunlight (even at midday) make you feel like you've entered another world. This is Rocky Hollow, which eventually widens and drops you back in the real world near the suspension bridge. On warm-weather weekends, be on this trail by 9 AM or be prepared for slow going and long backups at the ladders and other challenging locations.

Trail 4

Rating: ★ ★ ★ ★   **Configuration:** Loop
Distance: 2 miles   **Difficulty:** Challenging

Tour: This is an exceptional route, but few hikers tackle the full loop; most traffic is concentrated on the west and east sides. Follow the directions for Trail 3 but take the first right after departing the suspension bridge. Trail 3 and 4 share the route up amazing Rocky Hollow but, just past the Punch Bowl, Trail 4 climbs up stone stairs and follows a forested valley to the right, frequently crisscrossing a small stream, before climbing out of the valley and swinging to the south to a junction with Trail 8. The trails share a path for a quarter mile, then split, with Trail 4 going left to the Lusk Home, which has a parking area and vault toilet. Past the beautiful brick house, Trail 4 descends to the banks of Sugar Creek; a branch crosses Narrows Covered Bridge and connects with Trails 1 and 2 on the far side. Back on Trail 4, the route follows the base of a sandstone bluff on the north bank, heading west toward the suspension bridge. On the way, the path passes another piece of history, a small coal mine that was active until the 1920s. Past the mine, Trail 4 climbs briefly upward then descends to its end at the bridge.

Trail 5

Rating: ★ ★ ★ ★   **Configuration:** Partial Loop (complete with Trail 3)
Distance: 0.7 miles   **Difficulty:** Moderate

Tour: Trail 5 is not an independent route; it exists to connect Trails 3 and 9 and offers a somewhat easier alternative to those pathways. New Trail 12 gives Trail 5 additional importance, making it part of longer loops that include sections of Trail 10. To undertake a Trail 5 hike, follow the directions for Trail 3, trekking to the head of Bear Canyon and climbing the first two ladders. At the top, turn left and start your long climb up the infamous 140 Steps, a stone staircase that elevates you to the forested uplands. At the top, you soon encounter a junction with Trail 9; turn left to stay Trail 5. This wide path gently descends through a gorgeous old-growth forest filled with massive trees to a final downward climb on a series of stone steps. At the bottom is a second intersection with Trail 9. Turn left and follow the last section of Trail 5, which follows a bench just above Sugar Creek and winds through a beautiful riparian forest containing huge sycamores. The route ends at the junction with Trail 3 at the mouth of Bear Hollow.

Trail 6

Rating: ★ ★ ★ ★   **Configuration:** Partial Loop (complete with sidewalks near inn)
Distance: 0.5 miles   **Difficulty:** Easy

Tour: Trail 6 is an unexpected delight in the shadow of Turkey Run Inn. Park on the south side of the inn lot. The trail has an inauspicious beginning in the middle of the cabins, but things quickly change. You soon find yourself deep in the narrows of Turkey Run, a small stream, craning your neck to see the tops of the colorful sandstone walls. After passing under the old road bridge (now used by Trail 11) the

The Punch Bowl, next to the junction of Trails 3 and 4, has a pretty little waterfall.

canyon tightens even more, and the inn seems miles away. A short connector to the left provides access to Trail 7, which is a logical and scenic add-on to this hike. Trail 6 crosses a bridge, descends a staircase, and passes through a large sandstone formation. At the far side is a wonderful westward view up Sugar Creek: Sunset Point, beautiful any time of day. Nearby stands Lieber Cabin, first built in 1848 and moved to the park by Richard Lieber in 1918. After passing the start of Trail 1, Trail 6 ends on the north side of the inn.

Trail 7

Rating: ★ ★ ★ ★   **Configuration:** Loop
Distance: 0.7 miles   **Difficulty:** Moderate

Tour: Unless you start at the campground, it's impossible to hike Trail 7 without incorporating at least part of Trail 6, so they are often lumped together as a single route. Follow the directions for Trail 6; after the narrows, turn left on the connector to Trail 7. Turn left again to navigate the loop in the recommended clockwise direction. The "path" follows a creek bed up a sandstone canyon with relatively low walls and mature trees looming overhead, an especially colorful fall route. Stairs exit at the head of the ravine and Trail 7 takes to the woods. The campground connector joins from the left and the trail descends until Sugar Creek comes into view. After following the stream for a short distance, the path turns, descends stairs, and crosses a bridge back to its starting point.

Trail 8

Rating: ★ ★ ★   **Configuration:** Loop
Distance: 1.5 miles   **Difficulty:** Moderate

Tour: Trail 8 is only accessible via Trail 4 and shares sections with the latter path. It is an entertaining hike because it has different personalities on the two halves of its loop. Park at the Nature Center, cross the suspension bridge and turn left on Trail 4, which passes back under the bridge. After navigating a rugged stretch along the sandstone bluffs, turn left at the Trail 8 junction. This part of the loop follows a narrow, rocky path up a forested ravine before climbing a long staircase into an upland forest highlighted by enormous trees. The trail tops out at another junction with Trail 4 and the two paths turn south together. The paths split near Lusk Home; go left to see the house. While Trail 4 follows a rugged route near the water, Trail 8 stays in the uplands on a level, shady trail, perfect for running. After descending back into the valley, Trail 8 ends at Trail 4 near the coal mine.

Trail 9

Rating: ★ ★ ★ ★ ★   **Configuration:** Partial Loop (complete with Trail 5)
Distance: 1.0 miles   **Difficulty:** Very Challenging

Tour: In just 1 mile, Trail 9 packs a diversity of scenic highlights—some of the best in Indiana. You can't hike Trail 9 without first navigating parts of Trails 3 and 5. I suggest following Sugar Creek to the mouth of Falls Canyon and turning right on Trail 9. This stretch climbs a gorgeous slot canyon with moss-covered walls and a stream trickling over a richly patterned sandstone base. Ferns and wildflowers abound in pockets of green. The trail exits the chasm via steep stairs and emerges in a remarkable old-growth forest—why I think of 9 as "the big tree trail." The path makes a right turn into a scenic but sketchy section with fallen trees, rocks, roots, and an eroding bed that brings the steep drop-off to your left uncomfortably into play. Descending, the trail arrives at one of Turkey Run's unique locations: the head of Boulder Canyon. To your right is an elevated bowl pierced by a slot waterfall, to your left a boulder-clogged ravine. Explore, rest, and enjoy the quiet before following the trail uphill through the boulders (it's easier than it looks from below). After climbing more stairs, Trail 9 returns to the old growth—and the trees are even bigger in this upland section. It's one of Indiana's best forests. Trail 9 passes the start of new Trail 12 then ends at another intersection with Trail 5. Turn right for an easier return to Sugar Creek or stay straight to descend the 140 Steps into Bear Hollow.

Trail 10

Rating: ★ ★ ★   **Configuration:** Y-Shaped (Loop with Trail 3)
Distance: 1.4 miles   **Difficulty:** Moderate

Tour: Like other routes north of Sugar Creek, Trail 10 is accessible only by Trail 3 but follows the easiest course to the top of the bluffs. Turn left after the suspension bridge and take the second right turn. Trail 10 is wide, covered with crushed rock, and climbs steeply westward. Once on the uplands, it turns north/right and soon intersects Trail 3 again. Afterward, Trail 10 follows a level and relatively straight path through the woods—some of the easiest hiking at Turkey Run. When the path forks, go left to walk the spur to Camel's Back. Without much of a view it's an underwhelming destination, but the new Trail 12 crosses here. Return on Trail 10 to the junction and turn left. This section is more interesting, twisting down into and back out of a ravine before descending a shoulder into a valley, bound for trail's end at yet another intersection with Trail 3. Turn right to return to Trail 10 or left for a rugged descent down Rocky Hollow.

Scenic Trail 9 climbs its way out of aptly named Boulder Canyon.

Trail 11

Rating: ★ ★ **Configuration:** Point to Point
Distance: 0.5 miles **Difficulty:** Easy

Tour: This short path allows you to visit monuments honoring two shining lights in Turkey Run's history. Trail 11 starts on the south side of the inn and immediately passes the statue honoring journalist Juliet Strauss, whose persuasive writing built a case for establishing the state park. The wide path crosses the old highway bridge over the Narrows; peer over the edge to see Trail 6 at the bottom of the canyon. Make a sharp right turn into the woods to find two historic highlights. To the right is the old log church (still in active use) moved to the park by Richard Lieber in 1923. To the left is the beautiful grotto containing the memorial honoring Lieber. His ashes, and those of his wife and son, are interred here.

Trail 12

Rating: ★ ★ ★ **Configuration:** Point to Point
Distance: 1.8 miles **Difficulty:** Easy

Tour: Trail 12, new in 2025, was created by converting an existing service road on the north side of the park into a hiking path. It's a pretty, upland forest route and one of Turkey Run's easiest walks. Access Trail 12 by following Trail 5 west along Sugar Creek then north out of the valley. Turn left upon reaching Trail 9; Trail 12 begins a short distance away, heading north on a flat, wide right-of-way. The route first encounters Trail 10 adjacent to Camel's Back but continues northeast, winding past the upper ends of a series of ravines. Trail 12 turns south at a junction with two service roads then ends at a second intersection with Trail 10. Turn right for the easiest return to the suspension bridge or left to connect with more challenging routes on Trail 3.

23
Versailles State Park

A few years ago, my son, Kendal, and I were plotting a trip to celebrate my wife, Tari's, upcoming birthday. I discovered a KC and the Sunshine Band concert at a casino in southeast Indiana. Our shared love of 1970s music would make this event the perfect centerpiece of a fun three-day itinerary. Kendal had some outdoorsy ideas in mind to fill out the rest of the weekend, including a hike at Versailles State Park.

Though we are close in age, Tari and I lived very different lives during the 1970s. I was in Colorado and my family camped and hiked its way around the Rocky Mountains. Tari was an Iowa girl, and her family was more focused on horseback riding and working on their hobby farm. She'd hiked some but never camped before we got married.

Nonetheless, I knew that Tari would have a great time hiking on her birthday. She never took to camping with quite the same enthusiasm as me (maybe because of too many nights spent in a rain-soaked tent) but became my best hiking buddy. In addition to Indiana, we've traipsed on trails together all over the Midwest and West.

We arrived at Versailles on a cool March morning, passed photogenic Busching Covered Bridge, and picked up a property map at the gatehouse. We planned to hike Trail 1—better known as the Old Forest Loop—a three-mile trek.

After parking near Oak Grove Shelter, we found the trailhead and started walking counterclockwise on the loop. After crossing the park road, we worked our way up a ravine into a quiet, open forest. Unlike many people, I like winter hiking in the woods. Sure, I wish there was some green, but the lack of leaves and undergrowth opens vistas hidden during the warm-weather months—on this day, expansive views to the west of Laughery Creek valley.

The open forest also gave us a better perspective on the topography, which deserved attention on this trail. The path winds around several sinkholes, indicating that easily eroded limestone dominates the bedrock underneath. This rock, formed millions of years in the Ordovician Period, also emerges at various points along the

Trail 3 makes three crossings of Fallen Timbers Creek as it works its way upstream.

trail, including sections following and crossing waterways. Small streams trickled over stairstep layers, making for slick footing in places, but creating an entertaining walk.

An interesting rock feature soon caught our attention: fossils! This limestone got its start at the bottom of a warm sea. Creatures that died and fell into the soft muck were preserved for the ages. We saw a couple of fossils that looked like shells—brachiopods—but discovered later that serious searching in the park might also turn up crinoids, bryozoans, corals, and trilobites, marine animals that lived more than 400 million years ago.

Despite the "Old Forest" name, the trail does not pass through any *old growth* forest. Though Versailles has two small stands of preserved old growth south of U.S. 50, this part of the park was logged but replanted, probably around 1840. As a result, many of the trees are mature and *big*. They are also diverse, an interesting mix of oaks, beech, maple, and tulip.

As we walked through the brown, quiet environs, we knew that just a few weeks hence, this area would be dramatically different: the forest floor would explode with a colorful carpet of spring wildflowers followed by the rapid greening of both the forest floor and the canopy overhead.

We made a sharp turn not far from the former site of the fire tower built by the Civilian Conservation Corps in the late 1930s. The tower, which was one of at least 40 built in Indiana to help spot forest fires, was eventually torn down. A grassy knoll just off the trail marks its location.

Back on the Old Forest Loop, we continued northward, passing more sinkholes. Though described as "More Difficult" on the park map, we found the route moderate at best. Yes, the trail twisted and turned and the footing was slippery in places, but it didn't compare with some of Indiana's more challenging state park trails that we'd previously hiked. But considering this was a birthday outing, winding our way through a pleasant forest seemed the perfect hiking option.

We finally crossed the road again and found ourselves back at the parking lot. It was time to find lunch. After we piled into the car and started the drive to our next destination, I glanced at Tari and saw a satisfied smile on her face. Apparently, a hike in an Indiana state park is a great way to celebrate your birthday.

Versailles State Park History

The park's Ordovician limestone was formed more than 400 million years ago. The rock formation's western edge is marked by Laughery Creek, which runs from north to south through Versailles.

In addition to a multitude of marine fossils, the porous limestone at Versailles is home to a hidden underground drainage system. The surface sinkholes give you a clue to what's happening beneath the forest soil. Versailles is also one of four state parks with a cave. (O'Bannon Woods, McCormick's Creek, and Spring Mill are the others.) Bat Cave today gets very little attention, probably because park managers want to discourage visitors from trying to enter it. The cavern, located just north of Trail 3 above Falling Timber Creek, has been explored and mapped for more than 700 feet. The cave is not shown on current park maps, and the entrance has been blocked with an earthen berm.

With rich water, forest, and wildlife resources, southeast Indiana was long inhabited and visited by Miami, Delaware, Shawnee, and other native tribes. White settlers soon followed. Indiana became a state on December 11, 1816, and Ripley County was established just 16 days later. Versailles, just a mile west of the modern-day park, was selected as the county seat in 1818.

In July 1863, the town played an unwanted role in the Civil War. Confederate General John Morgan and 1,800 cavalry riders crossed the Ohio River below Louisville and started a raid to the northeast through Indiana and Ohio. Meeting little resistance, "Morgan's Raiders" easily captured Versailles on July 12. After taking whiskey, horses, food, and other essentials, the riders moved on. Chased by Union cavalry and with the size of his force dwindling, Morgan was finally defeated and taken prisoner on July 26 near Salineville, Ohio.

One local legend in the aftermath of the raid contends that a Confederate rider named Silas Schimmerhorn deserted near Versailles and took refuge in Bat Cave. Schimmerhorn was said to have shared his living quarters with a family of wolves, and he was sometimes seen at night, running naked with the wolves, raiding nearby farms for food. A local posse hunted "The Wolf Man of Versailles" but only found the cave, a bed, and a military rifle—not Schimmerhorn. Some people claim he can still be seen running through Versailles' woods at night...

Farming the hills of Ripley County was never easy—the land and its thin soil is better suited to trees than crops. Eliphalet Stevens and his wife, Margaret, settled on park land in 1839. They built a cabin, cleared the forests, and planted an orchard inside the area roughly encircled by modern-day Trail 2. They hauled wagonloads of fruit to Madison (27 miles south) and made a good living until a cholera epidemic in 1852 killed four of their 14 children as well as many of their neighbors.

Other early settlers were more successful. In 1837, Leander Webster walked into the area of the modern-day park and built a cabin and a water-powered sawmill along the banks of Falling Timber Creek. He became one of the area's leading citizens.

With the trees mostly cut and the poor soil played out, people living on the future park land struggled. By the Great Depression, the area was targeted for help thanks to an innovative New Deal program. Recreational Demonstration Areas (RDA), under the direction of the National Park Service, were developed to convert failing farmland into a better use—in this case, parks—that would help invigorate rural economies.

Trail 1 dodges sinkholes while exploring a wonderland of ferns, fungi, and big trees.

Working with the Ripley County commissioners, the Department of the Interior purchased 1,700 acres of poor-quality farmland east and north of town in October 1934. Work began immediately on the new Versailles Federal Park. In January 1935, Civilian Conservation Corps Company 596 joined the project. For the next two years, 200 young men built roads, campgrounds, and structures, including Oak Grove Shelter. They also planted thousands of trees. Much of the land had been clear-cut, so the beautiful forests you see today are largely the result of hard work by the CCC. Their efforts have been memorialized by a statue, dedicated in 2010, that can be found in front of the park office.

Versailles was one of 46 RDAs spread across 24 states. Indiana had two properties; Tippecanoe State Park emerged from the other. The new facilities were a success but a drain on the National Park Service budget; by 1942, President Franklin Roosevelt signed legislation that outlined how the RDAs would be transferred to the states. The Ripley County RDA was handed to Indiana in April 1943, becoming Versailles State Park, from its start a fully developed and popular recreational property.

Versailles State Park Today

Versailles State Park is located about 80 miles southeast of Indianapolis; Cincinnati, Ohio, is only an hour east. Versailles ranked 15th among parks in popularity, according to data from 2023-2024, with 331,000 visitors.

Much has happened to Versailles since its birth in 1934, including a significant expansion. It now encompasses 5,988 acres, making it the second largest property in the state park system. (Only Brown County is larger.) Versailles counts four state nature preserves within its modern boundaries. Versailles, Laughery Bluffs, and Dogwood are located south of U.S. Highway 50. The latter two properties both contain stands of old-growth forest. The fourth nature preserve, Falling Timber, is north of Campground B and accessible by Trail 3.

Versailles Lake, one of the modern park's centerpieces, was not part of the original RDA. Construction started on a dam across Laughery Creek in 1954. The resulting 230-acre reservoir was completed four years later. The lake is prone to flooding and muddy water, so swimming is not allowed. Instead, the lake is a popular fishing spot. Channel catfish, largemouth bass, and crappie are the top targets.

Today, Versailles State Park is well-known for trail-based recreation. While hiking trails dominate the central part of the property, more than 24 miles of horseback trails crisscross the southern and eastern parts of the park. A horse day use area and a horseman's camp with nine electric sites cater to visiting riders. Versailles also has become one of southeast Indiana's premiere destinations for mountain bikers. Thanks to the hard work of volunteers there are now more than 25 miles of well-maintained routes in the property's northern reaches, catering to riders of all abilities.

Versailles has been a popular camping spot since its earliest days. The main campground is split into three separate sections that offer a total of 226 sites, all with electric service. The campground sits in the middle of the park's trails, so it's convenient for hikers.

Lodging is limited in the vicinity of the park. Versailles has a single small hotel, though the town is a good option for gas, groceries, and restaurants. Lawrenceburg, Batesville, or Vernon, all about 24 miles away, have chain hotel options.

Hiking Versailles

Versailles State Park is an exceptional, overlooked hiking destination. Hilly topography and mature forests give it a wilderness-like personality. The are only nine miles of trails but they are well maintained, connect nicely, and there isn't bad stretch of path in the park. Versailles is also expanding its trail network with two new, outstanding additions in recent years.

The Oak Grove Shelter picnic area is a great central location for hiking any or all the trails. A complete tour of the park's trails from Oak Grove requires some short road walks and a few backtracks but it's a very manageable 13-plus miles. Several shorter combo hikes are also possible from this central spot. The best is a five-mile tour of Trail 1 and new Trail 5. Trail 2 and Trail 3 combine nicely for two different routes of roughly 2.5 miles each.

As mentioned earlier, Versailles also has a 25-mile network of mountain bike trails that are open to hikers and runners.

Trail Running

Versailles is a good running destination. The topography rolls but the hills are all manageable and the park has fewer stairs and boardwalks than other properties. Some of the trails are technical with roots and rocks and the waterway crossings have limestone that gets slick when wet. Just check your speed in those locales to keep yourself safe.

As noted above, the entire network can be covered in a single transit of 13 or so miles starting from Oak Grove. Shorter runs using multiple trails are also possible. Trails 1 and 5 combine for a run-friendly and scenic five-miler. Trail 3 up Fallen Timber Creek valley is a superb run (complete with three water crossings).

Beyond the trails, Versailles offers quiet, scenic road running. Consider running tours to the shelters north of Fallen Timber Creek, the Lake Versailles dam, and the site of the Old Fire Tower. The latter is a narrow, barely paved route through dense woods that can be combined with side trips on Trails 1 and 5.

Finally, there are the mountain bike trails. While I usually avoid hiking on them, I enjoy running on a nicely flowing mountain bike trail. Use common sense at Versailles. If cyclist traffic is minimal you might want to do some cautious exploring.

TRAIL GUIDES

Trail 1—Old Forest Trail

Rating: ★ ★ ★ ★ ★   **Configuration:** Loop
Distance: 3 miles   **Difficulty:** Moderate

Tour: This hike takes a leisurely, winding route through a gorgeous upland forest with some of the park's oldest and largest trees. Park at the Oak Grove Shelter; the trail starts on the south side of the lot near the restroom. I prefer navigating the loop counterclockwise, which keeps the major elevation changes near the beginning of the hike. The first section passes the historic CCC-era shelter then joins Trail 2 for a stretch. Trail 1 makes a hard left on its own, descends to and crosses the park road, and starts climbing up a pretty valley. Massive beech, white oak, and other trees dot the mature forest, which has a dense, fern-rich understory in the warm months. Keep an eye open for sinkholes, which appear periodically along the edge of the trail. Watch also for fossils in the limestone as you cross small waterways. The trail soon reaches the blufftop above Laughery Creek, but views of the valley are limited when the leaves

VERSAILLES STATE PARK

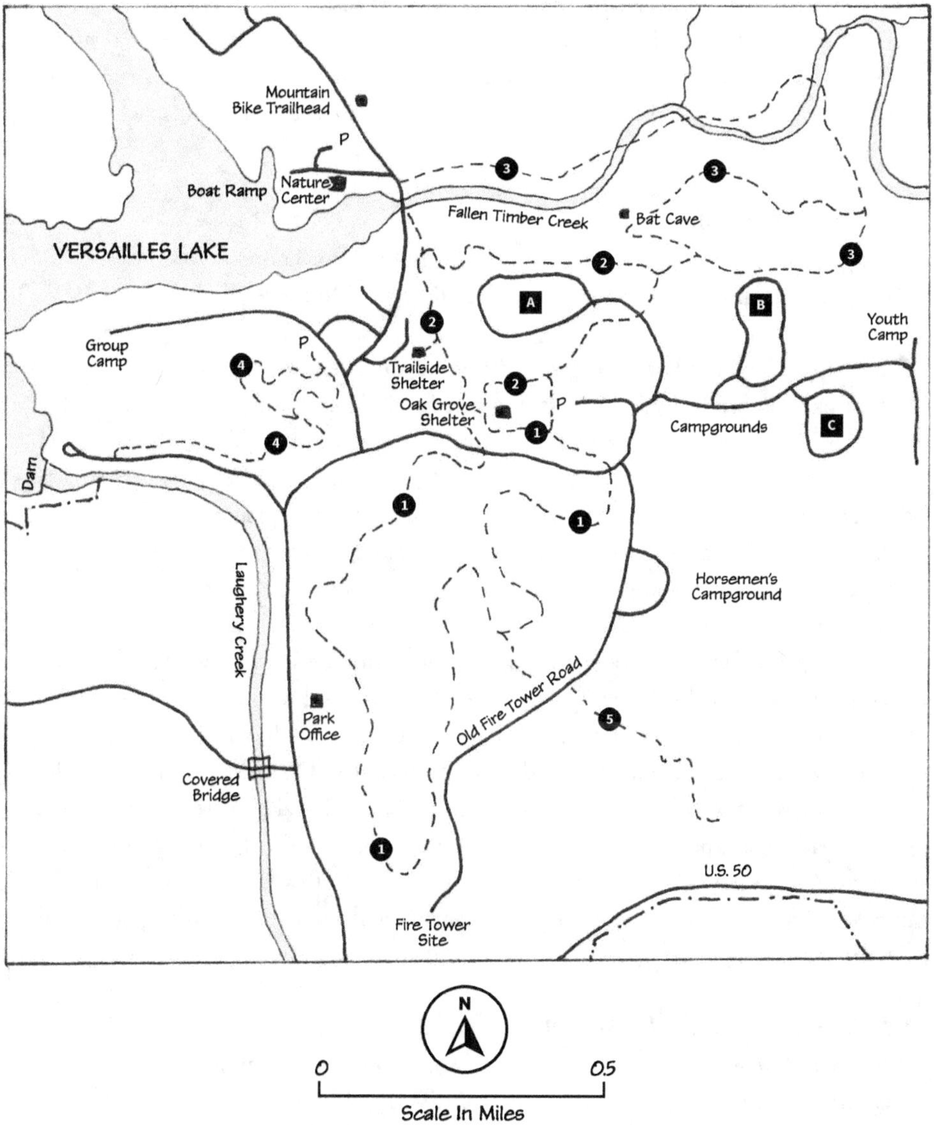

are out. At its halfway point, the trail makes a sharp northward turn then passes close to the Old Fire Tower Road; turn right and walk down the road a quarter mile to reach the grassy knoll where the tower once stood. A half mile north the trail crosses a pretty, small stream with a series of stairstep cascades; soon a path, marked by a locator map, joins from the right. This is the new (in 2025) Trail 5/Waterfall Trail (see below for more information), which makes a fine two-mile side trip. The final stretch of Trail 1 is a pleasant wander through the woods with a couple of small waterways thrown in for interest. After re-crossing the park road it's a short jaunt back to your starting point.

Trail 2—Orchard Loop

Rating: ★ ★ ★　　　　　**Configuration:** Loop
Distance: 1.25 miles　　　　**Difficulty:** Moderate

Tour: The official trailhead for Orchard Loop is on the north side of the Oak Grove Shelter parking lot, but you can also access it from Campground A, Trailside Shelter, and the Fallen Timber Creek bridge. It's valuable connector, linking hikers directly with Trails 1, 3, and (with a little road walking) Trail 4. Trail 2 has an ever-changing character. In places it's civilized, passing near campsites and picnic spots. Elsewhere, it has some of the park's most rugged, overgrown, and slippery trail segments. Depart from Oak Grove lot and turn left (clockwise) on the loop; the shelter soon comes into view. Trail 1 joins for a short stretch before Trail 2 departs and descends to the right on a wild-feeling stretch with tricky footing. At the bottom, a stairway goes to the left. It leads to the park road bridge over the Fallen Timber Creek; cross the bridge to reach the start of Trail 3. Back on Trail 2, the path switchbacks to the blufftop and emerges at Campground A. The trail follows the northern edge of the campground (campsites are just steps away), plunges back into the woods, and makes a steep climb up an eroded path to a junction. The left fork is the connector to Trail 3 and Campground B; turn right to stay on the main trunk of Trail 2. The path soon reaches a road crossing, with Campground A to your right. A short hike from here takes you back to your starting point.

Trail 3—Fallen Timber Creek Trail

Rating: ★ ★ ★ ★　　　　**Configuration:** Lollipop
Distance: 1.85 miles　　　　**Difficulty:** Moderate

Tour: Trail 3 follows Fallen Timber Creek on a wide, level path that was once a horse and buggy road. To reach it from the entrance gate, follow signs for the pool and mountain bike trails. Trail 3 starts on the right (east) side of the road just past Fallen Timber

Creek bridge. Park on the left near the Nature Center. There are three creek crossings (rock hops) in the heavily forested valley; prepare for wet feet in all but the driest seasons. Take the time to look for fossils in the rocks as you cross. The second crossing is near where early settler Leander Webster built a cabin and sawmill. It's also near the unmarked western boundary of Fallen Timber Creek Nature Preserve, through which the trail passes for a short distance. After the final creek crossing the trail makes a sharp right, climbs out of the valley and enters a side ravine with pretty stairstep cascades. A junction marks the start of the Trail 3 loop. Go straight to reach the campground. If you're planning to connect to Trail 2 and avoid the lollipop and stream crossings on a return trip, go right; it's much more scenic and includes a special highlight. Continuing straight on the main loop, the trail climbs to Campground B, passing close to some pretty, shaded spots on the area's north side. Following a flat, sometimes-sloppy path past the campground, you soon reach a junction with Trail 2; turn left for a return loop offering two options for returning to your car. Staying on Trail 3, keep your eyes open for a sharp right turn near the blufftop where a well-worn but unmarked path continues straight. Following the detour a short distance, scramble carefully over the edge and look to your right at a limestone outcropping. You'll see the entrance to Bat Cave, which has been covered to leave a less-than-human-size opening. Returning to the main trail, the narrow path winds through a beautiful blufftop forest back to the junction with the main trail and the return route to your car.

Trail 4—Otter Trail

Rating: ★ ★ ★   **Configuration:** Lollipop
Distance: 1.5 miles   **Difficulty:** Moderate

Tour: Trail 4 is one of Versailles' newer hiking paths. From the gatehouse, follow signs for the Group Camp. After passing the picnic areas, look to your left for a small gravel parking area. The trail starts at an inconspicuous marker on the left side of the lot. A junction marks the start of the loop; continue straight to navigate it clockwise. After passing first through a young forest the trail enters another luxurious, mature woodland reminiscent of other trails in the park. This journey is a gentle downhill, following and crossing small waterways; ferns and mushrooms dot the forest floor. The sound of flowing water gets louder as you move forward. The trail straightens, exits the woods near a restored prairie highlighted by summertime flowers, then ends in mowed grass by a fenced utility area. Walk to a paved road and turn right to visit the Versailles Lake dam and spillway, which you've been listening to as you walk. There is parking here, offering an alternative starting point for Trail 4. Steep stairs take you to the top of the dam and pleasant lake views. Return to forest trail and retrace your steps to a junction you passed on your outbound trip. Turn left to navigate the west side of the loop. This section is

Trail 4 leads to the spillway for Versailles Lake, created by damming Laughery Creek.

pretty but passes within sight of the park service buildings for much of its climb out of the valley. At the top, turn left at the junction to return to your car.

Trail 5—Waterfall Trail

Rating: ★ ★ ★ ★   **Configuration:** Point to Point

Distance: 1.0 miles (one way)   **Difficulty:** Moderate

Tour: Trail 5 made its debut in Spring 2025 and is a classic "good payoff at the end" route. It's a natural add-on to the Old Forest Loop (Trail 1) but can be accessed from the Old Fire Tower Road. There is a wide spot in the road where the new trail crosses, just south of the Horseman's Campground, with room to park a few cars. From this point, the hike is an easy one-mile out and back. For a longer hike (about five miles) that covers the whole trail, follow the directions for Trail 1 but turn left at the start to hike the loop clockwise. After 1.5 miles, look for a junction to the left with a locator map on a post marking the start of Trail 5. It's beautiful route, crossing small limestone-bottomed streams and passing huge beech and oak trees. The only negative is road noise from nearby U.S. 50 that intrudes during the latter part of the hike. After crossing the road near the halfway mark and climbing a particularly beautiful valley, the trail swings to the left and the waterfall comes into view. The flow is modest, even after rains, but the stacked limestone layers make for a pretty water feature. The trail stays on the blufftop above the falls, so views are somewhat limited. Nonetheless, take some time to rest and enjoy the idyllic setting before making your return trip.

24
Whitewater Memorial State Park

Outdoor adventures and family memories seem to go hand in hand. As a child, I was fortunate to live in Colorado, and my dad and mom enjoyed camping and hiking. Our family's frequent trips into the Rockies fueled my passion for the outdoors and turned me into a lifelong trail lover. Despite the mountain scenery, not all our hikes were a success. I remember one time Dad led us on a forced march along the side of a busy road in Rocky Mountain National Park. "I'm sure the trail starts just down this road," he kept saying. It didn't, but we survived, and today the family laughs about these misadventures.

I lost my dad in February 2021, a year that seemed intent on prolonging the misery of 2020. Even as Covid loosened its grip on the world, my father's sudden death left me in a funk that was hard to crawl out of. I needed a little help from my family and a nice outdoor adventure, maybe at an Indiana state park. When my son, Kendal, asked what I wanted to do for Father's Day that year, I already had something in mind. "Let's go hiking at Whitewater Memorial," I said. "And fishing!"

Whitewater Memorial State Park lies just a few miles west of the Ohio state line. Its dominant features are two lakes— Brookville, a huge flood control reservoir on the park's short western boundary, and Whitewater, a beautiful 200-acre reservoir wholly contained within the park that would be our focus for this trip.

We entered the park, drove across the dam, and parked in a small lot by the start of the Lakeshore Trail, our hiking route for the day. We rigged our rods, loaded up, and hit the trail.

Whitewater Lake has a wild feel, with an undeveloped shoreline and heavily forested surroundings. Lakeshore Trail plunges right into the trees after leaving the parking lot, then presents hikers with fork that is the start of a short loop. We went right, toward the lake, and planned to make our return trip on the other side of the loop.

If you think back to June 2021, there was another natural phenomenon making headlines in Indiana: the Brood X Cicada. I was hopeful that the charismatic insects

The Red Springs Trail winds through a lakeside forest in Hornbeam Nature Preserve.

were still active at Whitewater Memorial. They wouldn't return for another 17 years, so I wanted to see as many as I could before their short breeding season ended.

Good news! As we walked up the trail, cicadas sounded off all around us, their high-pitched vibrations drowning out other sounds. Most were high in the trees, but occasionally we would encounter a cicada crawling on trailside shrubs. With their buggy red eyes, they look intimidating but they're harmless; I stopped and gently picked one off a branch for a better look. After a short time, it flew off in search of a mate—the only reason it had emerged from its safe home in the soil below us.

A side trail soon departed to the right, and we followed it a short distance to the water's edge. Whitewater Lake, calm and clear, invited us to stay and fish a while. Did we catch any trophies? Not even close, but Kendal and I both caught several small bluegills and bass. It was enough action to keep us entertained for a while.

Another wonderful feature of Whitewater Lake is the quiet; only electric motors are allowed. Though a few boats worked the shoreline near us, we could barely hear them beyond the quiet conversations of the fishermen they carried.

When we grew tired of fishing, we packed our gear, returned to the main trail, and started hiking north. Lakeshore Trail is 2.7 miles long, so it's a 5.4-mile out-and-back round trip. For a long stretch north of our fishing spot, the trail hugged the shore. We tried a couple of casts along the way, but no luck. About one mile in, the trail abandoned the lake and followed a roller-coaster profile, mostly inland, that continued until its end.

Like most hikers, I love a great payoff at trail's end—a memorable viewpoint, waterfall, or rock formation. Unfortunately, Lakeshore Trail doesn't offer one. The path ends abruptly on a wooden platform next to a wetland, somewhat removed from one of the lake's coves.

Despite the uninspiring endpoint, Kendal and I took the opportunity to rest and talk. Feeling both alone in the woods and safe in each other's company, we opened up—more than we would have during a typical get-together back in the city. We'd both been through a lot in the previous 15 months, personally and professionally, and it felt good to share our feelings.

Eventually, we started our return trip back to the car, getting into the rhythm of the trail. For a little while at least, we focused on the amazing sights and sounds around us and forgot about the sometimes-scary world beyond the park boundary. The healing power of walking a trail through the woods in the company of a good partner had worked its magic.

Whitewater Memorial History

As its name implies, the state park lies in the basin of the Whitewater River, which played an important role in Indiana's early history. The landscape is rugged and cut by many valleys, the product of erosion caused by the runoff from melting glaciers that stalled just south of the modern-day park about 24,000 years ago.

The post-glacial soil was productive and soon covered with lush forests. The resource-rich lands attracted humans from the earliest times. Mounds State Recreation Area, 10 miles south of Whitewater Memorial, contains remnants of structures built more than 2,000 years ago by the Adena Culture. More recently, Woodland tribes including the Miami and Delaware frequented the area.

Everything changed in 1794 when Major General "Mad Anthony" Wayne won a decisive victory over a confederation of native tribes at the Battle of Fallen Timbers. A year later, the Treaty of Greenville ended the Northwest Indian Wars and opened a small slice of Indiana—including the Whitewater Valley—to white settlement.

While surrounding communities, including Brookville, Connersville, and Richmond, blossomed and grew to respectable sizes, Union County, in which Whitewater Memorial is located, stayed modest. It has farms and a few small towns but not many people; the population today is less than 7,000.

With fewer people came fewer pressures on the land, and this corner of the state retained a healthy share of its beautiful forests. But in the 1940s, east central Indiana lacked a state park. The Department of Conservation wanted to fill this gap and directed a committee to use scientific methods to select the best location for a new park. After gathering and evaluating a wealth of data, the committee announced that only one site in the region met their criteria: a parcel on Silver Creek in Union County's Liberty Township. Whitewater Memorial had taken its first step toward becoming a state park.

The Indiana state government was willing to develop and manage the new property, but first local entities had to raise money and purchase the land. In 1945 the Whitewater Memorial State Park Association was organized with representatives from Fayette, Franklin, Wayne, and Union counties. As its name implied, the association's goal was for the proposed park to honor men and women who had served in the armed forces during World War II.

On June 8, 1949, 1,514 acres along Silver Creek that had been acquired by the association were given to the state. The purchase price was $147,000. Of that amount, Union County contributed $12,250 in tax levies and $15,000 raised by public subscription. The remaining money came in the form of tax levies from the other three counties; Wayne County provided more than half of the purchase funds, $79,350.

Construction of the dam for Whitewater Lake was completed two years later, and the park was formally dedicated on October 29, 1951. The event was a patriotic affair attended by more than two thousand people. A huge storm in January 1952 filled the lake much more quickly than anticipated. Flooding with huge trees and other debris severely damaged the spillway area, requiring repairs.

The Lakeshore Trail offers access to fishing spots and exceptional water vistas.

The park officially opened on September 1, 1952. The most recent data (from Fiscal Year 2023-2024) report that 312,796 people visited Whitewater Memorial, ranking it 16th out of 24 properties in the state park system.

The final big change to the park came with the 1965 start of construction of Brookville Lake, a huge Army Corps flood control reservoir that now abuts the park's western boundary. Brookville was completed in 1974 and at 5,260 acres is the third largest body of water in Indiana. Before the reservoir, development in the state park was limited to land east of Whitewater Lake. Afterward, the park road was extended across the dam and new amenities added to the western area of the park, including family cabins, a boat ramp on Brookville, and three new hiking trails.

Whitewater Memorial Today

Whitewater Memorial State Park extends across 1,710 acres just south of Liberty, Indiana, about 80 miles east of Indianapolis near the Ohio state line. From the beginning, Whitewater Lake has been this park's focus and recreational heartbeat. Visitors go to the park to boat, fish, swim, or just gaze at the 200 acres of water and its forested shoreline.

Whitewater Lake has a boat ramp on its southeastern shore and a rental service offering rowboats, paddleboats, and canoes. Fishing is good in the lake; largemouth bass, bluegills, and catfish are the most popular species. Serious fishermen usually focus on huge Brookville Reservoir, which is on the park's western boundary and accessible by a boat ramp. Walleye, striped bass, and smallmouth bass are among the stars but big fish representing several species can be caught.

Whitewater Memorial is an important destination for nature lovers. The park is a key stop for migratory bird species and a noted location on the Indiana Birding Trail. Hornbeam Nature Preserve, so named because of it many hornbeam trees (a relatively uncommon species), covers 83 acres on the southeast shore of the lake. The preserve is a good destination for birdwatching and spring wildflowers.

There are a couple of options for overnighting at Whitewater Memorial. The campground is large, well maintained, and includes sections devoted to horseman camping and tenting youth groups. There are 214 electric and 41 non-electric sites in the main campground. Cattail Loop Trail and Memorial Loop Trail pass nearby for hikers.

If camping isn't your thing, the park has 20 family cabins located near the shore of Brookville Lake and close to Veterans Vista Trail. Outside the park, nearby motels are limited. There is a small, local property in Liberty (4 miles north) but you'll need to drive to Richmond (21 miles north) or Oxford, Ohio (16 miles southwest), for options from national chains.

Hiking Whitewater Memorial

With five trails, nearly 10 total route-miles, and several beautiful stretches of pathway, Whitewater Memorial is a fine hiking destination. On the negative side, the trails need maintenance (including repairs to damaged bridges) and invasive plants, especially

A Leopold bench makes a reasonable request of hikers on the Memorial Trail.

Asian honeysuckle, are a problem. Another weakness is that the trails don't connect very well, requiring drives from trailhead to trailhead or connector hikes along the side of a road.

The one place where you can park once and hike two trails is the Hornbeam Nature Preserve lot. The Lakeshore and Red Springs Loop trails both start at this lot and offer the most beautiful hiking in the park, a total of nearly seven miles.

Let's not forget the best reason for hiking Whitewater Memorial: nature. The forests are beautiful, the lake is teeming with life, and the variety of bird species is some of the best in Indiana. Plus, you'll probably have the trails to yourself, especially on weekdays.

Trail Running

The lack of connectivity discussed previously is less of a problem for runners who are happy to eat up miles and mix in paved road segments to connect the trails. Though I've yet to try it, I've mapped out a tour of all the trails, connected by road segments, that is about 15 miles.

All the trails are runner-friendly, but Lakeshore, a 5-mile, out-and-back affair is the most interesting. It's technical, with roots and rocks, and rolls nicely through the dense woods on the west side of Whitewater Lake. Memorial Loop is also a nice run, and Veterans Vista is arguably a better run than hike. The only trail section that is not runner friendly is the south side of Red Springs Loop. In addition to tight turns and roots, the surface is slick in many spots.

TRAIL GUIDES

The Whitewater Memorial property maps are confusing because they use a trail-numbering system that is never apparent in the park itself. All trails are signed with their names, not numbers. For that reason, I will follow suit and identify the trails by their names (listed alphabetically), though will provide the corresponding map numbers.

Cattail Alley Trail (Map Trail 13)

Rating: ★ ★ ★ **Configuration:** Point to Point
Distance: 1.0 miles (one way) **Difficulty:** Moderate

Tour: This trail connects the campground to the beach but it's rugged and overgrown in places; it's hard to imagine many swimmers making the trek. Hikers or fishermen, on the other hand, will love this scenic lakeside route. If you're not starting at the campground, drive to the beach and park at the north end of the lot, where Cattail

Alley starts. The trail plunges into a dense but young forest that matures as you travel north. Frequent side trails venture down to the lake—and at one point the main path touches the water for several yards—but generally the trail stays above the shoreline, winding around large trees. Multiple side paths cause some confusion but follow the most-worn trail and trend uphill if you're confused. The lake narrows to your left and a grassy/cattail expanse soon appears; a side trail takes you to Silver Creek, which was dammed to create the lake. The main trail makes a right turn at this junction and climbs straight uphill. This heavily overgrown section finally tops out in the campground near Site 194. Turn around and retrace your steps to return to your vehicle.

Lakeshore Trail (Map Trail 15)

Rating: ★ ★ ★ ★ **Configuration:** Point to Point (with extra loop)
Distance: 2.7 miles (one way) **Difficulty:** Moderate

Tour: This is my favorite trail at Whitewater Memorial. In addition to offering frequent lake views, the southern portion passes through Hornbeam Nature Preserve, a diverse hardwood forest that has a carpet of wildflowers in the spring. Cross the park road on the dam and park at the second lot you encounter on the right; the trail departs to the north. After an inauspicious start in a scrubby forest, the trail enters the mature woods of the nature preserve and presents you with a junction. Stay right; the upland loop to the left is a good option for the return trip. The forest in this area is dense and beautiful. After working around a lake inlet and crossing a small stream the trail climbs to the top of a shoulder, turns right, and descends almost to the water; a side trail takes you to a peninsula with ample shore access. The main trail follows a water-level route for the next half mile before turning inland and climbing higher into the forest—the start of a roller-coaster that continues to the trail's end, passing near two lake inlets. The trail terminates at the second inlet, finishing on a wooden platform at the bottom of a stairway. The view is unremarkable (the lake isn't that close) but it's a quiet spot to rest. To visit the side loop on the return trip, start looking for the unmarked junction after you pass the side trail to the peninsula. Cross a small stream; the side loop departs immediately to the right.

Memorial Loop Trail (Map Trail 12)

Rating: ★ ★ ★ **Configuration:** Loop
Distance: 2.5 miles **Difficulty:** Moderate

Tour: Sections of this trail are outstanding, passing through gorgeous forests and along Whitewater Lake. But other sections follow roads or are overgrown with invasives, so it's a mixed experience. This hike can be started at several different locations. Poplar

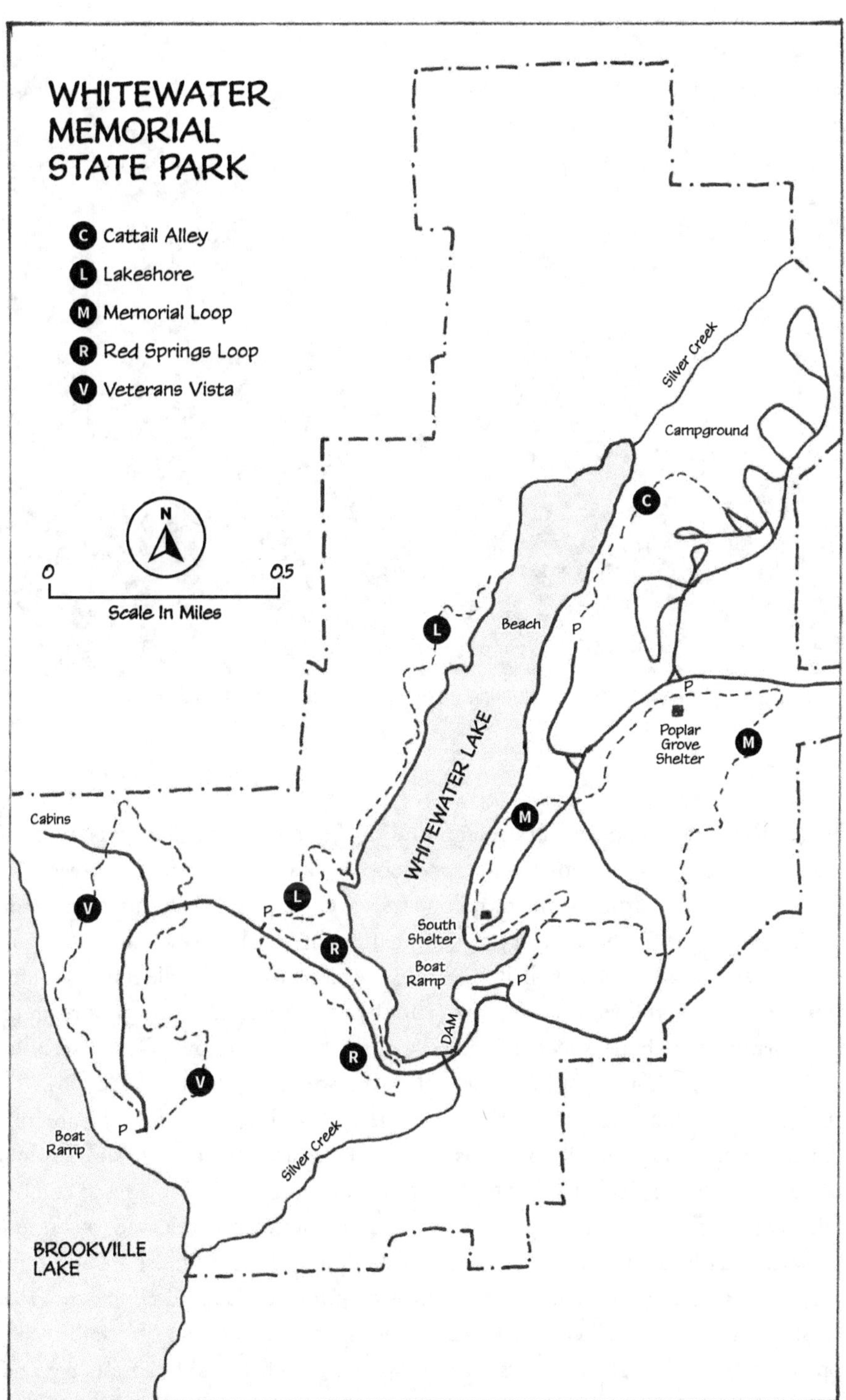
WHITEWATER MEMORIAL STATE PARK
C Cattail Alley
L Lakeshore
M Memorial Loop
R Red Springs Loop
V Veterans Vista
N
0
0.5
Scale In Miles
Silver Creek
Campground
C
Beach
P
P
Poplar Grove Shelter
M
L
WHITEWATER LAKE
M
Cabins
V
P
L
R
South Shelter
Boat Ramp
R
V
P
DAM
P
Boat Ramp
Silver Creek
BROOKVILLE LAKE

Whitewater Lake fisherman from a shoreline-hugging stretch of the Memorial Trail.

Shelter, near the gatehouse and campground, is the most convenient plus offers pit toilets and a large parking lot. To hike the loop clockwise depart from the east end. The unremarkable starting segment follows the entrance road but improves markedly after turning right and entering a gorgeous mature forest. The trees, wildflowers, and birdlife mesmerize for the next half mile until the path crosses a bridle trail and enters a long stretch of scrub woods overgrown with honeysuckle. After crossing a road, the forest matures, the honeysuckle dwindles, and the hiking improves. The descending path Ts near the shore of Whitewater Lake. The scenic trail to the left follows the lakeshore to the boat ramp parking lot, an optional starting point for a future hike. The main trail to the right circumnavigates a quiet lake arm very close to shore. Watch for herons, geese, and other water birds. On the far shore the trail turns and climbs a stair to South Shelter, yet another optional starting point. Cross the road to continue on a particularly pretty stretch of Memorial Loop that follows the shore and offers great views across Whitewater Lake. After turning inland, the trail climbs to a road crossing adjacent to a fish cleaning station, passes a side trail to the Naturalist Cabin (open in the summer), and follows a straight path through a scrubby forest edge back to the Poplar Shelter parking lot.

Red Springs Loop Trail (Map Trail 14)

Rating: ★ ★ ★ ★   **Configuration:** Loop
Distance: 1.2 miles   **Difficulty:** Moderate

Tour: The park road passes inside this loop, but it rarely intrudes during this hike through Hornbeam Nature Preserve that feels remarkably wild. The road also splits the loop into distinctly different halves. Park at the nature preserve lot (see Lakeshore Trail description) and depart on the Red Springs trail at the east end. This northern part of the loop is wide, flat, and winds through gorgeous big trees in a relatively dry forest. Sporadic views of the lake catch your attention on the left. After crossing the park road, the character of the trail changes markedly on the south side. Switchbacking downhill, the now-slick path is nearly covered in places by dense undergrowth. Everything feels damp and the mosquitoes are often thick. Soon you see why—the spring that gives the trail its name gushes out of the hillside below the trail, coloring the soil red and creating a small wetland. After the springs, the trail gently climbs a gorgeous valley dotted with huge trees. Look also for the small, smooth-bark Hornbeam (ironwood) trees that give the preserve its name. Eventually, the trail emerges from the valley and ends at the park road across from the nature preserve parking lot.

Veterans Vista Trail (Map Trail 16)

Rating: ★ ★   **Configuration:** Loop
Distance: 2 miles   **Difficulty:** Moderate

Tour: This trail's name is something of a misnomer; the only view is the one from the Brookville Lake boat ramp that's about a 100-yard detour west of the trail. Reach the start by driving to the end of the park road and parking on the east side of the boat ramp lot. Start where you see the Veterans Vista/Pit Toilet sign. Hiking the loop counterclockwise, the trail starts climbing immediately; its right-of-way is a grass path with a narrow dirt lane. Honeysuckle encroaches from both sides. Eventually the climb stops, the trail enters an open, mature forest, and the honeysuckle temporarily disappears. Big tulip-poplars, oak, and hickory tower overhead for the next half mile, but the trail returns to its former character for most of the remainder of the hike. In places, you must lean over to fit through the low "tunnel" created by the honeysuckle branches meeting overhead. After crossing the main and cabin access roads (and passing near one of the family cabins), you realize that you are very near Brookville Lake. The sounds of lapping waves and occasional glimpses of water through dense undergrowth are enticing, but a hoped-for shore access never appears. The trail soon returns to the scrub woods and emerges at the boat ramp lot.

Resources

The following sources provide additional information about Indiana state parks:

Website
Indiana State Parks and Lakes: https://www.in.gov/dnr/state-parks/parks-lakes/
The official website directs you to individual sites for the 24 state parks, with maps, campground guides, and other useful information.

YouTube Channel
Slone's Wilderness Expeditions
Mark Slone and his son, Kaden, have been posting enjoyable and informative hiking content since 2012. You'll find more than 60 Indiana state park–focused videos on their channel.

Podcast
IN the Parks
Schoolteacher Alison Martin's entertaining podcast, launched in 2024, features Indiana state-owned recreational resources, including many of the parks profiled in this book.

Book
The Complete Guide to Indiana State Parks
This illustrated volume by Nathan D. Strange, published in 2018, is a great resource if you're looking for a deeper dive into the history of individual properties.

Magazine
Outdoor Indiana
Though down to just four issues per year, this print publication is a must-read and includes a regular stream of state park content. Subscribe at outdoorindiana.org.

About the Author

Don Gulbrandsen first ventured onto trails during his childhood in Colorado and his passion for both hiking and trail running remains strong today. He moved to Indiana in 2007 and over the years has explored every numbered and named state park trail—many of them multiple times. He still enjoys hiking these routes, usually with a camera in hand, and is always amazed at the natural treasures he discovers along the way.

Don graduated from Iowa State University with a B.S. in Animal Ecology and North Park University with a Masters of Nonprofit Administration. Professionally, he worked for many years in the publishing industry before spending a decade in the nonprofit sector. Today, he works full time as a writer, editor, and book publisher. He is a certified Indiana Master Naturalist and a member of the Friends of Turkey Run and Shades State Parks. He lives in Indianapolis with his wife and hiking partner, Tari.